Moving from QBasic™ to C

Moving from QBasic™ to C

Greg Perry

A Division of Prentice Hall Computer Publishing
201 West 103rd Street, Indianapolis, Indiana 46290

For my hardworking New York friends, Joe and Rose Scognamillo. Rush may have introduced us to Patsy's, but the great food and even greater people keep us coming back!

FIRST EDITION

International Standard Book Number: 0-672-30250-0

Library of Congress Catalog Card Number: 93-86956

97 96 95 94 4 3 2 1

Interpretation of the printing code: the rightmost double-digit number is the year of the book's printing; the rightmost single-digit, the number of the book's printing. For example, a printing code of 94-1 shows that the first printing of the book occurred in 1994.

Composed in AGaramond and MCPdigital by Prentice Hall Computer Publishing

Printed in the United States of America

Trademarks

Publisher
Richard K. Swadley

Associate Publisher
Jordan Gold

Acquisitions Manager
Stacy Hiquet

Managing Editor
Cindy Morrow

Development Editor
Scott Palmer

Senior Editor
Tad Ringo

Production Editor
Cheri Clark

Editorial and Graphics Coordinator
Bill Whitmer

Editorial Assistants
Sharon Cox
Lynette Quinn

Technical Reviewer
Gary Farrar

Marketing Manager
Greg Wiegand

Cover Designer
Dan Armstrong

Book Designer
Michele Laseau

Director of Production and Manufacturing
Jeff Valler

Imprint Manager
Kelli Widdifield

Manufacturing Coordinator
Paul Gilchrist

Production Analyst
Mary Beth Wakefield

Proofreading/Indexing Coordinator
Joelynn Gifford

Graphics Image Specialists
Sue VandeWalle
Dennis Sheehan

Production
Nick Anderson
Ayrika Bryant
Karen Dodson
Terry Edwards
Rich Evers
Angela Judy
Shelly Palma
Kim Scott
Michelle Self
Susan Springer
Marcella Thompson
Suzanne Tully
Dennis Wesner

Indexers
Jennifer Eberhardt
John Sleeva
Suzanne Snyder

OVERVIEW

CONTENTS

Part II Working with Data

Part III Operating with Operators

Part IV Controlling the Flow

ACKNOWLEDGMENTS

Sams Publishing wants to do one thing: produce books that will teach clearly and thoroughly. It's an honor and a pleasure to have my name on a Sams book. I've gotten to know so many of you over the years, and my life is more blessed because of our relationship. I especially want to thank Stacy Hiquet for her devotion to producing quality books and for having faith in me. Sams Publishing has a jewel, and her name is Stacy.

Scott Palmer guided this book from beginning to end. It's nice to work with you, Scott. You seem to know what I need. You leave me alone when you can, and you steer me when I get off track.

Gary Farrar, the technical editor for this book, has an eye for detail that I could never master. I've never met anyone who could be so humble and at the same time let me know I messed up! Gary, I hope we have many future projects together. Any book that you are a part of will be a better book than it otherwise would or could be.

Cheri Clark seems to win top honors for keeping my writing clear and concise. At times, my writing is great. It's great, however, *not* because of my original words but because of Cheri's polishing. Cheri, keep up the fantastic work, and especially, *Dittos* forever and ever.

The remaining editors and production staff at Sams Publishing, in particular Tad Ringo, produced a professional book as always.

The most special thanks goes to my family. My beautiful bride, Jayne, somehow puts up with me and is my best friend. Glen and Bettye Perry are the best parents that a son could hope for.

Greg Perry

About the Author

Greg Perry is a speaker and writer in both the programming and the applications sides of computing. He is known for bringing programming topics down to the beginner's level. Perry has been a programmer and trainer for the past 17 years. He received his first degree in computer science, and then a master's degree in corporate finance. Besides writing, he consults and lectures across the country, including at the acclaimed Software Development programming conferences. Perry is the author of more than 20 other computer books as well as a book on rental property management. In addition, he has published articles in several publications, such as *Software Development, PC World,* and *Data Training.*

Other Sams Programming Books Written by Greg Perry

Teach Yourself OOP with Turbo C++ in 21 Days
QBasic Programming 101
Moving from C to C++
Absolute Beginner's Guide to Access
Absolute Beginner's Guide to C
Absolute Beginner's Guide to QBasic
Absolute Beginner's Guide to Programming
C++ Programming 101
Turbo C++ Programming 101

Introduction

The easiest way to learn a new subject is to base that learning on something you already know. Because you have this book, you must be a QBasic programmer wanting to get in on the C action. No problem! This book was designed for you.

Although C is considered to be a much more advanced language than QBasic, it is amazing how similar the languages can be. In almost every section of this book, you will be able to see a QBasic program or routine, and then you'll see the same program or routine converted to C.

This book teaches you C from a familiar point of view. Often, a new C command is taught through an equivalent QBasic example first, and then you'll see C code that does the same thing. Your current knowledge of programming is respected, yet when an advanced C feature appears, such as pointer variables, you'll get a thorough introduction to the concepts behind the new feature.

It's true that C is more efficient than QBasic. It's true that C programs run faster and are often more powerful than QBasic programs. However, this book does not treat the QBasic language as a beginning "toy" language. Full respect is given to QBasic, because QBasic is the best interpreted version of the BASIC language ever developed. Some powerful programs have been written in QBasic. Nevertheless, when you begin to need the efficiency and compiled security that QBasic can't provide, you will want to move to C for your programming.

Overview

This book is for current QBasic programmers. Part I, "Getting Accustomed to C," discusses the actual QBasic prerequisites for the reader, but if you have written several programs in QBasic, and fairly well understood what you were doing, you will be fine with this book. No time is spent here describing what a program is or the hardware in your computer unless that hardware directly relates in a special way to C.

The book is for beginners and experts.

If you are an expert QBasic programmer, this book is also aimed at you. You spent much of your QBasic career learning the ins and outs of variables, variable names, loops, and so on. Now that you've mastered those concepts, you can use that knowledge to learn C. You will learn C much more quickly than someone who is new to programming and trying to learn C as a beginner.

This book is divided into eight parts. The first part describes many of the overall language differences between C and QBasic. You'll learn in Part I why C is considered superior to QBasic for many purposes.

Part II, "Working with Data," discusses beginning C language features such as variables, variable names, input, and output. You'll find that C uses the familiar assignment operator, =, integer variables, and real number variables (variables that hold single-precision and double-precision data). You'll also learn the C-like language features that equate to QBasic's `PRINT` and `INPUT` statements. Of all the language differences between C and QBasic, I/O is perhaps the greatest.

Part III, "Operating with Operators," begins to show you why the C operators are more important to the language than the keywords. Unlike QBasic, which has more than 200 keywords, C has only 32 keywords. C, however, has more than twice the number of operators than QBasic, and the operators can be cryptic unless you learn how to use them.

Part IV, "Controlling the Flow," shows looping, decision, and other control statements. These control statements bear a remarkable similarity to QBasic. Although the syntax of a C `for` statement differs from that of QBasic's `FOR`, you'll be happily surprised at how easily you can convert from one to the other.

Part V, "Saving Time with Internal Functions," provides insight into another major difference between C and QBasic. C relies on internal functions much more heavily than QBasic. As a matter of fact, there are no I/O commands in C, whereas there are many I/O commands in QBasic. C performs its I/O through internal functions that you call.

Part VI, "Advancing Data Power," teaches you how C handles single-dimensional arrays, multidimensional arrays, pointer variables, and structures. Of these topics, only the pointer variables will be entirely new to you. QBasic has no equivalent language feature.

Part VII, "Using Disk Files," shows that C and QBasic share sequential file I/O methods that are almost identical. Random file access, however, is almost completely different in C from the QBasic language.

Part VIII, "Organizing Your Code," prepares you for a strong C future. You'll learn how to structure your programs so that they are maintainable. Separate functions enable you to create program building blocks that improve your debugging and maintainability.

Required Programming Tools

You need a computer and a C compiler to use this book. Because most of the sample program listings contain the program's output, you can learn C without a computer, but seeing the programs operate and playing "what if?" on C source code is the best way to learn a new programming language. This book also assumes that you already have a version of MS-DOS that supports QBasic.

This book does not target a specific C compiler. This book attempts to promote the ANSI C standard as much as possible, and most C compilers now support the ANSI C standard. If you have a C++ compiler, such as Borland C++, Turbo C++, or Visual C++, you'll be able to run any program in this book because such C++ compilers run C programs.

Companion Disk

A low-cost companion disk is available through the order form at the back of this book. This book contains approximately 200 programs, both in QBasic and C, and the disk will save you a lot of typing time. To keep the price of this book down, the disk is offered to you as an option and not bound into the book itself.

If you choose to order the disk, it will be sent to you quickly so that you can begin using it as soon as possible.

Conventions Used in This Book

This book uses the following typographic conventions:

- New terms appear in *italic*.
- Commands, function names, variable names, code lines, and so on appear in `monospace`.
- Placeholders, text that you'll replace with other values when you use a command, within code syntax appear in *`italic monospace`*.

- User input is shown in **`bold monospace`**.

You'll also see lots of the following helpful icons throughout the book:

Before any QBasic code that will be compared to C, you'll see the QBasic icon so that you'll know at a glance that you're looking at QBasic code.

Before any C code that is compared to QBasic, you'll see the C icon so that you'll know at a glance that you're looking at C code.

Throughout the book, you'll see lots of helpful tips that provide shortcuts, advice, and efficiency improvements.

Additional information, sometimes as an aside to the current topic, appears as notes to reinforce the chapter's concepts or to introduce some thought-provoking feature.

You'll be warned against many tricks and traps that often plague C programmers so that you can fend off the bugs before they appear.

Part I

Getting Accustomed to C

1

Welcome to C

You've mastered the QBasic programming language. You've written lots of QBasic programs, some small and some not so small. You've tackled the QBasic editor, the interpreter, `FOR` loops, and arrays. What do you do now? Learn C!

The C programming language offers many advantages over QBasic. This chapter begins your rewarding learning journey into C. Learning C will extend your programming power and provide you with more programming tool choices than QBasic provided. Along the way, you'll learn why C is today's language of choice in the world of programming. (You'll also develop some extremely marketable skills to help you land employment as an ace programmer!)

This book assumes that you understand the mechanics of the QBasic language. You don't have to be a QBasic expert to move to C. This book uses the QBasic language as a springboard for learning C; while learning C, you'll see familiar techniques in QBasic as the book compares and contrasts QBasic and C.

In this chapter, you will learn about the following topics:

- The advantages that C provides
- The history of C
- The ANSI C standard
- Assumptions this book makes about your prior QBasic knowledge

Despite the language differences, QBasic is an excellent introduction to C. QBasic is the best starter language, and C is an excellent advanced language. Although some C purists might disagree, QBasic contains many programming similarities to the C language. Some features, such as C's file I/O commands and functions, will make you think that C was designed partly from QBasic.

You can write any program in any programming language, although some languages are better than others for different reasons. (If one language did everything well, there would *be* only one programming language instead of more than a hundred.) This book shows you how to access C's power while demonstrating C's improvements over many of QBasic's features.

A Brief History of C

C increased in use greatly during the 1980s.

The 1980s saw a growth in one programming language unlike the growth of any programming language up to that time. The C programming language supplanted the formerly popular Pascal. Pascal is a good, well-structured programming language that began making headway into business and scientific data processing during the late 1970s and early 1980s. However, as C rapidly grew in usage, people discarded Pascal. Today, Pascal is still used some in applications programs, but on a much smaller scale than ever before. Pascal is still used in education, but it is not a serious contender in the programming marketplace.

Luckily for beginning programmers, C did not replace BASIC (QBasic's predecessor) on a widespread basis. Computer makers first supplied BASIC, and later QBasic, on almost every microcomputer sold since the very first PC. By its sheer number of installations, BASIC and BASIC-derived languages have maintained their stronghold as a beginner's programming language. BASIC was designed from the start to be a beginner's programming language. Through the years, software companies (especially Microsoft) added to BASIC while maintaining the language's original goal of easing new programmers into programming.

The designers of C, Brian Kerninghan and Dennis Ritchie, did not design C to be a beginner's language. Their primary goal was to write a high-level language that was efficient enough to be used for a new operating system called *UNIX.* Kerninghan and Ritchie worked for the Bell Laboratories (now the AT&T software labs), which was developing

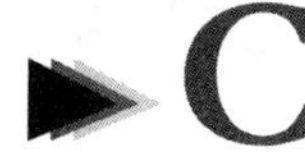

UNIX. Until that time, all operating systems were written in *assembly language,* a low-level programming language that uses abbreviated commands called *mnemonics.* Mnemonics are memory helpers. For example, many businesses change their phone numbers so that the letters on the phone spell an easy-to-remember name (such as 555-HELP or 555-CARS). Mnemonics helped assembly language programmers remember the commands of the language. Despite the mnemonics, assembly language is still difficult to master because of its close-knit relationship to the computer's internal hardware.

Computers get faster every year. Twenty years ago, computers were much slower than today's machines, and the operating systems had to be written to perform as quickly as possible. System designers used assembler to eke out as much operating system speed as possible. That speed carried a price tag—assembler programs are difficult to write and maintain.

High-level programming languages such as BASIC, COBOL, and FORTRAN did not provide the speed or efficiency needed for operating systems, even though their high-level abstraction (over assembler) provided for easy-to-write programs. If operating systems such as UNIX were to be written and maintained, and if they were to get much more complex, there had to be a change in the tools used to create such operating systems. A programming language had to be found that provided the easy maintenance and high-level advantages offered by BASIC, COBOL, and FORTRAN while being almost as efficient as assembler.

C is an efficient high-level language.

The people at Bell Laboratories could not find an efficient-enough high-level language, so they decided to write their own. They based their new language features on Algol (still used today, but primarily in the European community) and BCPL (rarely, if ever, still used). After a few attempts, an early incarnation of the C language resulted that took more than just the Bell Laboratories by storm.

It turns out that serious UNIX users and programmers have to delve into the system internals more frequently than users of other operating systems. As UNIX grew in popularity, so did C because so many people started using C. As C was getting more popular and was being used by more people, C was also getting modified a lot. C began appearing in several different versions.

In 1983, the *ANSI* (*American National Standards Institute*) formed the *X3J11* committee (why wasn't it simply called the *C group*?) to design a single standard version of C called *ANSI C.* C compiler writers wanted to sell compilers, so they began conforming to the ANSI C committee's standard. Through the years, the ANSI committee modified C a bit, primarily by adding to the language instead of changing it or removing functionality from it. Today's ANSI C standard provides a strong programming language that runs on several different platforms (meaning that it's available for microcomputers, minicomputers, mainframes, and supercomputers), while still maintaining C's original goal of being highly efficient. Although C is not as efficient as assembler, C achieves efficiency close to that of assembler. Some programmers call C a *high low-level language,* describing C's high-level programming constructs and low-level efficiency.

Keeping the Standard

Although C does exist in several versions, most C language vendors sell an ANSI C standard language and add extra features to the ANSI C foundation to differentiate their version of C from the rest. The two primary C language vendors are Microsoft Corporation and Borland, International. There is also an extension of C called C++. Most of today's C language vendors sell C along with their version of C++. Microsoft provides *Visual C++,* which includes C, as well as Microsoft C++/C 7.0 and QuickC. Borland offers Turbo C++ and Borland C++. If you own or purchase any of these programming languages, you'll get an ANSI C–compatible C programming language, and if you someday move from C to C++, you'll have those extensions as well.

> This book teaches the ANSI C language. After you learn how to program in ANSI C, you can easily learn any extensions to ANSI C provided by the individual language vendors.

Your QBasic Background

As you already know, this book assumes that you understand QBasic and have written QBasic programs. To "know QBasic" means different things to different programmers. It's difficult to determine how much QBasic you need to know before learning C. You don't have to be an advanced QBasic programmer, or have programmed in QBasic for many years, to learn C from this book. Nevertheless, you should have a fundamental grasp of a few basic QBasic language *constructs* (control statements) and language elements before moving on to the next chapter.

A short rundown of things you should already know about QBasic before learning C follows. Don't fret if you still use the QBasic on-line help or if you don't completely

understand every option of each command and function in the list. The most important thing to remember is that this book is not a beginner's programming book. For example, this book doesn't explain what a *loop* is, and this book doesn't explain everything there is to know about QBasic's `FOR` and `DO` loops. This book *does* show you how C's `for` and `do` loops work, and this book uses QBasic's equivalent statements to ease you into C.

> There is not always a one-to-one correspondence between C and QBasic. C is a smaller language than QBasic, but it offers stronger support for advanced programming capabilities. Those elements of C that have no QBasic equivalent are explained here in detail so that you'll finish this book with a solid grasp of C and ready to tackle any C program.

This book assumes that you have exposure to, and have at times used, the following QBasic elements:

- All major programming construct statements, such as `FOR`, `IF`, `DO`, `GOSUB`, and even `GOTO`
- The operators of QBasic, such as `+`, `-`, and `MOD`, and the relational operators, such as `AND` and `OR`
- Data and variable data-type differences, such as integers, characters, strings, and floating-point data (single-precision and double-precision values)
- Simple input and output statements, such as `PRINT`, `LPRINT`, and `INPUT`
- Built-in functions, such as `INT()`, `LEN()`, and `RIGHT$()`
- Arrays and multidimensional arrays
- User-defined functions and subroutine procedures, as well as `SHARED` data between procedures
- Calling and returning from procedures
- Passing and returning values between procedures
- The `TYPE` statement of record data definition

Summary

C is more efficient than QBasic. More companies use C than use QBasic because C produces extremely efficient programs that are easier to write than assembler programs. This book uses your current knowledge of QBasic to teach you C.

This chapter presented a history of C. By knowing the roots of the programming language, you'll have a better understanding of where C is headed. The ANSI C committee works diligently to keep the C language uniform so that programs you write today will run with tomorrow's C languages.

The rest of this book is devoted to moving you from QBasic to C. Put your programming engines in high gear, and get ready to learn C.

2

Distinguishing Between QBasic and C

There are some fundamental differences between C and QBasic. The most obvious difference is in the way the programs are prepared for execution. The QBasic language is called an *interpreted* language, and C is called a *compiled* language. This chapter explains those two differences.

You'll also learn some of the environmental differences between the languages. Although this book teaches ANSI C and attempts to be generic in its description of C, you'll learn a little about how to enter and run programs written using Turbo C++. (The same information applies to Borland C++). All the major C language vendors provide tools similar to those in Turbo C++ product, so by seeing how to run a Turbo C++ program, you'll have a good idea of how to run all C programs.

In this chapter, you will learn about the following topics:

- The difference between an interpreted language and a compiled language
- How to use a C editor such as Turbo C++

- How to convert your C program into an executable program
- Command-line compilation

This chapter doesn't teach any specifics of the C language. Instead, the chapter prepares you for using the C language. QBasic seems simple because of its interactive editor and pull-down menus. This chapter gets you ready to use C by explaining what it takes to run C programs after you type them into your computer.

What Is a Compiler?

You type source code.

You cannot program in C without having the C language on your computer. Unlike QBasic, which comes with PCs, C does not come supplied with computers. When you acquire C, you acquire a C *compiler.* The C program that you type into the computer is called the *source code* or the *source program.* Your computer cannot understand source code. A compiler translates your C source program into an executable program.

Your computer runs only compiled code.

It will be a while before computers understand a spoken language such as English. Until computers do understand human speech, people will have to keep using more formal, rigid programming languages such as QBasic or C. In reality, computers don't understand QBasic or C either! Each of these programming languages has to be translated down into a *binary format;* that binary format is all the computer actually understands. The term *binary* means *two-state.* Inside computers are hundreds of thousands of on and off switches that turn electric pulses on and off. These two states, on and off, form the binary states of computers.

As Figure 2.1 points out, the computer can understand only binary code. You don't want to program in binary code, however, because doing so is much too tedious, time-consuming, and error-prone. (You would really prefer to program in your native tongue, but the computer balks at that.) What language designers have done is design programming languages such as QBasic and C that are sort of English-like, but much more formal with many rigid language rules. Those rules let in-between translator programs, such as QBasic or C language translators, convert your high-level source code into low-level on and off states of electricity. Your programs that are translated into binary states of electricity are called *executable programs.*

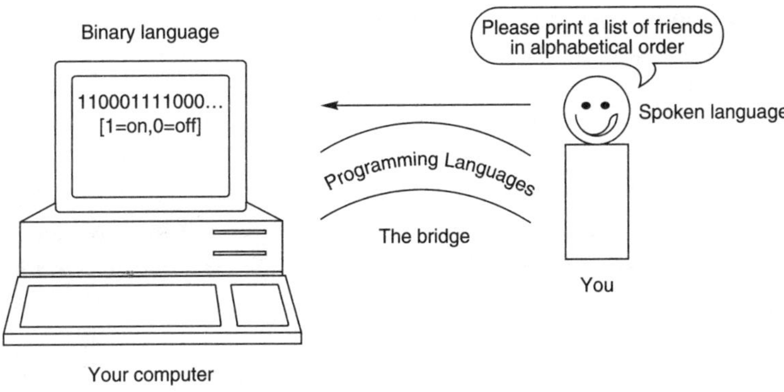

Figure 2.1. Computers want to hear binary; you want to speak your own language.

If you've programmed only in QBasic, you've never had to worry about the translation process that takes your QBasic source code and converts that source code into a binary executable program. All the translation happened under the hood. When you told QBasic to run your program, by selecting **R**un **S**tart from the pull-down menus or pressing the Shift+F5 shortcut key, QBasic translated your program from QBasic to binary automatically. You didn't have to think about, or even know about, the translation process. As a C programmer, you must learn a little more about the translation process.

There are two ways to translate a source program into an executable binary program:

- Interpret the source code one line at a time, running each line as each line is translated into binary.
- Compile the source code completely before running the program.

The first method is performed with a *program interpreter* (often just called an *interpreter*), and the second method is performed with a *program compiler* (often just called a *compiler*). QBasic uses the interpreter method, and C uses the compiler method.

Interpreters

Through the years, BASIC and its derivatives, such as QBasic, have been the most widely used interpreted languages. Another language developed by IBM approximately 30 years ago, APL, also was primarily an interpreted language, although APL isn't widely used today except in some mathematical and scientific circles. (*APL* is an acronym for *A Programming Language.* APL is a wonderful tool for mathematical processing, but it has lost a lot of ground since its heyday in the 1970s.)

Some operating-system command languages, such as the DOS batch language and the UNIX script language, are interpreted. These languages are not programming languages as are QBasic and C. These operating-system command languages control certain aspects of the operating system and are rarely used for applications programming.

Microsoft sells a QBasic compiler called *QuickBASIC.* The interpreted version, however, comes free with each copy of DOS, so that's the version most people have.

The reason the designers of the original BASIC language used an interpreter is that beginners have to do less to prepare an interpreted language for execution. The less beginners have to do, the more they can concentrate on programming. Here are some advantages of interpreters over compilers:

They're easier to use.
There is less to learn.
The computer acts as if it runs straight from the source code.

Interpreters are better for beginners.

BASIC was designed to be an interpreted language because BASIC was designed for beginners. The original BASIC was much different and less powerful than QBasic. As a matter of fact, in the early 1960s when BASIC was developed, no other programming language of the time (even those for large mainframe computers) could match today's QBasic for functionality. QBasic is many times better than its predecessor, yet Microsoft kept QBasic as an interpreter because of the advantage that interpreters offer for beginning programmers.

I Never Knew the Difference!

If you've never heard of binary code, or if you never before understood the term *compiling into executable code,* you never needed to learn those things. Running programs with an interpreter such as QBasic is much less demanding than running programs using compilers. Even though today's compiler vendors have made dramatic steps toward achieving the same ease of use as interpreted languages, you'll need to know more about the compilation of programs than you now know after you move to C, especially if you begin writing large programs and working on teams with other C programmers.

The reason interpreted languages provide an easier person-to-machine interface for beginning programmers is that the programmer seems to have more control over the

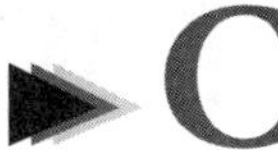

language than if using a compiler. When a person is ready to run an interpreted language program such as a QBasic program, he or she only has to *run* the program, via menu options or a command, and the program begins running. With a compiler, the programmer has to do more up-front work, and beginners aren't always ready to perform the extra work needed with compiled languages. (However, as you'll see later in this chapter, today's compiler vendors now offer environments that are almost as easy to use as the interpreted language environments such as QBasic.)

When a programmer runs an interpreted language, the interpreter immediately begins its translation of the high-level language to a low-level language. The interpreter translates a single line at a time and runs the interpreted line, then the interpreter interprets the next line and runs that line, and so on.

The term *interpreter* is an accurate term because a computer language interpreter works just like a human interpreter. Suppose that an American businesswoman traveling in Italy knows no Italian but has to communicate with branch offices there. She could hire an interpreter to help. When she walks in and hears, "Buon giorno," the interpreter translates the line and says, "Good morning." When she hears, "Come sta?" the interpreter translates, "How are you?"

Language interpreters translate a line at a time.

The interpreter does not wait until the end of the day to translate! The businesswoman needs the translation done *on-line,* to borrow from computer-speak. The translation would be meaningless if not done a line at a time. Computer language interpreters such as QBasic perform their translations of source code to binary a line at a time. Therefore, when you instruct QBasic to run your program, QBasic begins immediately at line one. It takes only a few microseconds to translate your program's first line into binary, and as soon as the translation takes place, the binary code executes. Then, the translation begins for the second line.

The nice thing about interpreters is that you don't have to prepare the program in any way before running it. QBasic is always there to run your program when you're ready.

Here's where the drawback to interpreters appears: If the same line has to be rerun, the interpreter has to re-interpret the line! QBasic does not store translated lines. If you write a loop, each statement in that loop is translated again and again for each loop iteration. In the following snippet of a QBasic program, QBasic converts the `PRINT` to binary 200 times!

```
FOR ctr = 1 TO 200
  PRINT "Counting at"; ctr
NEXT ctr
```

Unless the memory of the American traveling in Italy is extraordinary, she needs the human interpreter to do the same thing. If she hears, "Come sta?" two hours after the interpreter interprets the first occurrence of that phrase, she'll need the translation all over again.

Interpreted languages are inherently slow because their code has to be re-interpreted again and again. When you run a QBasic program, the interpreter must always be on the ball ready to translate as the program runs. Interactive translating means that every time you run a program, the program is translated a line at a time again.

If you write a QBasic program and distribute it to others, you must give them the source code (there are ways to protect QBasic source code, but the ways are not elegant or extremely secure, and are not routinely done). The source code has to be available because the QBasic interpreter works directly from source code.

> If you want security and speed, use a compiler.

Compilers

For *serious* programming (whatever that means!), programmers generally prefer a compiled language to an interpreted language. C is a compiled language. Using a compiled language means that you must do a little more up-front work (although, as mentioned earlier, today's compilers are extremely easy to use). The extra effort pays off because you don't have to translate the program a second time—that is, unless you change the source program.

Here are some advantages of compilers over interpreters:

Much faster program execution.

Sometimes smaller programs (not always; some compiled programs are huge in relation to the source code that generated them).

Source-code protection. People who run the program cannot see the source code underneath as they can with all QBasic programs.

Before you run a C program, you must go through several steps to get that program ready for execution. Figure 2.2 shows those steps.

When you buy a C compiler, you'll get all the tools needed to write and run C programs. You'll get an editor to create your C source program, and you'll get a compiler, which compiles your source program into something called an *object file.* The object file is not quite ready to be executed. As you write more powerful C programs, you can begin adding routines written by others called *library* routines that you want to integrate into your program. C library routines are little more than sets of C functions written and sold by others, such as I/O routines, advanced calculation routines, and modem communications routines. The writers of those libraries will not want to give you their source code, but they will give you the object code that you can combine with your program's object code by *linking* them together. The *linker* (or *link editor,* as it's sometimes called) converts your object file, and optionally other object files you are combining with your program, into a single executable file. When the file is executable, you can run the program from the DOS prompt or from Windows.

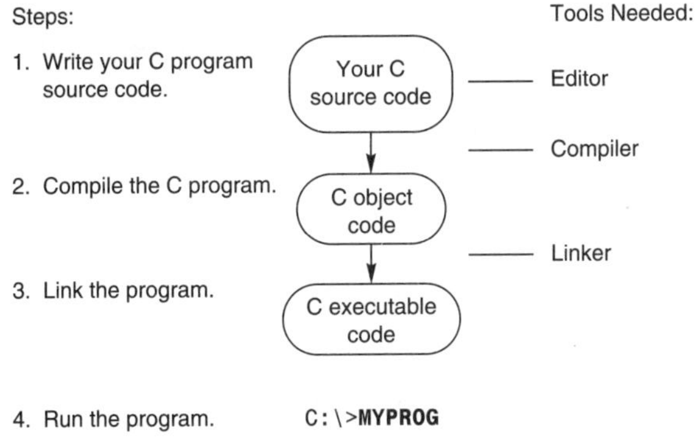

Figure 2.2. Steps needed to get a C program working.

> C source programs end with the .C filename extension. Although some compilers don't require .C at the end of program filenames, you should follow the standard. Typical C programs might be named MYPROG.C, ACCT.C, and so on. When your compiler compiles your program, it will create an object file with the filename extension .OBJ (such as MYPROG.OBJ or ACCT.OBJ). When your executable is linked, it will be named with the .EXE extension (such as MYPROG.EXE and ACCT.EXE). If your compiler finds any errors, the resulting .OBJ file will not be created; you'll have to fix the bug before recompiling. (Linker errors also are possible, in which case you'll not receive an .EXE file until you fix the linker error, which commonly is a misspelled function name.)

Remember earlier when you learned that a compiled program must go through a lot of steps before it's ready to run? As you can see now, these steps seem intimidating at the very least. Beginners simply aren't ready for the hassle required, so QBasic comes as an interpreted language. You get an editor with QBasic, but you don't have to worry about compiling, linking, and running. When you want the program to run, you select **S**tart from the **Run** menu, and the program takes off (albeit, more slowly than if you could have first compiled it).

Compiling All at Once

Compilation of the entire program takes place before *any* execution, unlike in an interpreted environment. Therefore, no recompilation is necessary during runs of the program. After a program is compiled, you can run it as many times as you like, and the program runs without another translation. The executable program is in binary form, so after the executable is created, no more translation is needed. If you save the executable to the disk, you can load and run the executable as many times as you like. The program will execute much faster than in an interpreted environment because the translation doesn't have to be repeated.

Here's the same loop written in C as shown before in QBasic:

```
for (ctr=1; ctr<=200; ctr=ctr+1)
  printf("Counting at %d \n", ctr);
```

Except for the language difference here and there (and there are relatively few differences between C's `for` loop and the QBasic `FOR` loop, as you can see), there is one primary difference between this loop and the previous QBasic loop. C translates the second line with `printf` *once* rather than 200 times as done in the QBasic `PRINT` shown earlier! That 200-to-1 improvement in speed produces a grand performance increase for C over QBasic!

You can make the analogy between a compiler and a speech translation just as you can do with interpreters. Suppose that while the businesswoman mentioned earlier is in Rome, she is given a report to take back to the United States. The problem is that the report is written in Italian. Therefore, she gives the report to her interpreter, and the interpreter sits down with the report and writes out a complete translation into English. After the businesswoman has the compiled translation, she can read the report over and over without ever needing to have it translated again.

Using C Compilers

Although languages such as QBasic are sometimes laughed at by the so-called experts, those experts are making strong headway into turning compiled languages into interpreted

language look-alikes. At least, they attempt to turn the tools used for compilers into a one-step source-to-executable sequence instead of requiring all the individual steps shown earlier in Figure 2.2.

Therefore, if you are just moving to a compiled language such as C, you'll be using compilers that make you feel at home. They'll have an editor and pull-down menus, and you'll be able to run a source program in a single step just as you've done in QBasic. If you need to perform the individual compile-link-and-run steps (and you'll have to someday if you write more advanced programs), you can step through the commands.

The most common and famous PC C compilers, made by Borland and Microsoft, both provide a QBasic-like interface you'll begin using to write, compile, and link C programs. (Those two companies are now cringing at that last sentence because they're not used to hearing their C products compared favorably to QBasic!) Borland's interactive editor/compiler is called the *IDE* (for *interactive development environment*), and Microsoft's is called the *PWB* (for *programmer's workbench*) or the Visual Workbench in Visual C++. Both companies offer a DOS-based version and a Windows version (supplied in the same box).

Figure 2.3 shows the DOS-based Borland C++/Turbo C++ IDE with a C program in the editor and a pull-down menu with the **R**un option selected. Figure 2.4 shows the same program with the Windows-based IDE. As you can see, there are more menu options than in QBasic, and the editors look slightly different from QBasic's—but the overall look and feel is similar to QBasic's environment.

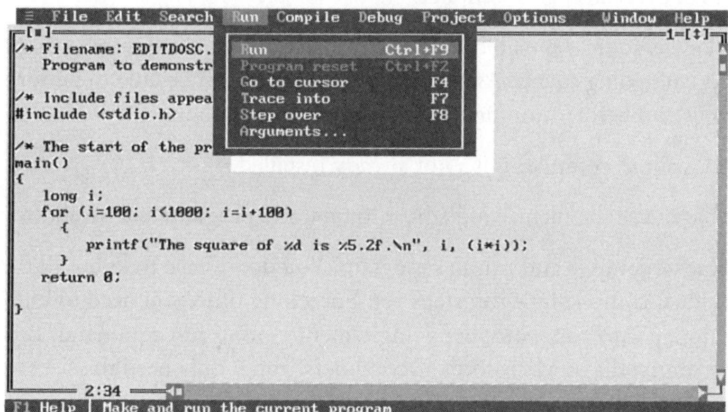

Figure 2.3. The Borland C++/Turbo C++ DOS-based editor/compiler.

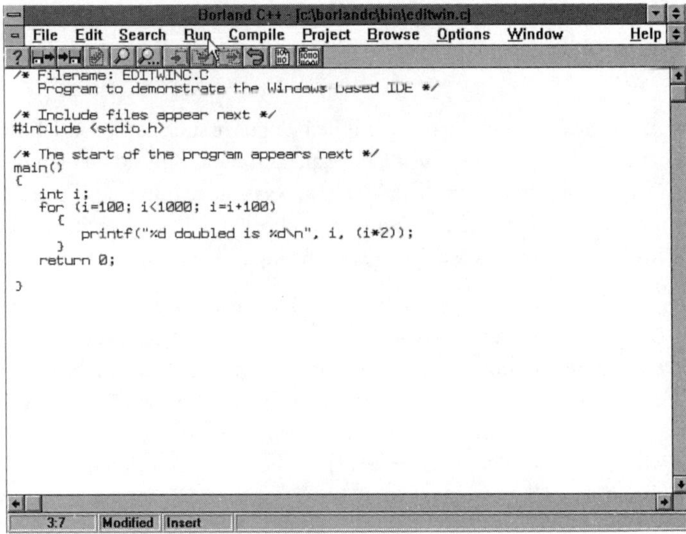

Figure 2.4. The Borland C++/Turbo C++ Windows-based editor/compiler.

The goal of this book is to teach you the language differences between QBasic and C so that you can get up and running with C as soon as possible. This book is not a tutorial on any one specific C compiler. As such, there is no time to delve into individual commands and features of everybody's C compiler.

Nevertheless, as soon as possible, you've got to get used to whatever C compiler's environment you are going to use. As a rundown, you've got to be able to perform all these tasks on your own before running any C program in this book:

1. Install your C compiler if it's not already installed.
2. Be able to use the menus and editor to type a C program and save it to disk.
3. Be able to compile and run the program. You don't have to know all the individual compile-link-run steps yet. For a long time, you need to know only how to tap into your compiler's single-menu option run command. If you use either Borland's or Microsoft's C compilers, you'll only need to select from the **R**un menu option.

Most C compiler vendors supply some kind of tutorial to get you started. Through the tutorial, whether it's a printed tutorial in the manual or an on-line tutorial from the on-line help system, you'll learn how to use the most common editor and menu options.

Before turning to the next chapter, make sure that you have installed your C compiler. You should also get used to using some of the editor's fundamental commands, such as entering text, changing text, and saving and loading files. You don't have to know all the ins and outs of an editor to write C programs. Most editors work just like QBasic's with minor exceptions. The following steps walk you through the use of Turbo C++'s editor for the entering, saving, and running of a simple program. These steps provide only an example for you to follow. Don't worry about understanding the C program at this time. The important thing is that you learn to enter, save, and run a C program before moving to the next chapter.

1. Start your compiler.

2. Open a new program source-code file. In Turbo C++, you would select **F**ile **N**ew from the pull-down menu.

3. Type the program in Listing 2.1. Be very careful to type it exactly as it appears. Unlike QBasic, uppercase and lowercase letters *are* different in C, so type them as they are shown.

Listing 2.1. A practice C program.

```
/* Filename: PRACT.C
   Easy practice program to get used to a C compiler */
#include <stdio.h>
main()
{
  printf("\n\n\n");
  printf("\aI'm going to learn C!\n");
  return 0;
}
```

4. After you type the program and check the typing for errors, save the program to disk. In Turbo C++, you'll select **F**ile **S**ave from the menu and type a new filename such as PRACT.C. Be sure to end the name with the .C extension.

5. Run the program. Select **R**un **R**un from the menu, and watch the program run after a brief delay. The brief delay is Turbo C++ compiling, linking, and executing your program automatically.

Get in the habit of saving your program before running it. If you write a program that freezes the computer (and in C it's very possible to hang the computer, requiring a complete reboot of the machine), you'll be able to recover the program and correct the problem if you've saved the program to disk.

Look through the other menu options available for your C compiler. You'll find a compile option, a link option, and many more features and commands. Most menu options have a shortcut key next to them. You can press the shortcut key instead of selecting from the menu to achieve the same result.

6. If you use Borland C++ or Turbo C++, you won't see your program's output right away. You'll either have to press Alt-F5 or select **U**ser screen from the **W**indow pull-down menu to see the output. Borland C++ and Turbo C++ always return to the source-code editor screen after a program executes. (QBasic did too, but QBasic first issued a `Press any key to continue` message to enable you to look at the output before returning to the editor.)
7. To exit Turbo C++, select **F**ile **Q**uit from the pull-down menu, and you'll then return to DOS.

The Windows-based C compilers work similarly to the Turbo C++ for DOS described here.

Command-Line Compilation

Most C compilers come with a *command-line* version as well as the interactive version. Although command-line compilers are not as easy for C newcomers, especially

for those moving to C from QBasic, advanced C programmers often prefer the command-line compiler.

The command-line compiler versions enable you to compile your program directly from the DOS prompt. Somehow, you have to type the C program before compiling it, so you have to use an editor to enter the program and save it to disk before using the command-line compiler. Before QBasic's interactive environment changed the way people viewed program editing and execution, command-line compilers were all we had to use. Today, command-line compilers are often used for advanced programming in which several source files must be compiled at once, such as for Windows programs that contain many small source programs that compile into a single executable file.

Summary

Already, you might think there's too much to worry about in using C. C does take a little more effort than QBasic, but as you learned in this chapter, most C compilers help you by mirroring much of the interactiveness that makes running QBasic programs so easy.

All QBasic programs are interpreted. All C programs are compiled. Interpreted programs are slower than compiled programs because each line in the program has to be retranslated over and over as the program executes. The compiled nature of C automatically makes C faster and more secure than QBasic programs.

You must compile a C program before you can run it, whereas you directly run a QBasic program when you are done with it. After it's compiled, your program must then be linked to an executable file before you can run the program. The interactive C compilers, such as Turbo C++ and Microsoft's C products, can perform all the separate steps for you, or you can order each step done individually using the menus.

Chapter 3, "Program Format Differences," begins the specific comparison of C and QBasic programs. You'll see how the overall format of a C program is more succinct than that of QBasic.

QBasic → C

3

Program Format Differences

This chapter begins to explore the overall look-and-feel differences between QBasic programs and C programs. Here you'll learn some of the high-level differences between the languages. The rest of the book will discuss specific commands and language elements.

C programs can be extremely cryptic. When a nonprogrammer looks at a QBasic program, QBasic might seem cryptic also, but not as much as C. C can be cryptic for programmers as well as nonprogrammers the first time they look at a C program. QBasic is wordier than C, but the wordiness has a slight advantage for newcomers to the language. C relies more on operators (special symbols such as `^`, `&&`, and `?:`, as well as more familiar ones such as `+`, `-`, and `*`) than does QBasic.

This chapter begins to explore the correct way to write programs. QBasic sometimes lends itself to sloppy unstructured programming techniques. C supports *structured programming* better than QBasic. Structured programming produces more organized code that is easier to change and modify in the future. The world changes constantly, and you'll have to update your programs accordingly. The better structured your programs are from the beginning, the faster you'll be able to change them later when the program's goals change.

In this chapter, you will learn about the following topics:

- The old-style and new-style BASIC and QBasic programs
- Structured and unstructured programming
- C's program format differences from QBasic
- QBasic remarks and C comments
- C preprocessor directives

Leaving the Old Style Behind

BASIC used to be rigid in style.

Just in case you moved to QBasic from older versions of BASIC, such as the GW-BASIC interpreter that came with pre-5.0 DOS versions, this section will try to replace the style you might still be accustomed to. Look at the program in Listing 3.1. The listing contains QBasic line numbers on each line and illustrates the rigid pre-QBasic programming style.

Listing 3.1. Old-style BASIC programming.

Line numbers

```
10 ' Filename: OLDSTYLE.BAS
20 ' This program shows the old way of writing BASIC programs
30 CLS
40 INPUT "What is the outside temperature in Fahrenheit"; FT
50 CT = (FT - 32) * (5 / 9)     ' Convert to Celsius
60 PRINT "In Celsius, the temperature is"; CT
70 PRINT : PRINT "Here are some other temperature conversions:"
80 PRINT "Fahrenheit"; TAB(12); "Celsius"
90 FOR I = 30 TO 100 STEP 10
100   PRINT I; TAB(12); (I - 32) * (5 / 9)
110 NEXT I
120 END
```

The old style of BASIC simply was too rigid. Each line required a line number (not required in QBasic), and *free-form* programs were not well supported. A free-form style of programming includes a great deal of *whitespace* such as blank lines and indentions that separate parts of the program. Pre-QBasic BASIC languages required a line number and some kind of BASIC statement on every line, even if the entire line was a remark.

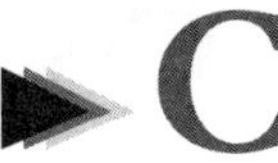

To make sure that you understand this program, here is the output from Listing 3.1:

```
What is the outside temperature in Fahrenheit? 212
In Celsius, the temperature is 100

Here are some other temperature conversions:
Fahrenheit Celsius
30        -1.111111
40         4.444445
50         10
60         15.55556
70         21.11111
80         26.66667
90         32.22223
100        37.77778
```

You probably don't use this older style of BASIC programming, but some people still have an attachment to it because QBasic hasn't been around for as long as the pre-QBasic interpreters. (QBasic has been here for less than 5 years compared to the 30 or so years that the older BASIC has been around.) Nevertheless, the program in Listing 3.1 is the epitome of how *not* to write a program. The program works, but its rigidness makes the program difficult to *maintain* (the term applied to changing the program later when it needs updating).

Listing 3.2 shows a better style of the same program as in Listing 3.1. Listing 3.2 produces the same output as before, but the program uses a more free-form QBasic-like style.

Listing 3.2. Rewriting the temperature program in QBasic's style.

```
' Filename: NEWSTYLE.BAS
' This program shows the newer way of writing BASIC programs

' Define a function so we don't have to repeat the formula
DEF fnFtoC (t) = (t - 32) * (5 / 9)

CLS
INPUT "What is the outside temperature in Fahrenheit"; userFah
celTemp = fnFtoC(userFah)  ' Pass value to the defined function
PRINT "In Celsius, the temperature is"; celTemp

PRINT
PRINT "Here are some other temperature conversions:"
PRINT "Fahrenheit"; TAB(12); "Celsius"
```

continues

Listing 3.2. continued

```
15: FOR temp = 30 TO 100 STEP 10
16:     PRINT temp; TAB(12); fnFtoC(temp)
17: NEXT temp
18:
19: END
```

Don't let these line numbers before the program statements confuse you. The line numbers shown here and in all the rest of this book's programs are reference numbers so that this book can explain individual lines of the program. The numbers shown back in Listing 3.2 were actually part of the BASIC program. Never type this book's line numbers (except for those in Listing 3.1 if you want to run that program) when you enter a program into your computer.

Add whitespace and separate a program into sections.

Just separating parts of the program into cohesive sections of code shows the structure of the logic. A user-defined function appears in line 5 so that the formula for temperature conversion doesn't have to appear twice as it did in Listing 3.1. A function procedure could have been used also, but a function procedure would be overkill for such a short formula.

For such a simple program, the comparison is rather trivial. After all, Listing 3.2 is not that different from Listing 3.1, but its free-form style is more modern and easier to maintain. Even though the program is longer, length takes a backseat to maintainability and readability. Throughout the rest of this book, you'll learn not only how to write C programs, but how to write them *correctly* so they produce correct results while being more readable. As mentioned in the introduction to this chapter, C is cryptic enough without adding to it any readability problems.

If you are still accustomed to using the older style of BASIC programming, make it a point to eliminate the line numbers from your next QBasic program and add whitespace to separate parts of the program into consistent sections. The QBasic programs in this book will assume the new and cleaner QBasic style, and all C programs in this book will also be written so that they are as easy to understand as possible.

If you use QBasic line numbers for `GOTO` or `GOSUB` labels, start using text labels instead. A text label ends in a colon, such as `calcPay:` and `prData:`. Better yet,

completely eliminate `GOTO` and `GOSUB` from your programs. Because C programmers rarely use `GOTO` and QBasic contains enough block-structured commands to write programs in an organized fashion, you no longer need `GOTO` or `GOSUB`. (See the sidebar entitled "Structured Programming" for more information about writing better program logic.)

There are many ways to write the same program, and if you find different ways to achieve the same results as the programs in this book, don't think that your program is wrong. Different people program using different styles. The best style is one that you and others can easily understand. Be sure to add ample remarks and leave lots of whitespace to make your programs more maintainable. Also be sure that you keep your program separated into different sections, in the way the language supports best. In this way, you'll have a bunch of interrelated modules rather than one long, continuous stream of code as is so common in BASIC and QBasic programs.

Structured Programming

As a programmer, you should get accustomed to breaking your program into logical units, whether those units are separate procedures, subroutines, or simply related parts of a small program separated with whitespace as done in Listing 3.1.

Structured programs are easier to maintain than unstructured programs. The old style of BASIC programming was difficult to structure very well because the language didn't support *block*-oriented language constructs. A block is one or more statements that you group together as a single statement. QBasic supports separated procedures and block structure to a point, but C is better. With QBasic, however, it's still too easy to insert a `GOTO` and branch around to other parts of the program when a more controlled loop or a block `IF` test would be easier to understand.

One of the first things you'll get used to in C is that there is not really a single long program with continuous lines as there can be in QBasic; all C code is stored in *functions.* A function in C is like a QBasic subroutine or function procedure. You *must* break a C program into functions. By forcing you to break your program into functions, and by providing lots of advanced language commands and multipart

continues

continued

program support, you'll write easier-to-maintain C programs than you wrote in BASIC or QBasic. This book shows only well-structured C programs, so you'll get in the habit of writing structured programs from the start. Perhaps then your C programs will not be as cryptic as other people's C programs!

Looking at a C Program

Listing 3.3 shows the temperature-conversion program written in C. Don't worry about the program specifics. Look at the general format of the program, and read the program's callouts to familiarize yourself with the format of C programs.

Listing 3.3. Rewriting the temperature program in C.

```
/* Filename: TEMPUR.C
   C version of the temperature-conversion QBasic program */
#include <stdio.h>
/* You must put a model of all non-main() functions here */
float fToC(float userFah);    /* Function that will convert */

main()
{
  float userFah, celTemp;
  int temp;    /* Loop counter */
  printf("What is the outside temperature in Fahrenheit? ");
  scanf(" %f", &userFah);

  /* Convert the temperature to Celsius */
  celTemp = fToC(userFah);
  printf("In Celsius, the temperature is %.2f.\n\n", celTemp);

  /* Loop through some more values to convert */
  printf("Here are some more temperature conversions:\n");
  printf("Fahrenheit   Celsius\n");
  for (temp=30; temp<=100; temp+=10)
    { printf("%4d\t%12.5f\n", temp, fToC(temp)); }

  return 0;  /* Return to DOS */
```

All programs require a main() function

All functions have names that end in parentheses

All complete statements end in semicolons

```
25: }
26: /* Conversion function appears next */
27: float fToC(float userFah)
28: {
29:   return ((userFah - 32.0) * (5.0 / 9.0));
30: }
```

Braces define a block of code

Right off the bat, you might find the C program a little less friendly than QBasic. Lots of extra symbols, such as braces and parentheses, are used in the program. Also, you'll see in line 29 that C prefers to keep data uniform; that is, the temperature conversion is calculated using floating-point values, so the decimal points are used on all numbers in the calculation.

Actually, QBasic programmers should use more consistent numeric values when writing expressions, but QBasic is more forgiving if you mix integers and floating-point values inside expressions.

A *floating-point* value in C is just like a single-precision floating-point value in QBasic. The value has a decimal point and a fractional value to the right of the decimal point, unlike integers, which have no decimal point.

The next few sections explain more about the style of the C program in Listing 3.3.

C Functions

Functions are the building blocks of all C programs. You cannot write a C program without a function. C functions are equivalent to all the following QBasic elements:

- Subroutines called with `GOSUB`
- Subroutine and function procedures called with `CALL`
- User-defined functions (defined with `DEF FN`)

A C function might return a value, or it might not. (All QBasic functions return values, but QBasic subroutines do not.) You can pass data to C functions via the parentheses just as you pass data to QBasic subroutine procedures and functions. In lines 15 and 22, the `fToC()` function is passed `userFah` and `temp`, respectively. All C function names end in parentheses. If you don't pass or receive data between functions, leave the parentheses empty. Therefore, these are function names:

```
main()     printf()     calcAvg()
```

But these are not:

```
myAge     minValue     count
```

Always enclose function bodies in braces. (A function body is the code that follows a function's opening definition line, which contains the function name.) For example, the first opening brace after `main()` indicates the start of `main()`'s function body, and the closing brace at the end of `main()` tells the C compiler where `main()` ends.

> The braces are similar to the `SUB` and `END SUB` commands in QBasic. If you have programmed using subroutine and function procedures and are used to passing data between procedures, the `main()` function in C coincides with the Main Module in QBasic.

Table 3.1 lists several similar-looking but different C symbols. The symbols are used for different purposes in C, so don't intermix them.

Table 3.1. Similar-looking symbols used in C programs.

Symbol	*Description*
`()`	Parentheses
`{}`	Braces
`[]`	Square brackets (or just *brackets*)
`<>`	Angle brackets

Function names must end in parentheses; you must enclose function bodies (and other blocks of code) within braces, and you could never begin a function with a brace and end it with a parenthesis.

> If you are not extremely familiar with QBasic user-defined functions, subroutines, or procedures, you'll still be fine. This chapter is attempting to give you an introduction to the language format differences. An in-depth discussion of function calls, and passing and returning values between functions, begins in Part VIII, "Organizing Your Code."

Lots of QBasic programs begin on the first line and end on the last without subroutines or procedures of any kind breaking up the program. By breaking your C program into functions, you better organize your code. Each function can perform a distinct task. When you later change or debug the program, you'll more easily be able to zero-in on the code that needs changing.

All execution of C programs begins at the `main()` function, and all C programs must contain one and only one `main()` function. In Listing 3.3, `main()` began on line 7. The lines before line 7 contained remarks and set up some of the program that followed. Not all C programs have to be broken into additional functions to `main()`, but most are. Some C programs are so small that they don't have to be broken down into more functions than `main()`. Most of the programs in this book stay as a single function, `main()`, because this book concentrates on the specifics of the language and the programs just aren't long enough to warrant extra functions. Only when you get to Part VIII will you see programs broken into several functions.

C comes supplied with lots of built-in functions. Many of them overlap QBasic's intrinsic built-in functions, such as `LEN()` and `SQR()` (the C equivalent functions are named `strlen()` and `sqrt()`). If you see a program such as the one in Listing 3.3 that uses a function but does not include a function body, such as `printf()` and `scanf()` in lines 11 and 12, those functions are supplied by the C compiler.

By the way, C has no commands for input or output (I/O). You might want to read that sentence again! QBasic contains about 40 commands related to I/O, and C has none. The lack of I/O commands is one reason why C has such a small vocabulary. When you have to perform I/O, you have to call built-in functions (or write your own). The two I/O functions that you'll see used most in this book are `printf()` and `scanf()`, which are rough equivalents to QBasic's `PRINT` and `INPUT` statements. Chapter 5, "Printing Output," and Chapter 8, "Getting Input," explain `printf()` and `scanf()` in more detail.

C Style

Turn off that Caps Lock key!

Perhaps the most important distinction between QBasic programs and C programs is that QBasic uses uppercase commands and C uses lowercase. C is extremely picky about lowercase. When you type a QBasic command in lowercase, such as `print`, QBasic converts that command to uppercase when you press Enter at the end of that line. C does no uppercase translation for you. You *must* type all commands and function names, except for those functions that you name and decide to give uppercase names to, in lowercase letters. Most C programmers also use lowercase for most of their variable names except for the uppercase letters they embed in some variable names (such as `grossPay`) to separate words within the variable name.

The C compiler complains when you use `IF` in place of `if`, `FOR` in place of `for`, and so on. The lowercase letters are perhaps the hardest thing for QBasic programmers to get used to when they move to C.

C is free form, and it doesn't matter how many blank lines or indentions you use within a C program. Put as much or as little whitespace in the program as you need to make the program readable. Sadly, the C program in Listing 3.4 is equivalent to the one in Listing 3.3 in every way and produces the same output, but you must admit that it begs for whitespace! It's legal to have more than one C statement on a single line, but as you can see, the readability suffers greatly if you do.

Listing 3.4. This program does not have nearly enough whitespace to make it readable.

```
/* Filename: SQUEEZE.C C version of the temperature-conversion QBasic
program */#include <stdio.h>
/* You must put a model of all non-main() functions here */float
fToC(float userFah);/* Function that will convert */main(){float
userFah,celTemp;int temp;/* Loop counter */
printf("What is the outside temperature in Fahrenheit? ");scanf(" %f",
&userFah);/* Convert temperature to Celsius */celTemp=fToC(userFah);
printf("In Celsius, the temperature is %.2f.\n\n", celTemp);/* Loop
through some more values to convert */
printf("Here are some more temperature conversions:\n");
printf("Fahrenheit   Celsius\n");for(temp=30;temp<=100;temp+=10){
printf("%4d\t%12.5f\n",temp,fToC(temp));}return 0;/* Return to DOS */}
/* Conversion function appears next */float fToC(float userFah){
return((userFah-32.0)*(5.0/9.0));}
```

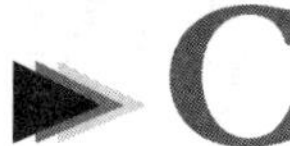

You'll see semicolons, `;`, at the end of several C statements in Listing 3.3 (just pretend that Listing 3.4 doesn't exist!). A semicolon ends a statement in C. That does not mean that all *lines* in C end in a semicolon, however. For instance, lines 1–4 in Listing 3.3 have no semicolon at their end, and neither do several other lines throughout the program.

A semicolon usually terminates a complete executable C statement. Function names that appear at the top of functions, braces that appear on lines by themselves, and program remarks aren't considered executable statements. Special C statements that begin with a pound sign, `#`, such as the statement on line 3 in Listing 3.3, don't constitute normal executable C statements either. As you get more accustomed to writing C programs, you'll begin to recognize when a line needs a semicolon and when it doesn't.

When you first begin writing C programs, you'll find it easier to start with another C program and change it than to start from scratch. Many parts of all C programs have similar formats. The C program outline in Listing 3.5 shows a skeleton of a C program from which you can begin writing many of your early and simple C programs. You'll have to fill in the areas marked `/* Your text here... */`, but the overall program structure is shown. (As you might have guessed, text between `/*` and `*/` constitutes program comments that document the program just like QBasic's `REM` statements do. The next section explains C comments in more detail.)

Listing 3.5. A C program outline that gives you a place to start.

```
/* Your text here usually includes the program's filename and
   a little about the program that follows */
#include <stdio.h>
/* Your text here might be more #include statements if needed */

main()
{
  /* Your text here would be the code that goes inside main() */
  return 0;
}
```

The `return 0;` that you've seen at the end of these C programs sends the program control back to the operating system or to your C program's editor, depending on how you start the program. If you run a fully compiled executable program from DOS, DOS takes control again at the `return 0;`, and the normal DOS prompt, such as `C:\>`, appears. If you run your program from within a compiler's integrated environment, such as from within Turbo C, the `return 0;` sends control back to the environment. `main()` is where all programs begin, and when the last line of `main()` finishes (the `return 0;`), the program ends. Many times, QBasic programmers are used to their programs ending at the program's last physical line, but C programs end when `main()` ends, even if other functions appear following `main()`. It's the programmer's job to ensure that `main()` or some other function properly calls all the functions listed after `main()`.

The `0` is sent back to DOS, where it's usually ignored. However, if you want your program to return other values at the end of program execution, you can list a different value at the `return`. DOS captures that return value in a DOS environment variable called `ERRORLEVEL`. If you are unfamiliar with checking `ERRORLEVEL` from within DOS batch files now, you'll probably never need to understand the `ERRORLEVEL` value. `ERRORLEVEL` is DOS-specific and beyond the scope of this book. (Any good book on DOS should explain all you need to know about `ERRORLEVEL`.)

For now, be sure to put the `return 0;` at the end of all of C's `main()` functions. If you fail to do so, probably your C compiler will still compile the program, and the program will run fine. However, you'll often get a compiler warning during the compile because the ANSI C standard requires the `return 0;` statement. After you master this book, especially Part VIII, "Organizing Your Code," you'll better understand the meaning of the C `return` statement, and you'll be better able to decide whether you want to use it or violate ANSI C (a small violation in this case) and omit `return 0`.

C Comments Are Just Like QBasic Remarks

Even if you don't put remarks in your QBasic program, you probably know that you should do so. Most programmers don't document their code enough (this author included). Most programmers, however, do document their programs somewhat. And the longer your programs become, the more apt you will be to put remarks in them, because you'll get tired of tracing through code looking for certain elements of the program when comments could have explained the parts of the program in English and saved you time.

This section of the book is not intended to berate you for not using remarks, however. Perhaps you work for a company that wisely requires them, or perhaps you were taught good programming techniques from an early age. The goal here is to explain how C supports the use of remarks.

A *comment* in C is analogous to a *remark* in QBasic. Both document your program's logic.

There are two ways to designate a QBasic remark: with `REM` or with the apostrophe, `'`. A C comment always begins with the two-character symbol, `/*`, and ends when `*/` appears. C comments can span several lines or reside on the same line as another comment or C statement. Most C programmers put C comments to the right of statements that are especially cryptic. QBasic programmers can use the apostrophe comment, `'`, to add comments to the right of their code lines too.

It's always a good idea to put the program's disk filename at the top of every program you write. If you run across a paper listing of a program and want to run or edit the program, you'll then be able to find the program on disk. Every program listing in this book includes a filename in a comment at the top. The filenames identify the associated filename on the book's companion disk if you decide to order one using the form at the back of the book.

Book companion disks are great when you want to see the results of code and learn a language as fast as possible. However, there's also a lot to be said for entering as much C code as you can when first learning the language. The more C programs you type, the faster the language will become second nature to you.

Listing 3.6 shows a QBasic program with the two kinds of QBasic comments. Listing 3.7 shows an equivalent program with C comments.

Listing 3.6. A QBasic program with two styles of remarks.

```
REM Filename: REM.BAS
REM A simple addition program
a = 1      ' Assign values to
b = 2      ' five variables
c = 3      ' so we'll have data
d = 4      ' to add together
```

continues

Listing 3.6. continued

```
e = 5

REM Add together the values for a sum
total = a + b + c + d + e

 REM Print the total
 PRINT "The total is"; total
END
```

Listing 3.7. A C program with comments.

```
/* Filename: COMMENT.C
   A simple addition program */
#include <stdio.h>

main()
{
   int a, b, c, d, e, total;
   a = 1;      /* Assign values to */
   b = 2;      /* five variables */
   c = 3;      /* so we'll have data */
   d = 4;      /* to add together */
   e = 5;

   /* Add together the values for a sum */
   total = a + b + c + d + e;

   /* Print the total */
   printf("The total is %d", total);
   return 0;
}
```

Here is the output from either of these programs:

```
The total is 15
```

A C comment can go just about anywhere within a C program. Don't make the mistake of doing this, however:

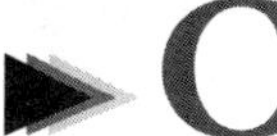

```
sales /* Assign a sales quota */ = 100000.00;
```

In this example, the comment obfuscates the C statement. Either put the comment above the C statement like

```
/* Assign a sales quota */
sales = 100000.00;
```

or add the comment to the right of the statement like

```
sales = 100000.00;     /* Assign a sales quota */
```

Don't nest C comments.

You cannot nest one comment within another. Although some of today's compiler vendors support nested comments, the ANSI C standard does not support nested comments. Therefore, the following lines are invalid:

```
/* This program provides support for customer service
   /* (And for customer invoicing also) */
   by providing input screens and handling routines */
```

The middle comment is not needed because C comments can span multiple program lines. Not only is the middle comment unnecessary, but it results in a compiler error. The C compiler will think that the first comment ends at the end of the second line when the `*/` is reached. C will then not know what to do with the words `by providing...` because the words aren't C commands.

Nested comments most often appear when programmers attempt to "comment-out" several lines of code. Suppose that you don't want the third and fourth lines in the following section of code to execute:

```
for (i=0; i<100; i=i+10)
  {
     printf("%d is counting...\n", i);  /* Print a message */
     i = j % 2;
     if (i > 55)
        { printf("The limit has been reached\n"); }
  }
```

You might attempt to comment-out the third and fourth lines like this:

```
for (i=0; i<100; i=i+10)
  {
/*      printf("%d is counting...\n", i);  /* Print a message */
     i = j % 2;    */
     if (i > 55)
        { printf("The limit has been reached\n"); }
  }
```

It would appear that you've kept those two lines from executing. Programmers often like to comment-out lines to test other areas of the program without the commented-out lines getting in the way for one reason or another. By commenting-out lines that already have comments, however, you introduce a compile bug! The C compiler sees the third line's comment as a nested comment. The subsequent */ seems to appear out of nowhere, and the compiler complains. If you want to comment-out lines of code, be sure that those lines don't already contain comments. If they do, remove the embedded comments, or make sure that the /* and */ align properly.

> Most of today's C compilers support a different kind of comment. The double-slash, //, begins a comment, and the end of the line ends the comment. C compiler writers have adopted this double-slash comment form from the C++ language. No statement can appear to the right of the // because C interprets all text after the // as the rest of the comment. This book stays with the more traditional /* */ comment style, but you should be aware that many C programmers are turning to the // because they don't have to worry about ending the comment or nesting comments because the end of the comment's line automatically ends a // comment.

Preprocessor Directives

Preprocessor directives aren't C commands.

Almost every C program you will see or write will contain *preprocessor directives.* QBasic doesn't have a concept related to preprocessor directives because QBasic is interpreted. A preprocessor directive is a command you give to the compiler that requests a change to the source code before the program is compiled. It's important to realize that preprocessor directives are not compiled, so they are not C statements in the normal sense of the word. Preprocessor directives are executed before your program is compiled. When you compile your program, if the program contains any preprocessor directives, the C compiler fulfills all the directives before doing any compilation. Figure 3.1 shows that the compiler fulfills preprocessor directive requests after you issue the compile request but before the compilation actually begins.

All preprocessors begin with a pound sign, #, and the standard is to start them in column 1 even though you can start them anywhere on a line because of C's free-form style.

The two most common preprocessor directives are

```
#include
```

and

```
#define
```

1. You write the C source code.	editor → source code
2. You compile the source code.	source code → C compiler
3. The compiler changes your source code according to the preprocessor directives.	preprocessor → processed source code
4. The compiler compiles and links your program.	compiler and linker → executable source code

(When you look at your source code again, it will be back the way you typed it.)

Figure 3.1. The compiler handles preprocessor directives right before compiling your program.

`#include` merges another file into yours.

The `#include` directive requires a filename. Its format is

```
#include <filename>
```

`#include` merges the file into your source code, in effect replacing the `#include` directive's line with the complete text in the included file. An included file is called a *header* file and normally ends with the .H filename extension. The header file must be an ASCII text file; you cannot include an executable program or an object file.

> If you wanted to (and you don't), you could type the entire contents of the header file in your source code, and then you wouldn't need to include the file. This is pointed out only to show you that `#include` does nothing more than merge text from another file into yours.

Header files contain common code that appears in many different C programs. You can write your own header files because they contain nothing more than C code. You probably won't be writing your own header files until you get more familiar with C and begin

to write larger programs. After you've written the same code over and over in many different programs, you'll begin to appreciate that typing the code once in a header file and including it from then on makes more sense than typing the code in lots of programs.

C programmers generally don't use header files for common routines and application code, however, even though they can if they want to. For example, if you wrote a function that prints a title at the top of each page that prints on the printer, you could put that function in a header file. When you need the code in any of your programs, you only need to include the file and it will appear in the code upon compilation, just as if you had typed the included code originally. Nevertheless, C programmers would generally prefer to compile such functions as separate stand-alone object files and link them into whatever programs need them later.

`#include` header files are most often used for common data and function definitions, not complete functions. There are common header files that come supplied with every C compiler. All C programs you've seen until this point in the book, and all C programs you see throughout the rest of this book, include the STDIO.H header file. STDIO.H contains some definitions that let C's input and output functions work better than if you didn't include the file. As this book teaches you more functions, you'll learn about additional common header files to include.

Include your header files before `main()`.

It will be a while (in Part VIII) before you can fully appreciate why header files are used so much and how they relate to your functions. In the meantime, make a habit of including STDIO.H and any other header files recommended throughout this book. By including the header files shown in this book's examples, you'll be writing more accurate C code. Even though you aren't ready to understand the internals of the header files such as STDIO.H, you should understand now that STDIO.H is nothing more than a C text file. Right before C compiles your program, C expands the source code that you type by replacing all your `#include` directives with the text that comes from the disk. C returns your source code to normal when the program is finished compiling.

Your header files are located in a special directory on your disk, probably under the directory name INCLUDE. As long as you use the angle brackets around the filename, C knows to search your INCLUDE directory for the header file.

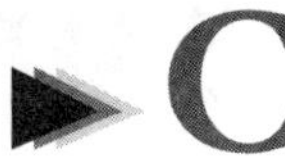

If you write your own header files, you can place them anywhere on the disk, not necessarily in the INCLUDE directory. If you store your own header files in directories other than INCLUDE, use quotation marks rather than angle brackets around the `#include` filename. For example, to include a header file named MINE.H stored in a directory named MYHEADRS on the C: disk drive, you would type this in your C program:

```
#include "c:\myheaders\mine.h"
```

You don't have to leave the path and filename in lowercase letters, but the standard is to do so.

You can look at the supplied header files such as STDIO.H because they are text just like your source code is. However, don't change the supplied header files in any way or you might have to reinstall your C compiler to get them back correctly.

`#define` replaces text with something else.

The second preprocessor directive mentioned here is being used less and less in the programming community, but because you'll still see it a lot, you should understand what it does. `#define` replaces all occurrences of source code text with something else. Here is the format of `#define`:

```
#define TEXT TextToReplace
```

`#define` is nothing more than a search-and-replace directive. If you've ever searched for text and replaced it in a word processor, such as issuing a command to replace all occurrences of *Mac* with *Mc,* you understand all there is to know about `#define`. The *`TEXT`* argument cannot contain spaces and is always a single word or word/number/symbol combination. The *`TextToReplace`* is your replacement text and can contain spaces and as many words as you need. All occurrences of *`TEXT`* will be replaced with *`TextToReplace`* when the preprocessor fulfills the `#define` request.

Generally, `#define` directives appear before `main()`, along with the `#include` directives (the order of directives is not important). The first argument is called a *defined constant.* Study Listing 3.8 and you'll see why.

Listing 3.8. Using a defined constant.

```
1:  /* Filename: DEFCONST.C
2:     Program that uses a defined constant */
3:  #include <stdio.h>
4:
5:  /* The defined constant appears next */
6:  #define PI 3.1416
7:
8:  main()
9:  {
10:   float area;       /* Holds the area of a circle */
11:   float rad = 2.5;  /* Radius of a circle */
12:   printf("The value of PI is %6.4f\n", PI);
13:   /* Perform the calculation */
14:   area = PI * (rad * rad);   /* Computes the area of a circle */
15:   printf("The area of a circle with a radius of %3.1f is %7.4f\n",
16:          rad, area);
17:   return 0;
18: }
```

The `#define` in line 6 informs the C preprocessor that all occurrences of `PI` are to be replaced, literally wherever they appear, with the value of `3.1416`. The replacement occurs *right before your program is compiled.* Therefore, when the C compiler finally gets your program, it appears as if you actually typed `3.1416` in place of `PI` in lines 12 and 14. `#define` defines *constants* because the value of `PI` remains constant after you define it in line 6.

> Words inside quotation marks, such as the `PI` on line 12, are *not* changed to the defined constant. C preserves all string data between quotation marks.

Here is the output of this program:

```
The value of PI is 3.1416
The area of a circle with a radius of 2.5 is 19.6350
```

The advantage of using `#define` is that if you need to change a defined value, you have to change it in only one place. For example, if you wanted to increase the precision of the area calculation, you would only change line 6 to this:

```
#define PI 3.14159
```

Then you would recompile the program. Lines 12 and 14 would then use the extended precision value `3.14159` rather than the value `3.1416` used earlier.

> Despite all you have already read about C's preference for lowercase words, the first argument in `#define`, *`TEXT`*, is always (by standard) uppercase. If you follow this standard, you'll be able to search through your C source code and easily distinguish between defined constants and regular variable names.

> The reason programmers are moving away from using `#define` is that a blind search-and-replace is done with no type checking performed. Programmers are beginning to initialize variables at the top of their programs and precede those variables with `const`, the constant qualifier, so that the variables cannot be changed later. Those variables are then used throughout the rest of the program as the defined constant value. In this way, rather than a blind preprocessed replacement, the data type checking and safety of variables stay in effect. You'll learn all about variable data types in the next chapter.

Summary

This chapter showed you lots of C code so that you can get used to the format of C programs. You learned how to code C comments as well as C preprocessor directives that act on your programs before they are compiled.

Table 3.2 briefly reviews the QBasic and C program format differences. The table helps summarize the concepts explained throughout this chapter.

Table 3.2. Comparing QBasic and C program formats.

QBasic Programs	*C Programs*
Uppercase commands	Lowercase commands
Nothing at the end of lines	Semicolons at the end of executable statements

continues

Table 3.2. continued

QBasic Programs	*C Programs*
Remarks that begin with `REM` or `'`	Comments enclosed between `/*` and `*/`
Can be one long program	Is composed of individual functions
`SUB`, `FUNCTION`, `END SUB`, and `END FUNCTION`	Braces
The Main Module	The `main()` function

Sometimes, program information is stored in external files called header files. You include header files with the `#include` preprocessor directive. You can also assign labels to constant values with `#define` so that all your program constants appear at the top of your programs instead of being scattered throughout the code.

4

Data Differences

Your data's types (integer, character, and so forth) are more important to C than to QBasic. If you never specify what type of variable you use, QBasic rarely complains. C, however, is much more picky. C requires that you make an effort to keep the right data in the right variables to avoid compiler errors, or worse, incorrect output.

This chapter begins to explore the kinds of data found in C. Luckily, a lot of the data overlaps that of QBasic. This chapter attempts to stay away from variables as much as possible and concentrate on just the data types available to C programmers. In the next part of the book, "Working with Data," you'll learn how to define and use variables that hold the data described here.

In this chapter, you will learn about the following topics:

- Character constants
- String constants
- Escape characters
- Integer constants
- Floating-point constants
- Scientific notation

The data described in this chapter is called *constant* data, or values that don't change and that are typed by you directly into the code, such as `"Hello"` and `87`. This data is sometimes called *literal* data. *Constant* has a special meaning in C (due to the `const` keyword), but this book often uses *constant* and *literal* interchangeably as is commonly done by the programming community.

Character Constants

QBasic does not have a *character* data type, but C does. In QBasic, if you want to represent a character constant, you treat the character as if it were a string that is one character long. All the following examples are QBasic characters, but more accurately, they are QBasic strings of one character.

```
"A"     "q"     "-"     "7"     "@"
```

Enclose all C characters in single quotation marks.

Although you can store an individual C character as a one-character string, C sets aside its own data type for characters. When you enclose a character in single quotation marks, C always interprets that character as if it were one character long. All the following examples are C characters:

```
'A'     'q'     '-'     '7'     '@'
```

Never enclose a string of more than one character within single quotation marks! The C compiler complains if you attempt to use any of these invalid characters:

```
'C is fun'     '1321 S. 48th Street'     'Grade: B'
```

Each memory location inside your computer is called a *byte* of storage, and each character consumes one of those memory locations, or one byte of memory.

String Constants

You must enclose all C strings, just as with all QBasic strings, inside double quotation marks. Here are three valid C strings:

Strings appear inside quotation marks.

```
"This is a string"  "1"  "funny ^%$@#$567764432 characters"
```

A C string literal can contain as many characters as needed, or none. Empty strings, called *null strings,* contain no characters and are sometimes used for initializing variables. Represent a null string constant with two side-by-side quotation marks, `""`.

> The different quotation marks used for characters and strings are easy to remember. Always enclose a single character within single quotation marks. Always enclose a string of characters (no matter what the length of the string is) in double quotation marks.

QBasic uses a different method for string storage than does C. QBasic keeps track of string lengths, and C does not. Understanding the method of string storage doesn't become critical until you store strings inside variables (see Chapter 7, "Character and String Data"), but mastering the storage of strings here gives you an added edge when you learn about string storage later.

All C strings end in a *binary zero.* Here are several other names for the string-ending zero:

All C strings end in ASCII 0.

Null zero
ASCII zero
\0 (You'll understand the meaning of the preceding backslash later)
String terminator

The reason *zero* is not used for the string-terminating character is that the ASCII value for the character '0' is 48. The complete ASCII table appears in Appendix A; you'll refer to it often while learning C. Turn back to the ASCII table now, and you'll see that the ASCII numbers are located at positions 48 through 57.

Now, look at the first entry in the ASCII table, the entry for ASCII 0 (not the character zero at ASCII 48). The character located at ASCII position 0 is the *null* character. ASCII 0 is a character and takes one byte of memory when stored, just as any other character consumes.

Here's the bottom line and one that QBasic programmers sometimes find difficult to accept when first moving to C: All strings end in the null zero, or the null character located at ASCII position zero.

C adds the terminating zero *every time you create a string.* You don't do anything special because C adds the terminator for you. For example, at first it appears that the following string contains three characters:

```
"abc"
```

In reality, however, it takes four characters, or bytes, of memory to hold that string. There is a null zero terminating the string. Figure 4.1 shows you how `"abc"` is stored in memory by a C program.

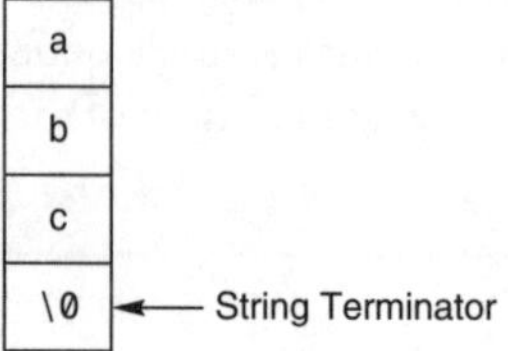

Figure 4.1. Storing `"abc"` *in memory; all strings end with an ASCII zero.*

> In all this book's figures that show memory contents, each box represents a location, or byte, of memory inside your computer.

As mentioned earlier, the importance of the terminating zero becomes much more critical when you learn how to store strings in variables. For now, remember that there is an ASCII zero value at the end of every string constant even though you do nothing to put the zero there.

As with QBasic strings, C strings can contain letters, numbers, or any other kinds of character data. Of course, even if a string contains only numeric digits, the string is not a number, just a string of digits that you must treat as if they were character data.

If a string contains numeric digits and at least one of those digits is a zero, the zero is just another character in the string and not the string-terminating zero. For example, the following string contains 15 characters and ends not at the zero in the middle but at the closing quotation mark:

```
"I have 20 pears"
```

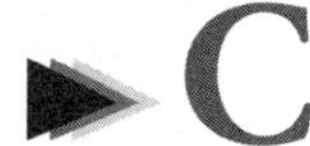

Figure 4.2 shows you what this string looks like in memory.

I		h	a	v	e		2	0		p	e	a	r	s	\0

Figure 4.2. Zeros inside a string don't terminate the string.

In QBasic, the `LEN()` function returns the length of whatever string you pass to it. The length of the string is the number of characters stored in the string. The QBasic statements

```
S1 = LEN("abc")
S2 = LEN("The rain in Spain")
S3 = LEN("")      ' Empty string
```

store the following values in `S1`, `S2`, and `S3`, respectively: 3, 17, and 0.

Of course, you rarely want to find the length of a string constant as done here. In both C and QBasic, you can find the length of strings stored in variables, but we're keeping this chapter free of variable-specific material as much as possible so that you can concentrate on the way C handles constant data.

String lengths don't include the string terminator.

The length of a C string also includes the number of characters in the string, but the length does *not* include the string terminator. To find the string length in C, use the built-in `strlen()` (for *string length*) function. The following code stores the length of the three strings in C variables:

```
s1 = strlen("abc");
s2 = strlen("The rain in Spain");
s3 = strlen("");  /* Empty string */
```

Don't confuse the length of C strings with the number of bytes needed to store C strings. The string length includes the number of characters up to, but not including, the null zero at the end of the string. The number of bytes needed to store a string *must* be enough to hold the string terminator. Therefore, the length of `"abc"` is 3, but it takes four bytes to store `"abc"`.

> **New Functions Mean Additional Header Files**
>
> When you learn about functions supplied with C, find out what header file to include at the top of your programs which use that function. For instance, the `strlen()` function requires the inclusion of the STRING.H header file. At the top of all programs that use `strlen()`, you'll want to add the following line:
>
> ```
> #include <string.h>
> ```
>
> As the preceding chapter explained, include all header files before `main()`. The order of the header files does not matter; you can include STRING.H before or after STDIO.H.

Escape Characters

There are some characters from the ASCII table that you simply cannot represent from the keyboard. For example, if you want to store a tab character in a character variable, you cannot use the Tab key as the tab character because the editor responds to the Tab keystroke by moving the cursor to the right. The tab character doesn't appear in such a way that you can store the tab character in a variable.

Escape characters are special.

Therefore, special characters called *escape characters* enable you to work with character data that you cannot easily represent without escape characters. An escape character is always preceded by a backslash, `\`, but the backslash is not part of the character.

Table 4.1 lists the C escape characters. You can use any of the escape characters anywhere in a C program that a regular single-quoted character can appear.

Table 4.1. The C escape characters.

Escape Character	*Description*
`\a`	Bell
`\b`	Backspace
`\f`	Form feed (vertical tab)
`\n`	Newline (translates to a carriage return/line feed sequence)

Escape Character	*Description*
`\t`	Tab
`\\`	Backslash
`\'`	Single quotation mark
`\"`	Double quotation mark

Although an in-depth discussion of C variables won't come for another couple of chapters, C assigns literals to variables using the equal sign (the *assignment operator*) just as QBasic does. Therefore, if you want to store a 10 in a variable named `n`, you do so like this:

```
n = 10;
```

When storing characters, you must use the quotation marks like this:

```
initial = 'T';
```

Use escape characters the same way. Here is how you would store a tab character in a variable:

```
myTab = '\t';
```

If you were to print `myTab`, the cursor would jump to the next tab stop on the screen.

> It might seem strange that *two* characters, `\` and `t`, reside inside the single quotation marks. Remember that the backslash tells C that an escape character is coming. C does *not* store two characters, a `\` and a `t`, but converts the `\t` to a single tab character (ASCII 9) and stores the single character.

All PCs have the capability to ring a bell. If you print the `\a` escape character, the bell sounds. QBasic enables you to ring the bell with the `BEEP` command, but C doesn't provide for a beep that easily. It's easy to remember that `\a` rings the bell if you think of the *a* as standing for *alarm.*

The newline escape character, `\n`, is the escape character used the most by C programmers. The newline character is a single character in memory, and you store the newline in a single character variable. However, when you print the newline character, C converts the newline to a carriage return/line feed sequence. The effect is simply that the cursor moves to the beginning of the next line down from the cursor's current line. In the next chapter, "Printing Output," you'll learn how to use the newline character to print multiple lines of output.

Rarely will you need the backspace escape character, but C provides it. When C was originally written, teletype machines were still used to enter and run programs. At that time, the backspace character enabled your program to back up the carriage so that one character could print on top of another, forming a new character if needed (such as a not-equal sign). However, most of today's output goes to the screen or to a more advanced printer that supports the entire ASCII character set.

> If you backspace on a video screen, you'll erase whatever character is backed over. Two characters cannot reside in the same screen location at the same time.

The form-feed escape sequence is nice because it enables you to send the printer to the top of the page before printing. If you want to ensure that you don't begin printing in the middle of a page, send the form-feed escape character, `\f`, to the printer using the printer output techniques you'll learn in the next chapter.

The last three escape characters, `\\`, `\'`, and `\"`, seem a little funny because they don't contain letters as the first ones do. The double backslash is the way to store or print a *single* backslash character. For example, to store the backslash character in a character variable named `b`, you would use this code:

```
b = '\\';    /* Store the backslash */
```

Without the escape character for the single quotation mark, there would be no way to represent a single quotation mark as a character. The following code is illegal:

```
sq = ''';    /* C does not allow this */
```

It's illegal because C always assumes that a pair of single quotation marks contains a character, and C won't know what to do with the third quotation mark. Therefore, the proper way to store a single quotation mark would be like this:

```
sq = '\'';    /* C allows this */
```

The backslash tells C that the next character, in this case the single quotation mark, is not an enclosing quotation mark but data.

You also need a way to represent the double quotation mark. Double quotation marks enclose strings, so you need an escape character for the double quotation mark if you want to represent it in a string.

When working with a C string, you can enclose any escape character in the string. For example, the following string literal contains embedded escape characters that represent quotation marks and a single quotation mark used for the possession:

```
"George said, \"It\'s mine!\""
```

Figure 4.3 shows how C stores this string in memory. Notice that the escaped characters each take only one byte of memory even though you have to type two characters (the backslash and the character) to represent each embedded character.

G	e	o	r	g	e		s	a	i	d	,		"	I	t	'	s		m	i	n	e	!	"	\0

Figure 4.3. Storing a string with escape characters.

All of this discussion on escape characters is well and good, but you're probably used to the QBasic function `CHR$()` that enables you to store *any* character in any variable. The argument to `CHR$()` is an ASCII number. For example, here is the QBasic code to store a bell ring (ASCII 7) in a string variable:

```
bell$ = CHR$(7)
```

The designers of C knew that Table 4.1 wouldn't suffice for every possible special character. There are too many characters in the ASCII table to represent with special escape characters. Therefore, there is a general-purpose escape character that you can use when you want to generate any ASCII character.

Look at the ASCII table stored in Appendix A, and you'll see the usual decimal numbers and character set. In addition, you'll see a *hexadecimal* column listing numbers that are represented in base 16 (people count in base 10). If you are unfamiliar with hexadecimal—many programmers are—that's OK, you can still use the hexadecimal column of numbers to simulate QBasic's `CHR$()` function in C.

All hexadecimal values begin with an `x` and continue with a two-digit code. To represent any ASCII character, enclose a backslash followed by the hexadecimal number inside the single quotation marks.

For example, to store the Spanish upside-down question mark, ¿, in a character variable, you would first look up the hexadecimal value of the upside-down question mark in the ASCII table. You'll see that the ASCII value is `A8`. Precede the `A8` with a backslash and `x` and enclose the characters in single quotation marks to create the special escape character for the Spanish upside-down question mark. The following C statement stores the character in a variable named `sqm`:

```
sqm = '\xA8';  /* Store an upside-down question mark */
```

By the way, you can type the x that precedes hexadecimal values and the letters inside in either uppercase or lowercase letters. Hexadecimal values are one of the few instances in the C language in which you can mix or match uppercase and lowercase letters.

Integer Constants

Integer constants look and act the same in C as they do in QBasic. Integers are whole numbers without decimal points. The following C statement stores the integer `17` in a variable named `code`:

```
code = 17;    /* 17 is an integer */
```

All the following examples are integer constants:

```
61      -9      0       888       32767
```

Leading zeros indicate octal numbers.

About the only difference between C integers and QBasic integers is that you shouldn't ever specify a leading zero if you want to designate a C decimal (base-10) integer. If you precede an integer constant with a zero, C assumes you're working with an *octal* (base-8) integer.

The C integer constant `011` is not the number 11 that you are used to. `011` is an octal number that translates to a decimal nine. Therefore, both `011` and `9` are stored as the same number internally because their internal in-memory bit patterns match. The numbers, however, look entirely different because the constant with the leading zero is octal.

As you might or might not know, QBasic includes the `OCT$()` function, which converts its numeric argument to an octal string. Because the return value is a string, however, you cannot perform math with QBasic's `OCT$()` octal return values.

If you precede an integer constant with an `0x0` or `0X0`, C interprets the number as if it were hexadecimal (base 16). The number `0x010` is not the decimal number 10 you are used to. `0x010` is equivalent to decimal `16`. As with octal, QBasic provides a hexadecimal function named `HEX$()` that converts its integer numeric argument to a hexadecimal string.

The following examples all represent the same number, 192, in decimal, octal, and hexadecimal, respectively:

```
192     0300      0xC0
```

In the preceding section, you learned how to store special characters using the hexadecimal value from the ASCII table. When printing escape sequences, you don't put the zero in front of the `x`, but you must use the zero for hexadecimal integers.

If all the octal and hexadecimal discussion in this chapter is beyond anything you've ever needed in programming, you can simply glance through it at this point. Octal is rarely used in today's computing environments. Hexadecimal is used a lot in internal systems programming, and many C programmers use hexadecimal at times. For now, however, if you understand that a leading zero indicates octal and a leading `0x0` indicates hexadecimal, you'll know all you need to know about integer constants.

Most C compilers store integers in 2 bytes of memory or 4 bytes, depending on the size of the integer. For example, all numbers from –32,768 to +32,767 are generally stored in 16 bits, or 2 bytes. Sixteen-bit integers are normally called *regular integers,* or just *integers.* Larger integer constants are usually stored in 32 bits, or 4 bytes, and are called *long integers.*

If you want to store a small integer constant as a long integer, you can append the `L` (or `l`) suffix to the constant. For example, `56` is a regular C integer, but `56L` is a C long integer. Sometimes, you want to assign a small number to a larger precision variable, and the `L` suffix ensures that C stores your integer constant as a long integer to keep consistent data types in your expressions.

Another suffix letter, `U` (or `u`), which declares the integer as an unsigned integer, is sometimes added to integers. Unsigned integers can be only positive. Unsigned integers are frequently used for weights and distances because neither weights nor distances can be negative. Unsigned integers hold a larger range than regular signed integers. The range of unsigned integers is `0U` to `65535U`, more extreme than the regular signed two-byte integer range, even though both signed and unsigned integers consume only two bytes of memory.

As with QBasic's numeric constants, never place a comma inside a number as you do when writing numbers by hand.

Floating-Point Constants

In QBasic, there are two kinds of *real* numbers, or numbers that contain decimal points and a fractional portion to the right of the decimal. QBasic's real numbers are either *single-precision* or *double-precision,* depending on their ranges.

C supports floating-point constants and double floating-point constants. Thirty-two bits, or 4 bytes, is the usual minimum amount of memory that holds C floating-point values. Many C compilers support 64-bit, or 8-byte, double floating-point constants.

The typical C compiler's floating-point values range approximately from –3.4 times 10^{+38} to 3.4 times 10^{+38} (the same as QBasic's single-precision values). The typical double floating-point values range from approximately –1.7 times 10^{+308} to 1.7 times 10^{+308}.

Most C compilers include a *long double* data constant for extremely high or small floating-point ranges (long double floating-point values are also known as *long doubles*). If you append the `L` suffix to the end of a floating-point constant, C stores the value as a long double floating-point value.

The amount of memory you need depends on the range of values you want to store. There is rarely a need for most people to work with real numbers more extreme than the regular floating-point constants provide. As mentioned earlier, the kind of constants you use depends often on the kind of variable you are using at the time.

All the data-type ranges presented in this chapter are common ranges but not required ranges. The ANSI C standard does not dictate ranges of numbers, and the ranges vary from compiler to compiler and among different kinds of computers.

Scientific Notation

QBasic supports two kinds of scientific notation, single-precision and double-precision. The letter representing the exponent tells you what kind of number you're working with. For example, the following numbers are single-precision scientific notation values:

```
5.434E+4      -7.80E+2      9.9001E-1
```

These numbers represent the following single-precision values, respectively:

```
54340.0      -780.0      0.99001
```

In both QBasic and C, the exponent can have a leading zero (but not a leading space). These values are equivalent:

```
6.5E+9      6.5E+09
```

Scientific notation offers a floating-point format that enables you to easily represent extreme values with sometimes a slight tradeoff in accuracy. For example, if you need to represent the number of grains of sand on a beach, it's much easier to write a number such as `5.6E+210` than to write out `56` followed by 209 zeros.

QBasic includes a slightly different notation for double-precision scientific notation. The following values appear to be the same as the previous list of three single-precision values, but these values will be stored in the double-precision's larger amount of memory:

```
5.434D+4      -7.80D+2      9.9001D-1
```

Even when you represent double floating-point values in scientific notation inside a C program, you'll use the `E` notation to specify the number. There is no need to distinguish between two kinds of scientific notation values in C. If the number you want to represent requires double or long double storage, C stores the number in the proper amount of storage.

Summary

This chapter covered all the kinds of data available in C programs. Much of this information overlaps that of QBasic's constant data types. You now know almost all there is to know about C constants. Although some of this chapter delved into numeric storage types, a topic that doesn't provide a lot of excitement for all programmers, you'll find that you are now better prepared to learn about I/O and variables in the next part of the book.

In this chapter, you learned about the following data types:

- Character
- String
- Integer
- Long integer
- Floating-point
- Double floating-point

Character constants must be enclosed in single quotation marks. Strings are enclosed in regular quotation marks. The length of a character is always one, but the length of a string constant varies in size. The length of a string is the number of characters in the string up to, but not counting, the string-terminating zero.

If you cannot represent a character from the keyboard alone, you can write an escape character that begins with \ and ends with the hexadecimal value of the character from the ASCII table.

Integers are simple to use, but don't precede them with a leading zero. C thinks that all integers preceded by 0 are octal constants. C also enables you to specify hexadecimal constants by preceding them with `0x0`.

Real numbers, such as floating-point and double floating-point values, are fairly easy to represent because of their similarity to QBasic's single-precision and double-precision constants. C also supports scientific notation, but there is only one form rather than two as in QBasic.

> It's only right to prepare you now for an upcoming shock: There are *no* string variables in C! You're coming from a QBasic background that supports string variables better than just about any other programming language. C does not support string variables. However, you'll see that you can represent string data inside variables through array mechanisms in Chapter 7, "Character and String Data."

In the next chapter, you'll learn how to print the data you learned about here.

Part II

Working with Data

5

Printing Output

You've got to have a way to see the data your program processes. In QBasic, PRINT and its companion commands, such as PRINT USING and LPRINT, display output. C has no output commands, but C compilers contain functions that display output.

When printing with QBasic's PRINT, you don't have to worry about the type of data you print. PRINT prints strings, integers, and floating-point values. The primary C output function, printf(), rarely prints your data correctly unless you tell the printf() function what kind of data you are trying to print.

The QBasic PRINT command can determine the kind of data to print because the command is part of the language. However, the printf() is not really part of C, although you'll never find a C compiler that does not support the printf() function. It is because printf() is a function that printf() cannot look internally at your data and decide how best to print that data. When you print a constant or variable with printf(), you have to describe that data. This chapter explores the way to use printf() correctly. printf() is a C function, just like INT() is a QBasic function.

In this chapter, you will learn about the following topics:

- Using printf()
- How printf() compares with PRINT and PRINT USING
- Format characters
- Printing to the printer

If the original designers of C were developing the language today rather than 20 years ago, they might design C's input and output methods a little differently. Today's input and output hardware is better defined than it was several years ago. Nevertheless, C's I/O functions give C a portability across different kinds of computers that QBasic will never enjoy. The QBasic I/O commands, especially the color, graphics, and sound commands, are tied directly to the PC and won't work on other kinds of computers, such as the Mac, or a larger system, such as a mainframe. When you purchase a C compiler for your computer, the compiler includes consistent I/O functions that work with any hardware. Therefore, the same C programs should, in theory and mostly in practice, work the same on virtually any computer you run them on.

Looking at *printf()*

Here is the format of the `printf()` function call:

```
printf(controlString [, otherDataToPrint] );
```

As you can see from the format, all `printf()` function calls require a *`controlString`* and optionally contain one or more additional arguments. The *`controlString`* must be a C string of some kind, whether a string constant or a string stored in memory accessible with a variable name. (You'll learn about storing C strings inside variables in Chapter 7, "Character and String Data.") The format of *`otherDataToPrint`* is a list of one or more data values, either constants or variables, that you want printed. The *`controlString`* determines how these values will look when printed.

`printf()`'s *`controlString`* works a lot like QBasic's `PRINT USING` format string. When the *`controlString`* contains formatting information, it determines how the output looks.

Printing Strings

It's easy to print C strings.

Strings are the easiest kind of data to print with `printf()`. Suppose that you wanted to print the text `Dittos, Inc.` on your screen. The following `printf()` does just that:

```
printf("Dittos, Inc.");
```

As you can see, the *`controlString`* does not really have to "control" anything. The *`controlString`* can be nothing more than a string value that you want to print.

C prints more literally than QBasic. QBasic does a little more work for you behind the scenes than C. In the preceding `printf()`, the cursor does not move down from the end of the string. In other words, the following three `printf()` function calls all write to the same line on the screen:

```
printf("Gene made a C+.");
printf("Terrie made an A-.");
printf("Jim flunked.");
```

Here is the output that these three lines produce:

```
Gene made a C+.Terrie made an A-.Jim flunked.
```

If you listed three QBasic `PRINT` statements that printed the strings, the strings would appear on three separate lines as expected. The QBasic `PRINT` statements

```
PRINT "Gene made a C+."
PRINT "Terrie made an A-."
PRINT "Jim flunked."
```

produce this output:

```
Gene made a C+.
Terrie made an A-.
Jim flunked.
```

> As you probably know, if you wanted to keep the cursor on the same line using QBasic, you would end each `PRINT` with a semicolon. The QBasic semicolon prevents the cursor from dropping to the next line. These three QBasic `PRINT` statements produce the same one-line output as the C `printf()`s:
>
> ```
> PRINT "Gene made a C+.";
> PRINT "Terrie made an A-.";
> PRINT "Jim flunked.";
> ```

To get a `printf()` to drop the cursor to the next line for subsequent output, all you have to do is insert a newline character, `\n`, inside the string. Any time a `printf()` *`controlString`* contains a newline escape character, C performs a carriage return/line feed sequence to move the cursor to the next line on the screen. The following `printf()` calls output the text on three separate lines:

```
printf("Gene made a C+.\n");
printf("Terrie made an A-.\n");
printf("Jim flunked.\n");
```

The following `printf()`s produce the same three-line output. Notice that it doesn't matter where the newline goes as long as you place the newline exactly where you want it to occur.

```
printf("Gene made a C+.");
printf("\nTerrie made an A-.");
printf("\nJim flunked.");
```

You can insert any of the escape-sequence characters inside printed strings. The `printf()`

```
printf("Paula said, \"I've got \xAB of my work done.\"\n");
```

prints this output:

```
Paula said, "I've got 1/2 of my work done."
```

Formatting Your Output

Numbers require formatting.

Numbers print properly only if you include a control string with *format characters* inside the control string. Format characters determine how printed values will look. Table 5.1 contains a listing of the most common C format codes.

Table 5.1. The C format codes.

Format Code	*Description*
`%d`	Decimal integer
`%f`	Floating-point number
`%e`	Floating-point number in scientific notation
`%g`	The shorter of fixed-point or scientific notation

Format Code	*Description*
`%c`	Character
`%s`	String

These format codes work like `#`, `%`, and other format codes that you've used inside `PRINT USING` format strings. The easiest way to learn the format codes is to see them used. The following sections look at each format code separately.

Printing Integers

You must use the `%d` format code to print integer values. The following `printf()` simply won't work:

```
printf(12345);     /* Invalid */
```

QBasic allows more freedom. QBasic's `PRINT` statement prints data values of any data type, but a string is the only kind of data that `printf()` prints without the need for format strings. (Actually, there is also a `%s` format code for strings that you'll learn about later in this chapter.)

To print the number `12345` in QBasic, this simple `PRINT` does the job:

```
PRINT 12345
```

To print `12345` in C, you must describe the format of the integer by inserting a `%d` in a control string like this:

```
printf("%d", 12345);     /* Prints 12345 */
```

If you want a carriage return/line feed sequence to appear after the number, include the newline escape character inside the control string like this:

```
printf("%d\n", 12345);    /* Prints 12345 and a newline */
```

If you want to surround the integer with text, you can do so by including the text in the control string like this:

```
printf("Your number is %d\n", 12345);
```

This `printf()` produces the following output:

```
Your number is 12345
```

You can also put text on either side of the integer like this:

```
printf("I am %d years old.\n", 12);
```

The preceding line produces this output:

```
I am 12 years old.
```

The `%d` tells C exactly where you want the integer to print within the control string. Figure 5.1 shows how the preceding `printf()` produces the output shown.

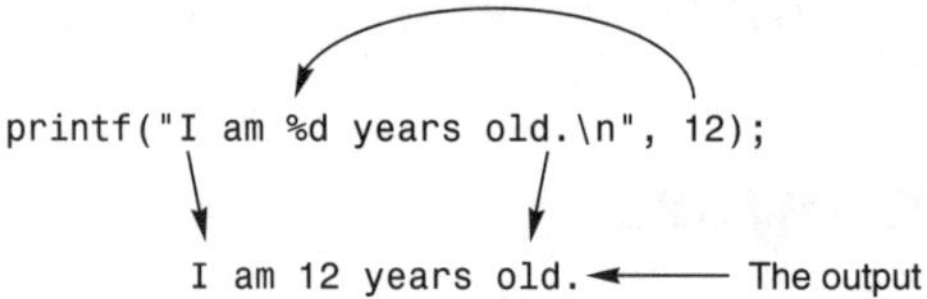

Figure 5.1. The control string determines the placement of the integer.

If you want to print a percent sign, `%`, somewhere within the string, you must use two consecutive percent signs so that C knows not to use the percent as a format code. The `printf()`

```
printf("There is %d%% gasoline in the mix.\n", 15);
```

produces this output:

```
There is 15% gasoline in the mix.
```

The control string determines exactly how the output should appear. If you include spaces in the control string, spaces appear in the output. The following `printf()` prints three values in a row, with two spaces between each value:

```
printf("%d  %d  %d", 10, 20, 30); /* Prints 10  20  30 */
```

The two spaces print only because the control code includes the spaces. The `printf()`

```
printf("%d%d%d", 10, 20, 30);  /* Oops, no spacing */
```

scrunches the numbers together like this:

```
102030
```

> All control strings must match the rest of your `printf()` argument list, or you'll get unpredictable output. In other words, both of the following `printf()`s are incorrect because the control strings specify a different number of integers than are actually printed:
>
> ```
> printf("The sum is %d and the average is %d.\n", 541);
> printf("The sum is %d and the average is %d.\n", 541, 42, 928);
> ```

If you want to specify a width for the printed integer, you can do so by inserting a width value between the `%` and the `d`. C prints the integer right-justified within that width. For example, suppose that you were printing a table of numbers and you wanted all the numbers to print aligned in columns. The `\t` would not position the numbers correctly. The next three `printf()`s show why:

```
printf("%d\t%d\t%d\n", 3, 19, 921);
printf("%d\t%d\t%d\n", 543, 8, 705);
printf("%d\t%d\t%d\n", 73, 893, 5);
```

The three `printf()`s produce this output:

```
3         19        921
543       8         705
73        893       5
```

The width specifier determines the minimum width of integers.

The numbers don't align properly even though they all begin in the same columns. Numbers should be right-justified within the space you print them. By putting a width value (called the *width specifier*) in the `%d` format code, you can accomplish well-aligned numbers. The `printf()`s

```
printf("%3d\t%3d\t%3d\n", 3, 19, 921);
printf("%3d\t%3d\t%3d\n", 543, 8, 705);
printf("%3d\t%3d\t%3d\n", 73, 893, 5);
```

produce this output:

```
  3        19       921
543         8       705
 73       893         5
```

In QBasic, you can use the `PRINT USING` to accomplish the same task. The following QBasic statements produce the same well-aligned output you saw previously.

```
PRINT USING "###     ###     ###"; 3; 19; 921
PRINT USING "###     ###     ###"; 543; 8; 705
PRINT USING "###     ###     ###"; 73; 893; 5
```

If the integer constant will not fit within the width you specify, C ignores the width specifier. QBasic prints a percent sign before the number to inform you that the width was ignored because it was too small.

Again, you rarely perform this much output using integer constants. However, all of this discussion applies also to integer variables, which you will learn all about in the next chapter.

If you want to print numeric values left-justified, include the minus sign, -, after the percent sign. For example, the `printf()`s

```
printf("%-3d\t%-3d\t%-3d\n", 3, 19, 921);
printf("%-3d\t%-3d\t%-3d\n", 543, 8, 705);
printf("%-3d\t%-3d\t%-3d\n", 73, 893, 5);
```

produce this output:

```
3       19      921
543     8       705
73      893     5
```

If you want to print a long integer value (with the `L` suffix discussed in Chapter 4) or a long integer variable, insert the `l` modifier before the `d` in the integer format code. The `printf()`

```
printf("Sum: %ld\n", 755012345L);
```

produces this output:

```
Sum: 755012345
```

Without the `l`, the integer `%d` could not print a number outside the range for normal integers that you read about in Chapter 4, "Data Differences." A regular integer `%d` format code can print only values that fall within the regular integer range from –32,768 to +32,767.

Listing 5.1 contains a QBasic program that prints data for a computer system. An equivalent C program follows.

Listing 5.1. A QBasic program that prints computer data.

```
' Filename: COMPDATA.BAS
' Prints computer data
PRINT "The computer system:"
PRINT "Name: Multi-Byte PC"
PRINT USING "RAM: ###K  ROM: ##K  Disk: ### Megabytes"; 640; 12; 200
PRINT USING "Age: # years"; 2
END
```

Here is the output from the program:

```
The computer system:
Name: Multi-Byte PC
RAM: 640K  ROM: 12K  Disk: 200 Megabytes
Age: 2 years
```

The C program in Listing 5.2 produces the same output as this QBasic program.

Listing 5.2. A C program that prints computer data.

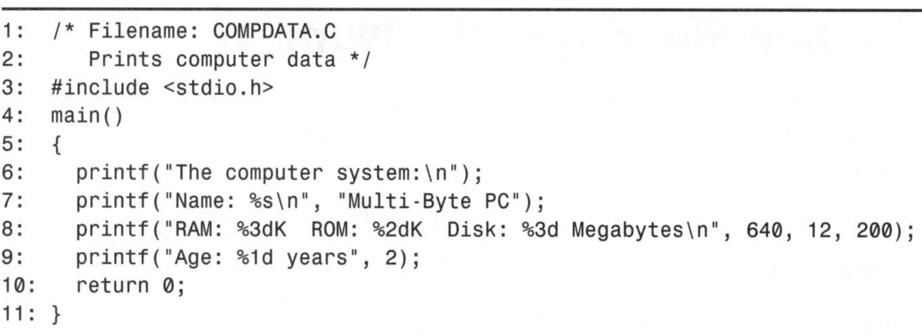

```
1:  /* Filename: COMPDATA.C
2:     Prints computer data */
3:  #include <stdio.h>
4:  main()
5:  {
6:    printf("The computer system:\n");
7:    printf("Name: %s\n", "Multi-Byte PC");
8:    printf("RAM: %3dK  ROM: %2dK  Disk: %3d Megabytes\n", 640, 12, 200);
9:    printf("Age: %1d years", 2);
10:   return 0;
11: }
```

Notice that line 7 uses a format code you have yet to see (except in Table 5.1). The `%s` is the format code for a string. Line 7's `%s` tells C that a data string will follow the control string; at the place of the `%s`, the string `Multi-Byte PC` is to print.

You can use the `%s` *format code to print strings.*

The `%s` is really not necessary for printing string constants. It would be more efficient and easier to understand if line 7 were written like this:

```
printf("Name: Multi-Byte PC\n");
```

However, when you learn how to store strings in variables, you'll need the `%s` to print the string data. Using `%s` here is overkill, but now you have seen `%s` and know that it's easy to understand.

There is no command in C to erase the screen that is equivalent to the QBasic `CLS` command. The designers of C wanted to keep C hardware independent. Most C compilers do provide an internal library function to erase your computer's screen, however. Borland's `CLS` equivalent is `clrscr()`, and you must include the CONIO.H header file. If you use a Microsoft C compiler, call the `_clearscreen(_GCLEARSCREEN)` and include GRAPH.H. (Be sure to type the two underscores if you use Microsoft's version of `CLS`.)

You can print results of C expressions like this:

```
printf("The answer is %d.", 15 * 7 / 2);
```

Expressions such as these, however, are best stored in variables, and then you can print the variables. Although both methods produce the same results, the variables provide for better maintainability of the code.

Printing Floating-Point Numbers

The `%f` formats floating-point values for the `printf()` function. The floating-point value or values that you place at the end of the `printf()` are positioned in the output by the `%f`. In other words, the `printf()`

```
printf("The average is %f dollars.\n", 634.58);
```

produces this output:

```
The average is 634.580000 dollars.
```

That output is *almost* what you want, right? Where did those trailing zeros come from? QBasic certainly never printed things like that! C always prints floating-point values to six decimal points unless you tell C to do otherwise.

It's true that QBasic formats data more automatically than C, but at the same time, QBasic doesn't give you the same ability to format data specifically as does C. Therefore, C

requires a little more work if you want to print floating-point values, but in the long run, you get better control over your output.

When you're printing values with decimal points, whether the values are floating-point, double floating-point, or long double floating-point, you usually must specify both a width specifier and a decimal-place specifier. Figure 5.2 illustrates how the format specifier `%6.2f` translates `634.58` into proper dollars-and-cents output.

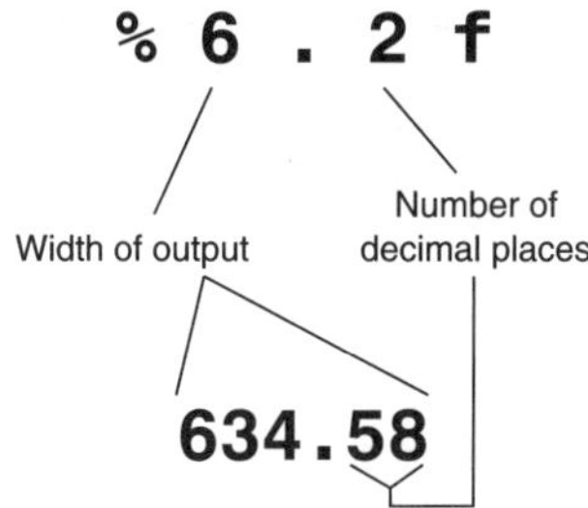

Figure 5.2. Specify both width and decimal positions for floating-point data.

The following C statement produces a corrected version of the previous `printf()`:

```
printf("The average is %6.2f dollars.\n", 634.58);
```

> As with the `%d` width specifier, if you don't specify enough positions for the width to print the entire value, C ignores your width request. Many C programmers leave off the width specifier completely unless they are printing floating-point data aligned in a columnar table format. Here is the preceding `printf()` without a width specifier but with a decimal-place specifier:
>
> ```
> printf("The average is %.2f dollars.\n", 634.58);
> ```

In QBasic, you could include the decimal point within the `USING` string to specify the number of decimal positions. The following `PRINT USING` produces the same output as the preceding `printf()` function call:

```
PRINT USING "The average is ###.## dollars."; 634.58
```

The QBasic program in Listing 5.3 expands on the computer data listed in Listing 5.1 by printing some floating-point values in addition to the integers printed in Listing 5.1.

Listing 5.3. Printing floating-point values.

```
' Filename: COMPDAT2.BAS
' Prints an expanded listing of computer data
PRINT "The computer system:"
PRINT "Name: Multi-Byte PC"
PRINT USING "Price: $####.##"; 2146.86
PRINT USING "RAM: ###K  ROM: ##K  Disk: ### Megabytes"; 640; 12; 200
PRINT USING "Age: # years"; 2
PRINT USING "Speed of the processor: ##.# mhz"; 33.1
END
```

Here is the output from the program:

```
Name: Multi-Byte PC
Price: $2146.86
RAM: 640K  ROM: 12K  Disk: 200 Megabytes
Age: 2 years
Speed of the processor: 33.1 mhz
```

Here is the equivalent C program. You'll soon think that C's `printf()` is easier to use than `PRINT USING`.

```
/* Filename: COMPDAT2.C
   Prints computer data */
#include <stdio.h>
main()
{
  printf("The computer system:\n");
  printf("Price: $%7.2f\n", 2146.86);
  printf("Name: %s\n", "Multi-Byte PC");
  printf("RAM: %3dK  ROM: %2dK  Disk: %3d Megabytes\n", 640, 12, 200);
  printf("Age: %1d years\n", 2);
  printf("Speed of the processor: %4.1f mhz\n", 33.1);
  return 0;
}
```

What? No Commas?

The QBasic `PRINT USING` can be powerful if you learn all its options. One of the most powerful features of `PRINT USING` is its capability to insert commas correctly in numerical output. The number 8495422 is a lot easier to read like this: 8,495,422.

> C does not include any comma-insertion mechanism. If you want commas inserted in your data, you have two options: (1) write the code to output a digit at a time and insert commas when appropriate or (2) get a C add-on library of functions someone wrote.
>
> Both of these methods might seem to be a lot of effort, and they are—compared to the built-in mechanism that QBasic provides for output. Programmers moving from QBasic to C are almost always frustrated by C's lack of built-in output capabilities.
>
> The designers of C wanted to make the language as low-level as possible to give programmers lightning-fast speed. In the process, they did not add any more than necessary because program speed would be hampered. It was the designers' *goal* to make C a language that programmers added to with user-written functions.
>
> In today's world, not being able to insert commas or print leading asterisks for check amounts makes a programming language seem lacking. C, however, remains stable and fast, and you can add whatever features you want to the language (instead of settling for what the designers wanted in this case, as you have to do with QBasic).
>
> Check out an on-line bulletin board system (BBS) for lots of free and shareware C libraries. Also available are many professional C add-in libraries that output C data in all kinds of formats. To use these libraries, you only include the library header file and call the functions within your code. When you compile the program, there is an extra linking step, explained in the documentation that comes with the function library.

If you want to print double-precision floating-point values or long double floating-point values, use the `%lf` specifier. The `printf()`

```
printf("%.2lf", 214678654476.66394);
```

produces this output:

```
214678654476.66
```

Printing Scientific Notation

If you write scientific and mathematical programs, you might want to print extremely large or small floating-point values in scientific notation. The `%e` format code enables you to do that.

The `printf()` function calls

```
printf("%e \n", 2.5);
printf("%e\n", -2.5);
printf("%e\n", 2543123.0);
printf("%e\n", .00000025);
printf("%e\n", -.00000025);
```

produce this output:

```
2.500000e+00
-2.500000e+00
2.543123e+06
2.500000e-07
-2.500000e-07
```

If you use an uppercase `E` in the format code, you get an uppercase `E` in the output. The `printf()`s

```
printf("%E \n", 2.5);
printf("%E\n", -2.5);
printf("%E\n", 2543123.0);
printf("%E\n", .00000025);
printf("%E\n", -.00000025);
```

produce this output:

```
2.500000E+00
-2.500000E+00
2.543123E+06
2.500000E-07
-2.500000E-07
```

Of course, using scientific notation for the first two values, `2.5` and `-2.5`, is overkill. Nevertheless, when printing floating-point data from variables, you won't always know whether a number is small enough to print regularly or whether it needs scientific notation. (The opposite of scientific notation is called *fixed-point.* `4.2E+23` is scientific notation, and `7.5` is fixed-point.) Therefore, you can use the `%g` specifier, and C outputs in either fixed-point or scientific notation, depending on which is shortest. The code

```
printf("%g\n", 2.5);
printf("%g\n", -2.5);
printf("%g\n", 2543123.0);
printf("%g\n", .00000025);
printf("%g\n", -.00000025);
```

produces this output:

```
2.5
-2.5
```

```
2.54312e+06
2.5e-07
-2.5e-07
```

As with %E, if you use %G with an uppercase G, C prints the E in uppercase if scientific notation is used for the output.

Printing Characters

The %c outputs a character constant or character variable. You can also use the %c format code to output escape characters if you want. Study the following printf()s to see how they output characters inside the printf() argument list:

```
printf("%c%c%c\n", 'A', 'B', 'C');
printf("Her initials are %c and %c.\n", 'M', 'P');
printf("Your score of %.1f gets a grade of %c.\n", 91.1, 'A');
```

Here is the output produced by these printf()s:

```
ABC
Her initials are M and P.
Your score of 9.1 gets a grade of A.
```

As with the other format codes, you'll use %c more with variables after you master variables in the next chapter than with character constants as shown here.

The %c is not equivalent to QBasic's PRINT USING ! format code, which prints the first letter from a string. With %c, you can print only characters. If you attempt to print the first letter from a string using %c, you'll get garbaged results.

Integers and characters are usually interchangeable.

In C, integers and characters are virtually interchangeable. If you use an integer when a character is expected, C uses the ASCII table to decide which character to work with. For example, if you print a 65 but use a %c like

```
printf("%c", 65);  /* C uses the ASCII table here */
```

C outputs the letter `A`. (In Appendix A's ASCII table, the code for 65 is the letter A.)

If you reverse the `printf()` and print a character but use `%d` for the format code, C uses the ASCII table to determine which integer to print. The `printf()`

```
printf("%d", 'A');  /* C uses the ASCII table here */
```

prints a `65`.

Many QBasic programmers use `CHR$()` and the `ASC()` functions to do what C does automatically. Here is the QBasic code to accomplish the output shown from the preceding two C `printf()`s:

```
PRINT CHR$(65)       ' Prints an A
PRINT ASC("A")       ' Prints a 65
```

Printing on Paper

QBasic's `LPRINT` statement makes printer output wonderfully easy. In C, there are several ways to print to the printer. The sad thing is that they don't all always work. This section presents the method used by almost every C programmer. If, however, you find that this method does not work with your compiler, you'll have to wait until Chapter 24, "Sequential Files" (sorry!), because having an understanding of C's file opening functions is necessary before you learn the more traditional C printer output method.

The `fprintf()` function is virtually identical to `printf()`. As with QBasic's `PRINT` and `LPRINT`, `printf()` and `fprintf()` look alike in many ways. As a matter of fact, `fprintf()` is identical to an equivalent `printf()` (except the output goes to paper) except for an extra argument that must precede the control string.

The following C program prints a name and address on the printer:

```
fprintf(stdprn, "Mark and Sherri Smith\n");
fprintf(stdprn, "6753 S. Illinois\n");
fprintf(stdprn, "Miami, FL  31232\n");
```

Here is the QBasic code to print the name and address:

```
LPRINT "Mark and Sherri Smith"
LPRINT "6753 S. Illinois"
LPRINT "Miami, FL  31232"
```

Although simple strings are printed here, you can also print formatted numbers to paper like this:

```
fprintf(stdprn, "I made only $%6.2f when I was 16.", 985.23);
```

The `stdprn` is a generic name for whatever primary printer is connected to your computer. Usually, the printer on the parallel port named `LPT1` will receive the output. If you want to output to a different parallel port or to a serial port, you'll learn how to redirect the output to a different device in Chapter 24.

> The QBasic `LPRINT` cannot be redirected to a different printer other than the printer at `LPT1`. Knowing this gives you a hint at why the lower-level C I/O functions might require a little more work than QBasic's I/O commands, but they offer more flexibility than QBasic I/O commands.

Summary

This chapter explored the output capabilities of C. The fundamental output function is `printf()`. Both beginning and advanced C programmers use `printf()` for much of their output. Many more output functions are available, but `printf()` provides an easy approach to getting data to the screen the way you want to see the data.

To use `printf()`, you must understand the format codes, such as `%d` and `%f`. `printf()` can print only strings unless you describe your output values with proper format codes. C replaces the format code with the data to print. The format codes must appear inside the `printf()`'s first argument known as the control string.

This chapter used numeric constants in the `printf()` functions because variables are introduced in the next chapter. However, you can use variables in place of the constants shown in this chapter to output computed values stored in the variables.

The `fprintf()` function is useful for sending output to the printer. `fprintf()` looks just like `printf()` except that an extra argument, `stdprn`, must appear before the formatting control string.

The next chapter describes how to define and use numeric variables. QBasic is more lenient than C because QBasic enables you to mix integers and floating-point values in the same variable (unless you define the variable to be a specific type before you use the variable). After you master C variables, you'll be able to write true data-processing C programs that let C calculate and store results as needed.

6 Numeric Variables

Now that you're familiar with many of C's data types, it's time to learn how to store data in variables. The nice thing about C is that you assign values to variables using the same assignment operator, =, that you use in QBasic. C, however, is not quite as lenient as QBasic because you must be careful not to put data of the wrong type into variables.

Before using variables in C, you must *define* those variables. Defining variables means that you tell C to reserve memory for a variable and assign a name for it. (QBasic enables you to start using a variable without defining the variable first.) There are only certain places within a C program where you can define a variable, and the placement of that variable determines how the rest of the program uses the variable.

In this chapter, you will learn about the following topics:

- Naming variables
- Numeric variable data types
- Floating-point variables
- Introductory operator usage
- Local and global variables

Only numeric variables are discussed here. In the next chapter, you'll learn how to store string data.

Naming Variables

All variables have names. Internally, the C compiler stores a variable's data at a specific memory location, but variable names are easier for programmers to remember and use than explicit addresses. Here are the variable-naming rules that follow the ANSI C standard:

- Variable names can range from 1 to 31 characters.
- Variable names can include alphabetic letters, numbers, and the underscore, _.
- Variable names cannot begin with a numeric digit; they can begin only with a letter or an underscore. Don't begin a variable name with an underscore, however, because it might clash with some internal variable and function names used by the C compiler.
- Variable names cannot be the same as a C keyword such as `if` or a built-in function such as `printf`. Appendix C lists the C keywords and internal functions.

When it comes time to write your own functions (Part VIII in this book), you'll see that you assign function names using the same naming rules that apply to variable names.

Functions are named just like variables.

The primary difference between QBasic variables and C variables is that QBasic variable names can be as long as 40 characters. Also, you cannot use two QBasic variables with the same name but different uppercase or lowercase combinations. To QBasic, `ageLimit`, `AGELIMIT`, and `agelimit` are all the same variable name. (Actually, if you do use a QBasic variable name a second time but use a different case, QBasic changes the first case of the name to that of the most recent one.)

QBasic enables you to use a period inside variable names. If you are used to doing that, guard against it when programming in C. The period is an important separating operator that you'll learn about in Chapter 22, "Structure Records," and you cannot use the period inside C variable names.

Variable Data Types

Table 6.1 lists all the data types available in C. (Chapter 7, "Character and String Data," discusses the character data type.)

Table 6.1. The C variable data types.

Data Type	*Typical Length**	*Range of Data*
`unsigned char`	8 bits	0 to 255
`char`	8 bits	–128 to 127
`unsigned int`	16 bits	0 to 65,535
`short int`	16 bits	–32,768 to 32,767
`int`	16 bits	–32,768 to 32,767
`unsigned long`	32 bits	0 to 4,294,967,295
`long`	32 bits	–2,147,483,648 to 2,147,483,647
`float`	32 bits	3.4e–38 to 3.4e38
`double`	64 bits	1.7e–308 to 1.7e+308
`long double`	80 bits	3.4e–4932 to 1.1e+4932

* The ANSI C standard does not guarantee the length of storage for data types, so your compiler might use a different number of memory bits to store data types. However, these lengths are typical for PC-based C compilers.

The *modifiers* such as `long` and `short` and `unsigned` modify the fundamental data types `char`, `int`, and `double`. A `short int` is identical to `int` in most C compilers.

unsigned holds only positive values.

You might wonder how character data can be termed `signed` because there's no such thing as a negative letter *A*. When reading characters from a file, C returns either a valid character *or* –1 to indicate that the end of file is reached. The `signed char` is a good data type for file I/O because it can hold incoming characters or a –1. You'll learn more about C's file I/O in Part VII of the book.

Sometimes, the `unsigned long` and `long` data types are called `unsigned long int` and `long int` data types. If the data type is not preceded by the `unsigned` modifier, the data type supports `signed` ranges (negatives can occur, as Table 6.1 demonstrates). `signed` is a valid modifier, but it is the default unless you specify `unsigned`. Programmers rarely use `unsigned`.

Use `unsigned` data types when you know that negatives won't occur. As Table 6.1 shows, the `unsigned` data types can hold larger values than the corresponding `signed` data types. Because distances, ages, and weights are never negative, they make good `unsigned` data types. However, if those positive-only values are not going to be extremely large, it doesn't make any difference if you specify them as `signed` or `unsigned`, so most programmers leave off the `unsigned` modifier.

Although there is not a direct one-to-one correspondence between the QBasic data types and C's, Table 6.2 shows you the closest equivalents between the two languages' data types.

Table 6.2. Comparing QBasic and C data types.

QBasic Data Type	*Approximate C Data Type(s)**
`INTEGER`	`short int`, `int` (and `signed int`), `unsigned int`
`LONG`	`long` (and `long int`), `unsigned long`
`SINGLE`	`float`
`DOUBLE`	`double`

* There is no QBasic equivalent for the `long double` data type in C. `long double` holds a much wider range of values than any of QBasic's data types.

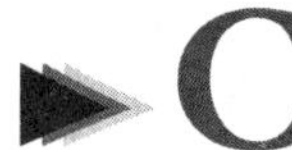

Defining Numeric Variables

QBasic does not require that you define a variable before using it. Listing 6.1 shows a QBasic program that assigns three values, first an integer, then a single-precision, and finally another integer to the same variable.

Listing 6.1. Changing the value you assign to a variable.

```
' Filename: NOTYPE.BAS
' Program that stores three values in the same variable.
' QBasic assumes that all variables are single-precision
' unless you override the data type with DIM or a suffix character.
'
' Assign an integer to the variable
var = 5 + 6
PRINT "var is"; var
' Assign a single-precision value to the variable
var = 5.6 * 120.9
PRINT "var is now"; var
' Assign an integer value again
var = 4432
PRINT "var is now"; var
END
```

Here is the output from Listing 6.1:

```
var is 11
var is now 677.04
var is now 4432
```

> QBasic assumes that all variables are single-precision unless you override that data type. You can assign a QBasic single-precision variable an integer or a single-precision value, and QBasic works with either. C is much more strict and requires that you store data types in correct variables defined for those types.

As you know, the QBasic `DIM` statement enables you to define variables as a specific data type. After you define a variable to be a specific data type (such as `INTEGER`), that variable can hold only that type of data.

If you thought that `DIM` only dimensioned arrays, you should make a quick review of QBasic. In earlier BASIC languages, `DIM` reserved array storage, but in today's QBasic language, `DIM` also defines variables so that they hold only one data type in the program that defines them.

You might also know that QBasic supports the use of data-type suffix characters. The variable `v1%` is an integer and can hold only integers accurately. The variable `v2#` is a double-precision variable. `v3!` is single-precision. `v4$` is a string variable (of which there are none in C, as you'll read about in the next chapter). Today's QBasic programmers rely more on the `DIM` statement than the suffix characters to specify variables of specific data types.

The QBasic program in Listing 6.2 shows the same program as the one in Listing 6.1 except that three variables are explicitly defined with `DIM` before they are used.

Listing 6.2. Defining variables before using them.

```
' Filename: TYPES.BAS
' Program that stores three values in three different variables.
'
DIM var1 AS INTEGER
' Assign an integer to the variable
var1 = 5 + 6
PRINT "var1 is"; var1
DIM var2 AS SINGLE
' Assign a single-precision value to the variable
var2 = 5.6 * 120.9
PRINT "var2 is"; var2
DIM var3 AS INTEGER
' Assign an integer value
var3 = 4432
PRINT "var3 is"; var3
END
```

Here is the output from the program:

```
var1 is 11
var2 is 677.04
var3 is 4432
```

In QBasic, it does not matter whether you define all variables at the top of a program or within the code body. For example, lines 4, 8, and 12 define variables with `DIM` in Listing 6.2. Listing 6.3 shows the same program with all three variables, `var1`, `var2`, and `var3`, defined at the top of the program. The placement of variable definitions isn't critical in QBasic as long as you define the variables before you use them. As you'll see in a moment, C *does* care where you define variables.

Listing 6.3. Defining variables at the top of the program.

```
' Filename: TOPTYPES.BAS
' Program that stores three values in three different variables.
' The variables are defined next.
DIM var1 AS INTEGER
DIM var2 AS SINGLE
DIM var3 AS INTEGER
' Assign an integer to the variable
var1 = 5 + 6
PRINT "var1 is"; var1
' Assign a single-precision value to the variable
var2 = 5.6 * 120.9
PRINT "var2 is"; var2
' Assign an integer value
var3 = 4432
PRINT "var3 is"; var3
END
```

Define all C variables before you use them.

All this review of QBasic becomes critical as you delve deeper into how C differs from the QBasic approach. In C, you must define all variables before you use them. Unlike with QBasic, you cannot just start storing data in a variable. To define a variable in C, you must follow these guidelines:

- You must tell C the name of the variable to reserve space for.
- You must tell C the data type of the variable.

Use the data types from Table 6.1 to define C variables. Here is the general format of C variable definitions:

```
dataType variableName;
```

For example, here is how you would define an integer and a long integer variable:

```
int i;          /* A regular integer */
long int j;     /* A long integer */
```

C variables are *undefined* until you assign them values. Unlike QBasic, which zeros all variables if you don't, C will not zero variables. Therefore, you have no idea what values are in the variables `i` and `j` until you assign them values.

Here are the first few lines in a C program's `main()` function that define the variables:

```
main()
{
  int i;
  long j;    /* The 'int' keyword is optional with longs */
  i = 7;
  j = 92834;
  /* Rest of program would follow... */
```

Only when the `7` is assigned to `i` does the programmer know what is in `i`. Many times, programmers want to define variables and then immediately zero the variables or assign other data to them. Therefore, the designers of C put the definition and initialization statements together. The preceding few lines of code can be shortened like this:

```
main()
{
  int i = 7;  /* Define AND initialize */
  long j = 92834;
  /* Rest of program would follow... */
```

Data Lengths

Just because you define a `long int` variable doesn't mean that you have to store large values in the variable. However, you know that you can store a wider range of values in `long ints` than in regular `ints` (or `short ints`, of course).

Figure 6.1 shows how the variables `amt1` and `amt2` are stored in memory given the following code:

```
int amt1 = 5;
long amt2 = 5;
```

Even though both `amt1` and `amt2` hold the same small value, it takes twice as many memory locations to hold `amt2` as `amt1`. Regular `int`s usually consume 16 bits (2 bytes) of storage, whereas `long int`s usually consume 32 bits (4 bytes). (Again, these are common sizes, but not universal.)

You already know to use the extended data types, such as `long` and `double`, when you want to hold values outside the range of the normal data types, such as `int` and `float`. However, don't use an extended data type unless you know that you might need the extra precision they provide; it takes much more machine time to process the extended data types than to process the regular data types. To keep efficiency, use the regular data types for all your variables unless you have a good reason to suspect that you'll need more storage.

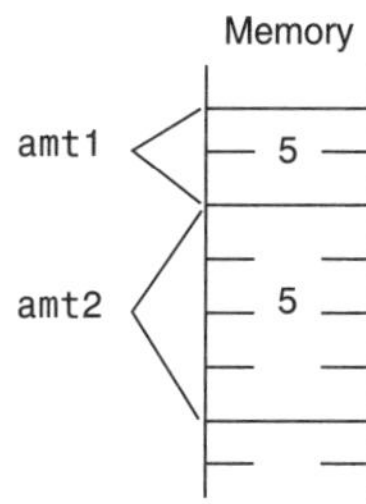

Figure 6.1. The memory space for the `long` *extended data type is twice as much as that for* `int`.

After you define a variable to be `int` or `long int`, be sure that you don't try to store a `float` value in that variable.

It's not that C doesn't enable you to store data of one type in another's variable. You can assign a double-precision value to a character variable, and C never complains. C's runtime type checking is disabled so that your programs run fast, but disabling the type checking means that you have more responsibility to store the right kind of data in the proper variables. By the way, if you assign a double-precision number to a character variable, you'll be storing garbage in that variable; there is no way that C can squeeze a double-precision value that consumes up to 64 bits of storage into an 8-bit character memory location. (If you assign an integer value to a `float` or `double` variable, C adds extra precision to convert the integer into a floating-point data value.)

Listing 6.4 shows you the C equivalent of QBasic's Listing 6.3. As you can see, the variables are all defined before they are used in the program.

Listing 6.4. Defining variables and assigning values in C.

```
/* Filename: TOPTYPES.C
   Defines variables and stores values in them */
#include <stdio.h>
main()
{
  int var1;      /* Variable definitions appear first */
  float var2;
  int var3;
  /* Assign values to the variables and print results */
  var1 = 5 + 6;
  printf("var1 is %d\n", var1);
  var2 = 5.6 * 120.9;
  printf("var2 is %.1f\n", var2);
  var3 = 4432;
  printf("var3 is %d\n", var3);
  return 0;
}
```

> Although Chapter 9, "Common Math Operators," explores C operators, the standard addition, subtraction, multiplication, and division operators are the same for both QBasic and C.

You can group more than one variable definition together. The following code defines several variables and initializes a few of them at the time of definition:

```
main()
{
  int i;
  int j = 9;
  int k;
  float x = 3454.54;
  char c = 'A';
  char d;
  char e = 'P';
  /* rest of C program would follow */
```

You can shorten the variable definition by putting all similar data-type definitions on the same line. The following code is equivalent to the preceding code:

```
main()
{
  int i, j = 9, k;
  float x = 3454.54;
  char c = 'A', d, e = 'P';
  /* rest of C program would follow */
```

Notice that no execution code (such as assignments or `printf()`s) appears before the variable definition lines. The placement of your variable definitions is explained in the next section.

Some Words About Variable Definition

Figure 6.2 shows a skeleton of a C program. The program has a `main()` function and a function named `anotherFun()`. (Don't worry about the specific coding of a function other than `main()` at this time.) The callouts to the figure show where you can define variables.

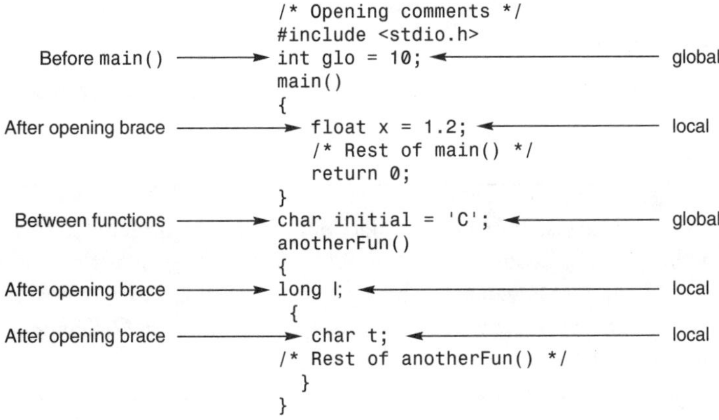

Figure 6.2. Outline of a C program showing variable definition locations.

Notice that there are several places in a C program where you can define variables. You can define variables before a function (or between two functions) and after the opening brace of a block of code.

All variables defined after any opening brace are called *local variables.* Local variables can be used only within their block of code. All variables defined before function names are called *global* variables. As with many QBasic program variables (and the predecessor BASIC renditions), all global variables can be used at any point in the program following their definition. You'll learn all about local and global variables in Part VIII of the book. For now, try to stay away from using global variables.

Often, a single C function such as `main()` contains one or more blocks of code (code between braces). You can define a variable after the opening brace of any block of C code, not just the opening brace that begins a function. Nevertheless, until you get more used to writing C programs, define all your variables after a function's opening brace to simplify your programming.

The largest type wins.

If you mix numerical data types within an expression, C converts the resulting expression to the largest, most extended data type possible. For example, suppose that `i` is an integer and `x` is a floating-point variable. If you want to multiply `i` and `x` together and store the result in a floating-point variable named `result`, you can do so like this:

```
result = i * x;
```

C converts the `i` to a `float` data type. If `i` contains a `7`, it contains a `7.000000` before being multiplied by `x`.

Sometimes, the conversion of `int` to a fractional data type produces small errors. The `7` might actually be converted to `7.000001`. Extremely accurate floating-point values are difficult to represent at the binary level. QBasic is a little better at hiding this rounding from you, but the problem affects QBasic as well as C statements that need a high level of precision.

If you want to control the data type, you can insert a *typecast* before a variable or constant. A typecast is actually a C operator, even though its syntax is a little strange. A typecast temporarily changes a variable's data type. To specify a typecast, place the data type

you want to convert to in parentheses. The following statement typecasts the `i` to `float` before the calculation takes place:

```
result = (float)i * x;  /* Multiply a float times a float */
```

When the expression is finished, `i` reverts to an integer. Although a typecast was unneeded in this expression because C automatically converts `i` to `float` before multiplying `i` by the `x`, you'll see many uses of the typecast operator throughout this book.

Summary

This chapter explained how to define and initialize variables in a C program. You must define all C variables before using them. Unlike QBasic, C must know what variables you will use in the program ahead of time. When defining variables, you assign a name and specify a data type that the variable will hold.

If you don't initialize your variables, C won't do it for you. You should explicitly initialize all variables, even those that you want a zero in, if you need an initial value in the variables.

There are several data types for character variables, integer variables, and floating-point variables. After you define a variable, you should do all you can to ensure that the variable gets the correct type of value. QBasic issues a `Type mismatch` error if you attempt to store a number in a string variable. C, however, does no type checking. Although the lack of type checking makes C more efficient than QBasic, that efficiency sometimes produces some hard-to-trace bugs! Be very careful when storing values in variables, and try to match data types in expressions when possible by using the typecast operator if needed.

There is something strangely missing from Table 6.1. There is no *string* variable data type! The next chapter explains how to get around the lack of string variables in the C language.

7

Character and String Data

QBasic and C are on the opposite ends of the scale when dealing with strings. QBasic is known for its advanced string handling, whereas C doesn't even support string variables! There is no way to store even a single word of text in a variable—that is, without the special kind of string storage you'll find described in this chapter.

Although there are no string variables in C, there is of course a way to store strings in other kinds of variables. Strings reside inside variables ending in a terminating null zero, just as string constants do. When printing strings, C knows where to print when it hits the string's null zero.

Store strings in character arrays.

C does provide several built-in string functions. Some rival those in QBasic, but you might still miss many of the QBasic string functions.

C supports the storage of strings in memory by enabling you to store strings in character arrays. A character array is an array of characters just like an integer array is an array of integer values. This chapter explains how to exploit character arrays so that you can store strings in them.

In this chapter, you will learn about the following topics:

- Character arrays
- Defining string-like arrays
- Defining and initializing string variables
- Putting data in string variables
- Some built-in string functions
- Printing strings

Array Review

As you should know from your QBasic programming, an array is a list of values called *elements.* Instead of a single stand-alone variable such as an integer variable, an array is a contiguous list of several variables, each with the same name (the array name) and distinguished by a subscript.

In QBasic, the `DIM` statement (for *dimension*) reserves arrays. To access an element from the array, you use a subscript in parentheses. Here is a simple `FOR` loop that dimensions an integer array and stores the values from 1 to 10 in the array:

```
DIM values(10)         ' Reserve the array
FOR n = 1 TO 10
  values(n) = n        ' Store 1 through 10
NEXT n
```

> If you don't understand this code, you might consider reviewing QBasic arrays and `FOR` loops before tackling C.

There is no direct `DIM` statement in C. When you define a variable, you must tell C using subscript notation that the variable will be an array. C doesn't use parentheses for subscripts; instead, you must use brackets to indicate the array subscript.

In the preceding snippet of QBasic code, the first array subscript was 0. The code, however, used only the subscripts 1 through 10 (`values(1)` through `values(10)`). All QBasic arrays begin at 0 even though many QBasic programmers don't use the 0 subscript.

If you want to change the beginning subscript in QBasic, you know that the `OPTION BASE` statement enables you to. QBasic reserves all arrays dimensioned after an `OPTION BASE 1` statement starting with a beginning subscript of 1, not 0. If you use an advanced `DIM` statement option, you can begin a QBasic array subscript at any number, even a negative number. The following `DIM` statement reserves eight array elements whose subscripts range from `-4` to `+3`:

```
DIM numbers(-4 TO 3)     ' Reserves 8 array values
```

All C array subscripts begin at 0!

Now that you've had this subscript power for so long in QBasic, throw it all away when moving to C. C supports *only* subscripts beginning at 0; you can't change the starting subscript from 0.

Zero Subscripts Are Efficient

As with most of the C language, the reason the designers of C force you to work with zero-based subscripts is that zero-based subscripts are more efficient than any other kind.

Remember from Chapter 2, "Distinguishing Between QBasic and C," that all programs (even QBasic programs) must be converted to binary before your computer can run the programs. At the binary level (sometimes called the *machine-language* level), all tables of data begin with a zero-based index. The term *index* is just another name for subscript.

Therefore, when a language supports beginning subscript values other than 0, the computer must make a calculation every time you access an array element to adjust your subscript back to a zero-based subscript.

Because C allows only zero-based subscripts, C arrays are translated directly into machine-language arrays, and no calculation has to be made to adjust your subscript to a zero-based subscript during program execution.

If you want to reserve an array in C, you only have to put the brackets and subscript to the right of variables when you define them. Here is the C-equivalent code to the QBasic `FOR` loop you saw earlier. For now, don't worry about the `for` loop differences in C from those of QBasic.

```
int values[11];      /* Reserve the array */
int n;
for (n=1; n<=10; n=n+1)
  { values[n] = n; }  /* Store 1 through 10 */
```

Why did 11 values have to be reserved? It was because C begins all array subscripts at 0. To make this code directly equivalent to that of the QBasic `FOR` loop, you had to tell C to give you 11 elements (0 through 10 are their subscript numbers) because you want to ignore the starting zero-based element here and store values in the remaining 10.

> The array definition in QBasic's `DIM` statement contains the highest subscript number to be used in the program. The number inside C's array definition brackets tells the C compiler the total number of elements you want to reserve, not the highest subscript number.

But You Want Strings!

This chapter will not concern itself anymore with numeric arrays because character string data is the focus here. However, before this chapter gets into strings, it helps to ease into thinking about arrays by looking at a simple integer array first. (Chapter 19, "Array Management," teaches you more about C's numeric arrays.)

It's time to move on to storing strings. QBasic does not support the use of character variables. If you want to store a character, you store that character in a string variable. C is the opposite; C supports the use of character variables but not string variables. If you want to store a string, you must store the string in an array of character variables.

It is your responsibility to ensure that the array holding your string is large enough to hold the terminating zero. Therefore, if you want to store a string of five characters in an array called `name`, you must reserve six elements like this:

```
char name[6];     /* 5-character string plus null zero */
```

The `6` inside the brackets tells C that `name` is not just a character variable but an array (a list) of six character variables. Each element in the array has a subscript running from 0 to 5. Figure 7.1 shows what `name` looks like in memory. (Remember that you don't know the values inside the elements until you initialize them.)

When defining QBasic strings using the common `$` string suffix character, you don't have to tell QBasic the size of the string. Here are valid statements from a QBasic program that store strings of different sizes in the same string variable:

```
myString$ = "ABC"
PRINT myString$          ' Prints ABC
```

```
myString$ = "ABCDEFGHIJKLMNOPQRSTUVWXYZ"
PRINT myString$          ' Prints the alphabet
myString$ = "#"
PRINT myString$          ' Prints a pound sign
```

Unless you designate a fixed-length QBasic string, your string variables can grow and shrink *dynamically* (during program execution).

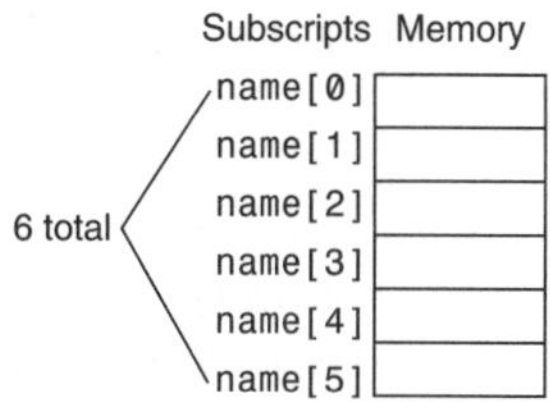

Figure 7.1. The `name` *array as it appears in memory.*

> One reason why many QBasic programs run more slowly than equivalent C programs is that the QBasic runtime speed is hampered by the resizing of strings. If you write a QBasic program that works with many strings of many different sizes, QBasic must take the time to find and release memory for all those strings (called *garbage collection*) behind the scenes while running the program. C doesn't have this behind-the-scene problem, but C doesn't support variable-length string variables either!

A wise man once said, "Sharp tools might be dangerous, but dull tools are useless." The designers of C didn't give you a lot of high-level tools such as variable-length string variables that require more work underneath to work. C offers a selection of low-level programming tools that enable you to write your own higher-level functions that work exactly the way you want them to, not the way the compiler writer designed them.

In QBasic, you can designate a maximum string length by using `DIM` to reserve a fixed-length string. The following QBasic `DIM` statement reserves a fixed-length string named `aString`, and the largest string you can store in `aString` is 20 characters:

```
DIM aString AS STRING * 20
```

After you define a fixed-length string, you lose the right (and ability) to store strings of longer length in the variable. After this `DIM` statement, you can store any string from 0 to

20 characters in aString. If you attempt to store a longer string in aString, QBasic *truncates* (chops off) the string to exactly 20 characters.

When defining C character arrays that will hold strings, you must also know in advance what the longest string you'll ever store in that array will be. If you don't know, you must be able to guess or make the array plenty large enough to hold whatever length of string you'll store there.

Here is how you reserve an array of 20 characters named aString in C:

```
char aString[20];
```

The character array named aString can now hold up to 20 characters. Only if there is a null zero at the end of the characters does aString hold a string. To C, aString is just an array of characters because there is no such variable data type as a string. However, if you make sure that there is a null-terminated string of characters inside aString, you use aString anywhere in a C program that you can use a string constant.

Remembering the following rule will simplify your C programming (and debugging) greatly: You must store all strings in character arrays, but not all character arrays hold strings. Figure 7.2 shows two character arrays, one named carray1 and the other carray2. Even though both arrays are five characters long, carray1 holds a character array only, whereas carray2 holds a character array that you can use as a string due to the null zero.

```
carray1      carray2
[0] a        [0] h
[1] b        [1] a
[2] c        [2] t
[3] d        [3] \0  <---- Null zero makes
                          carray2 a string
```

Figure 7.2. carray1 *holds characters, and* carray2 *holds a string of characters.*

A character array that holds a string does not always have a terminating zero in the *last* element of the array. If you want to store a string shorter than the array length, you can do so as long as the null zero appears at the end of the string.

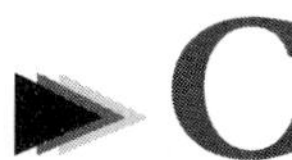

How do you get the null zero at the end of the string? The next section explains how to initialize strings inside character arrays.

Initializing Strings Inside Arrays

As you know, you can define a C integer variable like this:

```
int i;
```

Or you can define it like this:

```
int i = 10;
```

Which method you decide to use depends on whether you want an initial value put in the variable when you define the variable. Sometimes, you won't know the first value of a variable; some data comes from the user or a disk file or a calculation (or a combination of sources). Therefore, there are times when you define variables without initial values and times when you define them with initial values.

> A general rule is that all variables should have *some* initial value, even those that later will be properly initialized from the disk or user input. Usually, the initial value is zero or a null zero (`'\0'`) for character variables and arrays. C doesn't require an initial value, however, and the use of an initial value depends on your program's needs and your preference.

As with integers and the other kinds of numeric variables, you can define a character array without specifying initial contents as you've done in this chapter like this:

```
char myName[15];    /* Reserve memory for 15 characters */
```

If you want to specify initial character values when you define the array, you can do so in one of two ways:

- By filling the character array with a list of individual characters. Use braces to do this.
- By filling the character array with a string. Use a quoted string to do this.

Initializing Characters in an Array

Suppose that you were a teacher and needed to store 10 letter grades in an array. The following code does just that:

```
char grades[10] = {'C', 'A', 'D', 'B', 'B', 'C', 'A',
                   'B', 'D', 'A'};
```

This line of code tells the C compiler several things. You want an array of 10 characters reserved. You want the array named `grades`. The array will be accessible from `grades[0]` to `grades[9]` (remember that all C arrays have a zero-based subscript). The compiler initializes the array at the time of the array definition with the 10 letter grades in the order listed inside the braces. Figure 7.3 shows you what `grades` looks like in memory.

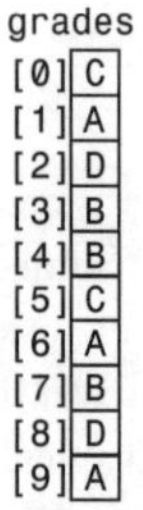

grades	
[0]	C
[1]	A
[2]	D
[3]	B
[4]	B
[5]	C
[6]	A
[7]	B
[8]	D
[9]	A

Figure 7.3. The array of 10 characters.

The `grades` array does not hold a string! The array simply holds 10 characters. Of course, if you want to initialize the array later in the program, an element at a time, you can do so like this:

```
/*
   Start of program here
 */

char grades[10];    /* Reserve the array */

/*
   Other code goes here
*/
grades[0] = 'C';
grades[1] = 'A';
grades[2] = 'D';
grades[3] = 'B';
grades[4] = 'B';
grades[5] = 'C';
grades[6] = 'A';
```

```
grades[7] = 'B';
grades[8] = 'D';
grades[9] = 'A';
/*
  Rest of program follows
 */
```

Don't assign data to arrays later in the program.

The thing that you *cannot* do is use the braces notation after the array is reserved! This is critical to understand. After you define a character array like

```
char grades[10];    /* Reserve the array */
```

you can never assign aggregate values to the array later using braces like

```
grades[10] = {'C', 'A', 'D', 'B', 'B', 'C', 'A', 'B',
              'D', 'A'};
```

because an array name can never appear on the left side of an assignment statement. C gives you the opportunity to assign aggregate (more than one) values to an array only at the time of the array definition.

Initializing Strings in an Array

If you want to initialize a character with a string rather than individual characters, you can assign the string directly to the array at the time of the array's definition like this:

```
char myName[5] = "Paul";
```

Notice that five elements, not four, were reserved. `Paul` contains four characters, and an extra element had to be used for the null zero at the end of the string. Figure 7.4 shows how `myName` appears in memory after its definition and initialization.

```
[0] P
[1] a
[2] u     5 elements total
[3] l
[4] \0
```

Figure 7.4. The `myName` array.

C knows that `Paul` is a string because of the quotation marks around the name. C always tacks on the null zero at the end of any string constant you specify inside quotation marks. Therefore, you never explicitly add a null zero when initializing strings.

Technically, you can add the null zero if you want to initialize the string one character at a time. The following array definition and initialization does *exactly* the same thing as the preceding one. This one requires more typing on your part, and there is not a good reason to initialize a string one character at a time when the quotation marks are so much easier to use.

```
char myName[5] = {'P', 'a', 'u', 'l', '\0'};
```

Use braces only when initializing arrays one element at a time. This line is incorrect:

```
char myName[5] = {"Paul"};
```

No subscript is needed if you define and *initialize.*

If you initialize an array at the time of its definition, you don't have to specify the subscripts. For example, the two statements

```
grades[10] = {'C', 'A', 'D', 'B', 'B', 'C', 'A', 'B', 'D', 'A'};
char myName[5] = "Paul";
```

are exactly the same as these statements, except C figures out how much array space to define:

```
grades[] = {'C', 'A', 'D', 'B', 'B', 'C', 'A', 'B', 'D', 'A'};
char myName[] = "Paul";
```

The reason that most C programmers omit the subscript is twofold. You don't have to take the time to count the elements yourself. Also, and perhaps more important, you won't risk an *incorrect* count. It is far too easy to type

```
char myName[4] = "Paul";    /* Oops, no room for null zero */
```

and forget to leave the extra space for the null zero. The biggest problem with this statement is that C will not generate an error. C actually does put the string, null zero and all, in the array named `myName`. Only the first four elements of the array are protected, however, and C might later store a value over the null zero. You can never safely use this four-element array as a string because you'll never know whether the null zero is still at the end of `Paul`.

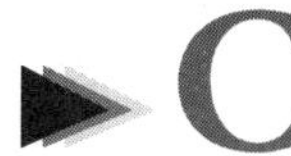

Always specify an initial subscript if you want to eventually put *more* values in an array than the initial data. For example, if you defined and initialized `myName` in the following way, later in the program you can store a string longer than `Paul` (up to 24 characters plus a null zero) in `myName`:

```
char myName[25] = "Paul";    /* Lots of extra room */
```

As with character arrays that hold individual characters, you cannot assign a string to an array after the array is defined. In other words, after you define the array like

```
char myName[25];    /* Just defines but does not initialize */
```

you can *never* assign `myName` a value later in the following ways:

```
myName[] = "Paul";    /* Not allowed */
myName[5] = "Paul";    /* Not allowed */
myName[25] = "Paul";    /* Not allowed */
```

The bottom line is a repetition of what this chapter mentioned earlier: You can never put an array name on the left side of an equal sign except when you initially define the array. Therefore, if you don't know an array's initial value when you define the array, you can never assign that array (as a whole) an aggregate string value later.

If C supported string variables as does QBasic, there would be nothing wrong with directly assigning string values to character arrays. However, C does not support string variables, and a character array is not the same thing as a string variable, even though a character array can hold a string.

There are two ways to assign a character array a string after you've defined the array. You can assign a single character from the string to the character array an element at a time like this:

```
myName[0] = 'P';
myName[1] = 'a';
myName[2] = 'u';
myName[3] = 'l';
myName[4] = '\0';   /* Without this, no string would be in myName */
```

There is no way that you'll want to store strings in character arrays a single character at a time. The process is simply too tedious. Therefore, C comes to the rescue with a function named `strcpy()` (for *string copy*). After you define a character array, you can store strings in the array like this:

```
strcpy(myName, "Paul");
```

The general format of `strcpy()` is

```
strcpy(targetArray, stringToAssign);
```

The *targetArray* must be a character array (or a character pointer, as you'll learn about in Part VI of the book). The *stringToAssign* can be a string constant or another character array that holds a string (or a character pointer).

> The `strcpy()` function requires that you include the STRING.H in all programs that use `strcpy()`. Therefore, along with STDIO.H and other header files, be sure to add the line
>
> ```
> #include <string.h>
> ```
>
> if the program uses `strcpy()` or any of the other C string functions described in this book.

Don't Overflow Arrays!

There are three rules that you *must* remember when working with strings in C:

- It is *your* responsibility to stay within array limits.
- It is *your* responsibility to stay within array limits.
- It is *your* responsibility to stay within array limits.

Such a rule is important enough to be seen three times in a row. The bottom line is this:

C does not guard against array overflow.

An example will drive home the point of this all-important rule in C. Suppose that you need a character array to hold someone's name, and an integer variable to hold someone's age. Right after `main()`'s opening brace, you might define the variables like this:

```
char name[8];     /* Will hold the person's name */
int age;          /* Will hold the person's age */
```

Later in the program, you are ready to assign values to these two variables. (Although the data might come from user input or from the disk drive, this example uses constants to clarify what takes place if you're not careful.) If you store values in `name` and `age` like

```
strcpy(name, "Tony Lo Bianco");   /* Uh oh... */
age = 36;
```

then the variable `name` will *not* hold the string `Tony Lo Bianco`! Why? The answer is that the `name` array was defined so that only 8 characters (including the null zero) will be stored in it, but `Tony Lo Bianco` has 15 characters (with the null zero at the end of the string). C protects only the first 8. As soon as the `36` is assigned to `age`, the 9th and 10th characters of `name` are overwritten (assuming a two-byte integer size). The string is then destroyed, and you cannot rely on `name` to hold a string.

It is interesting to see what happens if you reverse the assignments. If you attempt

```
age = 36;
strcpy(name, "Tony Lo Bianco");   /* Uh oh... */
```

then `age` gets wiped out as soon as the compiler stores the long string `Tony Lo Bianco` in the `name` array. Originally, `age` was defined after the `name` array, so `age` probably follows `name` in memory (although you can't be guaranteed of this because C is free to store variables in whatever order suits it best at compile time).

C does not ever check array boundary violations. (Some compilers give you the option of array checking, but the ANSI C standard does not support array size checking.) Even something as ridiculous as the following code runs without an error:

```
char name[10];
name[6349] = 'x';    /* Wow */
```

> Of course, there *will* be a problem because something important in memory probably got overwritten by the assignment of the `x`, but you won't receive an error message from the compiler.

There is no way you can get by with array violations in QBasic. As soon as you make the following mistake, QBasic will issue a `Subscript out of range` error message:

```
DIM values(10)
values(6349) = 15;
```

QBasic continually checks your program execution to make sure that you never attempt to write outside of an array's original definition. C does not perform runtime checking. The result is much faster program execution but much more danger on your part. You must make sure that you never write outside of an array, or the resulting logic error could be difficult to find at best. At worst, you'll lock up your computer because the out-of-range value might write over the operating system's stack or some other vital area of system memory.

Printing Strings

The `%s` format code enables you to print the contents of character arrays that hold strings. The `%s` works like this: All characters in the array, starting with the first element, print up to but not including the null zero. The string terminating null zero tells the `%s` format code exactly where to stop printing. Therefore, you must print only character arrays that hold null-terminated strings, not character arrays with individual characters that don't form strings.

If you wanted to print the contents of the array

```
char letters[] = {'A', 'B', 'C'};  /* Not a string */
```

then you would have to use the `%c` format code and print each element individually like this:

```
printf("%c", letters[0]);  /* Prints the A */
printf("%c", letters[1]);  /* Prints the B */
printf("%c", letters[2]);  /* Prints the C */
```

You cannot print the letters like this:

```
printf("%s", letters);  /* Will not work! */
```

C will not know where to end because there is no null zero at the end of the array. Actually, C will start printing the `A`, and continue printing *every* value of *every* memory location until C finds a null zero to stop on. If the ASCII null zero does not appear in memory for several hundred characters, the `printf()` will print several hundred characters!

If you know that there is a string in the array, however, you can use `%s` to print the string. Suppose the `letters` array were initialized like this:

```
char letters[] = "ABC";  /* A string */
```

The following `printf()` would properly print the string in the `letters` array:

```
printf("%s", letters);  /* Prints ABC */
```

Wrapping Up Strings

The programs in Listing 7.1 and 7.2 demonstrate string manipulation and output in QBasic and an equivalent program in C. Although there is a lot more to learn about strings, especially how to initialize them with user and disk-file input, the program in Listing 7.2 demonstrates the concepts you've learned about up to this point.

Listing 7.1. A simple QBasic string program.

```
' Filename: STRINGS.BAS
' Manipulates strings in QBasic

fruit1$ = "Apple"
' Remember that the plus sign acts as a string-concatenation
' operator when you apply the plus to strings.
fruit2$ = "O" + "r" + "a" + "n" + "g" + "e"
DIM fruit3 AS STRING * 20     ' A fixed-length string
fruit3 = "Pear"
DIM fruit4 AS STRING * 20     ' Not initialized yet

PRINT "Here are the fruits:"
PRINT fruit1$; ", "; fruit2$; ", "; fruit3

fruit4 = fruit1$    ' No string copy function needed in QBasic
PRINT "The 4th fruit holds: "; fruit4

fruit4 = "Kiwi"
PRINT "The 4th fruit now holds: "; fruit4

' Print a few individual fruit starting characters
PRINT "Fruit initials: "; LEFT$(fruit1$, 1); ", "; LEFT$(fruit2$, 1);
PRINT ", "; LEFT$(fruit3, 1); ", "; LEFT$(fruit4, 1)
END
```

The C program cannot be a perfect equivalent of the QBasic program because of the different methods of string storage in the two languages. C does offer a slight efficiency advantage, however, when printing individual characters from a string. You do not have to call a C function to print an array's first character, whereas you must use `LEFT$()` to print the first letter of a QBasic string.

Listing 7.2. A simple C string program.

```
1:  /* Filename: STRINGS.C
2:     Manipulates strings in C */
3:  /* Be sure to include STRING.H for the strcpy() function */
4:  #include <stdio.h>
5:  #include <string.h>
6:  main()
7:  {
8:    /* Initialize four arrays with fruit names */
9:    char fruit1[] = "Apple";
10:   char fruit2[] = {'O', 'r', 'a', 'n', 'g', 'e', '\0'};
11:   char fruit3[20] = "Pear";  /* More than enough space */
12:   char fruit4[20];  /* Will initialize later */
13:
14:   printf("Here are the fruits:\n");
15:   printf("%s, %s, %s\n", fruit1, fruit2, fruit3);
16:   strcpy(fruit4, fruit1);
17:   printf("The 4th fruit holds: %s\n", fruit4);
18:   strcpy(fruit4, "Kiwi");
19:   printf("The 4th fruit now holds: %s\n", fruit4);
20:   /* Print a few individual fruit starting characters
21:      just to show that the strings are stored in char arrays */
22:   printf("Fruit initials: %c, %c, %c, %c\n", fruit1[0], fruit2[0],
23:           fruit3[0], fruit4[0]);
24:
25:   return 0;
26: }
```

Here is the output from both programs:

```
Here are the fruits:
Apple, Orange, Pear
The 4th fruit holds: Apple
The 4th fruit now holds: Kiwi
Fruit initials: A, O, P, K
```

Lines 22 and 23 in the C program show that printing individual characters from C strings is easier and more efficient than printing them using the functions as done on lines 22 and 23 of the QBasic program.

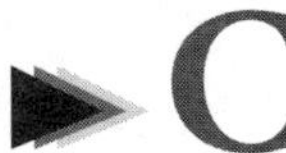

Summary

Whew! In this chapter, you learned what you must do to store strings in variables. There are no string variables in C, so you must store strings in character arrays. By using character arrays properly, you can store string data inside character arrays. However, there is a lot you must remember about character arrays, especially when defining and initializing them.

You must always keep in mind that a QBasic string variable can hold a multicharacter string, but you must define a character array to hold multibyte strings in C.

Table 7.1 lists the differences between QBasic arrays and C arrays that you learned in this chapter.

Table 7.1. Array differences between QBasic and C.

In QBasic	*In C*
Array subscripts appear in parentheses.	Array subscripts appear in brackets.
The `DIM` statement reserves an array.	A variable definition with brackets reserves an array.
Arrays begin at 0 or 1 (if you use `OPTION BASE`) or another number if you specify a different starting subscript with `DIM`.	Arrays always begin at subscript 0.
You can assign a value directly to a string variable.	Never assign values directly to a character array after you've defined the array. Instead, assign values an element at a time or use the `strcpy()` function.

It's easy to print C strings that are stored in character arrays. Use the `%s` to print strings, and use `%c` to print individual characters from the strings if you need to.

Although C strings seem cumbersome to QBasic programmers, C is highly efficient. QBasic performs a lot of string work behind the scenes, such as collecting leftover string space no longer needed as a program changes data in string variables. C requires more work on your part so that the programs you write are as efficient as possible.

The next chapter explains how to ask the user for values. With `scanf()`, you can grab keyboard data and store the data in variables.

8

GETTING INPUT

This chapter explains how to get input data from the user. You must learn how to convert your QBasic `INPUT` thinking into C's `scanf()` way of thinking. `scanf()` is to C what `INPUT` is to QBasic: they both get keyboard data from the user.

Before you go any further, be warned that you're not going to like C's `scanf()` function! Nobody does. C does not perform keyboard input as easily as QBasic. Although you might think that QBasic's `INPUT` statement is limited at times (and it is), C's `scanf()` is both limited and cryptic!

`scanf()` is one of the primary reasons that serious C programmers purchase powerful input functions from vendors that allow for better keyboard control, error correction, and full-screen data entry.

In this chapter, you will learn about the following topics:

- The `scanf()` function
- Prompting for input
- `scanf()` and `printf()` similarities
- The cryptic nature of `scanf()`

If scanf() is so bad (and it is), why should you take the time to learn it? scanf() does have a lot of similarities to printf(). In fact, as Figure 8.1 shows, these functions are mirror images of each other. scanf() uses almost all of printf()'s format codes and control string features. scanf() is a good function for you to use while learning the fundamentals of C because you've mastered printf(), and despite its drawbacks, scanf() is better at this point in your learning of C than any of the other input functions.

It might seem like a cop-out to say that you'll eventually use other people's input functions collected from electronic bulletin board systems or purchased from software companies, or that you'll write your own. But you will need to resort to extra help because none of C's input functions (except for disk file functions when you know the format of the incoming disk data extremely well) fulfills all input needs.

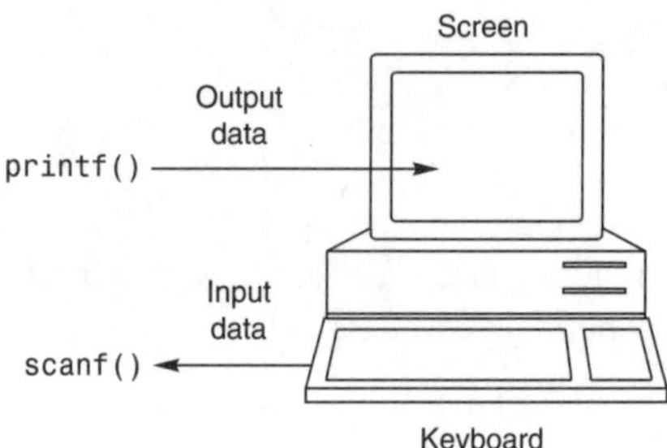

Figure 8.1. `scanf()` *gets keyboard input, and* `printf()` *displays screen output.*

An Overview of *scanf()*

As mentioned in the introduction, scanf() looks a lot like printf(). If you understand the way printf() uses format codes to format output, you'll understand how scanf() uses format codes to format input. Basically, the format of scanf() is this:

```
scanf(controlString, inputVariable [, inputVariable2...] );
```

As the scanf() format indicates with the brackets, you must fill at least one variable with scanf() input, and possibly more. Before using printf(), you need to have data in variables (possibly you want to print constants). scanf() fills variables with values.

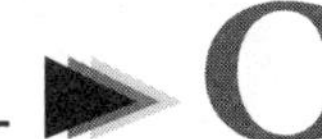

Therefore, any variables that appear in the *`inputVariable`* portion will be filled with values by the user at the keyboard. Whatever values `scanf()` variables contain before the `scanf()` will be wiped out after the `scanf()` finishes.

> The header file for `scanf()` is STDIO.H, just as it is for `printf()`.

If you want to get an integer value from the user, use the `%d` format code inside the `scanf()` *`controlString`*. If you want the user to enter an integer followed by a floating-point value, put both a `%d` and a `%f` in the *`controlString`*.

`scanf()` works a lot like `INPUT`.

So far, this description of `scanf()`, except for the talk about format codes, matches the description of QBasic's `INPUT` statement as well. `INPUT` accepts one or more values from the user at the keyboard. Those values go into variables, and whatever values are in those variables when the user finishes entering data are replaced with the new data. `scanf()`, however, never displays a question mark as QBasic's `INPUT` statement automatically does. If you want a question mark to appear, you have to print one with `printf()` before the `scanf()` statement.

> Escape characters such as `\n` and `\t` never appear inside `scanf()`. Use escape characters for output but not for input. Also, don't use width or decimal specifiers with `scanf()`. `%6.2f` works well with `printf()` to display two decimal positions inside a six-character field width, but you should use `%f` to get a floating-point value from the user. You cannot predict or control the number of decimal places the user enters, so don't try; you'll get hard-to-cipher bugs, or at best, C will simply ignore your width and decimal requests.

> As with QBasic's `INPUT`, always prompt the user before executing a `scanf()` function. In other words, don't call `scanf()` without asking the user a question, or without telling the user what to answer.

No Automatic Prompt

The designers of QBasic really tried to design the language to protect beginning programmers as much as possible (from themselves). QBasic includes lots of handy and powerful I/O commands. INPUT, the cornerstone of most standard QBasic keyboard input, optionally enables you to specify a prompt string within the INPUT statement. As you know, the two statements

```
PRINT "How old are you";
INPUT age
```

can become this one statement:

```
INPUT "How old are you"; age
```

QBasic enables you to include the printed prompt in the INPUT statement because the designers of QBasic knew that you should rarely, if ever, get keyboard data without prompting the user first. The PRINT/INPUT combination was so common that they were combined into the INPUT statement. If you were to run a QBasic program with the preceding INPUT, you would see this line on the screen when program execution got to the INPUT:

```
How old are you?
```

QBasic would then wait for a response. When the user types a number in response to the question (the prompt) and presses Enter, the user's typed number is assigned to the age variable, and the program can continue execution.

C's scanf() also halts until the user's next Enter keystroke. However, unlike in QBasic, scanf() does not have a combined form that enables you to specify a prompt at the time of the scanf(). Therefore, your C construct to ask for the age as shown earlier would look something like this:

```
printf("How old are you? ");  /* No automatic ? like QBasic */
/* The scanf() that receives the user's age would go here */
```

Oh No, Not Efficiency Again!

As you probably already know, if you don't respond to a QBasic INPUT properly, QBasic displays a Redo from start error message. For example, if you are supposed to enter four values but you enter three or five, QBasic displays the Redo from start message. QBasic then automatically issues the INPUT again and waits for a better input from you.

If you use C's `scanf()` to get four values, but you enter only three, C keeps right on going. When you press Enter, no matter what kind of response you typed, the line following the `scanf()` executes, and the program continues on its merry way, even if there are variables with bad values, no values, or whatever!

Efficiency raises its ugly head yet again. Instead of worrying about the user, C decides to "let the user take care of things," which is typically a dangerous practice. However, you chose C because of its efficiency and its widespread use as a direct result of that efficiency. Therefore, you have more burden on your back while writing your programs because you've got to check for many different things (or else, after mastering the fundamentals of C from this book, use someone else's input routines).

Later in this book, you'll learn some functions that accept single keystrokes without needing an Enter keystroke (similar to QBasic's `INKEY$`). With these functions, you can collect the user's input a character at a time and build numeric values you need. You'll have more control over your input by doing so. (Do you see why this book makes the strong case for learning the C basics, then purchasing some more reasonable add-in C programming functions? Others have taken the time to write and debug the routines that can improve all your input control functions that you'll begin incorporating into your own programs.)

scanf()'s Bane: Ampersand Signs (&)

You might as well get the most painful part of `scanf()` behind you. Here is the cardinal rule when using `scanf()`:

> If you use `scanf()` to accept non-array variable input, such as integers, single characters, and floating-point values, you *must* add an ampersand, `&`, before the variable name inside the `scanf()`'s parentheses. If you use `scanf()` to accept array values, such as keyboard-typed words that you want captured in character arrays as strings, *don't* precede the array name with an ampersand.

Put an `&` before `scanf()`'s non-array variables.

Suppose that you want to ask the user for a floating-point value. Here is a way to do that:

```
printf("How much is the cost? ");
scanf(" %f", &cost);
```

Notice that an ampersand precedes the `cost` variable. Without the ampersand, `cost` will not hold the user's input.

There is a good reason for the ampersand, but the reason involves the use of pointers, and you've probably never learned about pointers because QBasic does not support their use. It's going to be several chapters (Chapter 21, "Pointers Are New to You") before you fully understand why the ampersand is needed. That's OK. Just be sure to put the ampersand before non-array variables, and your programs will be able to accept keyboard input.

Suppose that you want to ask the user for a string value, such as a first name. Here is the combination `printf()` and `scanf()` that does that:

```
printf("What is your first name? ");
scanf(" %s", name);
```

The `name` must be defined earlier as a character array. Whatever name the user enters will be stored in the `name` array when the user presses Enter. No `&` is needed because an array is being filled from keyboard input.

The program in Listing 8.1 shows a QBasic program that accepts user input into several kinds of variables. To maintain as much relationship as possible to C, all the variables in the QBasic program are explicitly declared using `DIM AS` *`type`*. Subsequent `INPUT` statements enable the user to fill those different kinds of variables with values. Take a look at the QBasic program and the C equivalent following it.

Listing 8.1. Getting user input with QBasic.

```
' Filename: GOODINP.BAS
' Gets values from the user using INPUT
CLS
DIM c AS STRING         ' The rest of the program will
DIM n AS INTEGER        ' get values for these variables
DIM x AS SINGLE         ' from the user.
DIM word AS STRING

INPUT "Enter an integer number: ", n    ' Comma suppresses the ?
PRINT "You entered"; n
PRINT    ' Blank line

INPUT "Enter a floating-point number: ", x
PRINT "You entered"; x
PRINT
```

```

INPUT "Enter a character: ", c
PRINT "You entered "; c
PRINT

INPUT "Enter a single word: ", word
PRINT "You entered "; word
PRINT
END
```

Listing 8.2 contains the same program written in C using `scanf()` to get the input.

Listing 8.2. Getting user input with C.

```
/* Filename: GOODINP.C
   Introduces input using scanf() */
#include <stdio.h>
main()
{
  char c;              /* This program requests that */
  int n;               /* the user enter values into */
  float x;             /* these variables. */
  char word[25];
  /* Prompt for values and print them back to the user */
  printf("Enter an integer number: ");
  scanf(" %d", &n);
  printf("You entered %d\n\n", n);
  printf("Enter a float number: ");
  scanf(" %f", &x);
  printf("You entered %f\n\n", x);
  printf("Enter a character: ");
  scanf(" %c", &c);
  printf("You entered %c\n\n", c);
  printf("Enter a single word: ");
  scanf(" %s", &word);
  printf("You entered %s\n\n", word);
  return 0;
}
```

Here is the output from either program:

```
Enter an integer number: 13
You entered 13
```

```
Enter a floating-point number: 5.435487
You entered 5.435487

Enter a character: e
You entered e

Enter a single word: abc
You entered abc
```

scanf() Limitations

Notice that all the `scanf()`'s control strings shown in the preceding section contain a blank before the percent sign. Sometimes there will be a leftover whitespace character, such as a space or tab, on the input buffer. The space inside the control string makes C skip this whitespace.

The C program shown in Listing 8.3 is identical to the one in Listing 8.2 in every way except that every leading space is removed from the `scanf()` control strings. If you run this program, you'll find that simply removing the spaces causes problems.

Listing 8.3. Eliminating the leading control-string blank causes problems.

```
/* Filename: BADINP.C
   Input using scanf() needs a leading blank */
#include <stdio.h>
main()
{
  char c;              /* This program requests that */
  int n;               /* the user enter values into */
  float x;             /* these variables. */
  char word[25];
  /* Prompt for values and try to print them back to the user */
  printf("Enter an integer number: ");
  scanf("%d", &n);            /* NO leading space! */
  printf("You entered %d\n\n", n);
  printf("Enter a floating-point number: ");
  scanf("%f", &x);
  printf("You entered %f\n\n", x);
  printf("Enter a character: ");
  scanf("%c", &c);            /* Oops, scanf() doesn't work! */
  printf("You entered %c\n\n", c);
```

```
20:   printf("Enter a single word: ");
21:   scanf("%s", &word);
22:   printf("You entered %s\n\n", word);
23:   return 0;
24: }
```

Although no leading space appears before the first `scanf()` in line 12, the input problem doesn't rear its ugly head until line 18's `scanf()`. When you enter numeric values using `scanf()`, as done in lines 12 and 15, C reads all input up through the number but does not read the Enter keystroke. The `\n` character generated by the Enter stays on the input buffer. Line 15's `scanf()` works because a number is being requested, and C reads past the `\n` until C finds a valid floating-point number. (Technically, using a leading blank before a `scanf()` that accepts numeric input is not necessary, but using the leading blank is a good habit to apply to all `scanf()` control strings.)

Here is the output from Listing 8.3. Notice that C did not wait for the user's response to the character input from line 18.

```
Enter an integer number: 6
You entered 6

Enter a floating-point number: 1.234567
You entered 1.234567

Enter a character: You entered


Enter a single word: abc
You entered abc
```

You must keep in mind that C treats the `\n` newline sequence as a single character. In Chapter 4, "Data Differences," you learned that all the escape sequences are treated as single characters. Without the leading blank before line 12's `scanf()`, C grabs the Enter keystroke, the `\n` character, and uses the newline as the character to be stored in the variable named `c`! Notice the extra blank line before the `Enter a single word:` prompt; the blank line is the newline character being displayed.

Use `scanf()` only to get single words.

Any time you accept input for a single character, you must add the leading blank in the control string before the `%c`, or C will read the preceding input's newline as the data character. If you are in the habit of adding the leading space before all `scanf()` control strings, you'll never have to worry about the buffered newline with `scanf()` again.

The `scanf()` function cannot input strings with embedded spaces. Even though a character array can hold a string with embedded spaces, `scanf()` cannot accept strings of more than one word at a time. Of all of scanf()'s drawbacks, this one is probably the most limiting if you need to get text from the user. Luckily, there are some functions that do accept string input of more than one word at a time, but you won't learn about them until Chapter 16, "Some I/O Functions." Nevertheless, scanf() will get you by for a while so that you can learn more about C and how C compares with QBasic.

scanf() cannot check for array boundaries.

If the user enters a word that is longer than the character array size, scanf() doesn't inform you that an array boundary problem occurred. (Remember that C thinks you should worry about such trivial matters as array overflow!)

If you define a character array named lastName like

```
char lastName[5];
```

and you use scanf() to get the name from the user like

```
scanf(" %s", lastName);
```

the user can enter only strings of four or fewer characters (not five because there must always be room for a null zero). If the user enters a longer name, such as McDaniels, the characters following the letter n in the input name will overwrite other data areas, possibly and probably overwriting other variables somewhere else in the program.

> When using scanf() for string input, be sure to reserve an array large enough to hold the longest string the user will ever enter. Also, be sure to warn the user that no spaces are allowed in the string.

The array problem is yet another scanf() problem that you'll learn how to solve with other functions as you read through this book.

The Control String Dictates the Input

The scanf() control string is a picture image, to C, of what the user is going to enter at the keyboard. If you want the user to use scanf() to enter formatted input, such as a person's three initials, the control string must look like the user's response.

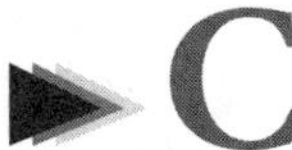

Consider the following code:

```
scanf(" %c. %c. %c.", &init1, &init2, &init3);
```

Assume that `init1`, `init2`, and `init3` are all character variables. The format code dictates *exactly* what the user is to type. The user had better type the following keystrokes, or the `scanf()` will not work correctly:

A single letter
A period
A space
Another letter
A period
A space
Another letter
A period
A space
The Enter key

If the user leaves out any space or types something other than a period, the three input variables `init1`, `init2`, and `init3` will not be initialized with good values. The user cannot enter `GMP`, `G M P`, `G.M.P.`, or any other combination of keystrokes that differs from the list just shown.

> The user does not have to type the leading space before the first `%c` because that space exists solely to skip over whitespace that might still be in the input buffer. If the user did happen to type a space before the input, that space would be harmlessly skipped over.

Don't Count on the User

Now that you understand `scanf()`, you can go about your merry way getting values from the user at the keyboard. If you think about `scanf()` for very long, however, you'll begin to realize that `scanf()` can never be trusted as much as QBasic's `INPUT`.

Although `INPUT` is not the best user-input statement in the world, at least QBasic monitors `INPUT`, issuing the `Redo from start` message when the user types something he or she should not type. C never informs you that bad input took place. Look back over the preceding section, and think about that user sitting at the keyboard needing to enter initials. Users don't always type what they should. Users make mistakes, and many of them are afraid of computers. Even if you print message prompts that tell the user in crystal-clear language what to type (a letter, followed by a period, followed by a space, then another letter, and so on), the user might not understand and could easily enter data that's not correct.

Therefore, be wary of `scanf()`, but go ahead and use it for now. While you're learning more of C, you must have some way to get keyboard data so that you can write and test code. This book uses `scanf()` for several chapters until you're ready for some other input routines. However, even the other input routines are only marginally better than `scanf()`. C was never designed to be a slick I/O language; its power lies in its efficiency. After you write C code "for real," look into add-on routines you can acquire that handle I/O better.

In Chapter 16, "Some I/O Functions," you'll learn about some character-oriented input functions that enable you to build your own array-checking string input functions. Before purchasing other people's C input functions, you'll want to try your hand at writing your own.

Summary

This chapter introduced the `scanf()` function. Every newcomer to C learns `scanf()`. Every newcomer to C uses `scanf()`. Virtually every introductory C textbook uses `scanf()` to get data from the keyboard. Despite all its appearances in the introductory C community, most C programmers look forward to the day they can swap `scanf()` for other, more powerful input functions. Usually, programmers write their own improved input functions, buy some, or download some from the many available on electronic bulletin board systems around the country.

In the meantime, your primary objective at this time is moving from QBasic to C, and `scanf()` is so similar to `printf()` that you can use `scanf()` for a while. In using `scanf()`, however, be sure to remember these important points about the function:

- Precede all non-array variables with an ampersand.
- Leave a leading blank before the `scanf()` control string.

- The user must follow the control string's format exactly, or the resulting input might be incorrect.
- `scanf()` will not enable the user to enter string data into character arrays if the string contains more than one word separated by a whitespace (such as a blank or tab).

The following chapter introduces a new part of the book that explains how to use C's operators.

Basic C

Part III

Operating with Operators

9

Common Math Operators

This chapter will be easy for you. Many of C's fundamental math operators work just like their QBasic equivalents. C's operators follow a hierarchy of order just as QBasic's operators do. As with QBasic, division is performed before addition unless parentheses override the natural order of the operators.

Appendix B contains a complete list of C operators and their order of precedence. Sometimes, C can be a little trickier than QBasic when performing calculations. A lot of this part of the book will devote itself to explaining some of the problem areas you might encounter.

In this chapter, you will learn about the following topics:

- The fundamental math operators
- How the division operator performs both integer and floating-point division
- C's equal sign works only for assignment, not for equality testing
- C's compound operators streamline your expressions

Start with the Easy Operators

Table 9.1 lists the four primary C operators. As you can see, they look just like their QBasic equivalents.

Table 9.1. C's four primary math operators.

Operator	*Description*
+	Addition
-	Subtraction
*	Multiplication
/	Division

Due to C's free-form nature, extra spacing throughout a C program is usually up to you, but spacing sometimes makes a difference when you're writing C expressions. Be especially careful not to put two plus signs or minus signs together without a space between them. If you type the lines of code in Listing 9.1 exactly as you see them, QBasic automatically inserts a space between the minus signs on line 6.

Listing 9.1. QBasic watches over you when you're writing expressions.

```
1:  ' Filename: NOSPACE.BAS
2:  ' QBasic inserts a separating space for
3:  ' you between two minus signs.
4:  a = 9
5:  b = 7
6:  c = a --b        ' QBasic inserts the space here
7:
8:  PRINT "The answer is"; c
9:  END
```

By the way, here is the output from the program:

```
The answer is 16
```

> Mathematically, subtracting a negative value is the same as performing an addition operation.

++ and - - are C operators.

C contains two operators that QBasic does not have. The *increment* operator looks like this: ++. The *decrement* operator looks like this: - -. If you didn't leave the separating space when adding a positive value or subtracting a negative value, C would think you were using an increment or decrement operator, and the resulting answer would not be to your liking.

The next chapter will explain more about ++ and - -. For now, just be sure that you leave spaces between two like addition or subtraction operators, and both you and C will be happier.

> Of course, two minus signs or two plus signs rarely appear together in an expression. Nevertheless, you bought this book to explain the differences, similarities, and problems that moving from QBasic to C involves. Early in your C programming foray, you don't want to get tripped up on an error such as two back-to-back operators that compute differently than you expect them to.

Listing 9.2 contains a simple QBasic program that computes payroll figures. Listing 9.3 shows the equivalent program in C. The order of operator precedence is the same in both languages for the primary math operators, as the table in Appendix B shows. Therefore, the conversion of simple expressions from QBasic to C is easy.

Listing 9.2. Calculating payroll with QBasic.

```
' Filename: PAYCALC.BAS
' Perform QBasic payroll calculations
PRINT "** Payroll Calculation **"      ' Print a title
PRINT
PRINT
INPUT "How many hours did you work"; hrs
```

continues

Listing 9.2. continued

```
7:  INPUT "How much did you earn per hour"; rate
8:  INPUT "What is your tax rate (i.e., .28)"; taxRate
9:  ' Compute the gross pay
10: grossPay = hrs * rate
11: ' Parentheses would clarify but are not needed
12: netPay = grossPay - grossPay * taxRate
13: PRINT USING "You'll get paid ####.##"; netPay
14: END
```

As the comment on line 11 states, line 12 does not require parentheses because QBasic computes multiplication before subtraction (as does C). However, putting redundant parentheses around the last part of the expression does help clarify the code by showing the calculation ordering like this:

```
netPay = grossPay - (grossPay * taxRate)
```

Listing 9.3. Calculating payroll with C.

```
/* Filename: PAYCALC.C
   Perform C payroll calculations */
#include <stdio.h>
main()
{
  float hrs, rate, taxRate, grossPay, netPay;
  printf("** Payroll Calculation **\n\n\n");
  /* Prompt and get values from the user */
  printf("How many hours did you work? ");
  scanf(" %f", &hrs);
  printf("How much did you earn per hour? ");
  scanf(" %f", &rate);
  printf("What is your tax rate (i.e., .28)? ");
  scanf(" %f", &taxRate);
  /* Compute the gross pay */
  grossPay = hrs * rate;
  /* Parentheses would clarify but are not needed */
  netPay = grossPay - grossPay * taxRate;
  printf("You'll get paid %6.2f", netPay);
  return 0;
}
```

Here is a sample session from either of the preceding programs:

```
** Payroll Calculation **

How many hours did you work? 40
How much did you earn per hour? 10
What is your tax rate (i.e., .28)? .1
You'll get paid 360.00
```

Exploring Division a Little More

There are three kinds of division.

The division operator, /, sometimes works differently in C than in QBasic. Both C and QBasic support three kinds of division-related operations:

- Regular floating-point division
- Integer division
- Modulus (remainder from integer) division

Table 9.2 shows how QBasic and C perform each of these division-related operations. As you can see, C uses the slash, /, for both floating-point and integer division.

Table 9.2. Comparing QBasic's and C's division operators.

Description	*QBasic Operator*	*C Operator*
Floating-point division	/	/
Integer division	\	/
Modulus (remainder)	MOD	%

Suppose that you had to divide a bonus of $725 between four salespeople. The following QBasic `PRINT` statement tells how much each person should get:

```
PRINT USING "Each gets ###.##"; 725 / 4
```

The output from this statement looks like this:

```
Each gets 181.25
```

The following C statement produces the same result:

```
printf("Each gets %5.2f", 725. / 4.);
```

Notice the decimal points following the two values in the `printf()`. If neither decimal were there, the `printf()` would produce an incorrect result. Here is the rule for C's floating-point division:

> One or the other side of the division operator must contain a floating-point constant or variable for floating-point division to take place. If integers appear on both sides of the division operator, *integer division* occurs.

Knowing this rule leads you into the method C uses to replace the \ operator in QBasic. QBasic uses \ for integer division, but C automatically performs integer division if two integers appear on both sides of the division operator.

Suppose that you needed to divide 30 cookies among seven children. No child should get more cookies than another, and you can't break any or the broken cookies would crumble. Therefore, integer division ensures that each child gets the same number of cookies, and you'll keep any leftovers for yourself. Here is how you would print the answer in QBasic:

```
PRINT "Each gets"; 30 \ 7
```

Here is the code in C:

```
printf("Each gets %d", 30 / 7);
```

Both of the preceding lines of code produce this output:

```
Each gets 4
```

> Constants are often used in this chapter's examples to illustrate the operators. However, in your "real" programs, you'll be operating more with variables for which the answers are not always as obvious as they are in these teaching examples.

Modulus arithmetic is useful for computing the remainder of integer divisions. For example, to see how many cookies from the preceding discussion you would have left for

yourself, compute the modulus of the integer division. `MOD` computes modulus for QBasic, and `%` computes modulus for C. This is how you would print the leftover number of cookies in QBasic:

```
PRINT "You get"; 30 MOD 7
```

Here's the equivalent C statement:

```
printf("You get %d", 30 % 7);
```

Here's the output from both statements:

```
You get 2
```

C's Repetitive Assignment

Given the next set of QBasic statements, what value do you think is stored in `ans`?

```
a = 5
b = 10
c = 15
d = 20
e = 25
ans = a = b = c = d = e = 30
```

If you first think that QBasic would give you an error here, you would be incorrect. This multiple use of the equal sign is a valid QBasic statement (although neither common nor very readable). QBasic stores a `0` in `ans`! (If you thought `30`, that's OK, because that's the way C handles the multiple equals.) Even `e` does not have a `30`, but retains its old value of `25`.

To QBasic, the equal sign is used for two purposes:

- For assignment such as this statement:

  ```
  n = 19 * 7;
  ```

- For equality comparisons such as this statement:

  ```
  IF age = 18 THEN PRINT "Now an adult"
  ```

The QBasic equal sign is an example of an *overloaded operator*. The equal sign has two purposes, and QBasic distinguishes between the two by the context in which you use the equal sign. That is, if the equal sign has a value or expression on its right side, an assignment occurs. If the equal sign contains code other than a single value or expression to the right of the equal, QBasic knows that a comparison must be made.

More will be said about QBasic's equality comparison operator in Chapter 12, "The *if* Statement." For now, you only need to know that QBasic's comparison equal produces a True or False result (something is either equal or not equal). You are used to seeing the equal sign used for equality testing after an `IF`, but you've probably never seen several equals stacked together as in the earlier example. Figure 9.1 shows you how QBasic interprets this multiple assignment problem.

```
a = 5
b = 10
c = 15
d = 20
e = 25
ans = a = b = c = d = e = 30
                       \/ False (0), e is not equal to 30
  ans = a = b = c = d = 0
                     \/ False (0), d is not equal to 0
    ans = a = b = c = 0
                   \/ False (0), c is not equal to 0
      ans = a = b = 0
                 \/ False (0), b is not equal to 0
        ans = a = 0
               \/ False (0), a  is not equal to 0
          ans = 0 Here, ans is assigned the zero
```

Figure 9.1. Multiple equals always produce True or False results.

In QBasic, True is always `-1` and False is always `0`. Therefore, as Figure 9.1 shows, none of the variables is equal to 30, so a False (`0`) results from each equal sign. When QBasic evaluates all but the `ans = 0` (the zero came from the `b = 0` test done in the expression evaluation step before the last one), the `0` is stored in `ans`.

An equal only means assignment in C.

All that review of QBasic's equal sign was important. First of all, you have to realize that an equal doesn't always mean assignment in QBasic; sometimes = means to test for equality. However, in C, the equal sign *always* means assignment, and there is never an exception. C has another operator for equality testing that you'll read about in Chapter 11, "Relational and Logical Operators." Therefore, you'll never be confused in C because an equal sign never appears that doesn't mean assignment.

Here is a section of C code equivalent to the multiple assignment operators. The results are greatly different.

```
a = 5;
b = 10;
c = 15;
d = 20;
```

```
e = 25;
ans = a = b = c = d = e = 30;   /* Multiple assignments! */
```

When this code finishes, ans contains a 30 and so do all the other variables. Figure 9.2 shows the assignment propagation that takes place in such a list of assignment statements.

```
a = 5
b = 10
c = 15
d = 20
e = 25
ans = a = b = c = d = e = 30    30 replaces the 25 in e
  ans = a = b = c = d = 30    30 replaces the 20 in d
    ans = a = b = c = 30    30 replaces the 15 in c
      ans = a = b = 30    30 replaces the 10 in b
        ans = a = 30    30 replaces the 5 in a
          ans = 30    30 is stored in ans
```

Figure 9.2. All C equal signs mean assignment of the righthand expression to the variable on the left.

The operator precedence table in Appendix B shows that the assignment statement associates from right to left. Be sure to read multiple assignments from right to left because that's what C does!

The multiple assignments offer an easy solution for you if you want to zero out a lot of variables at one time. The following statement assigns 0 to eight different variables:

```
var1 = var2 = var3 = var4 = var5 = var6 = var7 = var8 = 0;
```

All C assignments perform a two-step job: First they assign a value to the variable on the left of the equal sign, and then the assignment returns a result.

Although the assignment statement does not return values in the way that functions return values, an assignment statement does become a value, and the value it becomes is the value of the expression being assigned. In other words, Figure 9.2 illustrates that not only does each assignment assign the 30 to the next variable in line, but that entire assignment *becomes* a 30 so that the next part of the expression can continue. The `e = 30` part of the multiple assignment first stores a `30` in `e`, and then the expression becomes `30` so that the *next* variable in line can receive the `30`. After all the multiple assignments complete, the final job, `ans = 30`, not only assigns a `30` to `ans`, but produces an assignment return of `30`; however, nothing is done with the leftover `30` in the final assignment iteration.

If you feel confused, a quick C expression will clarify things considerably. The following expression performs two assignments:

```
num = 10 + (x = 5);
```

The first thing that C does is assign the `5` to `x`. No matter what was in `x` before this expression, a `5` is in `x` when the expression completes. C then has to have something to add to the `10`. The `x = 5` assignment returns the `5` so that the rest of the expression can continue. The `5` is added to the `10`, and the result is stored in `num`. Figure 9.3 shows how C interprets this expression.

```
num = 10 + (x = 5);
num = 10 + 5
num = 15
15          This 15 is ignored
```

Figure 9.3. After an assignment is done, the assignment returns its assigned value for the rest of the expression.

QBasic would have treated the `x = 5` as if its answer were True or False, then added the resulting `-1` or `0` (for True or False) to `10`, and then stored the result in `num`. `x` would remain unchanged in QBasic.

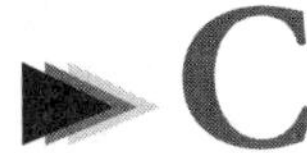

C ignores the final assignment value. For example, when a C single assignment appears on a line by itself like

```
x = 19;
```

the assignment puts the 19 in x and then becomes the value 19. However, nothing is left to be done with the 19, so the compiler discards it. In other words, there is literally a 19 left on the line (returned by the assignment) after the assignment takes place. The following printf() demonstrates the point:

```
printf("%d", (x = 19));
```

This printf() prints a 19. Also, the 19 was assigned to x. Therefore, in C, you can combine assignments with other statements. In QBasic, you would have to use these two statements to achieve the same goal:

```
x = 19
PRINT x
```

> Enabling you to combine an assignment with an expression or output which uses that assigned value is another way C lends itself to quick and efficient programming.

Compound Assignments

Any time you want to update a QBasic variable's value, such as adding to a total, dividing by a factor, or keeping track of counts, you put the value on each side of the equal sign. For example, suppose that you want to count the number of times a customer orders a product. Somewhere in your code, you'll find a line that looks like this:

```
custOrder = custOrder + 1    ' Add 1 to the count
```

If you need to find the total amount of payroll as you process employee records, you might see a line like this:

```
totalPay = totalPay + custPay(i)   ' Total the payroll
```

C supports the updating of a variable's value just as QBasic does. The following C statement increases cost by 15 percent:

```
cost = cost * 1.15;  /* Increase the cost by 15% */
```

Computers process data easily. Updating a variable's value is common, and if you've written many programs, you no doubt have put the same variable name on both sides of the equal sign.

C supplies five new operators called *compound operators* that streamline such assignments. Table 9.3 lists the compound operators and shows how they replace their corresponding regular operators.

Table 9.3. Compound assignment operators.

Compound Operator	*Example*	*Regular Operator Equivalent*
`+=`	`count += 1;`	`count = count + 1;`
`-=`	`numLeft -= 1;`	`numLeft = numLeft - 1;`
`*=`	`price *= 1.10;`	`price = price * 1.10;`
`/=`	`x /= .5;`	`x = x / .5;`
`%=`	`remain %= 2;`	`remain = remain % 2;`

> The compound operators are yet another way that C makes it easy to write programs succinctly.

Listing 9.4 shows a QBasic program that asks the user for five integer values, and Listing 9.5 shows the C equivalent program. As the user enters the values, compound assignments total the values. (These kinds of repetitive programs will be easier when you learn how to write C loops starting in Chapter 13, "The *while* Loops.")

Listing 9.4. A QBasic totaling program.

```
' Filename: TOTAL.BAS
' Adds five numbers together as the user enters them
DIM num AS INTEGER      ' Define the variables to keep consistent
DIM total AS LONG       ' with C as much as possible
total = 0            ' Not needed in QBasic, but recommended
                     ' to show your intentions
PRINT "I'll add five values as you enter them."
PRINT
```

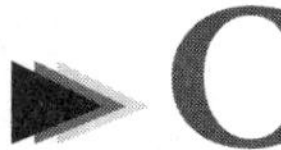

```
9:  INPUT "What is the first number"; num
10: total = total + num
11: INPUT "What is the next number"; num    ' 2nd number
12: total = total + num
13: INPUT "What is the next number"; num    ' 3rd number
14: total = total + num
15: INPUT "What is the next number"; num    ' 4th number
16: total = total + num
17: INPUT "What is the next number"; num    ' 5th number
18: total = total + num
19:
20: PRINT "The total is"; total
21: END
```

In QBasic, you have to repeat the variable name on each side of the equal sign when updating variables as done on lines 10, 12, 14, 16, and 18.

Listing 9.5. A C totaling program.

```
/* Filename: TOTAL.C
   Adds five numbers together as the user enters them */
#include <stdio.h>
main()
{
  int num;
  long int total=0;      /* long total; would work also */
  /* Request the numbers */
  printf("I'll add five values as you enter them.\n\n");
  printf("What is the first number? ");
  scanf(" %d", &num);
  total += num;
  printf("What is the next number? ");    /* 2nd number */
  scanf(" %d", &num);
  total += num;
  printf("What is the next number? ");    /* 3rd number */
  scanf(" %d", &num);
  total += num;
  printf("What is the next number? ");    /* 4th number */
  scanf(" %d", &num);
  total += num;
  printf("What is the next number? ");    /* 5th number */
  scanf(" %d", &num);
  total += num;
  printf("The total is %ld\n", total);
  return 0;
}
```

Here is the output from both of the preceding programs:

```
I'll add five values as you enter them.

What is the first number? 1
What is the next number? 2
What is the next number? 3
What is the next number? 4
What is the next number? 5
The total is 15
```

Be wary of mixing data types within the same expression. Lines 12, 15, 18, 21, and 24 all combine a regular integer with a long integer. However, the long integer is receiving the value, and C has no trouble storing a smaller data type into a larger data type's variable. Be cautious, however, when attempting to do the opposite because you can lose precision. Sometimes, the answer to an expression could require more storage than the smaller variable will allow room for. Chapter 10, "More C Operators," explores how you can use typecasting to ensure that your data types convert properly from one data type to another.

As you can see, the compound operators don't always save you a tremendous number of keystrokes, but they provide another method you can use for faster programming. There are times, however, when the compound operators do turn out to save you lots of keystrokes and debugging time. Suppose that in QBasic you were adding 10 to an integer array value and used a calculation to access the subscript like this:

```
value(n + index / factor) = value(n + index / factor) + 10
```

In C, you would have to type the array value only once, like this:

```
value[n + index / factor] += 10;
```

Although C's integer arrays aren't specifically covered until Chapter 19, "Array Management," they work much as they do in QBasic, except that you must use brackets rather than parentheses for the subscripts.

Watch the Precedence

Turn now to Appendix B to find C's order of operators table. Look for the compound operators. You'll see that they are extremely low in the table, lower than the regular `+`, `-`, `*`, and `/` by five or six levels.

Although conceptually `n += 5;` means the same thing as `n = n + 5;`, technically C handles their operations a little differently. When working with simple expressions, you won't notice the difference. However, see whether you can determine the value of `n` when the following code finishes:

```
n = 2;
n *= 6 - 3;
```

The value that goes into `n` is `6`, not `9` as a lot of programmers might think at first. Conceptually, the second line can be thought of as this:

```
n = n * 6 - 3;
```

But then the order of operators kicks in to tell the compiler to perform the `*=` *after* the subtraction! Therefore, C actually compiles the second line with the following precedence shown by parentheses:

```
n = n * (6 - 3);
```

Therefore, even though subtraction is low in the order of operators, subtraction is still much higher than the `*=` operator.

Summary

In this chapter, you learned how C's primary math operators work. Most of the time, you'll feel right at home working with C expressions because they operate much like QBasic's. However, there are some exceptions (some people would prefer the more accurate term *gotchas!*).

C's division operator, `/`, performs both integer division and regular floating-point division. Integer division occurs when integers appear on both sides of the division, and floating-point division occurs when a `float` (or `double`) appears on one or both sides of the division operator.

The C's equal sign performs only assignment. You do not use the equal sign for equality testing as QBasic's double-duty equal sign does. (You'll learn about an additional operator

C uses for equality testing in Chapter 11, "Relational and Logical Operators.") It's because C's assignment statement performs only one job (assignment) that C's equal sign can be used more places than QBasic's. You can set an entire series of variables equal to the same value. You also can embed assignments inside other expressions to assign two values at one time like this:

```
x = 20 * (y = 10);  /* Y gets the 10 and x gets 200 */
```

Don't overdo assignments, however. If you find that expressions are easier to read and maintain if you break them out onto separate lines (and they usually are), program maintenance should rule out over efficiency in most cases.

The compound operators enable you to update variables without having to repeat the same values on both sides of the equal sign. QBasic doesn't offer any operators similar to the compound operators. You'll find that compound operators are easy to use when you must track totals and update variables, but always keep in mind that their precedence is low and that other operators will execute almost always before the compound operators.

The next chapter explores more of C's operators. Many of the concepts in the next chapter have no QBasic equivalents, so you'll learn a lot of new ways to do what you maybe had to work around with QBasic.

More C Operators

C has so many operators that it takes more than one chapter to cover them all. This chapter teaches you about additional C operators that will come in handy as you begin to write more powerful C programs.

In this chapter, you'll learn two of the most famous C operators, ++ and --. You might recall that the preceding chapter warned you against omitting the separating space when adding a positive number or subtracting a negative one like this:

```
a = b -- c;    /* Don't do! */
x = y ++ z;    /* Don't do! */
```

C interprets ++ differently from + + and - - differently from -- because of the *increment* and *decrement* operators, ++ and --. This chapter shows you how the increment and decrement operators improve your program's efficiency and help streamline your coding.

The typecasting operator enables you to mix data types within the same expression. C can be more picky about mixing data types than QBasic. Although C doesn't complain when you mix data types, your program results can differ greatly depending on how you mix data types in the same expression. Typecasting becomes even more important in Part VIII of the book when you learn how to pass data back and forth between functions.

Some of the operators taught here are extremely useful. Others you might never use because of their technical nature. C gives you the ability to work with individual bits inside memory with C's *bitwise* operators. (You might not know this, but you can do some of this same *bit-fiddling* in QBasic, as you'll see.) Unless you write systems programs (such as the utilities used by your operating system) or *embedded programs* (such as the programs that control outside devices such as automobile controllers), you'll probably safely be able to stay away from the bitwise operators. Nevertheless, read through their section in this chapter to get an idea of how they work.

In this chapter, you will learn about the following topics:

- The increment and decrement operators
- The typecasting operator
- The `sizeof` operator
- The bit-manipulating operators

Incrementing and Decrementing

In the preceding chapter, you learned the `+=` and `-=` operators, which save you typing time. Instead of typing

```
count = count + 1;
```

when you want to add one to a variable, you can type this:

```
count += 1;
```

++ adds one to a variable.

The ++ enables you to add one to a variable also. The following statement does the same thing as the preceding two statements:

```
count++;
```

The increment operator can go on either side of the variable. The following statement is identical to the preceding one:

```
++count;
```

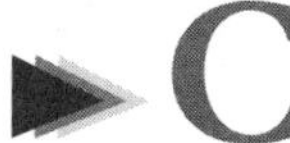

If the increment (or decrement) operator appears on the left side of the variable, it is known as a *prefix* increment (or decrement). A *postfix* increment (or decrement) operator occurs when you place the operator on the right side of the variable.

- - subtracts one from a variable.

If you want to subtract one from a variable, use the decrement operator, `--`. Here is the prefix decrement being applied to `count`:

```
--count;
```

When this expression completes, `count` will be one less than it was before the decrement. Here is the postfix version:

```
count--;
```

You can use either prefix or postfix for incrementing and decrementing variables. You'll always get the same results using prefix or postfix as just shown. However, when you combine increment and decrement operators within expressions containing other operators, the results can change between prefix and postfix versions. You'll see examples of why in the next section.

Use ++ and - - for efficiency.

The increment and decrement operators are more efficient than either their `+=` and `-=` counterparts or the extended notation (such as `count = count + 1;`). Both `++` and `--` compile into a single efficient machine-language statement, whereas the other operators don't always compile as efficiently. Some increment statements, depending on the compiler, compile `count = count + 1;` into three machine-language statements, adding much more overhead to the compiled program, especially if the expression executes inside a loop.

Watch Out for Some ++ and - - Side Effects

Whether you use postfix or prefix, the result is the same: a variable is either incremented or decremented. The *timing,* however, of that increment or decrement changes depending on which notation, prefix or postfix, that you use. If a variable is sitting all by itself in the expression, such as `--count;` or `count--;`, you don't have to worry about the timing because nothing but the one variable is affected. However, expressions such as these produce different results depending on your use of prefix or postfix:

```
int n = 5;
total = n++ + 3;
```

The increment of n occurs *after* the 3 is added to n, not before. Therefore, total holds 8, not 9. When total is assigned a value, then and only then does n get incremented to 6.

Here is the equivalent QBasic code:

```
n = 5
total = n + 3
n = n + 1          ' Add 1 only after total gets its value
```

Not only is C's increment more efficient than its QBasic equivalent, but there is less you have to type. Therefore, using ++ (and --) speeds both your program development and your program's runtime efficiency. However, don't forget about the *timing* of the increment and decrement, or your answers might not come out as expected.

The following code stores a 9 in total:

```
int n = 5;
total = ++n + 3;
```

If you use prefix, the increment (or decrement) occurs *before all other operations on the line.* The equivalent QBasic code is this:

```
n = 5
n = n + 1          ' Add 1 before total gets its value
total = n + 3
```

The result in n is the same for both the postfix and the prefix sets of code just shown. n always gets incremented by one. However, the timing of that increment affects the rest of the expression surrounding n. Be careful when using increment and decrement with other operators to use the correct version. If you're in doubt, place the increment or decrement on the line before or after the rest of the expression like this:

```
n++;
total = n + 3;
```

Or you can use this:

```
total = n + 3;
n++;
```

Never increment or decrement a constant or an expression. ++ and -- apply only to variables. Therefore, both of the following statements are invalid:

```
n = ++9;          /* Invalid */
x = (c + 4)--;    /* Invalid */
```

The Real Order of Increment and Decrement

Before going further, note that the order of operators table in Appendix B is flawed. Yes, there is an error in the table. The error did not occur because someone messed up. The error is the result of this author's insistence that the *practical* use of increment and decrement differs from the theoretical use and that the *correct* order of operator table will mess up anyone trying to learn C.

If you were to study the true ANSI C's order of operators charts, you would find that *postfix* increment and decrement appear on level one and that *prefix* increment and decrement appear on level two (both much earlier than the arithmetic operators). Yet, even though postfix appears in the table before prefix, prefix definitely computes before postfix. In practice, postfix evaluates long after all other operations finish in an expression.

The "correct" order of precedence was designed to help decipher ambiguous statements such as this:

```
count = a+++b;
```

First of all, any programmer that writes such a statement ought to be corrected because all sorts of ambiguities arise from such statements. Is the b being incremented before being added to a, or does the a have postfix increment with b being added to a? The ANSI C order of precedence clearly states that postfix has precedence, so such an ambiguous (to humans) expression would be evaluated like this by the C compiler:

```
count = a++ + b;
```

Nevertheless, it is the argument of this author (and the thousands of C students who have thanked him over the years) that from a practical standpoint, postfix is always performed last in an expression. The ANSI order of operators explains how the expression is interpreted, but not calculated; the a is not incremented until after its original value is added to b and the total is stored in count. That is why the order of operators listed in

Appendix B shows prefix at level 1, breaking the ANSI C standard in one respect. As a programmer, you should know that C evaluates all prefix increments and decrements before anything else in the statement. Postfix increments and decrements execute after the rest of the statement's operators have done their job.

Typecasts

The typecast operator doesn't really look like an operator. Chapter 6, "Numeric Variables," introduced the typecast operator when it showed how to change integer variables to floating-point variables. However, the core of the typecast discussion was saved for this section of the book.

A typecast temporarily converts a value or variable from one data type to another. If you do not use a typecast but mix data types in an expression, C performs an implicit typecast. For example, if `x` is a `float` variable, C changes the integer answer, `18`, to `18.000000` before saving it in the floating-point variable `x` here:

```
x = 3 * 6;   /* Multiply two ints and store in a float */
```

C converts from the smaller to the larger data types.

There is nothing wrong with letting C perform implicit typecasting in many situations. There are several defined rules as to how C converts its data types to other data types when mixed in expressions, but the bottom line is this: Generally, unless you explicitly use your own typecast, C converts the smallest of data types into the largest. As just shown, the integer is converted to the floating-point value. The same holds true for expressions such as this:

```
x = 3.2 * 6;
```

C converts the `6` to `6.000000` before finishing the multiplication.

All this discussion is useful because you must know how the language handles mixed data types. Nevertheless, this discussion seems trivial. Of course C converts the smaller to the larger in such expressions. If C decided to convert the `3.2` to an integer `3`, the answer would be dramatically different (`18` as opposed to `19.2`). Also, if `x` in the preceding discussion were an integer variable, the `19.2` would be truncated down into an integer `19` before being stored in `x` even though the values in the expression multiply as floating-point values.

QBasic performs implicit mixed data typing in the same way as C; QBasic uses the largest data type needed to compute expressions.

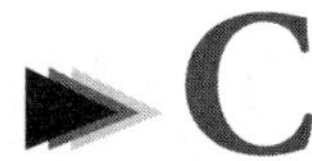

Typecasting gives you added control over the automatic data type conversion in expressions. Sometimes, you don't want a variable to be treated as if it were its originally defined data type. For example, suppose you need a program to perform modulus arithmetic with floating-point values. Modulus, by its very definition, works only with `int` values. Therefore, if `x` and `y` were `float` variables, the following C expression would not work:

```
leftOver = x % y;
```

However, by applying an `(int)` typecast to each variable, the modulus works like this:

```
leftOver = (int)x % (int)y;
```

To declare a typecast, put any valid data type (`int`, `float`, `long double`, and so on) inside parentheses right before the variable, value, or expression that you want to change. It's important to realize that the variables `x` and `y` are not really changed, but they are only converted to an integer temporarily for that one expression. If you were to use `x` or `y` on the next line in the program, it would still contain its original floating-point value.

Typecasting is not needed much for mixing data types. Usually, the default implicit data typecasting suffices for your expressions. You would use typecasting only when you want to type *down* an expression because C handles typecasting *up* to a higher precision value when needed. Typecasting is used mostly for parameter passing between functions and dynamic memory allocation. You'll learn more about these C features throughout this book.

The QBasic `INT()`, `CINT()`, `CSNG()`, and `CDBL()` functions convert numbers to various data types and back again. Keep in mind that the typecast in C is an operator and the QBasic routines are functions, but the result of each is the same. For example, to perform the QBasic modulus result of the two floating-point variables described earlier, you can do this:

```
leftOver = INT(x) MOD INT(y);
```

Before moving on to the next section, study the short C program in Listing 10.1. The program performs division using different typecast placements. As you can see, the result differs depending on how the typecast is used. You'll sometimes typecast a specific variable, especially when performing division, so that you can control when rounding takes place instead of leaving the rounding up to the default implicit data typecasts.

Listing 10.1. Rounding differs depending on your typecasts.

```
/* Filename: TYPECAST.C
   Perform division based on typecasting */
#include <stdio.h>
```

continues

Listing 10.1. continued

```
main()
{
  int n;
  float x = 10.0;
  float y = 3.9;
  /* No typecast */
  n = x / y;
  printf("After n = x / y, n contains %d.\n", n);
  /* Typecast one of the floats */
  n = (int)x / y;
  printf("After n = (int)x / y, n contains %d.\n", n);
  /* Typecast the other float */
  n = x / (int)y;
  printf("After n = x / (int)y, n contains %d.\n", n);
  /* Typecast both floats */
  n = (int)x / (int)y;
  printf("After n = (int)x / (int)y, n contains %d.\n", n);
  /* Typecast the entire expression */
  n = (int)(x / y);
  printf("After n = (int)(x / y), n contains %d.\n", n);
  return 0;
}
```

Here is the output from Listing 10.1:

```
After n = x / y, n contains 2.
After n = (int)x / y, n contains 2.
After n = x / (int)y, n contains 3.
After n = (int)x / (int)y, n contains 3.
After n = (int)(x / y), n contains 2.
```

Using *sizeof*

C programmers have to be more concerned with internal data lengths than QBasic programmers do. QBasic runs only on PCs, and the size of integers, single-precision, and double-precision variables always remains the same. Programs can compute the amount of storage needed for different kinds of data based on those preset QBasic sizes. However, C was designed to be used on all kinds of computers, hence C programmers can never rely on integers, floating-points, or doubles to be the same size from computer to computer.

C contains the sizeof operator. sizeof looks like a function but is an operator, and as such, it appears in the order of operator table in Appendix B. sizeof returns the size of whatever value follows it. Most C programmers put the sizeof argument in parentheses, but the parentheses aren't required. Listing 10.2 contains code that finds and prints the size of several C data types.

Listing 10.2. Using *sizeof* to find internal data sizes.

```
1:  /* Filename: DATASIZE.C
2:     Finding data sizes with the sizeof operator */
3:  #include <stdio.h>
4:  main()
5:  {
6:    int i = 0;
7:    long int l = 0L;
8:    float f = 0.0;
9:    double d = 0.0;
10:   long double ld = 0.0L;
11:
12:   /* sizeof() returns a long int value */
13:   long int size;
14:   size = sizeof(i);   /* Get size of integer variable */
15:   printf("The size of an int variable is %ld.\n", size);
16:   size = sizeof(l);   /* Get size of long integer variable */
17:   printf("The size of a long int variable is %ld.\n", size);
18:   size = sizeof(f);   /* Get size of float variable */
19:   printf("The size of a float variable is %ld.\n", size);
20:   size = sizeof(d);   /* Get size of double variable */
21:   printf("The size of a double variable is %ld.\n", size);
22:   size = sizeof(ld);   /* Get size of long double variable */
23:   printf("The size of a long double variable is %ld.\n", size);
24:   return 0;
25: }
```

As you can see from the assignment statements to the long int variable in lines 14, 16, 18, 20, and 22, sizeof returns a long integer value. You can use sizeof to find the size of arrays, and array sizes can easily be larger than a regular integer would hold.

Most readers will be using a PC-based C compiler because QBasic is a PC-based product. Here is the output of Listing 10.2 if you were to run the program on a PC using Turbo C:

```
The size of an int variable is 2.
The size of a long int variable is 4.
```

```
The size of a float variable is 4.
The size of a double variable is 8.
The size of a long double variable is 10.
```

On different kinds of computers (PCs, minicomputers, and mainframes), Listing 10.2 gives different results because different computer hardware internally stores data in differing amounts of memory.

`sizeof` returns the byte count for any kind of value.

`sizeof` returns the value of *any data,* not just variables. Listing 10.3 produces the same output as that of Listing 10.2. Listing 10.3 finds the size of data-type names rather than variables.

Listing 10.3. Using *sizeof* to find internal data sizes of data types.

```
/* Filename: DATASIZ2.C
   Finding data sizes of data types with the sizeof operator */
#include <stdio.h>
main()
{
  /* sizeof() returns a long int value */
  long int size;
  size = sizeof(int);    /* Get size of integer value */
  printf("The size of an int value is %ld.\n", size);
  size = sizeof(long int);  /* Get size of long integer value */
  printf("The size of a long int value is %ld.\n", size);
  size = sizeof(float);    /* Get size of float value */
  printf("The size of a float value is %ld.\n", size);
  size = sizeof(double);    /* Get size of double value */
  printf("The size of a double value is %ld.\n", size);
  size = sizeof(long double);  /* Get size of long double value */
  printf("The size of a long double value is %ld.\n", size);
  return 0;
}
```

`sizeof` returns the original character array size that you defined, not the string length inside the array. `myName` always has a size of `10` even though a much shorter string is stored in it here:

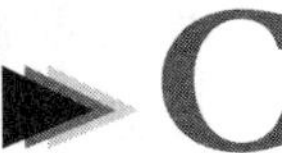

```
char myName[10] = "Joe";   /* String length 3,
                              sizeof(myName) is 10 */
```

`sizeof` does not look at what is inside a variable. `sizeof` concerns itself only with the amount of storage needed to hold a variable of any given data type, including the array size that you originally defined if you apply `sizeof` to an array.

Getting Technical: The Bitwise Operators

C's *bitwise* operators work with the internal bits of a value, not with the value itself. Using the bitwise operators, you can change or look at individual bits. If you've never needed to work with bits before, you can skim this section and return to it when you need the material.

A complete understanding of bitwise operators requires knowledge of your computer's internal architecture. You must especially understand how characters and integers are formed internally through the combination of on and off bits.

Many veteran QBasic programmers are often surprised to learn that QBasic can manipulate internal bits in data. Before looking at the C bitwise operators, take a look at how QBasic supports bit manipulation.

You've probably used the QBasic `AND` and `OR` operators for multiple `IF` comparisons. The following QBasic statement prints "Yes" only if both `x` and `y` are more than zero:

```
IF (x > 0 AND y > 0) THEN
  PRINT "Yes"
END IF
```

The following statement prints "Yes" if `x`, `y`, or both are more than zero:

```
IF (x > 0 OR y > 0) THEN
  PRINT "Yes"
END IF
```

XOR is an exclusive OR operator.

There is a third QBasic operator, `XOR`, called the *exclusive* `OR` operator, that you can also use for logical comparisons. `XOR` returns true if one side or the other side is true *but not both.* For example, `XOR` returns true if `x` is more than zero or if `y` is more than zero in the following QBasic `IF` test:

```
IF (x > 0 XOR y > 0) THEN
  PRINT "Yes"
END IF
```

However, if *both* `x` and `y` are more than zero, "Yes" does not print. The `XOR` operator is sometimes called the *mutually exclusive* operator because it returns true only if one of its two sides is true.

Many people program with QBasic for years and never know that `AND`, `OR`, and `XOR` all work as bit-manipulators as well as logic comparison operators. The program in Listing 10.4 shows an example of how to use QBasic for bit-manipulation. The program's explanation follows the code.

Listing 10.4. Using *AND, OR,* and *XOR* to mask bits.

```
1:  ' Filename: BITMASK.BAS
2:  ' Print the answer of masked bits in an integer variable
3:  DIM i AS INTEGER
4:  i = 7
5:  PRINT i AND 1
6:  PRINT i OR 1
7:  PRINT i XOR 1
8:  END
```

Here is the output from the program:

```
1
7
6
```

In QBasic, an integer takes two bytes of memory. Two bytes requires 16 bits of storage. The `i` variable is defined as an integer in line 3 because if the variable were not explicitly defined as an integer, QBasic would automatically use single-precision for it.

In two bytes, the value `7` takes on this bit pattern:

```
0000000000000111
```

The bit pattern for the number `1` is this:

```
0000000000000001
```

> Again, if internal binary representations of decimal values confuse you, you can skim this section and return to it if you ever need to work with bits in the future.

Lines 5, 6, and 7 of Listing 10.4 perform three bit-by-bit comparisons between `1` and the integer variable. (The `1` is treated as an integer by QBasic in this case because `AND`, `OR`, and `XOR` work only with integer values on each side.) Figure 10.1 shows how the three `PRINT` expressions produce their values.

```
 0000000000000111     0000000000000111     0000000000000111
              AND                   OR                  XOR
 0000000000000001     0000000000000001     0000000000000001
=0000000000000001    =0000000000000111    =0000000000000110
```

Figure 10.1. Manipulating the bits of the variable `i`.

As you can see, QBasic's `AND`, `OR`, and `XOR` operators perform double duty, just as the equal sign does. You can use `AND`, `OR`, and `XOR` for `IF` comparisons, and you can use them for bit-manipulation as well.

> It's easy to distinguish between the two uses of the QBasic `AND`, `OR`, and `XOR` operators. If integers appear on both sides of an `AND`, `OR`, or `XOR`, a bit comparison occurs. If logical tests such as
>
> `IF (x > 0 AND y > 0)`
>
> appear on both sides of an `AND`, `OR`, and `XOR`, a logical true or false result occurs.

QBasic also supports the use of the bit-manipulating `NOT` operator. As with `AND`, `OR`, and `XOR`, `NOT` works as both a logical comparison and a bit manipulator. The following statement is true if `A` is not equal to `B`:

`NOT` is also a QBasic bitwise operator.

```
IF NOT(A = B)
```

In most cases, using `NOT` muddies the program's readability. It's a lot clearer to test the previous expression like this:

```
IF (A <> B)
```

Sometimes, however, the `NOT` is readable, especially when you're testing for end-of-file conditions (as in `IF NOT(EOF(1))` to make sure that file #1 is not at the end of file).

When applied to an integer value, `NOT` reverses the bits in the value. Doing this often produces a *1's complement* value (which often appears as a negative number). If you're not familiar with 1's complement, you'll probably not need `NOT`! The following QBasic statement prints `-8`:

```
PRINT NOT(7)
```

This book concentrates on explaining C, not QBasic, but if you have worked with these QBasic bit-manipulation operators before, you'll find that the switch to C's bitwise operators is easy. Table 10.1 lists the C bitwise operators and shows the QBasic equivalents.

Table 10.1. The C bitwise operators.

C Operator	*QBasic Equivalent*	*Description*
&	AND	Bitwise And
¦	OR	Bitwise Or
^	XOR	Bitwise exclusive Or
~	NOT	Bitwise Not (1's complement)

Instead of using the keywords `AND`, `OR`, `XOR`, and `NOT`, you only have to use the operators between the values you want to bitwise compare. The program in Listing 10.5 uses the C bitwise operators to show you how C would produce the values shown throughout this section.

Listing 10.5. Using C's bitwise operators.

```
/* Filename: BITWISE.C
   Demonstrating the use of C's bitwise operators */
#include <stdio.h>
main()
{
```

```
    int i = 7;    /* Data for the bitwise comparisons */
    int ans;      /* Result for the bitwise comparisons */
    /* Bitwise Or */
    ans = i ¦ 1;
    printf("7 ¦ 1 is %d\n", ans);
    /* Bitwise And */
    ans = i & 1;
    printf("7 & 1 is %d\n", ans);
    /* Bitwise Xor */
    ans = i ^ 1;
    printf("7 ^ 1 is %d\n", ans);
    /* Bitwise Not */
    ans = !i;
    printf("!i is %d\n", ans);
    /* Bitwise 1's complement */
    ans = ~i;
    printf("~i is %d\n", ans);
    return 0;
}
```

Here is the output from the program in Listing 10.5:

```
7 ¦ 1 is 7
7 & 1 is 1
7 ^ 1 is 6
!i is 0
~i is -8
```

Don't confuse C's `!` (Not) operator with `~`. C's `!` operator always works to negate true or false relational tests such as the C statement `while !(x = 0);`. C's `!` is not an equivalent operator to QBasic's `NOT` even though both are called the same thing. The equivalent of QBasic's bitwise `NOT` is `~` in C.

Summary

You've now tackled almost every operator that C has to offer. C includes many operators, such as the increment and decrement operators, that have no equivalent operator in QBasic. As you saw in this chapter, using the C operators often leads to smaller and more efficient programs than writing the code without the operators as QBasic requires.

The typecasting operator enables you to change the data type of a value so that you can use that new data type in an expression. When mixing data types, you might want to typecast one data type to another to maintain consistency in the expression. Throughout the rest of this book, you'll see how to use the typecast operator in specific situations that streamline your C programming.

QBasic does not need a `sizeof` operator because QBasic is only run on PCs; QBasic's data sizes always consume the same amount of memory from program to program. C, however, was designed to be run on any kind of computer, large or small, and `sizeof` enables you to find out how much memory a data type consumes on the computer running the program. Knowing your data sizes enables you to plan memory requirements.

The last part of this chapter explained the bitwise operators. The bitwise operators manipulate internal bits within a value instead of working with the complete value itself. Not every programmer will need the bitwise operators, but if you ever do need them, C provides them.

You have yet to see an entire group of C operators. So far, you don't know how to perform relational testing such as is done in `if` statements. The nice thing about C's relational and logical (for And or Or logic) operators is that they work almost exactly like QBasic's. The next chapter shows you how to use C's logical and relational operators so that you'll be prepared to use them when you learn C's `if` and `while` statements.

11

Relational and Logical Operators

This chapter compares and contrasts C's relational and logical operators to those of QBasic. The relational operators perform data testing. With the relational operators, you determine how one value compares to another (less than, greater than, and so on).

The logical operators enable you to combine one or more relational operators in the same test. For example, you can determine whether someone makes a certain pay amount *and* whether that person sold more than a certain sales quota. Depending on the result of both comparisons, your program can make a decision and execute a certain path of code. Without the logical operators, you would have to make individual comparisons (test the salary and then in the next statement test the sales).

This chapter does not delve very deeply into C's `if` statement, although `if` is the perfect vehicle for teaching the relational and logical operators. This chapter teaches the differences in the way QBasic and C handle true and false conditional tests. Sometimes, you'll see the first line of a C `if` statement used to clarify an operator, but concentrate on the operator at this point. The next chapter puts this chapter's material into practice by showing the complete C `if` statement in action.

In this chapter, you will learn about the following topics:

- C's relational operators
- C's logical operators
- True and false differences between C and QBasic

Making a Relation

Computers shine when it comes to comparing data. Your computer speeds through a series of hundreds of values and instantly finds the lowest, highest, or whatever you request. Being able to test one data value against another lets the computer make decisions based on the results it finds; if one value is less than another, one section of code might execute, whereas another would execute if the reverse were true.

In QBasic, you use the relational operators inside `IF` statements and `DO` loops to control program flow. You might want to loop a certain number of times until a condition is reached. Your program might need to print a report based on the user's input.

The relational true or false result dictates the program's course.

All decisions break down into a series of true or false relationships. One of the difficulties that beginning programmers experience is being able to take a complicated series of decisions and separate those decisions into several simple true and false decisions. For example, determining which employee gets a raise from a file with multiple employee data might be nothing more than a series of individual tests to see which employee in the file sold the most goods.

A value always appears on each side of the relational operators. Here is the format of a relational operator's use:

```
(expression1 op expression2)
```

Again, it's important to point out that as in QBasic, C's relational operator expression usually appears after an `if` or `while` statement. You'll learn about those statements in the next part of the book.

Make sure that the *expression* on each side of the operator evaluates to the same data type when testing for equality relationships. Never attempt to test whether an integer is equal to a floating-point value because those data types are hard to compare for equality.

> Testing for equality between two `floats` rarely works properly either. It is difficult to store floating-point values accurately inside the computer. `7.854` does not always compare equal to `7.854`! It sounds crazy, but that's one of the problems with computers and their floating-point comparisons.

Table 11.1 lists the C relational operators (the operators used in place of *op* in the format line given earlier) and their QBasic equivalents. Most of the relational operators are identical in both languages. Pay special attention to the first and last C operators listed in the table.

Table 11.1. The C relational operators.

C Relational Operator	*QBasic Equivalent*	*Description*
==	=	Equal to
>	>	Greater than
<	<	Less than
>=	>=	Greater than or equal to
<=	<=	Less than or equal to
!=	<>	Not equal to

You might recall that C does not use the assignment operator, `=`, for equality testing. The equal sign is used only for assignment. The `==` operator is C's test for equality. In QBasic, if you want to test whether `i` is equal to `j`, you do this:

```
IF (i = j) THEN
```

In C, you write the equality test like this:

```
if (i == j)
```

One of the hardest habits to break when moving from QBasic to C is using the single equal sign to test for equality. Some C compilers issue a warning if you embed a single equal sign inside an `if` test like this:

```
if (i = j)
```

The compiler warns you because you probably meant to use a double equal sign to test the two values. Nevertheless, don't rely on the compiler to find this error for you because not all C compilers flag this problem.

If you ever use a single equal sign inside a test being made with `if` or `while`, C performs the assignment. Therefore, after `if (i = j)`, `i` is assigned the value of `j`.

Whereas QBasic's not-equal operator is <>, C uses the `!=` operator. Figure 11.1 sums up all of C's relational operators by illustrating several true comparisons.

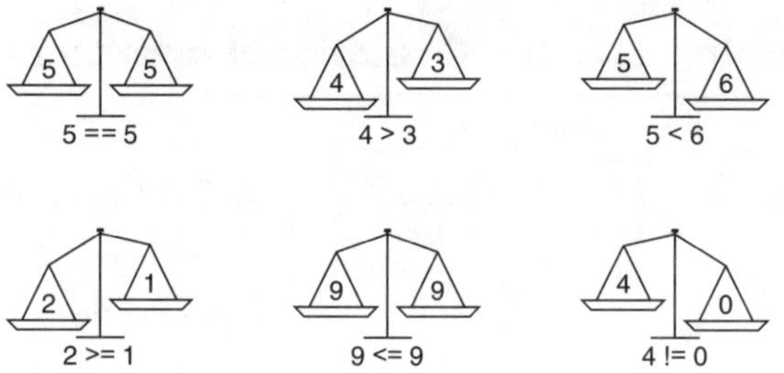

Figure 11.1. Illustrating C's relational operators.

Logical Comparisons

In one respect, the last part of the preceding chapter introduced logical operators. You saw in that chapter how QBasic gives the logical `AND`, `OR`, and `XOR` operators double duties: Both are logical operators and bitwise operators. C's bitwise operators do not overlap its logical operators. Therefore, C includes a set of bitwise operators that are different from the logical operators you'll use to combine relational comparisons.

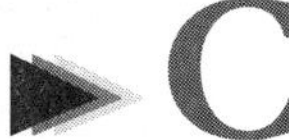

Logical operators combine relational operator tests.

Table 11.2 shows the C logical operators and their QBasic equivalents.

Table 11.2. The C logical operators.

Logical Operator	*QBasic Equivalent*	*Description*
`&&`	`AND`	And
`¦¦`	`OR`	Or
`!`	`NOT`	Not

&& and ¦¦ combine relational tests.

Only true and false relations appear on either side of `&&` and `¦¦`. The `&&` logical operator returns a true result if and only if both sides of the operator are true. The `¦¦` logical operator returns a true result if one or the other side (or both sides) of the `¦¦` is true.

There are no C logical operator equivalents to QBasic's `XOR` or `EQV` operators, so those operators are not discussed here.

You can recognize the `&&` and `¦¦` operators because of their similarity to the bitwise `&` (for bitwise *and*) and `¦` (for bitwise *or*) described in the preceding chapter.

The `!` operator does not combine two or more relational tests. `!` is known as a *unary* operator because it operates only on single values (as do `++` and `--`). The `&&` and `¦¦` are sometimes called binary operators because they take two arguments. Be sure that you don't confuse binary operators with the bitwise operators you learned about in the preceding chapter. Bitwise operators such as `&` and `¦` compare the bits that make up values, and binary operators such as `+` and `*` work on full values.

The following QBasic `IF` statement evaluates to true if both sides of the `AND` are true:

```
IF (sales > 5000 AND hrsWorked > 40) THEN
```

Only the first lines of QBasic `IF` and C `if` statements are shown in this chapter to focus on the operators themselves. Chapter 12, "The *if* Statement," delves into the details of `if` and explains the `if` statement using complete example programs.

Here is the same code in C:

```
if (sales > 5000 && hrsWorked > 40)
```

The following QBasic `IF` statement evaluates to true if one side *or* the other side of the `OR` is true, or if both sides are true:

```
IF (sales > 5000 OR hrsWorked > 40) THEN
```

Here is the same code in C:

```
if (sales > 5000 || hrsWorked > 40)
```

Suppose that you wanted to test to see whether a salesperson did *not* meet a sales quota. You can use C's `!` operator like this:

```
if !(sales >= 5000)
```

Don't overdo `!`. Reversing `!` logic to remove `!` often makes for clearer code. Sometimes, however, the `!` is needed to eliminate an extra test. You'll learn in Chapter 17, "Character and String Functions," about C's `strcmp()` function that compares strings for equality. It sounds crazy now, but `strcmp()` returns *false* if its two string arguments compare equal to each other. (One would think that an equal string comparison would produce a true result.) Therefore, you must negate the result of `strcmp()` if you want to test for equality. The following `if` test is true *if and only if* the two strings `st1` and `st2` are equal to each other:

```
if !strcmp(st1, st2)
```

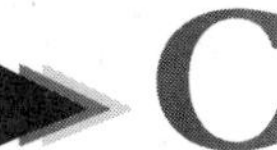

If you want to ease the transition from QBasic to C, add the following `#define` preprocessor directives at the top of your C programs (before `main()`):

```
#define AND &&
#define OR  ||
#define NOT !
```

Instead of `if` statements such as

```
if ((a > b) && (c < d))

if ((sales < 10000) || (quota < 9000))
```

you can write the following, more readable code:

```
if ((a > b) AND (c < d))

if ((sales < 10000) OR (quota < 9000))
```

True and False Values

QBasic uses integer values for true and false results. In QBasic, false always equates to zero, and true is always –1. Therefore, the following QBasic `IF` statements are true:

```
IF (1) THEN    ' Rest of the IF would follow, of course
IF (-1) THEN
IF (829) THEN
```

You wouldn't normally test a constant value. Constants are used here to demonstrate true values.

Zero always produces a false result in QBasic. The following `IF` fails because its test value is zero, hence the relational value is false:

```
IF (0) THEN
```

In C, a true value is any nonzero value. A false value is always zero. Therefore, the following `if` tests are true:

```
if (1)      /* Rest of if would follow */
if (-1)
if (829)
```

The following `if` is false:

```
if (0)
```

Knowing that zero always means false in C, and that a nonzero value always means true, is more important to C programmers than the same information is to QBasic programmers. You must remember that *all* assignments do two things: They assign values to variables, and they also return a result. A non-C programmer would think that the following `if` produces a false result:

```
n = 25;
if (n = 1)        /* A true if statement! */
```

The `if` *will* be true! The parentheses hold an assignment expression, not an equality test using `==`. Therefore, the `1` is assigned to `n`, which overwrites the original value of `25`. Is `1` true in C? Yes it is. The assignment's return value of `1` is used as the `if` test, and you know that a nonzero value always produces a true result in C.

Be careful when you see stand-alone equal signs. In QBasic, this identical code would produce a false result:

```
n = 25
IF (n = 1) THEN       ' False occurs
```

QBasic would interpret the equal sign as an equality test, and because `n` is not equal to `1`, the `IF` is false.

Will the following C `if` produce a true or false result?

```
n = 0;
if (n = 0)
```

The answer could surprise you. The `if` will be false. (Equivalent QBasic code would produce a true result.) Remember that the equal sign does both of these things: (1) assigns the `0` to `n` and (2) returns the result of the assignment, `0` in this case. Therefore, the result of the `if` test is zero, and zero is always false.

You can assign comparisons directly to other variables in C. All the relational and logical operators produce a 1 or 0 result, indicating true or false. Study the following comments to understand what each variable receives when the expressions finish:

```
ans = 5 > 8;    /* ans gets 0 (false) */
ans = 5 < 8;    /* ans gets 1 (true) */
ans = 0 == 0;   /* ans gets 1 (true) */
ans = (9 > 10) ¦¦ (20 == 20);    /* ans gets 1 (true) */
ans = (7 = 5) && (19 < 4);    /* ans gets 0 (false) */
```

Knowing about C's `1` and `0` results helps you streamline your programs. Sometimes, you can replace a C `if` statement with a highly efficient assignment statement. Listing 11.1 computes a salesperson's pay, giving that person a bonus if and only if a certain sales quota is met. Notice that there is no `if` statement in the entire program.

Listing 11.1. Using true and false to streamline coding.

```
1:  /* Filename: BONUS.C
2:     Shows that true is 1 and false is 0 */
3:  #include <stdio.h>
4:  main()
5:  {
6:    float sales, total;
7:    printf("How much were the sales last month? ");
8:    scanf(" %f", &sales);
9:    total = (sales * .1) + ((sales > 5000.0) * 50.0);
10:   printf("Your total pay will be $%.2f.\n", total);
11:   return 0;
12: }
```

Even though no `if` statement appears in Listing 11.1, the program produces different results depending on the user's input. The program is designed to reward top salespeople with a $50 bonus if their sales exceed $5,000. Here is a sample run of the program:

```
How much were the sales last month? 4000.00
Your total pay will be $400.00.
```

The salesperson got paid a total of 10 percent of sales. However, if the sales were exceptional, totaling over $5,000, an added bonus of $50 is given, as shown here:

```
How much were the sales last month? 6000.00
Your total pay will be $650.00.
```

The program calculates the bonus pay properly because of the relational test on line 9. The expression `(sales > 5000.0)` is either true or false. If true, the expression results in a value of `1`. Therefore, if the sales did exceed $5,000, a `1` is multiplied by `50.0`, producing the `50.0` bonus that is added to the pay. If the result of the comparison is false, the expression results in a value of `0.0` times `50.0` results in a zero value, so nothing is added to the pay.

In the next chapter, you'll learn how to write complete C `if` statements, but as you can see here, `if` is not always needed if you can take advantage of the `1` or `0` true and false comparisons.

Include as many parentheses in program statements as needed to clarify your code. If you removed line 9's parentheses, the program would produce the same results because the default operator hierarchy calculates the total correctly. However, grouping the expression's components with parentheses as done on line 9 helps separate parts of the expression into readable groups.

Don't try to eliminate most of your `if` statements as done in Listing 11.1. You won't be able to eliminate them all using this technique—and remember that clear coding is more important than short and "cute" tricks of the language. Nevertheless, Listing 11.1 is a valid use of the `1` and `0` result from relational comparisons, and using the results of comparisons in this way makes for an efficient program. Writing out an `if` statement to perform the calculation (as done next in QBasic) would not necessarily help this program's readability. The true and false result of relational and logical operators is a part of the C language. Although you shouldn't overdo its use, you shouldn't steer away from it when simple, clear, and efficient code results.

Listing 11.2 shows the QBasic version of Listing 11.1 using an `IF` statement to compute the bonus.

Listing 11.2. Using an *IF* to calculate a bonus.

```
' Filename: BONUS.BAS
' Computes a bonus pay based on sales using IF
INPUT "How much were the sales last month"; sales
' An IF is needed to calculate sales
IF (sales > 5000) THEN
  total = (sales * .1) + 50
ELSE
  total = sales * .1
END IF
' Print the results
PRINT USING "Your total pay will be $###.##."; total
END
```

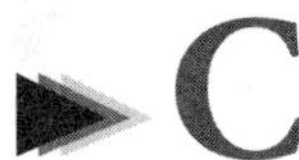

Notice that the QBasic program isn't any longer than the C equivalent, but the C compiler has to do much less work than the QBasic interpreter because an `if` statement doesn't have to be resolved in Listing 11.1, whereas it does in Listing 11.2.

Some careful readers might say that QBasic's true and false values, `-1` and `0`, could be used to rewrite Listing 11.2 to remove the `IF` statement similar to the way C handled things in Listing 11.1. Although they would be correct, such readers would have to admit that an extra calculation is required because of the *negative* 1 that QBasic uses for a true test. Multiplication is fairly costly in runtime overhead, and a separate `IF` statement is probably as efficient, and certainly clearer, than trying to take advantage of QBasic's true and false values as shown in Listing 11.3.

Listing 11.3. Using QBasic's true and false to calculate the bonus.

```
1:  ' Filename: BONUSTF.BAS
2:  ' Computes a bonus pay based on sales using QBasic's -1 and 0
3:  INPUT "How much were the sales last month"; sales
4:  ' An IF is needed to calculate sales
5:  total = ((sales * .1) + ((sales > 5000) * 50 * -1))
6:  ' Print the results
7:  PRINT USING "Your total pay will be $###.##."; total
8:  END
```

Line 5 is now so convoluted that readers probably have to admit that C's positive value of `1` for true makes much more sense than QBasic's `-1`. If the multiplication of the `-1` were removed in line 5 and the `50` were changed to `-50`, the program's readability would suffer, and the efficiency gained would not be worth the trade-off of the code's readability.

When stacking more than one relational test together, you must continually be aware of the true and false results of the individual parts of the test. In other words, the following `if` statement will compare as false even though it looks as though a true result is assured:

```
if (20 == 20 == 20)      /* Rest of if would follow */
```

Why will this `if` compare as false? Isn't `20` always equal to `20`? Although `20` *is* equal to `20`, the first comparison of `20 == 20` returns a `1` (true) result! The `1` is then compared against the third `20`, and they are found to be not equal.

Summary

You're now ready to jump into the C control statements (`if`, `while`, and so on) because you've mastered the relational and logical operators. The good news is that C's relational and logical operators work a lot like QBasic's.

The most important difference is the test for equality between the two languages. QBasic uses the equal sign for both assignment and equality testing. C reserves the equal sign for assignment and uses the double equal, ==, for equality testing. There is no ambiguous use of = in C; if you see an equal sign, assignment is taking place without exception. This leads to frustrating programming for newcomers to C who attempt to perform equality comparisons like this:

```
if (x = 10)
```

Luckily, most C compilers issue warnings when they spot such statements because the programmer probably meant to code the first part of the `if` like this:

```
if (x == 10)    /* Notice the double equal */
```

Rather than the keywords `AND` and `OR`, C uses the operators `&&` and `||` (two side-by-side vertical bars) for logical operators. The logical operators enable you to combine two or more relational tests into a single statement. QBasic's `NOT` operator equivalent in C is `!`.

The last part of this chapter taught you the differences between C's true and false results and QBasic's true and false results. C converts all relational true results to `1` and all false results to `0`. Knowing about C's true and false values enables you to use relational tests directly inside expressions without using an `if` statement all the time. There is nothing wrong with using `if`, but for some short relational tests, you'll find that you can use the `1` and `0` in place of a longer and less efficient `if` statement in your C expressions. The next chapter explains all about `if`.

Part IV

Controlling the Flow

QBasic C

12

THE *IF* STATEMENT

This chapter explains how to use C's `if` statement so that your programs can make decisions based on data values. C's `if` works a lot like QBasic's `IF`, but there are some differences of which you must be aware.

This chapter assumes that you've mastered the relational and logical operators taught in the preceding chapter. You should also understand how C interprets all nonzero values as true and zero values as false. The result of a relational or logical test is always `1` or `0`, indicating true or false.

C includes an `else` statement that handles the false leg of the `if` statement. As with QBasic's block `IF-ELSE-END IF`, C executes either a single statement or an entire block of code for the `if` or the `else` legs of the `if`.

C includes an operator, called the *conditional operator,* that can sometimes replace simple `if-else` logic if you want maximum efficiency. The conditional operator is the only C operator that requires three arguments. Such an operator is called a *ternary operator.* (QBasic does not include any ternary operators.)

In this chapter, you will learn about the following topics:

- The `if` statement
- The `else` statement

- Combining tests with logical operators
- Short-circuiting logical `if` tests
- Using the conditional operator, `?:`

The *if*

`if` makes a decision.

Here is the format of the simple C `if` statement that doesn't include an `else` leg:

```
if (relational test)
  { block of one or more C statements }
```

The parentheses around the *`relational test`* are required in C. QBasic doesn't require the parentheses around the *`relational test`*, but many QBasic programmers use them for clarity. Therefore, the first line of a QBasic statement

```
IF sales > minSales THEN
```

looks like this when converted to C:

```
if (sales > minSales)
```

When moving to C, you have to break the habit of using `THEN`. C doesn't support the `THEN` keyword as QBasic does.

The braces aren't always required but are always recommended.

If the body of the `if` statement, the *`block of one or more C statements`*, contains a single C statement, the braces are not required. Therefore, both of the following sets of C code are equivalent:

```
if (p > 1)
  { x++; }

if (p > 1)
  x++;                /* Same as preceding code */
```

Always use braces, even when the body of the C `if` statement contains only a single statement as this one does:

```
if (x > y)
  { printf("The sum is greater.\n"); }  /* Notice the braces */
```

Using the braces helps reduce future maintenance errors. If you omit the braces around an `if`'s body when the body contains a single statement, you might forget to add the braces later when you add statements to the `if` body. It's important to note that the following code's `if` body contains only a *single* statement; the assignment to `n` is always performed because it's not part of the `if` even though the assignment is indented beneath the `if`'s body.

```
if (c == d)
  printf("The initials are the same.\n");
  n = 0;     /* Always executes! */
```

Don't put a semicolon at the end of the `if`'s relational test. If you do, C thinks that the body of the `if` is null. Consider this `if`:

```
if (amount <= 19.99);    /* Incorrect semicolon */
  { amount *= 1.15;
    total++; }
```

The semicolon at the end of the `if`'s relational test changes this `if` statement dramatically from the programmer's intent. If the value in `amount` is less than or equal to `19.99`, the `if` statement completes the body of the `if`, which is *null* because no code exists between the closing parenthesis and the semicolon. The program then *always* executes the two statements following the `if`. The braces around the two statements don't imply that the statements are part of the `if`. The semicolon keeps the block of two statements from being part of the `if`. Removing the semicolon fixes everything as shown here:

```
if (amount <= 19.99)    /* Removed the semicolon */
  { amount *= 1.15;
    total++; }
```

Now the body of the `if` is the block of two statements, and those two statements execute only if `amount` is less than or equal to `19.99`.

The program in Listing 12.1 shows a QBasic `IF` statement that asks the user for his or her age. If the user is 18 or over, a couple of messages print on-screen.

Listing 12.1. The QBasic *IF*.

```
' Filename: IF1.BAS
' Demonstrates the QBasic IF
PRINT "**Adults Only!**"
INPUT "How old are you"; age
IF (age >= 18) THEN
  PRINT "Have a good Italian wine for dinner."
  retireYrs = 65 - age
  PRINT "You only have"; retireYrs; "years before retirement!"
END IF
END
```

Listing 12.2 shows the same code in C.

Listing 12.2. The C *if*.

```
/* Filename: IF1.C
   Demonstrates the C if statement */
#include <stdio.h>
main()
{
  int age, retireYrs;
  printf("** Adults Only!**\n");
  printf("How old are you? ");
  scanf(" %d", &age);
  if (age >= 18)
    { printf("Have a good Italian wine for dinner.\n");
      retireYrs = 65 - age;
      printf("You only have %d years before retirement!\n",
              retireYrs);
    }
  return 0;
}
```

Here is sample output of both programs:

```
**Adults Only!**
How old are you? 21
Have a good Italian wine for dinner.
You only have 44 years before retirement!
```

Adding *else*

`if` without `else` is sometimes limiting. If there were no `else` keyword, you would have to list several `if` statements back-to-back. For example, in Listing 12.2, what if you wanted to print a message for those people under 18? Without `else`, you would have to test the `age` variable again to execute code for users under 18. Such code is both inefficient and difficult to maintain. Listing 12.3 shows how you would rewrite Listing 12.2 so that a message is printed for those under 18.

Listing 12.3. Multiple *ifs* are required if you omit *else*.

```
1:  /* Filename: IFELSE1.C
2:     Demonstrates the C if without else */
3:  #include <stdio.h>
4:  main()
5:  {
6:    int age, retireYrs;
7:    printf("** Adults Only!**\n");
8:    printf("How old are you? ");
9:    scanf(" %d", &age);
10:   if (age >= 18)
11:     { printf("Have a good Italian wine for dinner.\n");
12:       retireYrs = 65 - age;
13:       printf("You only have %d years before retirement!\n",
14:               retireYrs);
15:     }
16:   /* The next statement is redundant when 'else' is available */
17:   if (age < 18)
18:     { printf("Have a bottle of diet raspberry iced tea.\n");
19:       printf("Made from the best stuff on earth!");
20:     }
21:   return 0;
22: }
```

The `if` on line 17 is redundant because an `else` is available in C. Using `else` takes care of the `if` statement when the relational test is false.

Here is the format of the `if` statement with an `else` leg that handles the false condition:

```
if (relational test)
  { block of one or more C statements }
else
  { block of one or more C statements }
```

Figure 12.1 shows a sample `if-else` with callouts to review your understanding of `if-else` logic.

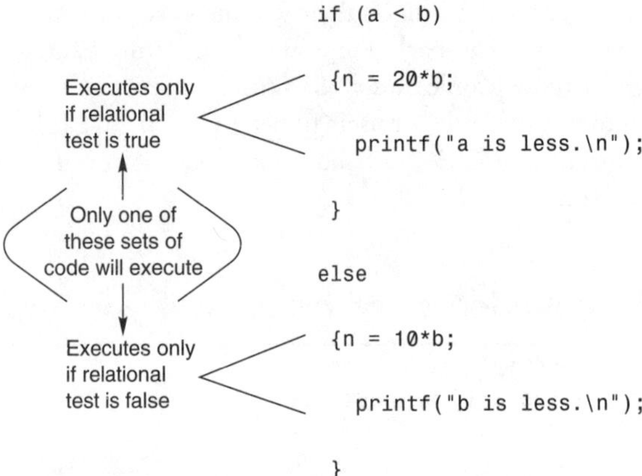

Figure 12.1. Diagramming `if-else`.

There is little to distinguish C's `if-else` from QBasic's `IF-ELSE`, other than the `if` differences described earlier in this chapter. If the `else` leg of the `if-else` contains only a single statement, you don't have to enclose the statement within braces. As with the `if` body of code, it's highly recommended that you enclose all bodies of `else` code in braces, even if the body is a single statement.

Listing 12.4 contains the age-checking program in QBasic using an `IF-ELSE` compound statement. Listing 12.5 shows the same program in C using `if-else` to show you that C's `if-else` is easy to understand.

Listing 12.4. Using the QBasic *IF-ELSE*.

```
' Filename: IF2.BAS
' Demonstrates the QBasic IF-ELSE
PRINT "**Adults Only!**"
INPUT "How old are you"; age
IF (age >= 18) THEN
  PRINT "Have a good Italian wine for dinner."
  retireYrs = 65 - age
  PRINT "You only have"; retireYrs; "years before retirement!"
ELSE
  PRINT "Have a bottle of diet raspberry iced tea."
  PRINT "Made from the best stuff on earth!"
```

```
END IF
END
```

Listing 12.5. Using the C *if-else*.

C VERSION

```
/* Filename: IFELSE2.C
   Demonstrates the C if-else */
#include <stdio.h>
main()
{
  int age, retireYrs;
  printf("** Adults Only!**\n");
  printf("How old are you? ");
  scanf(" %d", &age);
  if (age >= 18)
    { printf("Have a good Italian wine for dinner.\n");
      retireYrs = 65 - age;
      printf("You only have %d years before retirement!\n",
              retireYrs);
    }
  else
    { printf("Have a bottle of diet raspberry iced tea.\n");
      printf("Made from the best stuff on earth!");
    }
  return 0;
}
```

Here is the program's output when the user is less than 18 years old:

```
**Adults Only!**
How old are you? 17
Have a bottle of diet raspberry iced tea.
Made from the best stuff on earth!
```

if Within an *if*

Any statement can appear within the block of an `if` or `else`, even another `if` statement. QBasic requires an `ELSEIF` statement if you want to embed a second `IF` within the `ELSE` condition, but C does not.

`if` statements can appear within `if` or `else` blocks.

Embedded `if` statements, called *nested* `if` *statements,* are useful when you need to test more than one condition. The programs in Listing 12.6 and 12.7 demonstrate QBasic and C versions of programs that print a different enrollment message for new students based on which third of the alphabet their last names begin with. If the last names begin with the letters *A* through *H,* they must enroll in a different room than if their names begin with *I* through *R* or *S* through *Z.*

> The programs both assume that the user enters an uppercase letter of the alphabet. For now, assume that the user does enter what is asked for. When you finish this part of the book and the next that covers C's built-in functions, you'll be able to validate user input after letting the user enter either uppercase or lowercase letters. It's important that you concentrate on the `if` at this time.

Listing 12.6. Using a nested *IF* in QBasic.

```
' Filename: NESTIF.BAS
' One of three messages prints depending
' on the first letter of the student's last name
PRINT
PRINT "** Enrollment Search **"    ' Title
PRINT "What letter does your last name begin with?"
INPUT "(Enter a single uppercase letter): ", initial$
' A nested IF follows
IF (initial$ <= "H") THEN
  PRINT "Please enroll in Room 42."
ELSEIF (initial$ <= "R") THEN
  PRINT "Please enroll in Room 16."
ELSE PRINT "Please enroll in Room 12."
END IF
PRINT "Good luck this semester!"
END
```

Listing 12.7. Using a nested *if* in C.

```
/* Filename: NESTIF.C
   One of three messages prints depending
   on the first letter of the student's last name */
```

```
#include <stdio.h>
main()
{
  char initial;
  printf("\n\n** Enrollment Search**\n");  /* Title */
  printf("What letter does your last name begin with?\n");
  printf("(Enter a single uppercase letter): ");
  scanf(" %c", &initial);
  /* Nested if follows */
  if (initial <= 'H')
    { printf("Please enroll in Room 42.\n"); }
  else
    { if (initial <= 'R')
        { printf("Please enroll in Room 16.\n"); }
      else
        { printf("Please enroll in Room 12.\n"); }
    }
  printf("Good luck this semester!");
  return 0;
}
```

Here are two sample runs from either of the programs:

```
** Enrollment Search**
What letter does your last name begin with?
(Enter a single uppercase letter): F
Please enroll in Room 42.
Good luck this semester!

** Enrollment Search**
What letter does your last name begin with?
(Enter a single uppercase letter): T
Please enroll in Room 12.
Good luck this semester!
```

Don't nest too many `if` statements, or your code will become unreadable and a maintenance nightmare. If you have more than two or three conditions to check, consider using a `switch` statement. The `switch`, which is C's equivalent to QBasic's `SELECT CASE`, is explained in Chapter 15, "*switch* Selections."

> The nested `if-else` statement offers another reason to put brackets around all `if` and `else` bodies of code, even if the code consists of single-line bodies. The brackets show which `else` code goes with which `if`. The following nested `if-else` statements would be more difficult to follow without the braces:
>
> ```
> if (a > b)
>   { if (c > d)
>        { printf("apple"); }
>     else
>        { printf("pear"); }
>   }
> else
>   { printf("orange");}
> ```

The Shortcuts of Logical Testing

As with QBasic's `IF`, you can combine relational tests with the logical operators. The `&&` and `||` operators can appear within an `if` statement's relational test, and you can combine as many relational tests as you like as long as you enclose the entire test in parentheses.

Remember logical and relational precedence.

As Appendix B shows, C's relational operators have precedence over the logical operators. The same holds true for QBasic. Therefore, the `if` statement

```
if (a < b && b < c || c < d)
```

compares like this according to the default order of operators:

```
if ((a < b) && (b < c) || (c < d))
```

You must, however, *always* include the overall surrounding parentheses. C issues a compiler error if you attempt something like this:

```
if (a < b) && (b < c) || (c < d)    /* No enclosing () */
```

> QBasic does not need such parentheses around such a compound relational test, but using them helps clarify your compound relational tests.

Compound `if` testing is yet another way that C achieves more efficiency than QBasic. C does not look at the right side of an `&&` or `||` if the left side provides enough information to determine the truth of the expression. Consider the following `if` statement:

```
if ((a < b) && (c < d))
  { printf("True happened.\n"); }
```

If `a` is *not* less than `b`, the `if` condition can *never* be true! There is no reason for C to look at the right side of the `&&`, and therefore, C does not bother with the right side. A false `&&` and any other result is still false.

QBasic interprets both sides of the equivalent `IF` statement completely, even though doing so is redundant if the left side is false. Therefore, in the statement

```
IF ((a < b) AND (c < d)) THEN
  PRINT "True happened."
END IF
```

QBasic compares the `c` to the `d` even if the relational test on the left side of the `AND` is false.

The efficiency of the compound relational test is sometimes called C's *short-circuiting feature.* The `if`'s short-circuiting also occurs if the left side of a `||` operator is true. True `||` or *anything* is true. Therefore, if `a` is less than `b` in the following `if`, then C never compares the `c` and `d` because their comparison won't affect the outcome of the `if`:

```
if ((a < b) || (c < d))
  { printf("True happened.\n"); }
```

QBasic, however, would process both sides of this equivalent `OR`:

```
IF ((a < b) OR (c < d)) THEN
  PRINT "True happened.\n"
END IF
```

Here are the bottom-line rules for C's short-circuiting:

- If the left side of an `&&` is false, the entire expression is false, and C does not process the right side of the `&&`.
- If the left side of a `||` is true, the entire expression is true, and C does not process the right side of the `||`.

The short-circuiting feature helps make your C programs run faster, but there are also drawbacks to its use. Be sure that you don't put anything other than a relational test on the right side of a logical operator. You cannot be assured that the right side of either of the following `if` tests will execute:

```
if ((a < b) && (c++ < d))    /* Increment might not happen! */
if ((x > y) ¦¦ (p = f > 1)) /* Assignment might not happen! */
```

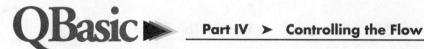

If you want the increment or assignment to occur, you must code them on the line before the `if`. C might never process the right side of the `&&` or `¦¦`, depending on what the left side's results are.

To review compound logical `if` tests, the programs in Listing 12.8 and 12.9 show a QBasic and C program that helps secure your house at night.

Listing 12.8. Using QBasic's *IF* with a logical test.

```
' Filename: LOGIF.BAS
' Performs a logical operation inside an IF statement
' Ask a series of security questions
INPUT "Did you lock the doors (Y/N)"; door$
INPUT "Did you pull the shades (Y/N)"; shad$
INPUT "Did you set the alarm (Y/N)"; alarm$
IF ((door$ = "Y") AND (shad$ = "Y") AND (alarm$ = "Y")) THEN
  PRINT "You are now secure for the evening."
ELSE PRINT "You should be more careful."
END IF
END
```

Listing 12.9. Using C's *if* with a logical test.

```
/* Filename: LOGIF.C
   Performs a logical operation inside an if statement */
#include <stdio.h>
main()
{
  char door, shad, alarm;
  printf("\nDid you lock the doors (Y/N)? ");
  scanf(" %c", &door);
  printf("Did you pull the shades (Y/N)? ");
  scanf(" %c", &shad);
  printf("Did you set the alarm (Y/N)? ");
  scanf(" %c", &alarm);
  /* if with logical operator appears next */
```

```
  if ((door == 'Y') && (shad == 'Y') && (alarm == 'Y'))
    { printf("You are now secure for the evening.\n"); }
  else
    { printf("You should be more careful.\n"); }
  return 0;
}
```

Here is the output from both programs:

```
Did you lock the doors (Y/N)? Y
Did you pull the shades (Y/N)? Y
Did you set the alarm (Y/N)? Y
You are now secure for the evening.
```

The Conditional Operator

C provides an operator that sometimes takes the place of `if-else` statements. By using the *conditional operator,* which is written like `?:`, you'll gain extra efficiency because C does not have to process `if` and `else` keyword statements.

The conditional operator requires three arguments.

Here is the format of the conditional operator:

```
relationalExpression ? statement1 : statement2;
```

The `?:` operator requires three arguments. The first argument is a relational test that determines which of the remaining two arguments will execute. It's important to note that `?:` replaces simple `if-else` logic, so the `?:` makes a decision (the *`relationalExpression`*) and executes code according to that decision.

Here is an example of the conditional statement:

```
(a < b) ? min = a: min = b;
```

The three arguments are `(a < b)`, `min = a`, and `min = b`. Notice that a semicolon doesn't appear in the `?:` until the end of the statement. The second and third arguments can be any executable C statement, including function calls such as `printf()`.

The preceding `?:` expression stores the minimum of `a` or `b` in the variable named `min`. Here is the C `if-else` code required to duplicate this single `?:` expression:

```
if (a < b)
  { min = a; }
else
  { min = b; }
```

Obviously, the conditional expression is more succinct and efficient than the `if-else`. Figure 12.2 shows how the conditional works by explaining the preceding `?:` expression.

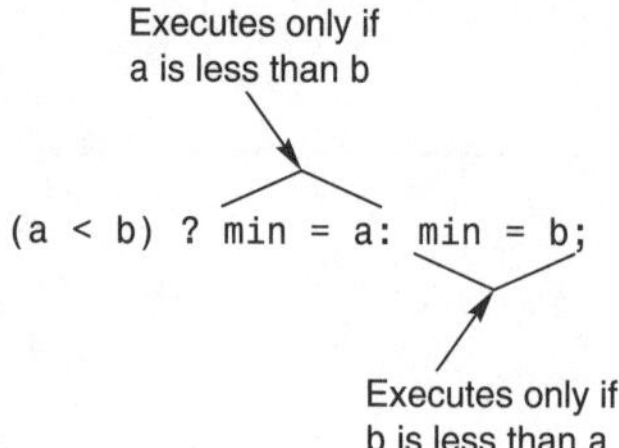

Figure 12.2. Diagramming the conditional, `?:`*.*

Often, you can consolidate conditional expressions. The following expression stores the minimum of `a` or `b` in `min` with only one assignment operator and without repeating the `min` variable:

```
min = (a < b) ? a : b;  /* Stores the minimum value */
```

Don't overdo the conditional operator. If the `if-else` logic gets very complex, especially if you need nested `if` statements, use the easier-to-read `if-else` statements. The nested conditional

```
(t == b) ? ((i <= 1) ? p = 2: p = 4; ) : x = 14 * t;
```

is much easier to read when written as a nested `if` as follows:

```
if (t == b)
  { if (i <= 1)
       { p = 2; }
    else
       { p = 4; }
  }
else
  { x = 14 * i; }
```

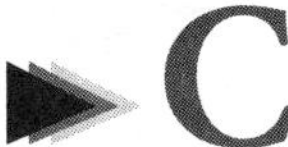

> There is no QBasic equivalent to the conditional operator, except for the `IF-ELSE` written out in its regular form.

Listing 12.10 contains a C program that prints both the minimum and the maximum of two entered values. The program uses a regular `if-else` statement. Listing 12.11 is the same C program using the conditional operator to improve the efficiency.

Listing 12.10. Finding the minimum and maximum with *if*.

```
/* Filename: MINMAXIF.C
   Finds the minimum and maximum of two values with if */
#include <stdio.h>
main()
{
  int val1, val2;
  int min, max;
  printf("\nWhat is the first number? ");
  scanf(" %d", &val1);
  printf("What is the second number? ");
  scanf(" %d", &val2);
  /* Store the maximum and minimum values */
  if (val1 < val2)
    { min = val1;
      max = val2; }
  else
    { min = val2;
      max = val1; }
  /* Print the results */
  printf("The maximum value is %d.\n", max);
  printf("The minimum value is %d.\n", min);
  return 0;
}
```

Listing 12.11. Finding the minimum and maximum with ?:.

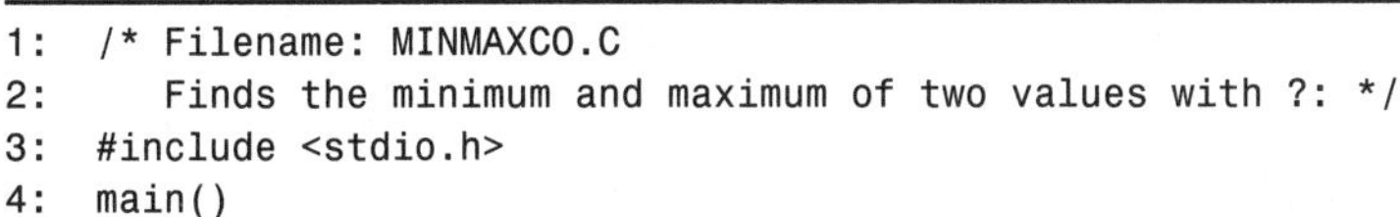

```
/* Filename: MINMAXCO.C
   Finds the minimum and maximum of two values with ?: */
#include <stdio.h>
main()
```

continues

Listing 12.11. continued

```
5:  {
6:     int val1, val2;
7:     int min, max;
8:     printf("\nWhat is the first number? ");
9:     scanf(" %d", &val1);
10:    printf("What is the second number? ");
11:    scanf(" %d", &val2);
12:    /* Store the maximum and minimum values */
13:    (val1 <= val2) ? (min = val1) : (min = val2);
14:    (val1 <= val2) ? (max = val2) : (max = val1);
15:  /* Print the results */
16:    printf("The maximum value is %d.\n", max);
17:    printf("The minimum value is %d.\n", min);
18:    return 0;
19: }
```

As you can see from lines 13 and 14, you often have to repeat the same conditional test because only single statements can appear as the second and third arguments to `?:`. When you learn how to write your own functions, you'll be able to extend the power of `?:` by using a function call for the second and third `?:` arguments.

Here is the output from the two programs:

```
What is the first number? 3
What is the second number? 6
The maximum value is 6.
The minimum value is 3.

What is the first number? 443
What is the second number? 236
The maximum value is 443.
The minimum value is 236.
```

> If the user enters the same value, that value is stored in both `min` and `max`.

Summary

You can now convert your QBasic style of `IF-ELSE` coding to C's `if-else` style. The two languages provide almost identical statements (except for QBasic's reluctance to allow lowercase keywords and C's refusal to allow uppercase). C requires that you put parentheses around the `if` relational test and does not support a `THEN` keyword.

C also provides more efficiency when you use logical operators to combine one or more relational tests. C will not process the right side of a logical expression if the left side provides the true or false answer.

Another way you can improve the efficiency of your C programs is to use the conditional operator, `?:`. The conditional operator is the only operator that takes three arguments, a relational test and the true and false code legs of that test. Use conditional operators to replace simple C `if-else` statements.

The next chapter continues the discussion of C control statements by comparing QBasic's `WHILE` loops (QBasic has several versions of `WHILE`) to C's two versions, `while` and `do-while`. The `if` statement is a powerful decision statement, but you cannot write loops with `if` statements. The `while` keyword provides the loop capabilities you need in order to process several iterations of code.

13

THE *while* LOOPS

C simplifies looping with its two `while` statements. QBasic contains several kinds of loops that work just like C's `while` loop:

```
WHILE-WEND
DO WHILE-LOOP
DO UNTIL-LOOP
DO-LOOP WHILE
DO-LOOP UNTIL
```

As a matter of fact, QBasic has so many different ways to loop that it's difficult to describe them all. QBasic simply doesn't need so many looping statements. C contains only two versions of a `while` loop. This chapter teaches you about how C's `while` and `do-while` statements can control virtually any loop that you need in any program. After mastering C's `for` loop in the next chapter, you'll know all there is to know about looping with the C language.

In this chapter, you will learn about the following topics:

- The `while` loop
- The `do-while` loop
- Looping early with `continue`
- Exiting loops early with the `break` statement
- Exiting programs early with the `exit()` function

The *while* Loop

QBasic offers too many loops!

Basically, all the QBasic `WHILE` loops and the C `while` loops continue looping while a certain condition is true or while a certain condition is false. In QBasic, the `WHILE-WEND`, the `DO WHILE-LOOP`, and the `DO-LOOP WHILE` loops continue looping, or *iterating* as it's often called, while a condition such as a relational test is true. Both of QBasic's `DO UNTIL-LOOP` and `DO-LOOP UNTIL` loops iterate *until* a certain relational test is true.

If you have programmed in QBasic for a while, you've probably stopped using the `WHILE-WEND` loop. The `DO` loop combinations are more flexible than the older `WHILE-WEND`. (QBasic supports `WHILE-WEND` for compatibility with older versions of BASIC such as GW-BASIC.)

You'll find, however, that C's `while` loop more closely mirrors that of `WHILE-WEND` than any of the four `DO` loops. While diving into C's `while` loops, you'll take a few moments to see examples of each of QBasic's loops along the way for comparison.

> Reviewing all the forms of the QBasic loops will do two things. First, you'll know what this chapter refers to when one of the QBasic loops is mentioned. Also, you'll appreciate C's smaller offering of loops, and you'll see that both of C's loops take care of any processing that QBasic uses five loops for.

The program in Listing 13.1 asks the user for a number from 1 to 10 and then prints the square of the number. The `WHILE-WEND` loop ensures that the user enters a number within the proper range.

Listing 13.1. The QBasic *WHILE-WEND*.

```
' Filename: WHWEND.BAS
' Demonstrates QBasic's WHILE-WEND loop
INPUT "Please enter a number from 1 to 10: ", num
' Make sure the number is within range
WHILE (num < 1 OR num > 10)
  BEEP
  PRINT "You must enter a number between 1 and 10"
  INPUT "Please enter a number from 1 to 10: ", num
WEND
' Compute the square
sq = num * num
```

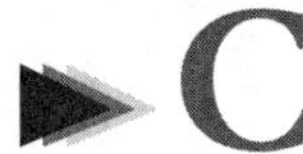

```
12: PRINT
13: PRINT "The number squared is"; sq
14: END
```

One of the common problems with `WHILE-WEND` loops, and with any loop that tests for a true condition at the top of the loop, is that you have to prompt the user in two different places in the program with the same prompt. Lines 3 and 8 both do the same thing. You'll see that a more flexible loop construction enables you to issue the prompt only once.

Here is a sample run from Listing 13.1. The output also matches that of the next several listings.

```
Please enter a number from 1 to 10: 25
You must enter a number between 1 and 10
Please enter a number from 1 to 10: 6

The number squared is 36
```

The closest QBasic `DO` loop to `WHILE-WEND` is the `DO WHILE-LOOP`. Listing 13.2 contains the same program as Listing 13.1, except the `DO WHILE-LOOP` is used rather than `WHILE-WEND`.

Listing 13.2. The QBasic *DO WHILE-LOOP.*

```
' Filename: DOWHLOOP.BAS
' Demonstrates QBasic's DO WHILE-LOOP
INPUT "Please enter a number from 1 to 10: ", num
' Make sure the number is within range
DO WHILE (num < 1 OR num > 10)
  BEEP
  PRINT "You must enter a number between 1 and 10"
  INPUT "Please enter a number from 1 to 10: ", num
LOOP    ' Signals the end of the loop
' Compute the square
sq = num * num
PRINT
PRINT "The number squared is"; sq
END
```

The `DO WHILE-LOOP` tells QBasic to loop while a certain relational test is true. The QBasic `DO UNTIL-LOOP` executes *until* a certain relational test is true. In other words, as long as the test is false, the loop continues. (The inclusion of this loop in QBasic is redundant because all you have to do is reverse the logic in the other loops just described to achieve the same effect.) Listing 13.3 contains an example of the number-squaring program rewritten to use the `DO UNTIL-LOOP`.

Listing 13.3. The QBasic *DO UNTIL-LOOP*.

```
1:  ' Filename: DOUNLOOP.BAS
2:  ' Demonstrates QBasic's DO UNTIL-LOOP
3:  INPUT "Please enter a number from 1 to 10: ", num
4:  ' Make sure the number is within range
5:  DO UNTIL (num >= 1 AND num <= 10)
6:    BEEP
7:    PRINT "You must enter a number between 1 and 10"
8:    INPUT "Please enter a number from 1 to 10: ", num
9:  LOOP    ' Signals the end of the loop
10: ' Compute the square
11: sq = num * num
12: PRINT
13: PRINT "The number squared is"; sq
14: END
```

The top of the loop (line 5) tells QBasic to loop until the user's value is between 1 and 10. Notice that even though you're now familiar with this program's goal, the reverse logic used with the `DO UNTIL-LOOP` might seem backward now that you've seen the more positive `WHILE-WEND` and `DO WHILE-LOOP`.

C's `while` loop tests at the top of the loop.

C's `while` loop will work for any of the preceding three QBasic loop statements, `WHILE-WEND`, `DO WHILE-LOOP`, and `DO UNTIL-LOOP`. Here is the format of C's `while` loop:

```
while (relationalTest)
  { block of one or more C statements }
```

As with the `if` statement shown in the preceding chapter, you must enclose the `relationalTest` in parentheses. If you combine more than one relational test with logical operators, you must enclose the entire combined test in parentheses. The body of the `while` does not require braces if the body consists of a single statement, but you should be in the habit of using the braces even if the body contains only a single statement.

Always change something about the `relationalTest` in the body of the `while` loop, or the loop will loop forever.

Don't put a semicolon at the end of the `while`'s *`relationalTest`*, or C will think the body of the loop is null. The result will be that C enters an infinite loop! Nothing inside the null body will change the *`relationalTest`* so that the loop can fall out. Only the individual statements within the body of the `while` loop end with semicolons.

Listing 13.4 contains the C version of the number-squaring program. Although the prompt has to be repeated (lines 13 and 14), you'll have to admit that C's single `while` loop is cleaner than QBasic's `DO` versions. The ending `LOOP` statement is not required in the C `while` loop because the loop knows to end at the closing brace.

Listing 13.4. The C *while* loop.

```
1:  /* Filename: WHILE.C
2:     Demonstrates C's while loop */
3:  #include <stdio.h>
4:  main()
5:  {
6:     int num, sq;
7:     printf("Please enter a number from 1 to 10: ");
8:     scanf(" %d", &num);
9:     /* Make sure the number is within range */
10:    while (num < 1 ¦¦ num > 10)
11:      { printf("\a");    /* Ring the bell */
12:        printf("You must enter a number between 1 and 10\n");
13:        printf("Please enter a number from 1 to 10: ");
14:        scanf(" %d", &num);
15:      }
16:    /* Compute the square */
17:    sq = num * num;
18:    printf("\nThe number squared is %d", sq);
19:    return 0;
20: }
```

You'll probably never want or need an infinite loop, but if you ever do, you can use this code to set one up:

continues

continued

```
while (1)
  { /* Your infinite loop statements here */
  }
```

`1` always means true, so this loop continues forever (until someone presses the Ctrl+Break key combination that stops the program). Perhaps you might want an infinite loop to display a scrolling advertisement on-screen that continues throughout the day. Most of the time, however, infinite loops are the result of *unintentional* code!

Don't ever confuse the `if` with the similar-looking `while` statement. As in QBasic, `if` executes its body at most one time, whereas the body of a `while` loop might execute many times, as Figure 13.1 shows.

```
                  if (a > b)
                  {/*The body of
Executes at          the if statement
most 1 time          goes here*/
                   }

                  while (a > b)
                   {/*The body of
Can execute           the while loop
several times         goes here*/
                   }
```

Figure 13.1. `if` is not a loop, but `while` is.

The *do-while* Loop

The `do-while` loop tests at the bottom of the loop.

QBasic includes two loops that test the loop relational test at the bottom of the loop. C's `do-while` loop does so too. The choice of `while` or `do-while` loop depends on your application. Sometimes, routines are easier to code with the loop testing appearing at the

bottom of the loop. To base the do-while loop on your current QBasic knowledge, following is a review the two remaining QBasic loops.

The DO-LOOP WHILE loop continues looping *while* the conditional test, which appears at the bottom of the loop, is true. The program in Listing 13.5 shows the number-squaring program using the DO-LOOP WHILE construction.

Listing 13.5. The QBasic *DO-LOOP WHILE* loop.

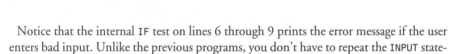

```
1:  ' Filename: DOLOOPWH.BAS
2:  ' Demonstrates QBasic's DO-LOOP WHILE
3:  DO
4:    INPUT "Please enter a number from 1 to 10: ", num
5:    ' Make sure the number is within range
6:    IF (num < 1 OR num > 10) THEN
7:      BEEP
8:      PRINT "You must enter a number between 1 and 10"
9:    END IF
10: LOOP WHILE (num < 1 OR num > 10)
11: ' Compute the square
12: sq = num * num
13: PRINT
14: PRINT "The number squared is"; sq
15: END
```

Notice that the internal IF test on lines 6 through 9 prints the error message if the user enters bad input. Unlike the previous programs, you don't have to repeat the INPUT statement if there is an error when using a DO-LOOP WHILE loop.

QBasic's DO-LOOP UNTIL loops *until* a relational test is true, and the test appears at the bottom of the loop. Listing 13.6 shows a program that uses DO-LOOP UNTIL.

Listing 13.6. The QBasic *DO-LOOP UNTIL* loop.

```
' Filename: DOLOOPUN.BAS
' Demonstrates QBasic's DO-LOOP UNTIL
DO
  INPUT "Please enter a number from 1 to 10: ", num
  ' Make sure the number is within range
  IF (num < 1 OR num > 10) THEN
    BEEP
```

continues

Listing 13.6. continued

```
8:      PRINT "You must enter a number between 1 and 10"
9:    END IF
10: LOOP UNTIL (num >= 1 AND num <= 10)
11: ' Compute the square
12: sq = num * num
13: PRINT
14: PRINT "The number squared is"; sq
15: END
```

yellow highlighted transactionsNotice that the conditional test on line 10 is just the reverse of that of the `DO-LOOP WHILE` in Listing 13.5. QBasic is really too bloated because both of these loops are possible with only one of the loop construction statements. The designers of C kept C much smaller than QBasic, and in doing so, they did not include superfluous commands. You can use the `do-while` loop any time you want to test a relational condition at the bottom of a loop. Here is the format of the `do-while` statement:

```
do
  { block of one or more C statements }
while (relationalTest);
```

Notice that there is a required semicolon at the end of the closing parenthesis in the `do-while` loop. Figure 13.2 shows the distinction between C's `while` and `do-while` loops.

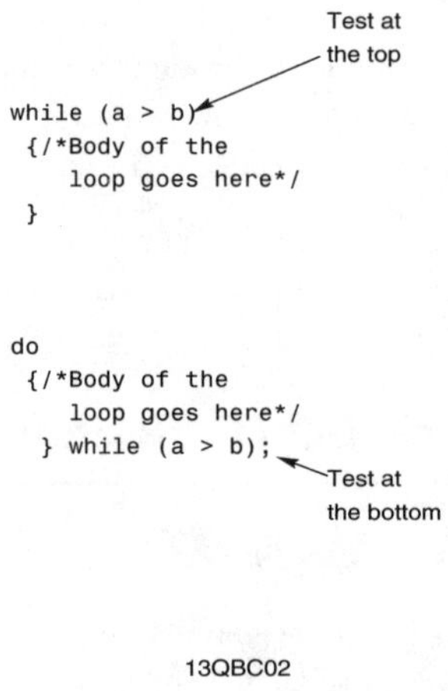

```
while (a > b)
 {/*Body of the
    loop goes here*/
 }

do
 {/*Body of the
    loop goes here*/
  } while (a > b);
```


Figure 13.2. The only difference between C's `while` and `do-while` is the location of the test.

Listing 13.7 shows the final installment of the number-squaring program. Listing 13.7 uses the `do-while` loop to test the user's number.

Listing 13.7. The C *do-loop* loop.

```
/* Filename: DOWHILE.C
   Demonstrates C's do-while loop */
#include <stdio.h>
main()
{
   int num, sq;
   do
   { printf("Please enter a number from 1 to 10: ");
     scanf(" %d", &num);
     /* Make sure the number is within range */
     if (num < 1 || num > 10)
       { printf("\a");    /* Ring the bell */
         printf("You must enter a number between 1 and 10\n");
       }
   } while (num < 1 || num > 10);
   /* Compute the square */
   sq = num * num;
   printf("\nThe number squared is %d", sq);
   return 0;
}
```

Looping Early with *continue*

There are rare times when you need to loop again, earlier than the normal iteration of the loop. For example, perhaps you want the first half of the `while` loop body to execute *each* time through the loop, but you want the second half of the loop body to execute only some of the time. C provides the `continue` statement that enables you to end the body of one loop iteration early and start another iteration.

> QBasic does not support any kind of `continue` feature.

The program in Listing 13.8 prints the total of all numbers up to the user's entered value and then prints only the odd and even number totals. For example, if the user enters `7`, the program adds the numbers from 1 to 7, producing 28. Then the program adds the odd numbers from 1 to 7, producing a total of 16 (1 + 3 + 5 + 7), and adds the even numbers from 1 to 7, producing a total of 12 (2 + 4 + 6).

Listing 13.8. Using *continue* in a loop.

```
/* Filename: CONTIN.C
   Demonstrates C's continue statement */
#include <stdio.h>
main()
{
   int num, numSave;
   long odd=0, even=0, all=0;  /* Will hold totals */
   do
   { printf("Please enter a number from 1 to 100: ");
     scanf(" %d", &num);
     /* Make sure the number is within range */
     if (num < 1 || num > 100)
       { printf("\a");    /* Ring the bell */
         printf("You must enter a number between 1 and 100\n");
       }
   } while (num < 1 || num > 100);
   numSave = num;    /* Save the user's value */
   /* Compute the sums */
   while (num > 0)
     {  all += num;
        if (num %2 == 0)  /* Test for even */
         { even += num;
           num--;
           continue; }   /* Loop again */
        odd += num;
        num--;
     }
  printf("Here are the totals:\n");
  printf(" Total from 1 to %d: %d\n", numSave, all);
  printf(" Odd total from 1 to %d: %d\n", numSave, odd);
  printf(" Even total from 1 to %d: %d\n", numSave, even);
  return 0;
}
```

Here is the output from the program:

```
Please enter a number from 1 to 100: 7
Here are the totals:
 Total from 1 to 7: 28
 Odd total from 1 to 7: 16
 Even total from 1 to 7: 12
```

The `continue` statement on line 24 ensures that the odd-number summing code on lines 25 and 26 don't execute if the even-number summing code executed. The `if` statement on line 21 forces the execution to skip over the even summing code if an odd number is being added. The body of the `while` loop is basically divided into three parts: The program always sums each number from 1 to the user's entered value; the `if` ensures that the even summing occurs only half the time through the loop; and the `continue` ensures that odd summing occurs only half the time.

> You could rewrite Listing 13.8 without using the `continue` statement. As usual, there are several ways to write the same program. The `continue` statement isn't used a lot, but it does save you the trouble of adding a `goto` or a long `if` block of code as you would have to do in QBasic.

Exiting Loops Early with *break*

The `break` statement is the opposite of `continue`. Instead of iterating a loop early, `break` ends the current loop. As with `continue`, `if` typically precedes a `break`. The following loop is not really a loop:

```
do while (a < b)
  { break;     /* Always terminates */
    a++;       /* Never executes */
  }
```

The `break` statement is not part of an `if`, so the `break` always executes when the loop begins its first iteration. The loop always terminates immediately.

If you nest loops, `break` terminates the innermost loop, not every loop in progress.

There is no `break` *equivalent in QBasic.*

`break` is useful when you are processing disk data; you can break the loop reading and processing of the data when you reach the end of file. You'll also see how `break` is used to augment the `switch` statement that you'll read about in Chapter 15, "*switch* Selections." Figure 13.3 shows how `break` compares to `continue`.

The program in Listing 13.9 includes a loop that contains both `while` and `continue` statements. It's rare to see both in the same loop as done here. The program loops from 1 to 100 and finds the first number divisible by both 5 and 8. When the number is found, the loop breaks and the program ends. If the program encounters a number divisible by 5, or divisible by 8, a message prints, and the program continues.

```
while (a < b)
 {printf("The loop is in progress...\n");
   a++
   if (a == 10)
      {continue;}
   if (a == 20)
      {break;}
 }
printf("The loop is done.\n");
```

Loop again earlier than usual

Completely exit the loop

Figure 13.3. `continue` *loops again, and* `break` *terminates the loop.*

Listing 13.9. Using both *break* and *continue*.

```
/* Filename: BRCONT.C
   Finds the first number divisible by both 5 and 8 */
#include <stdio.h>
main()
{
   int num=0;
   do
   { num++;   /* Keep the loop going with a new number */
     if (((num % 5) == 0) && ((num % 8) == 0))
       { printf("Found it; %d is the number\n", num);
         break; }  /* End the loop */

     /* See if number is divisible by 5 */
     if ((num % 5) == 0)
       { printf("The number %d is divisible by 5\n", num);
```

```
            continue;   /* Loop again */
          }
        /* See if number is divisible by 8 */
        if ((num % 8) == 0)
          { printf("The number %d is divisible by 8\n", num);
            continue;   /* Loop again */
          }
      } while (num <= 100);
    return 0;
}
```

Here is the output from this program. See whether you can trace the program flow as you read through the output.

```
The number 5 is divisible by 5
The number 8 is divisible by 8
The number 10 is divisible by 5
The number 15 is divisible by 5
The number 16 is divisible by 8
The number 20 is divisible by 5
The number 24 is divisible by 8
The number 25 is divisible by 5
The number 30 is divisible by 5
The number 32 is divisible by 8
The number 35 is divisible by 5
Found it; 40 is the number
```

The program in Listing 13.9 is rather simple to write when you're using C's `break` and `continue` statements. Writing the same program in QBasic would take several extra `IF-ELSE` statements because of QBasic's lack of `break` and `continue` statements.

Exiting Programs Early with *exit()*

The `break` statement terminates a loop early. There is a built-in function in C called `exit()` that corresponds to QBasic's `STOP` statement. `exit()` terminates the entire program's execution. If you ever need to quit a program early, use `exit()`. `exit()` requires a value inside its parentheses, and `1` works fine.

The `exit()` value is passed to the operating system, where it is usually ignored, but you can test the value in the MS-DOS system's `ERRORLEVEL` variable if you want to do so.

You should include the header file named STDLIB.H in every program that uses `exit()`.

The program in Listing 13.10 shows a common use of `STOP` in QBasic. Often, you'll end the program early with `STOP` if an error occurs. The program asks the user for two numbers and prints the result of the numbers divided by one another. If the second number is `0`, the program prints an error message and quits with a `STOP` statement.

Listing 13.10. Use *STOP* if an error occurs.

```
' Filename: STOP.BAS
' Stopping the program early if an error occurs
PRINT "**Division Practice**"    ' Title
PRINT
INPUT "What is the first number"; num1
INPUT "What is the second number"; num2
IF (num2 = 0) THEN
  PRINT "The second number cannot be zero."
  STOP   ' Stop program early
END IF
PRINT num1; "divided by"; num2; "is"; (num1 / num2)
END
```

Here is the output from two sample runs:

```
**Division Practice**

What is the first number? 4
What is the second number? 6
 4 divided by 6 is .6666667

**Division Practice**

What is the first number? 4
```

```
What is the second number? 0
The second number cannot be zero.
```

The program in Listing 13.11 shows the C version of the preceding program. Notice that `exit()` in line 15 stops the program's execution. If you run this program from within an integrated environment, such as Turbo C, the `exit()` function call returns to the environment.

Listing 13.11. Use *exit()* if an error occurs.

C VERSION

```
1:  /* Filename: STOP.C
2:     Stopping the program early if an error occurs */
3:  #include <stdio.h>
4:  #include <stdlib.h>
5:  main()
6:  {
7:    int num1, num2;
8:    printf("**Division Practice**\n\n");    /* Title */
9:    printf("What is the first number? ");
10:   scanf(" %d", &num1);
11:   printf("What is the second number? ");
12:   scanf(" %d", &num2);
13:   if (num2 == 0)
14:     { printf("The second number cannot be zero.\n");
15:       exit(1);    /* Stop program early */
16:     }
17:   printf("%d divided by %d is %f", num1, num2, (num1 / num2));
18:   return 0;
19: }
```

Summary

This chapter explained how to use C's `while` and `do-while` looping statements. Unlike QBasic's five loop versions, C's two versions of a `while` loop are all you need to write whatever loop you want. The `while` loop continues looping as long as a relational condition is true and tests the condition at the top of the loop. The `do-while` tests for the condition at the bottom of the loop.

After you learned how to loop, you saw how `break` and `continue` give you added control over loops. `continue` causes an early iteration of the loop to execute. All the code within the loop's body that follows `continue` is ignored for that iteration. The `break` statement terminates the current loop. Both `break` and `continue` are usually preceded by `if` statements.

Not only can you exit a loop early with `break`, but you can exit an entire program with the `exit()` function. `exit()` requires a value in its parentheses such as `0` or `1`. The value is passed back to the operating system. DOS can check the return value or ignore it, depending on the application.

The next chapter explains how to use C's `for` loop. C's `for` works almost exactly like QBasic's, except that C's is a little shorter and easier to use.

14

THE *for* LOOP

There's great news for you in this chapter! You'll see that QBasic's `FOR` loop is almost identical to C's `for`. There is almost a one-to-one correspondence between the two languages' *determinate loops.* (`FOR` loops are sometimes called determinate loops because you can often determine ahead of time how many times the loop will iterate. `WHILE` loops keep looping until a condition becomes true or false, and you cannot predict ahead of time how many times they will iterate; `WHILE` loops are therefore referred to as *indeterminate loops.*)

C's `for` loops don't need an ending `NEXT` statement because of C's block structure. When execution reaches the ending brace of the `for` statement, `}`, C knows that the end of the `for` loop has been reached.

In this chapter, you will learn about the following topics:

- The `for` loop
- Changing the way you specify `for` loops
- Nesting `for` loops
- Using `break` and `continue` in `for` loops

The *for* Loop

You already understand `FOR` loops because of your background in QBasic. This discussion might as well cut to the chase and present C's `for` loop to you so that you can begin to make the shift to C's `for` statement. Here is the format of C's `for` loop:

```
for (startExpression; testExpression; incrementExpression)
  { block of one or more C statements; }
```

The parentheses around the `for`'s controlling statement are required; the C compiler complains if you omit the parentheses. The strangest thing about C's `for` loops is the use of two semicolons inside the `for` controlling statement. The semicolons are required.

If the *`block of one or more C statements`*, the *body* of the `for` statement, consists of only a single statement, the braces are not required (as with the `if`, `while`, and `do-while` statements that you learned in the past couple of chapters). However, many C programmers use the braces even if the body of the `for` contains only a single statement.

Don't ever put a semicolon at the end of the `for` statement's parentheses. If you do, the body of the `for` will be null, and the compiler will do absolutely nothing for the duration of the loop!

Figure 14.1 graphically shows the similarities between a QBasic `FOR` statement and an equivalent C `for` statement. The figure shows how C's loop-controlling parenthesis expressions control the loop.

The `STEP 1` is optional in the QBasic `FOR` loop, but it's shown in the figure to illustrate how the third element of C's `for`-controlling parentheses matches that of QBasic's.

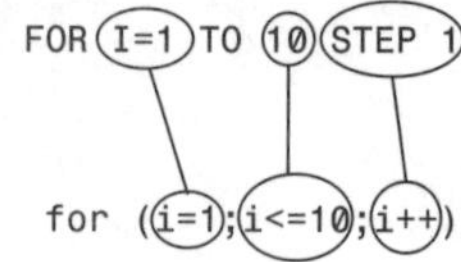

Figure 14.1. Comparing QBasic's `FOR` with C's `for`.

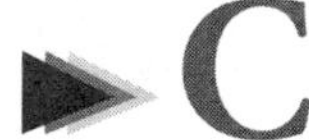

C's and QBasic's loops have equivalent sections.

C's `startExpression` is the expression that begins the loop. The loop variable must be initialized, and the first position inside `for`'s parentheses is the location of the control variable's initialization.

The `testExpression` is C's way of knowing when the `for` loop ends. The loop continues as long as the `testExpression` is true; when the `testExpression` is false, the `for` loop terminates. There is not exactly a corresponding `testExpression` in QBasic's `FOR` statement, but the `TO` value determines the loop termination; when the `FOR` control variable becomes more extreme than the `TO` value (either higher than or lower than, depending on the direction of the loop), the QBasic `FOR` loop ends.

Finally, the `for` (and `FOR`) loop must know what to do with the control variable each time the loop iterates. The `incrementExpression` modifies the control variable just as the `STEP` statement in QBasic's `FOR` does. The `incrementExpression`, however, can perform any calculation on the `for` loop's control variable, whereas QBasic's `STEP` allows only for incrementing or decrementing.

It helps to remember these rules: The `startExpression` occurs only once, at the beginning of the loop. The `testExpression` occurs at the top of every loop iteration. The `incrementExpression` occurs each time the loop ends and starts another iteration. Figure 14.2 clearly shows the execution path of the `for` loop.

```
for (i=1;i<=10;i++)
 {
  /* Body of for
     loop goes here
  */
 }
```

Figure 14.2. The execution path of C's `for` *loop.*

C's `FOR` loop might never execute depending on the control variable's initial value and the `testExpression`. Notice from Figure 14.2 that the `testExpression` occurs *before the first iteration of the loop's code body*. Therefore, if the `testExpression` is false upon entering the loop the first time, the `for` loop ends without a single iteration, and the code following the `for` loop's last statement begins its execution.

Incrementing in a *for*

Probably the most common kind of `for` loop increments the control variable in the *`incrementExpression`* section. One of the simplest `for` statements simply increments a control variable from `1` to `10` and prints the results. Here is the QBasic code to do that:

```
FOR ctr = 1 TO 10
  PRINT ctr
NEXT ctr
```

Here is the same code in C:

```
for (ctr=1; ctr<=10; ctr++)
  { printf("%d\n", ctr); }
```

As you can see, C's `for` loop takes slightly longer to set up, but the trade-off comes in the elimination of the `NEXT` statement. C doesn't provide nor need a `NEXT` statement because of the braces enclosing the body of the loop.

Increment by any value.

The increment doesn't have to be by one. The *`incrementExpression`* can increment the control variable by any value. The QBasic equivalent is the `STEP` value. Here is the QBasic code to print the numbers from `5` to `25`, counting by fives:

```
FOR ctr = 5 TO 25 STEP 5
  PRINT ctr
NEXT ctr
```

Here is the C code to increment the control variable by 5:

```
for (ctr=5; ctr<=25; ctr+=5)
  { printf("%d\n", ctr); }
```

The QBasic program in Listing 14.1 asks the user for five values inside a `FOR` loop. The program totals each of the values inside the loop and then prints the average after the loop ends.

Listing 14.1. A QBasic *FOR* loop to average five numbers.

```
' Filename: AVG5.BAS
' Program that uses a FOR loop to input 5 values
DIM total AS INTEGER
DIM avg AS INTEGER
total = 0        ' Initialize the total
PRINT "I'll now ask for the values..."
FOR num = 1 TO 5
  PRINT "What is value"; num;
  INPUT value
```

```
   total = total + value
NEXT num
avg = total / 5
PRINT
PRINT "The total is"; total
PRINT "The average is"; avg
END
```

Here is the output from this program:

```
I'll now ask for the values...
What is value 1 ? 1
What is value 2 ? 2
What is value 3 ? 3
What is value 4 ? 4
What is value 5 ? 5

The total is 15
The average is 3
```

The C program in Listing 14.2 shows the C version of Listing 14.1. Assuming that you've already mastered QBasic's `FOR` statement (and you should have by the time you start this book), there is little new to learn when you're converting to C.

Listing 14.2. A C *for* loop to average five numbers.

```
/* Filename: AVG5.C
   Program that uses a FOR loop to input 5 values */
#include <stdio.h>
main()
{
  int total=0, avg=0, num, value;
  printf("I'll now ask for the values...\n");
  /* Loop starts next */
  for (num = 1; num<=5; num++)
    { printf("What is value %d? ", num);
      scanf(" %d", &value);
      total = total + value;
    }
  avg = total / 5;
  printf("\nThe total is %d\n", total);
  printf("The average is %d\n", avg);
  return 0;
}
```

Knowing that C's integer variables and character variables can often be interchanged enables you to print the ASCII table easily by using a `for` loop to loop from `32` to `255`, as done in Listing 14.3. (The first 31 ASCII codes are unprintable.)

Listing 14.3. Printing the ASCII codes.

```
/* Filename: ASCIIFOR.C
   Prints the ASCII codes in a for loop */
#include <stdio.h>
main()
{
  int ascii;
  for (ascii=32; ascii<255; ascii++)
    { printf("%d\t%c\n", ascii, ascii); }  /* Notice that two
                                              different format codes
                                              are used to print both
                                              an ASCII value and the
                                              ASCII character */
  return 0;
}
```

> Be sure that you locate the Pause key (if your keyboard has one) before running the program in Listing 14.3 because the ASCII codes scroll quickly off the screen.

Decrementing in a *for*

Although the third parameter of the `for` controlling expressions has the name *`incrementExpression`*, you can decrement the control variable in the expression. You can decrement the control variable by 1 or by any other value.

Here is a QBasic `FOR` statement that decrements a variable named `ctr` from `10` to `0`:

```
FOR ctr = 10 TO 0 STEP -1
  PRINT ctr
NEXT ctr
PRINT "Countdown!"
```

The `STEP` is required when you decrement a variable in QBasic. Here is the C code to decrement the control variable by 1:

```
for (ctr=10; ctr>=0; ctr--)
  { printf("%d\n", ctr); }
printf("Countdown!\n");
```

The program in Listing 14.4 shows a QBasic program that computes the *factorial* of a number the user inputs. The program contains two loops, a `WHILE` loop and a `FOR` loop. A factorial is the product of the number times the next lowest number times the next lowest number and so on until `1`. In other words, 5 factorial is computed like this:

```
5! = 5 * 4 * 3 * 2 * 1
```

> The exclamation point, `!`, is the mathematical symbol for factorials. Factorials are often used to compute gaming combinations and risk measurements.

Listing 14.4. A QBasic *FOR* loop that calculates factorials.

```
' Filename: FACT.BAS
' Computes a factorial by counting down a FOR loop
DIM fact AS LONG
fact = 1      ' Initialize the product variable
DO
  INPUT "What number do you want a factorial for (1-8) "; num
  IF (num < 1 OR num > 8) THEN
    PRINT "The number must be between 1 and 8"
    PRINT "Try again"
  END IF
LOOP WHILE (num < 1 OR num > 8)
' FOR loop now computes the factorial
FOR f = num TO 1 STEP -1
  fact = fact * f
NEXT f
PRINT "The factorial of"; num; "is"; fact
END
```

Here is the output from the program:

```
What number do you want a factorial for (1-8) ? 33
The number must be between 1 and 8
Try again
What number do you want a factorial for (1-8) ? -1
The number must be between 1 and 8
```

```
Try again
What number do you want a factorial for (1-8) ? 6
The factorial of 6 is 720
```

Listing 14.5 shows the C version of the factorial program.

Listing 14.5. A C *for* loop that calculates factorials.

```
1:  /* Filename: FACT.C
2:     Computes a factorial by counting down a for loop */
3:  #include <stdio.h>
4:  main()
5:  {
6:    int num, f;
7:    long int fact = 1;      /* Initialize the product variable */
8:    do
9:      { printf("What number do you want a factorial for (1-8) ? ");
10:       scanf(" %d", &num);
11:       if ((num < 1) || (num > 8))
12:         { printf("The number must be between 1 and 8\n");
13:           printf("Try again\n");
14:         }
15:     } while ((num < 1) || (num > 8));
16:
17:   /* FOR loop now computes the factorial */
18:   for (f=num; f>=1; f--)
19:     { fact = fact * f; }
20:   printf("The factorial of %d is %ld\n", num, fact);
21:   return 0;
22: }
```

Omitting Some of the Control

You don't have to specify each of the three expressions inside the `for`'s parentheses. There might be times when the initial expression is already specified. Consider the C program in Listing 14.6. The program is the same factorial computation as in Listing 14.5, except that the `for` loop on line 18 does not have an initial expression. The loop uses the user's input variable directly (`num`) and counts down from the user's value instead of adding another variable (`f`) just for the countdown. Unlike in Listing 14.5, however, the `printf()` does not print the user's entered value because the `for` loop changed the variable so that it no longer holds what the user typed.

Listing 14.6. A C *for* loop without an initial value.

```
/* Filename: FACTDIFF.C
   Computes a factorial by counting down a for loop */
#include <stdio.h>
main()
{
  int num;
  long int fact = 1;      /* Initialize the product variable */
  do
    { printf("What number do you want a factorial for (1-8) ? ");
      scanf(" %d", &num);
      if ((num < 1) || (num > 8))
        { printf("The number must be between 1 and 8\n");
          printf("Try again\n");
        }
    } while ((num < 1) || (num > 8));

  /* FOR loop now computes the factorial */
  for (;num>=1; num--)  /* No initial expression specified!!! */
    { fact = fact * num; }
  printf("The factorial is %ld\n", fact);
  return 0;
}
```

If you ever omit one of the expressions in the control parentheses, be sure to leave the semicolon so that C can separate the unspecified expressions from the specified ones.

If you omit the *testExpression*, you have to include an `if` and `break` somewhere in the loop to exit the `for` loop early. As with `while`, `break` terminates a `for` loop.

If you omit the *incrementExpression*, the body of the `for` loop has to change the control variable somehow (increment or decrement by whatever value is needed).

Most often, all three expressions are specified, and if one is omitted, it's usually the first one because the control variable was initialized previously in the program.

The program in Listing 14.7 demonstrates how the `for` loop can be controlled from within the body of the loop. See whether you can figure out the result of the program before looking at the output that follows it.

Listing 14.7. A controlled C *for* loop without any expressions inside the parentheses.

```
/* Filename: NOSEMIS.C
   Includes a controlled for loop without expressions */
#include <stdio.h>
main()
{
  int start=1, end=8, step=2;
  for (;;)    /* No control expressions here */
    {
      printf("%d\n", start);
      start += step;              /* Increment expression */
      if (start > end)            /* Test expression */
        { break; }                /* Quits if needed */
    }
    return 0;
}
```

Here is Listing 14.7's output:

```
1
3
5
7
```

As with the `while` loops, you can specify an infinite `for` loop if you want one for demonstration programs or other kinds of programs that should continue running. Here is the way you specify an infinite `for` loop:

```
for (;;)
  { /* Put body of
       for loop here */
  }
```

To ensure that the loop continues indefinitely, be sure that you don't include a `break` statement in the body of the `for`.

You can use the `continue` statement to iterate a `for` loop early if you want. However, `continue` is rarely used with `for` loops.

`break` lets the `for` quit early.

`break` is often used when the `for` loop assumes a certain number of iterations, but the data is such that you don't want to iterate as many times as the control variables indicate. For example, the program in Listing 14.8 loops from 1 to 20, asking the user for values to average. (The first half of the program is similar to Listing 14.2.) If, however, the user enters `-99` for a number, the `-99` is considered to be a trigger value that forces an early exit from the loop. The user, by entering `-99` for the value, tells C to ignore the remaining `for` loop iterations.

Listing 14.8. Giving the user a chance to exit early.

```
/* Filename: MAX20AVG.C
   Asks the user for up to 20 numbers to average */
#include <stdio.h>
main()
{
  int count, num;
  float avg=0.0;
  /* Loop 20 times or until user signals with -99 */
  for (count=1; count<=20; count++)
    { printf("What is the next value to average (-99 to quit) ?");
      scanf(" %d", &num);
      if (num == -99)
        { break; }
      avg += (float)num;     /* Add to running total */
    }
  avg /= (float)count-1.0;     /* Compute average based on
                        values entered (and adjust the count) */
  printf("The average is %.1f.\n", avg);
  return 0;
}
```

As the following output shows, the user wanted to quit after entering only six values, and a correct average was done. If the user had kept entering values other than `-99`, the program would have asked for 20 values in all before computing the average of those 20 numbers.

```
What is the next value to average (-99 to quit) ? 10
What is the next value to average (-99 to quit) ? 20
What is the next value to average (-99 to quit) ? 30
What is the next value to average (-99 to quit) ? 40
```

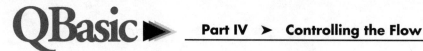

```
What is the next value to average (-99 to quit) ? 50
What is the next value to average (-99 to quit) ? 60
What is the next value to average (-99 to quit) ? -99
The average is 35.0.
```

Nested *for* Loops

As in QBasic, you can nest `for` loops within other `for` loops. The outer loop controls the inner loop. As in QBasic, the innermost loop iterates faster than the outermost loop. Listing 14.9 contains a short QBasic program that prints the quarter and minute countdown in a football game. There are four quarters and 15 minutes in each quarter. Listing 14.10 shows the C code that does the same thing.

Listing 14.9. A nested QBasic *FOR* loop that prints a football timer.

```
' Filename: FOOTBALL.BAS
' Prints the quarters and minutes on a
' football clock using a nested FOR loop
PRINT "Quarter  Minute"
FOR quarter = 1 TO 4                ' Outer "slower" loop
  FOR minute = 15 TO 1 STEP -1      ' Inner "faster" loop
    PRINT " "; quarter; "       "; minute
  NEXT minute
NEXT quarter
END
```

Listing 14.10. A nested C *for* loop that prints a football timer.

```
/* Filename: FOOTBALL.C
   Prints the quarters and minutes on a
   football clock using a nested for loop */
#include <stdio.h>
main()
{
  int quarter, minute;
  printf("Quarter  Minute\n");    /* Title */
```

```
   for (quarter = 1; quarter<=4; quarter++)  /* Outer "slower" loop */
     {
       for (minute=15; minute >=1; minute--) /* Inner "faster" loop */
         {
            printf("  %d        %d\n", quarter, minute);
         }
     }
   return 0;
}
```

> The ANSI C standard enables you to nest as many as 15 levels of `for`, `while`, or `do-while` loops. Although many C compilers enable you to nest more than 15 levels, stay within the ANSI limits to ensure future compatibility.

Summary

This chapter showed you that C's `for` loop is a lot like QBasic's `FOR` except for some syntax differences. Both are determinate loops because they continue looping a predetermined number of times (although you can change the number of iterations within the loop bodies by modifying the control variables).

With C's `for` loop, you can count up, count down, or adjust the control variable by any value using any expression. QBasic's `FOR` loop is limited by a positive or negative `STEP` value.

Now that you know how to loop, it's time to study one final C control statement called `switch`. As with the `for` statement, you'll think that the designers of C used QBasic as their model when writing the C language. `switch` is identical to the QBasic `SELECT CASE` statement. The next chapter shows you how to reduce the number of embedded `if-else` statements by using `switch` when appropriate.

15

switch SELECTIONS

QBasic's `SELECT CASE` has a distant cousin in C. C's `switch` statement mirrors QBasic's `SELECT CASE` in many ways. However, `SELECT CASE` is one of the situations in which QBasic surpasses C in power. QBasic's `SELECT CASE` provides more ways of selecting from among several choices than does C's `switch` statement. Even though C's `switch` is hampered a bit in comparison, however, C's `switch` is still a powerful means by which you can replace difficult to read and maintain nested `if-else` conditions.

When it comes to multiple-choice decisions, you've got two programming options. Your first option is to break the multiple-choice selection into many two-part true or false conditions and embed them inside a nested `if-else`. But as the preceding paragraph implied, it's best not to embed too many `if` and `else` statements because the logic gets too obfuscated. The logic needed in virtually all multiple-choice conditions is much cleaner when handled by your second option, the `switch` statement.

In this chapter, you will learn about the following topics:

- The `switch` statement
- The limitations of C's `switch` compared to QBasic's `SELECT CASE`
- How `break` adds flexibility to `switch`

This chapter wraps up the part of the book on control statements. After you tackle `switch`, you'll know all of C's controlling statements.

The preceding note lied! There's another control statement, `goto`, that mirrors QBasic's `GOTO`. However, you're best advised to stay away from `goto`. Using `goto` in place of the more structured control statements taught in this book leads to unstructured programs that are difficult to maintain.

The *switch* Statement

`switch` statements are great for menu logic.

One of the most common uses of `switch` logic is menu processing. A menu offers the user a selection of several choices. Although you can choose among the choices through `if-else` logic, `switch` more closely fills the need of menu logic.

Before going much further, you need to understand how C's `switch` is slightly more limiting than QBasic's `SELECT CASE`. As you probably know, QBasic provides three forms of `SELECT CASE`:

- A regular `SELECT CASE` statement that selects a match based on a single value. Here is an example of such a `SELECT CASE` that might be used to process a user's selection from a menu:

```
' Assumes that user entered a value in response to a menu
SELECT CASE (userChoice$)
  CASE "A"                     ' User pressed A
    CALL firstOptionLogic      ' Calls a procedure
  CASE "B"                     ' User pressed B
    CALL secondOptionLogic     ' Calls a procedure
  CASE "C"                     ' User pressed C
    CALL thirdOptionLogic      ' Calls a procedure
  CASE "Q"                     ' User pressed Q
    STOP                       ' End program
  CASE ELSE                    ' Invalid user choice
END SELECT          ' Rest of program would follow
```

The procedure called depends on the user's answer to the menu stored in the string variable named `userChoice$`.

- A relational `SELECT CASE` statement that selects a match based on the result of a relational test. Here is an example of a relational `SELECT CASE` that prints a message in response to the number of years an employee has been employed:

```
' Assumes user's # years worked is stored in yrsWrkd variable
SELECT CASE (ABS(yrsWrkd))   ' Positive values only
  CASE < 5          ' Handles 0 through 4
    PRINT "You get only two weeks of vacation."
  CASE < 10         ' Handles 5 through 9
    PRINT "You get three weeks of vacation."
  CASE < 15         ' Handles 10 through 14
    PRINT "You get four weeks of vacation."
  CASE ELSE
    PRINT "You get five weeks of vacation!"
END SELECT
```

Although you could handle this same logic with 15 separate single-value `SELECT CASE` statements, it would be foolish to try.

If you want to use relational `SELECT CASE` in your C programs, you cannot use `switch`. Instead, you must use embedded `if-else` logic.

- A range `SELECT CASE` statement that selects a match based on the result of a range of values. Here is an example of a range `SELECT CASE` that performs the same logic as the relational `SELECT CASE` last shown, except that the years worked are expressed as ranges rather than with relational logic:

```
' Assumes user's # years worked is stored in yrsWrkd variable
SELECT CASE (ABS(yrsWrkd))   ' Positive values only
  CASE 0 TO 4           ' Handles 0 through 4
    PRINT "You get only two weeks of vacation."
  CASE 5 TO 9           ' Handles 6 through 9
    PRINT "You get three weeks of vacation."
  CASE 10 TO 14         ' Handles 10 through 14
    PRINT "You get four weeks of vacation."
  CASE ELSE
    PRINT "You get five weeks of vacation!"
END SELECT
```

Don't give up on C just because it lacks two of the three kinds of `SELECT CASE` logic available in QBasic. As you've seen throughout this book, C excels in so many areas over QBasic, especially in speed and flexibility, that the few times you have to simulate relational `SELECT CASE` or range `SELECT CASE` logic in C are worth all the advantages that C offers.

Now that you have a good idea what to expect from C's `switch` statement, here is the format of `switch`:

```
switch (testExpression)
  { case (expression1) : {block of one or more C statements; }
    case (expression2) : {block of one or more C statements; }
    case (expression3) : {block of one or more C statements; }
    case (expression4) : {block of one or more C statements; }
      /* More can follow */
    default: {block of one or more C statements; }
  }   /* The closing brace is required */
```

As with `if`, `while`, `do-while`, and `for`, the parentheses around *`testExpression`* are required. The individual `case` *`expressions`* don't require the parentheses, but you'll find that the cases are easier to follow if you use the parentheses.

The *`block of one or more C statements`* portions do not *have* to be enclosed in braces. The `switch` blocks demonstrate one of the few times when a block of C statements that work together doesn't have to be enclosed in braces. However, as with the parentheses around the individual `case` *`expressions`*, you'll more easily be able to group each `case`'s code visually if you enclose them in braces.

Be careful that you don't put a semicolon at the end of the `switch` *`testExpression`*, or the C compiler will issue a compile error.

`switch`'s `default` case is analogous to that of QBasic's `CASE ELSE`; either takes over if the preceding cases did not find a match.

The `switch` *`expression`* must be an integer or character data type. You cannot specify a `switch` statement based on a floating-point or double floating-point value. Equalities to

such data types are difficult to represent internally in today's computers. (Although computers are highly accurate, if one double-precision value differs from another by .0000000000000000001, the two values are not considered to be equal by the computer even though statistically they are often considered to be equal.)

To introduce the `switch` to you, Listing 15.1 contains a QBasic program that enables the user to select from a menu and prints a message accordingly. Listing 15.2 shows an equivalent C program using a `switch` statement.

Listing 15.1. A QBasic *SELECT CASE* statement that handles a menu selection.

```
1:  ' Filename: SELECT.BAS
2:  ' A QBasic program that displays a menu and prints a message
3:  DO          ' Repeat until user enters a value from 1 to 4
4:    PRINT "** Menu **"
5:    PRINT "Here are your choices:"
6:    PRINT "1. Watch television"
7:    PRINT "2. Read a book"
8:    PRINT "3. Go to a movie"
9:    PRINT "4. You don't know"
10:   INPUT "What do you want to do"; choice
11: LOOP UNTIL ((choice >= 1) AND (choice <= 4))
12: ' Got a good value from the user
13: SELECT CASE (choice)
14:   CASE 1:
15:     PRINT "There's nothing on but reruns."
16:   CASE 2:
17:     PRINT "Try one from Sams Publishers!"
18:   CASE 3:
19:     PRINT "It's raining outside."
20:   CASE 4:
21:     PRINT "Go for a walk."
22: END SELECT
23: END
```

> The loop in lines 3 through 11 ensures that the user enters a number from 1 to 4. The loop guarantees that the `SELECT CASE` works without a `CASE ELSE` statement. Listing 15.2 contains the same check in C.

Listing 15.2. A C *switch* statement that handles a menu selection.

```
/* Filename: SWITCH1.C
   A C program that displays a menu and prints a message */
#include <stdio.h>
main()
{
  int choice;
  do        /* Repeat until user enters a value from 1 to 4 */
   { printf("** Menu **\n");
     printf("Here are your choices:\n");
     printf("1. Watch television\n");
     printf("2. Read a book\n");
     printf("3. Go to a movie\n");
     printf("4. You don't know\n");
     printf("What do you want to do? ");
     scanf(" %d", &choice);
   }
  while ((choice < 1) ¦¦ (choice > 4));
  /* Got a good value from the user */
  switch (choice)
  { case (1): { printf("There's nothing on but reruns.\n");
                break;}
    case (2): { printf("Try one from Sams Publishers!\n");
                break;}
    case (3): { printf("It's raining outside.\n");
                break;}
    case (4): { printf("Go for a walk.\n");
                break;}
  }
  return 0;
}
```

Here are three sample runs from either Listing 15.1 or Listing 15.2:

```
** Menu **
Here are your choices:
1. Watch television
2. Read a book
3. Go to a movie
4. You don't know
What do you want to do? 23
** Menu **
Here are your choices:
1. Watch television
```

```
2. Read a book
3. Go to a movie
4. You don't know
What do you want to do? 1
There's nothing on but reruns.
** Menu **
Here are your choices:
1. Watch television
2. Read a book
3. Go to a movie
4. You don't know
What do you want to do? 3
It's raining outside.
```

> QBasic's `SELECT CASE` and C's `switch` statements don't need a `default` condition as long as you ensure (as these programs do) that the value tested with `SELECT CASE` or `switch` falls within the expected range of values.

Just to show you how the `default` case works, Listing 15.3 contains the same C code without the checking of the user's value before the `switch` statement. In other words, a value such as `78` could get to the `switch` statement, so the `default` case takes care of values that aren't matched earlier in the `switch` statement.

Listing 15.3. A C *switch* statement with a default condition.

```
/* Filename: SWITCH2.C
   A C program that displays a menu and prints a message
   The default part of switch is used for exceptions */
#include <stdio.h>
main()
{
  int choice;
  printf("** Menu **\n");   /* No loop */
  printf("Here are your choices:\n");
  printf("1. Watch television\n");
  printf("2. Read a book\n");
  printf("3. Go to a movie\n");
  printf("4. You don't know\n");
  printf("What do you want to do? ");
  scanf(" %d", &choice);
```

continues

Listing 15.3. continued

```
  /* Didn't ensure that we got a good value from the user */
  switch (choice)
  { case (1): { printf("There's nothing on but reruns.\n");
                break;}
    case (2): { printf("Try one from Sams Publishers!\n");
                break;}
    case (3): { printf("It's raining outside.\n");
                break;}
    case (4): { printf("Go for a walk.\n");
                break;}
    /* The default occurs if none of the other cases matched */
    default:  { printf("Sorry, I didn't understand your answer.\n");
                break;}
  }
  return 0;
}
```

Finally, Listing 15.4 contains the same C code with an embedded `if-else` to show you how convoluted multiple-choice selections can get without `switch`.

Listing 15.4. Using an embedded *if-else* to handle multiple choice.

```
/* Filename: NOSWITCH.C
   A C program that displays a menu and prints a message
   using embedded if-else logic */
#include <stdio.h>
main()
{
  int choice;
  printf("** Menu **\n");    /* No loop */
  printf("Here are your choices:\n");
  printf("1. Watch television\n");
  printf("2. Read a book\n");
  printf("3. Go to a movie\n");
  printf("4. You don't know\n");
  printf("What do you want to do? ");
  scanf(" %d", &choice);
  /* Didn't ensure that we got a good value from the user */
  if (choice == 1)
    { printf("There's nothing on but reruns.\n"); }
  else
```

```
    { if (choice == 2)
        { printf("Try one from Sams Publishers!\n"); }
      else
        { if (choice == 3)
            { printf("It's raining outside.\n"); }
          else
           { if (choice == 4)
               { printf("Go for a walk.\n"); }
            else
              { printf("Sorry, I didn't understand your answer.\n"); }
           }
        }
    }
  return 0;
}
```

switch Does Windows

The program in Listing 15.4 shows how much more convoluted an embedded `if-else` can be than a `switch`. Multiple-choice logic fits neatly within `switch`'s format.

Think how difficult Listing 15.4 would have been to write if the menu had 25 choices! Such embedded nestings of `if-else` logic would become unreadable.

Most Microsoft Windows programs are written in C. Although such programs are way beyond the scope of this book (Windows programming is very difficult and requires a complete mastering not only of C but of the Windows internal architecture as well), you might be interested to know that most Windows programs consist of huge `switch` statements that handle all the *events* going on inside Windows. (An event is a mouse movement, mouse click, keystroke, window resizing, menu selection, and so on.) In any one Windows program, there might be a hundred or more events to handle. A nested `if-else` with 100 levels of nesting would never be readable or maintainable.

As you might gather, C's single `switch` statement might seem more limiting than QBasic's three versions of `SELECT CASE`, but `switch` is plenty powerful enough to handle any programming job.

Why the Use of *break*?

break keeps cases from running into each other.

You should have spotted a bunch of break statements in the C programs shown earlier in this chapter, and you probably wondered why they were there. The QBasic SELECT CASE doesn't include a STOP statement at the end of each of the CASE statement bodies. QBasic's SELECT CASE does not need a STOP because each SELECT CASE occurs independently of the others. C's switch statement, however, does not treat each case as a separate, stand-alone body of code.

For example, if you were to remove the break statements from lines 19, 21, 23, and 25 in Listing 15.3, and the user responded to the menu prompt by typing 1, this would be the output of the program:

```
There's nothing on but reruns.
Try one from Sams Publishers!
It's raining outside.
Go for a walk.
Sorry, I didn't understand your answer.
```

In other words, the break on line 19 would normally keep the other case bodies from executing. Without the breaks, C lets the execution fall through all the remaining cases. If the user responded with a 3 and the breaks were removed, this would be the output:

```
It's raining outside.
Go for a walk.
Sorry, I didn't understand your answer.
```

Figure 15.1 shows the switch statement's execution path if you removed the embedded break statements. The figure assumes that choice contains the value 2. Figure 15.2 shows the execution path with the break statements. The break ensures that one and only one case selection executes.

Assume that choice is equal to 2

```
switch (choice)
{case (1): {printf("There's nothing on but reruns.\n");}
 case (2): {printf("Try one from Sams Publishers!\n");}
 case (3): {printf("It's raining outside.\n");}
 case (4): {printf("Go for a walk.\n");}
  default: {printf("Sorry, I didn't understand your answer.\n");}
}
```

Figure 15.1. Without embedded break *statements, the* switch *execution falls through.*

```
                        Assume that choice is equal to 2

switch (choice)
{case (1): {printf("There's nothing on but reruns.\n");
            break;}
 case (2): {printf("Try one from Sams Publishers!\n");
            break;}
 case (3): {printf("It's raining outside.\n");
            break;}
 case (4): {printf("Go for a walk.\n");
            break;}
 default: {printf("Sorry, I didn't understand your answer.\n");
           break;}
```

Figure 15.2. With embedded `break` *statements, the* `switch` *executes only one case body.*

The first two `case`s were skipped over because they didn't match the user's value, but as soon as a match was found, every `switch` option from that point forward executes unless a `break` stops the `switch`. Even though `switch` is not a loop, `switch` requires a `break` statement after each `case` that you don't want falling through to subsequent `case`s.

> The definition of the `break` statement now must be modified. In the preceding two chapters, you learned that `break` terminates the current loop. That still holds true, but as you are learning here, `break` also terminates a `switch` statement.

It might seem as if C packs an extra workload onto you by requiring the use of `break` at the end of each `case` body. However, in requiring `break` at the end of stand-alone `case`s, C adds more flexibility than QBasic's `SELECT CASE` statement. With `SELECT CASE`, you have no choice; there is nothing you can do to execute more than one of the `case` options. But you can execute more than one option with C's `case`.

Consider the program in Listing 15.5. The user selects from a menu of choices. Notice that the user must enter a letter of the alphabet. The user's Caps Lock key might or might not be pressed when the user enters a choice. Therefore, by using two back-to-back `case` statements, with the first one in the pair containing a null code body and lacking a `break`, this code lets the execution fall through to the next code body. The program prints a message if the user types either the uppercase or the lowercase equivalent letter to the answer desired.

Listing 15.5. Using an embedded *if-else* to handle multiple choice.

```
/* Filename: ALPHMENU.C
   Using a switch statement to select from either
   uppercase or lowercase selections */
#include <stdio.h>
main()
{
  char choice;
  printf("** Menu **\n");    /* No loop */
  printf("Pick your computer brand:\n");
  printf("A. Apricot QY/7\n");
  printf("B. Banana System 1\n");
  printf("C. Cherry CRT/P6\n");
  printf("D. Don't know\n");
  printf("Which one is yours? ");
  scanf(" %c", &choice);
  /* Didn't ensure that we got a good value from the user */
  switch (choice)
  {  case 'a' : /* No code body for this case! */
     case 'A' : { printf("You can upgrade to a PC for $2000.00\n");
                  break; }   /* Don't fall through to 'b' */
     case 'b' : /* No code body for this case! */
     case 'B' : { printf("You can upgrade to a PC for $75.00\n");
                  break; }   /* Don't fall through to 'c' */
     case 'c' : /* No code body for this case! */
     case 'C' : { printf("You can upgrade to a PC for $1325.00\n");
                  break; }   /* Don't fall through to 'd' */
     case 'd' : /* No code body for this case! */
     case 'D' : { printf("A new super-powered PC is $4300.00\n");
                  break; }   /* Don't fall through to default' */
     default  : { printf("I didn't understand your answer\n");
                  break; }
   }
   return 0;
}
```

Notice that it doesn't matter if you enter a `c` or `C`, as the following output shows:

```
** Menu **
Pick your computer brand:
A. Apricot QY/7
B. Banana System 1
C. Cherry CRT/P6
D. Don't know
```

```
Which one is yours? C
You can upgrade to a PC for $1325.00
** Menu **
Pick your computer brand:
A. Apricot QY/7
B. Banana System 1
C. Cherry CRT/P6
D. Don't know
Which one is yours? c
You can upgrade to a PC for $1325.00
```

In QBasic, none of the three versions of `SELECT CASE` works as easily as C's for such selections. You would have to either repeat pairs of `CASE` bodies (one for uppercase and one for lowercase) or convert the selection to the same letter's case with `UCASE$()` or `LCASE$()`. It is because of QBasic's limit that C actually provides a more flexible `switch` statement than any of QBasic's three `SELECT CASE` statements.

Some astute QBasic programmers might think that a compound relational `CASE` statement such as the following statement would work:

```
CASE (IS = "A") AND (IS = "a")
```

The QBasic relational `SELECT CASE`, however, does not support logical operators such as `AND` and `OR`; you can specify only simple relational tests after a `CASE` statement.

After you learn how to use C's string-manipulation functions, you'll find additional ways to streamline programs such as Listing 15.5. As with QBasic, there are internal functions that convert characters to uppercase or lowercase. By converting the user's answer to one expected case, you can eliminate the extra `case` statements.

If there's one `case` body that will be selected more often than another, put it first. C won't have to search through the list of `case` bodies as much if you put the `case`s most likely to execute toward the top of the `switch` statement. You can even move the `default` to before the first of the `case` statements to improve efficiency if specific `case` statements aren't as likely to occur.

The last `break` *is recommended.*

It's because you can rearrange `case` statements for efficiency that you should keep the `break` that resides in the `default` body of the `switch` statement. The `break` is superfluous if the `default` appears last, as happens in this chapter's `switch` statements. The `break` simply tells C to exit the `switch`, but because the `default` is the last statement within the `switch`, the `switch` would exit anyway after the `default` code finishes. However, if you leave the `break` in the `default` portion of the `switch` and then later rearrange the `default` case, you're more likely to have the `break` when it is truly needed than if you have to remember to add it at another time.

Just to review the differences between QBasic's `SELECT CASE` and C's `switch`, Listing 15.6 contains a program based on QBasic's online help example you get when you press F1 (the context-sensitive QBasic help shortcut key) while the cursor rests on a `SELECT CASE` statement. The program demonstrates all three versions of QBasic's `SELECT CASE`. The program in Listing 15.7 shows the same code in C. Although C cannot duplicate the relational and range selection that `SELECT CASE` provides, you can see that it is relatively easy to simulate in C when only a few values compose the range being selected.

Listing 15.6. Demonstrating all three of QBasic's *SELECT CASEs*.

```
' Filename: RISK.BAS
' Program from QBasic's online help that uses each of the
' three QBasic SELECT CASE statements.
PRINT "** Risk Measurement **"
INPUT "Enter acceptable level of risk (1-5): ", Total
' Print one of three messages based on the risk.
SELECT CASE Total
  CASE IS >= 5
    PRINT "Maximum risk and potential return."
    PRINT "Choose stock investment plan."
  ' Notice that QBasic knows to skip remaining CASE statements
  CASE 2 TO 4
    PRINT "Moderate to high risk and potential return."
    PRINT "Choose mutual fund or corporate bonds."
  CASE 1
    PRINT "No risk, low return."
    PRINT "Choose IRA."
  CASE ELSE
    PRINT "You must have entered an incorrect risk level."
  END SELECT
END
```

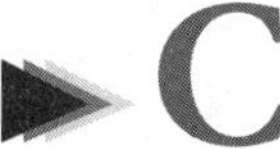

Listing 15.7. With just a little effort, you can simulate QBasic's *SELECT CASEs*.

```
/* Filename: RISK.C
  Program that simulates as much of the three
  QBasic SELECT CASE statements as possible. */
#include <stdio.h>
#include <stdlib.h>
main()
{
  int total;
  printf("** Risk Measurement **\n");
  printf("Enter acceptable level of risk (1-5): ");
  scanf(" %d", &total);
  /* You must ensure with an if that user didn't enter 0 or less */
  if (total <= 0)
    { printf("You must have entered an incorrect risk level.\n");
      exit(1);  /* Exit the entire program */
    }
  /* Print one of three messages based on the risk. */
  switch (total)
  {  case (1) : { printf("No risk, low return.\n");
                  printf("Choose IRA.\n");
                  break; }
     case (2) : /* Handle the 2 through 4 */
     case (3) :
     case (4) : { printf("Moderate to high risk and potential ");
                  printf("return.\n");
                  printf("Choose mutual fund or corporate bonds.\n");
                  break; }
     default :  /* If here, the number is 5 or more */
                { printf("Maximum risk and potential return.\n");
                  printf("Choose stock investment plan.\n");
                  break; }
     }
  return 0;
}
```

The only part of Listing 15.6's `SELECT CASE` that cannot be fully represented by Listing 15.7's `switch` statement is `total` values less than or equal to zero. Clearly, if you study Listing 15.6, you'll see that the program does not intend for the user to enter negative values. However, just in case the user enters a zero or a negative number, the `CASE ELSE` prints an error message. The `default` part of Listing 15.7 could not handle a zero or negative in this way because the `default` is taken up by all numbers equal to or greater than 5.

QBasic has the advantage in line 8 of Listing 15.6 of checking for all values equal to or more than `5` (using a relational `SELECT CASE`), whereas the `CASE ELSE` on line 18 is reserved for zero and negatives.

To sum this up, QBasic's relational `SELECT CASE` and range `SELECT CASE` statements do allow a selection from more than one range of numbers, but C's `switch` can handle only one unknown range with a `default`. All other values tested for in a `switch` statement must be eliminated with `if` before the `switch`.

Summary

This chapter concludes the teaching of C's control statements. The `switch` statement mirrors the simple `SELECT CASE` in QBasic. Unfortunately, C doesn't support an equivalent statement to QBasic's range `SELECT CASE` or QBasic's relational `SELECT CASE`, but as shown in this chapter, you can program around this slight limitation.

Actually, C offers a little more flexibility with `switch` than any of QBasic's `SELECT CASE` statements because the `switch` doesn't have to provide for just one choice at a time. If you don't put `break` statements at the end of each `case` body, C executes down through the remaining `case` bodies' code until a `switch` statement forces the program to end or until the end of the `switch` is reached. Most of the time, you'll want to insert a `break` at the end of each `case` code body because you'll usually want just one of the `case` bodies to execute. Whatever you want, C gives you your choice.

The next chapter is the first of three chapters that compare C's built-in functions to those of QBasic. Most C compilers provide a standard library of common ANSI C-compatible functions.

Part V

Saving Time with Internal Functions

Some I/O Functions

This chapter introduces you to some of C's I/O (*input/output*) functions. Actually, you've already seen three C functions that perform I/O: `printf()`, `fprintf()`, and `scanf()`. There are several more I/O functions that come with all ANSI C-compatible compilers, and this chapter shows you some of them.

With `scanf()` as one of the crudest examples, C simply doesn't provide a lot of fancy I/O routines. You have to use what C gives you to write your own I/O code. Of course, you'll also want to look into several of the many electronic bulletin boards across the country and shop programming magazines for I/O libraries of routines that others have written. You can use these already-written powerful functions in your own programs to greatly augment the power of your programs. The designers of QBasic gave you much more powerful I/O than the designers of C did, but C does provide incredible flexibility and speed—and the rest is up to you.

Meanwhile, you must see what C has to offer before worrying about finding additional I/O routines elsewhere. This chapter shows you some of C's I/O functions and shows how some of them compare to QBasic's own routines.

In this chapter, you will learn about the following topics:

- The `getchar()`, `putchar()`, `getc()`, `putc()`, and `putch()` functions
- How `getch()` mimics QBasic's `INKEY$` function
- The `gets()` and `puts()` string I/O functions

C's I/O Attempts Hardware Independence

C's I/O reads and writes data to standard devices.

The QBasic I/O commands are extremely hardware dependent. That is, the `COLOR` command requires a PC color monitor, the `LPRINT` command requires a printer, and the `CLS` applies only to a CRT. Although it might seem strange to you at first, C does not have any I/O commands. All of C's I/O is achieved through functions such as `printf()` that are supplied with all C compilers. Instead of reading from and writing to specific hardware devices, C's I/O functions read from and write to generic devices, called *standard devices,* listed in Table 16.1. As you can see from the table's second column, the default C devices for PCs are usually the devices you want to use anyway, so the term *standard devices* isn't all that crucial to PC programs.

Table 16.1. C's standard I/O devices and their typical DOS equivalents.

Standard Device	*DOS Device*	*Description*
`stdout`	`CON:`	Screen
`stdin`	`CON:`	Keyboard*
`stdprn`	`LPT1:`	Parallel printer port #1
`stdaux`	`COM1:`	Serial port #1
`stderr`	`CON:`	The screen (errors go here by default)

*The PC knows whether to read from the keyboard or write to the screen (both are known as `CON:`)

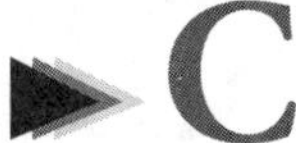

When C was first developed, PCs weren't invented yet. There were many kinds of hardware devices, and there were very few standards of any kind. Instead of offering a command that wrote to every device possible, C offered the standard I/O functions that were not targeted for any specific hardware; by not specifying *any* hardware, C worked on *all* hardware. The operating system running each individual C compiler could take the standard device and route it to a specific device on the system. Figure 16.1 shows that C writes to standard devices, and the operating system routes those generic devices to specific devices.

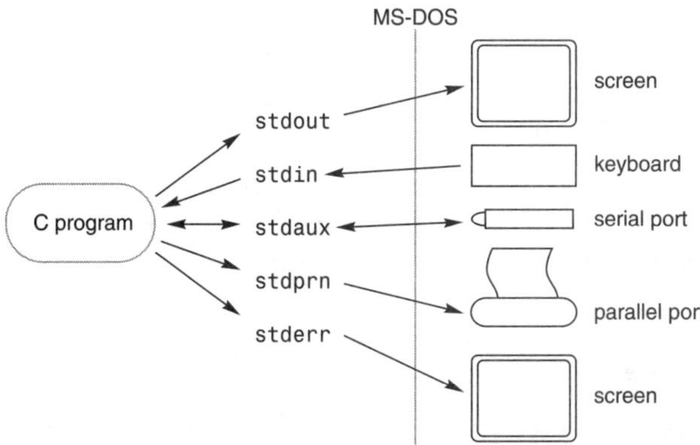

Figure 16.1. C's generic I/O occurs on specific devices according to the operating system's routing.

As Figure 16.1 shows, some standard devices are output only, some are input only, and one, the serial port, is both input and output.

If you do nothing to change the default, all standard output with a PC-based C compiler goes to the screen. If you do nothing to change the default, all input comes from the PC's keyboard. There are some MS-DOS commands that you can use to redirect input and output to other devices and files. If you know of MS-DOS's redirection operators, >, <, and >>, you can route your compiled program's I/O to other devices and files.

Using some advanced file-related C functions that you'll learn about in Part VII of this book, you'll learn better ways than MS-DOS's redirection operators to direct I/O to specific devices from within your C programs.

The distinction between an I/O function and an I/O command is relatively minor to general programmers. In other words, if you think of `printf()` as being a screen output command just as you think of QBasic's `PRINT` as being a screen output command, you'll be OK, and you don't really have to know the difference until you advance further into C's file I/O functions.

You'll Usually Get More

Although C compiler vendors are free to add their own I/O functions to the ANSI C's repertoire of common I/O functions, you can always count on having the standard functions described in this book such as `printf()` because these common functions are in the ANSI C collection of functions required in all ANSI C compilers.

Most compiler vendors do indeed offer a wide range of additional I/O functions, some of which are very specific to hardware. For example, Borland provides a `CLS`-equivalent function that erases the PC's screen and returns the cursor to the upper-left corner of the screen. The ANSI C committee would never approve such a function for their standard, although any additions to ANSI C are accepted as long as the compiler includes support for the ANSI C specification as well.

The ANSI C committee is attempting to protect you in their seemingly limiting disapproval of outside functions. The ANSI C standard tries to ensure that your programs, if written using the ANSI C language and functions, will work on all hardware platforms and all future ANSI C-approved compilers. You're free to use as many of your compiler's additional functions and features as you like, but be aware that those functions might not be around forever, and if you use them, you might have to modify your programs to conform to future compiler releases.

You might remember the `stdprn` device name from Chapter 5, "Printing Output." The `fprintf()` used `stdprn` to print to the printer. If you substituted `stdout` or `stdaux` for `stdprn` in the `fprintf()` function call, output would go to those devices. (The serial device doesn't always accept output until you set the serial port properly with the DOS `MODE` command. In addition, you have to understand the workings on serial communications, which would take an entire book or two itself, to read or write to the serial port properly.)

The `stderr` is a good place to send error messages using `fprintf()`. The following `fprintf()` function call writes an error to the screen:

```
fprintf(stderr, "You selected an incorrect option.\n");
```

Many C programmers send error messages to the screen directly with `printf()`, and that's probably OK. However, through MS-DOS redirection commands, the screen's standard device, `stdout`, might be rerouted to a device other than the screen. The `stderr` device *always* goes to the screen, so you can be sure that your user will see your error messages if you print to the `stderr` device. In MS-DOS-based programs, writing with `printf()` or `fprintf(stderr, ...)` virtually always guarantees the same screen output because the standard output device is rarely diverted from the screen.

Stay with it!

Doesn't this standard input and output seem like a lot of work? It really isn't, but using `LPRINT` when you want to print to the printer is a lot easier in QBasic than worrying about device names in C. C is different from QBasic, but C offers flexibility that QBasic doesn't. The same C program works on almost every computer with a C compiler no matter how big or small the computer is. QBasic programs, on the other hand, work only on PC-compatibles. A QBasic program will not work on any other computer, even a different computer that uses a version of BASIC, because QBasic is tied directly to the PC hardware.

Device Versus Character I/O

C specializes in character I/O.

Most of the I/O functions you'll learn about in the rest of this chapter are *character-based* I/O functions. The functions usually input or output a single character at a time. One QBasic semi-equivalent to these functions, `INKEY$`, accepts a character from the keyboard and enables you to store that character in a variable.

The `printf()` and `scanf()` functions are not character-based I/O functions. They are known as *formatted I/O* functions. The QBasic `PRINT` and `INPUT` also output and input formatted data, such as integers, strings, and floating-point values, as you know. Although C's `printf()` and `scanf()` do more work than the character-based functions, the character I/O functions offer building-block functions that enable you to write your own functions that perform input or output exactly the way you want them to.

The powerful input and output routines that you can buy or download from many electronic bulletin board systems are usually written using these character-based I/O functions as their foundation. Even numeric input and output functions can be written by accepting or printing a digit, comma, and decimal point, one at a time.

This book's goal is to move you from QBasic to C, and to do that, you have to get accustomed to the character I/O features of C. You've been spoiled by QBasic's powerful but rigid I/O commands. C will eventually spoil you by its efficiency and power to enable you to write routines that work exactly the way you want them to work.

Most of the I/O functions introduced in this chapter require that you include the STDIO.H header file. If another header file is needed, this chapter will let you know.

getc() and *putc()*

Perhaps the most common character-based I/O functions are `getc()` and `putc()`. Simply stated, `getc()` gets a character at a time from a standard input device, and `putc()` outputs a character at a time to a standard output device. Following are the formats of the two functions:

```
getc(stdDevice);
```

and

```
putc(stdDevice, character);
```

`getc()` gets a character from the `stdDevice`, and `putc()` outputs its `character` argument to the `stdDevice` argument. The `stdDevice` must be capable of input when used with `getc()` and capable of output when used with `putc()`. Therefore, you cannot use the `stdout` device with the `getc()` function.

There is no direct QBasic equivalent command or function to `getc()` or `putc()`. QBasic's `INKEY$` function mirrors another input function, `getch()`, that you'll read about later in this chapter.

The `getc()` function is a *buffered input* function, which means that you must press Enter before the first character you typed is sent to your program. Figure 16.2 helps show what goes on at a `getc()` function call.

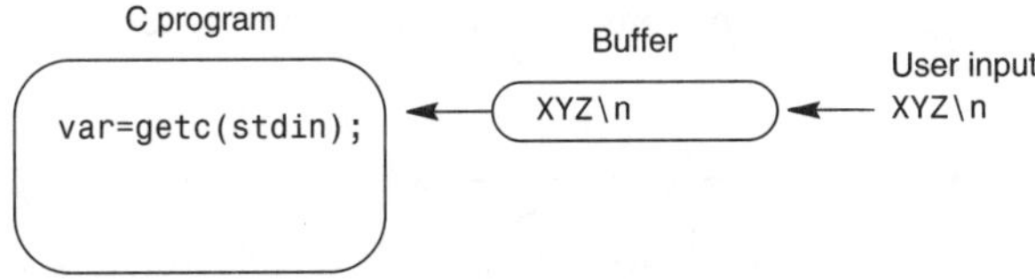

Figure 16.2. `getc()` *gets input into a buffer before Enter releases the buffer to your program.*

Suppose that you were to call `getc()` five times, assigning each of its values to five variables like this:

```
v1 = getc(stdin);
v2 = getc(stdin);
v3 = getc(stdin);
v4 = getc(stdin);
v5 = getc(stdin);
```

Here are the steps that C takes when the first `getc()` executes:

1. The program pauses execution at the first `getc()` while waiting for the user.
2. Suppose that the user presses the *A* key. The ASCII value for *A* goes to the buffer, not to the variable `v1`. `getc()` echoes the input character, so the *A* appears onscreen.
3. Suppose that the user then presses *B*, *C*, *D*, and *E*. The letters appear on-screen as the user presses them because `getc()` echoes its input to the screen. The program's execution is *still* held at the first `getc()` even though the user has pressed several letters in response to the single `getc()`. The variable `v1` has yet to get one character. The input buffer looks like this:

   ```
   ABCDE
   ```

4. The user presses Enter. The Enter keystroke releases the buffer to the program until it's emptied. The *A* goes to the variable `v1`, and the buffer now looks like this:

   ```
   BCDE\n
   ```

5. The second `getc()` executes and gets its value from the buffer. The buffer looks like this:

   ```
   CDE\n
   ```

6. The remaining `getc()` functions execute and receive the rest of the buffer until the `\n` is reached.

Press Backspace to correct input when using `getc()` and `putc()`. When you press Backspace, C erases the last character in the buffer at the time of the Backspace.

The `putc()` output is also buffered. There is no noticeable difference between buffered and unbuffered output, so the distinction isn't as critical as it is with input.

Listing 16.1 contains a program that uses both the `getc()` and the `putc()` functions. An explanation follows the program.

Listing 16.1. A C program that reads and writes single characters.

```
/* Filename: GETPUTC.C
   Demonstrates getc() and putc() functions */
#include <stdio.h>

main()
{
  int v1,v2,v3,v4,v5; /* Not character variables! */

  /* Read characters */
  v1=getc(stdin);
  v2=getc(stdin);
  v3=getc(stdin);
  v4=getc(stdin);
  v5=getc(stdin);
```

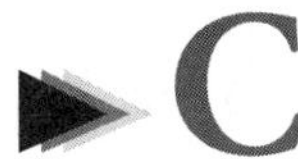

```
15:    /* Output each of the characters */
16:    putc(v1,stdout);
17:    putc(v2,stdout);
18:    putc(v3,stdout);
19:    putc(v4,stdout);
20:    putc(v5,stdout);
21:    return 0;
22: }
```

The first thing you'll notice is that the variables `v1` through `v5` are integer variables (line 7) even though they are used to receive data from the `getc()` character input function. Remember that C's integers and characters share a lot of work, and you can often use them interchangeably. Character I/O functions can return a `-1` if they are directed to receive input from a file that has reached the end-of-file condition. You'll learn about file I/O in Part VII, but in the meantime, use integer variables for character input. You can use the integers as if they are characters, such as printing them with the `printf()` `%c` format code or with `putc()`, as shown in Listing 16.1.

What do you think the output of this program is when the user runs it and types `ABCDE`? Here is the output:

```
ABCDE
ABCDE
```

Why does `ABCDE` appear twice? Remember that `getc()` echoes as you type data. Therefore, the first set of `ABCDE` appears as the user types the letters. The Enter keystroke also goes to the screen and forces the cursor to the next line. The five `putc()` function calls in lines 16 through 20 repeat the five characters.

> It's interesting to note that if you ran this program and pressed more than five characters before pressing Enter, all the characters would appear on the first line, but only the first five would appear on the second because only five `getc()`s occur in the program.

Notice also that you must do something with the `getc()` return value. In Listing 16.1, the `getc()` return value is stored in a variable, `v1` through `v5`. You don't have to do anything with a return value from `putc()` because no value is input, so none has to be captured.

It's interesting to see how succinctly you can write C code. The program in Listing 16.2 produces the same effect as the preceding program. Instead of storing the input in individual variables, the program immediately sends the `getc()` return values to `putc()`.

Listing 16.2. A C program that more efficiently reads and writes single characters.

```
/* Filename: EMBEDDED.C
   Demonstrates efficient getc() and putc() functions */
#include <stdio.h>

main()
{
  /* Read and output characters */
  putc(getc(stdin),stdout);
  putc(getc(stdin),stdout);
  putc(getc(stdin),stdout);
  putc(getc(stdin),stdout);
  putc(getc(stdin),stdout);
 return 0;
}
```

getchar() and putchar()

Most of the time, you'll want to get input from the keyboard (`stdin` if you haven't redirected `stdin` elsewhere) and send output to the screen (`stdout` if you haven't redirected `stdout`). C provides two more functions that work *exactly like* `getc()` and `putc()`, called `getchar()` and `putchar()`. The only difference between the `getchar()` and `putchar()` functions and the `getc()` and `putc()` functions is that the latter don't use device names. The `stdin` and `stdout` devices are assumed by `getchar()` and `putchar()`. Here are the formats of the two new functions:

```
getchar();
```

and

```
putchar(character);
```

Listing 16.3 contains a program that works just like that in Listing 16.1, except the simpler `getchar()` and `putchar()` functions take the place of `getc()` and `putc()`.

Listing 16.3. Reads and writes single characters with *getchar()* and *putchar()*.

```
/* Filename: GETPUTCH.C
   Demonstrates getchar() and putchar() functions */
#include <stdio.h>

main()
{
  int v1,v2,v3,v4,v5; /* Not character variables! */

  /* Read characters */
  v1=getchar();
  v2=getchar();
  v3=getchar();
  v4=getchar();
  v5=getchar();
  /* Output each of the characters */
  putchar(v1);
  putchar(v2);
  putchar(v3);
  putchar(v4);
  putchar(v5);
  return 0;
}
```

Notice that `getchar()` and `putchar()` are simpler when you're performing I/O from and to the standard devices. You don't have to specify the devices.

Just to show you that `getchar()` doesn't actually receive input until you press Enter, it's interesting to note that the program in Listing 16.4 contains a `putchar()` after each `getchar()`, yet no change to the output takes place. The reason is that the first `getchar()` doesn't release the program's execution until Enter releases the buffer.

Listing 16.4. Even rearranging *getchar()* and *putchar()* doesn't change the output.

```
/* Filename: REORDER.C
   Demonstrates getchar() and putchar() functions
   after rearranging their order from the previous program */
#include <stdio.h>

main()
```

continues

Listing 16.4. continued

```
{
   int v1,v2,v3,v4,v5; /* Not character variables! */

   v1=getchar();
   putchar(v1);
   v2=getchar();
   putchar(v2);
   v3=getchar();
   putchar(v3);
   v4=getchar();
   putchar(v4);
   v5=getchar();
   putchar(v5);
   return 0;
}
```

getch() and *putch()*

`getch()` works almost exactly like QBasic's `INKEY$`.

The `getch()` and `putch()` functions are *unbuffered character I/O functions.* As soon as you type a key, the `getch()` has done its job, and the program continues. The `getc()` and `getchar()` would not release the program until the user pressed Enter. Using `getch()`, your program can act on your user's response as soon as the user types a letter.

The `getch()` and `putch()` functions are *not* ANSI C compatible! Use them at your own risk. They are used by so many of today's C compilers, however, that *not* describing them here would be doing you a disservice. The `getch()` function requires unbuffered input hardware, and not all computers, such as multiuser mainframe computers, can always provide unbuffered input. Therefore, ANSI C will probably not adopt `getch()` or `putch()` any time soon because `getch()` cannot be supported on all kinds of computer equipment. Most if not all PC-based C compilers do support `getch()`, however.

The getch() and putch() functions are described by the CONIO.H header file that you must include at the top of any program that uses these two functions.

Some menus and input data are best left buffered so that your user can press Backspace and correct an incorrect choice before pressing Enter to select that choice. Other menu programs (and other input routines) might want to respond to the user's keystrokes as soon as the user presses the keys. If you've used INKEY$, you'll recognize the similarities. Unlike INPUT, INKEY$ grabs the user's input as soon as the user presses a key.

There is one major difference between QBasic's INKEY$ function and C's getch() function. getch() waits until the user presses a key. INKEY$ does not wait; if a key is not being pressed as soon as the INKEY$ executes, the program continues.

Unbuffered output is just like buffered output. The buffering differences between the getchar() and getch() functions are much more pronounced than the differences between putchar() and putch().

Listing 16.5 contains a C program that accepts five characters from the keyboard as done previously in this chapter. The program uses getch() and putch().

Listing 16.5. Reads and writes single characters with *getch()* and *putch()*.

```
/* Filename: GETCHPUT.C
   Demonstrates getch() and putch() functions */
#include <stdio.h>
#include <conio.h>

main()
{
  int v1,v2,v3,v4,v5; /* Not character variables! */

```

continues

Listing 16.5. continued

```
  /* Read characters */
  v1=getch();
  v2=getch();
  v3=getch();
  v4=getch();
  v5=getch();
  /* Output each of the characters */
  putch(v1);
  putch(v2);
  putch(v3);
  putch(v4);
  putch(v5);
  return 0;
}
```

You should run this program yourself and type five letters. Here is one sample output:

```
ABCDE
```

Notice that the program didn't repeat the letters twice as all the other programs did. `getch()` doesn't echo its input to the screen. Listing 16.6 shows the same program, except the characters are output as soon as they are grabbed with `getch()`.

Listing 16.6. Reads characters with *getch()* and immediately prints them with *putch()*.

```
/* Filename: FASTPUT.C
  Demonstrates getch() and putch() functions */
#include <stdio.h>
#include <conio.h>

main()
{
  int v1,v2,v3,v4,v5; /* Not character variables! */

  /* Read characters */
  v1=getch();
  putch(v1);
  v2=getch();
  putch(v2);
  v3=getch();
  putch(v3);
```

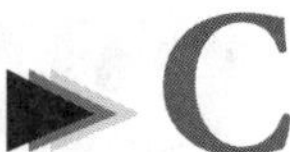

```
    v4=getch();
    putch(v4);
    v5=getch();
    putch(v5);
    return 0;
}
```

When you run Listing 16.6, you'll see that the characters appear on-screen, via the `putch()` calls, as soon as you press a key, and the program ends as soon as the fifth character is printed.

Figure 16.3 shows how `getch()`'s input goes directly to the program as the user presses keys. There is no time for corrections here; if the user presses Backspace, the ASCII code for the Backspace key is sent to whatever variable is accepting the keystrokes.

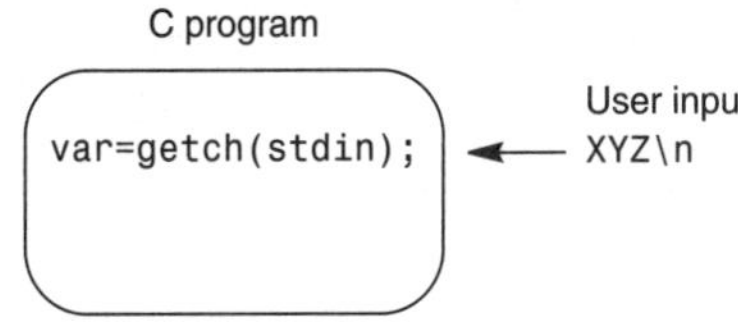

Figure 16.3. `getch()` input goes directly to the program.

Listing 16.7 contains a QBasic version of the program that accepts five characters and displays them on-screen.

Listing 16.7. Simulating *getch()* with QBasic's *INKEY$*.

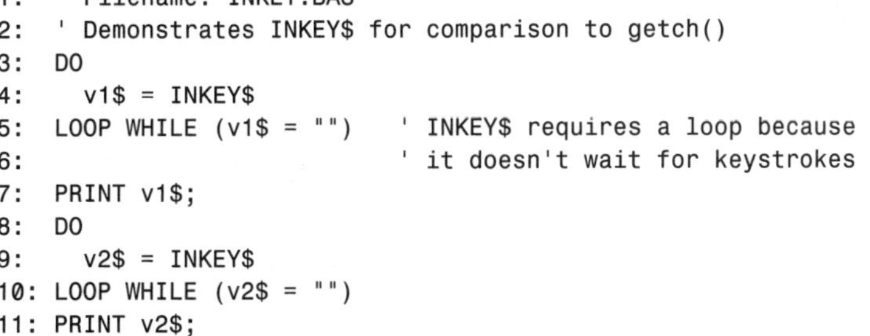

```
' Filename: INKEY.BAS
' Demonstrates INKEY$ for comparison to getch()
DO
  v1$ = INKEY$
LOOP WHILE (v1$ = "")     ' INKEY$ requires a loop because
                          ' it doesn't wait for keystrokes
PRINT v1$;
DO
  v2$ = INKEY$
LOOP WHILE (v2$ = "")
PRINT v2$;
DO
  v3$ = INKEY$
```

continues

Listing 16.7. continued

```
LOOP WHILE (v3$ = "")
PRINT v3$;
DO
   v4$ = INKEY$
LOOP WHILE (v4$ = "")
PRINT v4$;
DO
   v5$ = INKEY$
LOOP WHILE (v5$ = "")
PRINT v5$;
END
```

> Using `INKEY$` takes a lot more work than using C's `getch()` function because `INKEY$` can grab input only inside a loop.

The Easy Ones Now: *gets()* and *puts()*

The functions `gets()` and `puts()` are simple. `gets()` accepts a string as input (into a character array), and `puts()` prints a string. Here are the formats of the functions:

`gets(`*`characterArray`*`);`

and

`puts(`*`string`*`);`

The regular `INPUT` and `PRINT` commands in QBasic would equate to `gets()` and `puts()` because both `INPUT` and `PRINT` can read and write strings.

Listing 16.8 contains a program that accepts three strings and prints them on-screen.

Listing 16.8. Using *gets()* and *puts()*.

```
/* Filename: GETSPUTS.C
   Demonstrates gets() and puts() */
#include <stdio.h>
main()
{
  char first[25];     /* To hold three strings */
  char middle[25];
  char last[25];
  /* Ask for each name */
  puts("What is your first name? ");
  gets(first);
  puts("What is your middle name? ");
  gets(middle);
  puts("What is your last name? ");
  gets(last);
  /* Print the strings */
  puts("Here you are:");
  puts(first);
  puts(middle);
  puts(last);
  return 0;
}
```

Here is the output from the program:

```
What is your first name?
Tony
What is your middle name?
Lo
What is your last name?
Bianco
Here you are:
Tony
Lo
Bianco
```

Use `gets()` to input strings even if those strings contain embedded blanks. You might recall that `scanf()` cannot get strings with embedded spaces.

The `puts()` automatically appends a newline, `\n`, to all output, so never add a newline character to the string being printed unless you want a blank line between strings.

`gets()` does *not* check for array overflow! Therefore, if the user were to enter a string longer than 24 characters, that input could overwrite important parts of memory because only 25 are reserved for each string, including the terminating zero. Therefore, you must be sure that you reserve enough memory to hold the largest string ever to be input with `gets()`.

Summary

This chapter explained how C performs I/O. C reads from and writes to standard devices rather than to specific devices. Doing so lets the same C program run on virtually any computer it is compiled on.

The low-level character I/O functions C provides read and write a character at a time. The buffered functions, `getc()`, `puts()`, `getchar()`, and `putchar()`, all read and write to a buffer, and a newline character releases the buffer to the I/O device. The unbuffered `getch()` (and `putch()`) gets characters directly from the input device, which makes the function mirror `INKEY$` in many respects.

Finally, `gets()` and `puts()` provide easy string I/O capabilities. You'll see more uses of all these functions throughout the rest of this book, especially when you get to the file I/O routines in Part VII.

17

QBasic

C

Character and String Functions

This chapter explains how to use C's character and string functions. The functions explained here are ANSI C compatible. C provides character functions because it supports the character data type (variables can be character variables as you know). Although C does not support string functions, there are several C functions that manipulate strings. The string functions can work with strings represented in these three ways:

- String constants, such as `"a string"`
- Character arrays that contain zero-terminated strings
- Character pointers that hold the address of strings

You've seen strings represented by the first two methods. You'll learn about character pointers in the next part of the book. The most important point to remember about the C string functions is that they work only with properly terminated strings that end in zero.

Most of the strings discussed in this chapter have QBasic equivalents. Alas, QBasic's string power exceeds that of C, and QBasic includes many string functions that C does not provide. However, you can write your own string functions using the fundamental string functions described here as a basis. You'll find that the seemingly limited string-handling capability of C is compensated for by C's efficiency.

The character functions described here require that you include the CTYPE.H header file. All the string functions described in this chapter require that you include the STRING.H header file. In this chapter, you will learn about the following topics:

- Character functions that test and change character data
- The full impact of the `strcpy()` function
- How to concatenate strings
- How to search for substrings within other strings

The Character Functions

There are no QBasic character functions.

The character-testing functions test character data and return true (1) or false (0), depending on their result. The character-testing functions are easy to use and don't require a tremendous amount of discussion. QBasic does not contain these character-testing functions because a character is not one of the QBasic fundamental data types.

Table 17.1 lists the character-testing functions and gives a description of each. All of Table 17.1's character functions require a single character argument. The argument can be a character variable or a character constant.

Table 17.1. The character-testing functions.

Function Name	*Description*
`isalpha()`	Returns true if the argument is an alphabetic letter.
`islower()`	Returns true if the argument is a lowercase letter.
`isupper()`	Returns true if the argument is an uppercase letter.
`isdigit()`	Returns true if the argument is a numeric digit.
`isalnum()`	Returns true if the argument is an alphabetic letter or a numeric digit.

Listing 17.1 contains a C program that asks the user to press a key. The user's keystroke is grabbed with the `getch()` I/O function described in the preceding chapter. Each character-testing function from Table 17.1 is applied to the user's character value, and a message prints according to the result of those tests.

> If you use a Microsoft Windows-based C compiler, you cannot use `getch()` or `getche()` because the Windows-based languages don't support the two functions.

Listing 17.1. The character-testing functions at work.

```
/* Filename: CHARTEST.C
   Applies the character-testing functions to the user's input */
#include <stdio.h>
#include <conio.h>
#include <ctype.h>
main()
{
  char userChar;
  printf("Please press a key...");
  userChar = getch();
  printf("%c\n", userChar);  /* Echo the character */
  /* Use the conditional operator to print results of tests */
  /* A character? */
  printf("Your character ");
  /* Prints "not" or doesn't print anything */
  isalpha(userChar) ? printf("is ") : printf("isn't ");
  printf("an alphabetic character.\n");
  /* Lowercase? */
  printf("Your character ");
  /* Prints "not" or doesn't print anything */
  islower(userChar) ? printf("is ") : printf("isn't ");
  printf("a lowercase letter.\n");
  /* Uppercase? */
  printf("Your character ");
  /* Prints "not" or doesn't print anything */
  isupper(userChar) ? printf("is ") : printf("isn't ");
  printf("an uppercase letter.\n");
  /* A digit? */
  printf("Your character ");
  /* Prints "not" or doesn't print anything */
  isdigit(userChar) ? printf("is ") : printf("isn't ");
  printf("a numeric digit.\n");
  /* A letter or digit? */
  printf("Your character ");
  /* Prints "not" or doesn't print anything */
  isalnum(userChar) ? printf("is ") : printf("isn't ");
  printf("a numeric digit or letter.\n");
  return 0;
}
```

The character-testing functions return either true or false. The program uses the conditional operator, `?:`, to test for true or false, so the character-testing functions are used as the conditional operator's first argument in lines 16, 21, 26, 31, and 36. The word `is` or `isn't` is printed according to the result of the conditional operator.

Here is the result of running Listing 17.1's program three times, entering a different kind of character each time.

```
Please enter a key...a
Your character is an alphabetic character.
Your character is a lowercase letter.
Your character isn't an uppercase letter.
Your character isn't a numeric digit.
Your character is a numeric digit or letter.
Please enter a key...5
Your character isn't an alphabetic character.
Your character isn't a lowercase letter.
Your character isn't an uppercase letter.
Your character is a numeric digit.
Your character is a numeric digit or letter.
Please enter a key...$
Your character isn't an alphabetic character.
Your character isn't a lowercase letter.
Your character isn't an uppercase letter.
Your character isn't a numeric digit.
Your character isn't a numeric digit or letter.
```

C provides two additional character functions that change their arguments. `toupper()` and `tolower()` (whose header file is also CONIO.H) work just as you would guess: `toupper()` converts its argument to uppercase, and `tolower()` converts its argument to lowercase. If the argument cannot be converted, for instance if the argument is not a character or the argument is already in the target case, nothing is done to the argument.

> The QBasic `UCASE$()` and `LCASE$()` functions convert their string arguments to uppercase and lowercase respectively. If you want to convert strings to a specific case, you must do so one character at a time using several calls to `toupper()` or `tolower()`.

Notice that the following section of code prints an uppercase `G`:

```
char initial = 'g';
printf("Initial is %c.", toupper(initial));
```

The following section of code prints a lowercase p (the p was not changed because it was already lowercase):

```
char initial = 'p';
printf("Initial is %c.", tolower(initial));
```

Use toupper() or tolower() to make the test for a user's yes or no answer easier. For example, without these functions, you would have to perform a compound relational test like this:

```
printf("Do you want to continue (Y/N)? ";
userAns = getch();
if ((userAns == 'y') || (userAns == 'Y'))
  /* The Yes code goes here */
```

But with toupper(), the test is easier:

```
printf("Do you want to continue (Y/N)? ";
userAns = getch();
if (toupper(userAns) == 'Y')
  /* The Yes code goes here */
```

Copying Strings: A Review

QBasic doesn't need a string copy function because in QBasic, a string is a built-in data type. Any time a data type is built into the language, a simple assignment operator is enough to copy the contents of one string to another.

In Chapter 7, "Character and String Data," you learned about C's strcpy() function. It would be a good idea to review strcpy() now that you're more familiar with the language. Here is the format of strcpy():

```
strcpy(targetArray, stringToAssign);
```

Figure 17.1 shows how the strcpy() function works. The *targetArray* must be a character array. You could not copy a string into a string constant. The *stringToAssign* can be a string constant, an array, or a character pointer to a string.

```
strcpy(targetArray, stringToAssign);
```

Figure 17.1. The `strcpy()` *function copies the second argument to the first one.*

The `strcpy()` function changes the first argument. The second argument, the *`stringToAssign`*, is left unchanged.

The following code copies the string `"Bo Snerdley"` to the character array named `answerPerson`:

```
strcpy(answerPerson, "Bo Snerdley");
```

In QBasic, a simple assignment of the two strings works like this:

```
answerPerson$ = "Bo Snerdley"
```

As is always the case in C, the target string is never checked to ensure that it contains enough room for the *`stringToAssign`*. It's up to you to make sure that the *`targetArray`* is large enough to hold the string. The following code would do that:

```
if (strlen(name) >= (strlen("Smith")+1) )
  { strcpy(name, "Smith")); }
else
  {fprintf(stderr, "The assigned string is too long to copy.\n"); }
```

Remember that the length of a string is the number of characters up to, but not including, the terminating zero. C's `strlen()` function works just like QBasic's `LEN()` function and returns the length of its string argument. `1` had to be added to the result of the `strlen()` call to ensure that the target string was large enough to hold the copied string and the terminating zero.

Is C Really More Efficient?

If all things were equal, QBasic's simple assignment of strings would be much more efficient than C's `strcpy()`. Any time you have to call a function, function-call overhead is added to the program, and function calls take time (arguments must be passed, received, and returned).

Remember, though, that C is a compiled language. The fact that C is compiled rather than interpreted like QBasic is enough to add lots of efficiency to the language. Furthermore, QBasic loses additional efficiency in the way strings are represented.

QBasic strings change in size throughout a program's execution. The same QBasic string variable, `sv$`, might be assigned a one-character string, then a 100-character string, and you'll never have a problem with string sizes. QBasic easily and dynamically changes the sizes of string variables as needed to hold whatever data you assign to them (although there is a 255-character limit to QBasic's string size). Supporting variable-length strings is very powerful and makes for easier programming, but variable-length string handling requires a lot of overhead and slows down programs considerably.

C is at the opposite end of the efficiency spectrum from QBasic. C does not support variable-length strings. After you define a character array to be a certain size, you cannot lengthen that array. It's up to you to ensure that you don't store too long a string in a character array that is not set up to hold a string of that size. In return for some extra effort on your part, you'll get highly efficient runtime code.

String Concatenation

+ concatenates in QBasic.

When you concatenate strings, you append one string to another. You might want to concatenate a last name to a first name, or the string `", Inc."` to the end of a company name. As is usually the case with string handling, QBasic's string concatenation is a little simpler than C's. The plus sign, `+`, is all you need to use when you want to concatenate one string to the end of another like this:

```
fullName$ = firstName$ + lastName$
```

In both QBasic and C, you must make sure that you embed a space between the strings you are concatenating. Using QBasic's plus sign, you can add the embedded space between two strings like this:

```
fullName$ = firstName$ + " " + lastName$
```

QBasic distinguishes between the addition plus sign and the concatenation plus sign by the context in which you use the sign. If numbers appear on both sides of the plus sign, QBasic adds the numbers numerically. If strings appear on both sides, QBasic concatenates the strings.

strcat() concatenates in C.

The `strcat()` function concatenates two strings in C. Here is the format of `strcat()`:

```
strcat(targetArray, stringToAdd);
```

Unlike QBasic's string-concatenating plus sign, you can only concatenate to the end of a string one value at a time. The *targetArray* must be long enough to hold its initial contents plus the contents of the *stringToAdd*. Suppose that you reserved a three-character array in a C program like this:

```
char fullName[15];    /* Reserve arrays for strings */
char firstName[10];
char lastName[10];
```

You could assign the first- and last-name strings initial values using `strcpy()` like this:

```
strcpy(firstName, "Tony");
strcpy(lastName, "Bianco");
```

There is plenty of room in `fullName` to hold the two other strings concatenated together. You must concatenate the two strings to the `fullName` array one at a time. However, before doing so, you should make sure that `fullName` holds an empty string. Remember that C does not initialize variables for you. The following statement assigns a null string to `fullName`:

```
strcpy(fullName, "");
```

The null string assignment of `""` stores an ASCII 0 (the string terminator) to the array's first element. You can also put a null string into a character array like this:

```
fullName[0] = '\0';
```

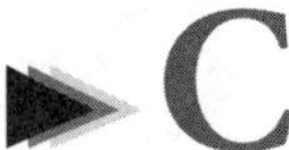

After you initialize `fullName`, you can concatenate the strings to it. Here is the code which does just that:

```
strcat(fullName, firstName);  /* Add the first name */
strcat(fullName, " ");        /* Add a blank */
strcat(fullName, lastName);   /* Add the last name */
```

Figure 17.2 shows the contents of the `fullName` array after the strings are added to it.

> As Figure 17.2 shows, only the data up to each string's null zero is added when concatenated. In other words, not all 10 elements of `firstName` are sent to `fullName` because only the first four elements contain string data.

fullName	
[0]	T
[1]	o
[2]	n
[3]	y
[4]	
[5]	B
[6]	i
[7]	a
[8]	n
[9]	c
[10]	o
[11]	\0
[12]	?
[13]	?
[14]	?

Figure 17.2. After concatenating the strings.

> If the *targetArray* is not long enough to hold the fully concatenated string, you will overwrite other memory and probably receive errors, or at worst, your computer will freeze up.

Comparing Strings

Again, QBasic shines over C when it comes to built-in string-comparison power, but C excels in efficiency. Whereas QBasic compares strings directly as in

```
IF (s1$ = s2$) THEN
```

C requires that you use the string comparison function, `strcmp()`. Here is its format:

```
strcmp(string1, string2);
```

Both *`string1`* and *`string2`* can be string constants, arrays, or character pointers pointing to strings. `strcmp()` does not change either argument. The return value of `strcmp()` will be as explained here:

- The return value will be 0 if the strings are equal.
- The return value will be less than 0 if *`string1`* compares lower (in ASCII order) than *`string2`*.
- The return value will be more than 0 if *`string1`* compares higher (in ASCII order) than *`string2`*.

Be careful when using `strcmp()`! When the strings compare as equal, `strcmp()` returns a `0`, which means *false* in C! Therefore, if you want to test for equality, be careful that you don't do so like this:

```
if (strcmp(string1, string2))  /* Rest of if would follow */
```

`strcmp()` returns a true (nonzero) value only if the strings are *not* equal. When you use `strcmp()` is one of the few times when using `!` (the NOT operator) is clearer than coding without the `!`. The proper `if` test to see whether two strings compare would be this:

```
if (!strcmp(string1, string2))     /* Notice the NOT */
```

You won't be able to predict the value of `strcmp()`.

If the strings are different, you cannot determine exactly what return value `strcmp()` will return. All you know is that the return value is less than zero if and only if *`string1`* is less than *`string2`*. You don't know what negative number will result, but you do know the order of the comparison. Consider the following `if`:

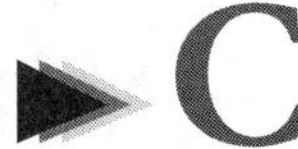

```
if (strcmp(lastName1, lastName2) < 0)
  { printf("%s goes to the front of the line.", lastName1); }
else
  { printf("%s goes to the front of the line.", lastName2); }
```

When you use `strcmp()`, pretend that there is an imaginary minus sign between the string arguments. The imaginary minus sign tells you exactly how the strings compare according to the ASCII table. For example, consider this example:

```
if (!strcmp("A", "a"))     /* Rest of if would follow */
```

Looking at the ASCII table, you find that `"A"` has the value of 65 and `"a"` has the value of 97. An imaginary minus sign subtracting 97 from 65 yields a negative value. Sure enough, `"A"` is less than `"a"` in the ASCII sequence, and `strcmp()` returns a negative value when you compare these two one-character strings.

The program in Listing 17.2 contains the QBasic code that determines whether the user enters a secret password correctly. The QBasic code is shorter than the C code in Listing 17.3, which does the same thing. Shorter is not always better, as you've seen throughout this book. String comparison really is one of those things you'll wish C could do without a requiring a function such as `strcmp()` because you have to stop and think about return values.

Listing 17.2. A QBasic program that compares strings.

```
' Filename: STRCMP.BAS
' Compares the user's entered string against a secret password
INPUT "What is the secret password"; pswd$
IF (pswd$ = "money") THEN
  BEEP
  PRINT "You win $25!"
ELSE
  PRINT "Sorry, you get a free ball-point pen."
END IF
END
```

Listing 17.3. A C program that compares strings.

```
1:  /* Filename: STRCMP.C
2:     Compares the user's entered string against a secret password */
3:  #include <stdio.h>
4:  #include <string.h>
5:  main()
6:  {
7:    char pswd[25];
8:    printf("What is the secret password? ");
9:    gets(pswd);
10:   if (!strcmp(pswd, "money"))
11:     { printf("\a");      /* Ring the PC's bell */
12:       printf("You win $25!\n");
13:     }
14:   else
15:     { printf("Sorry, you get a free ball-point pen.\n"); }
16:   return 0;
17: }
```

Notice that `gets()` was used on line 9 to get the user's password. `gets()` is a lot easier to code than `scanf()` when you're writing string input routines.

Here is the output from either program when the correct password is entered:

```
What is the secret password? money
You win $25!
```

Searching for Substrings

C does not duplicate `INSTR()` exactly.

C contains functions that work somewhat like QBasic's `INSTR()` function. As you might recall, `INSTR()` returns the location of one string, called the *substring,* within another. There is no function available in ANSI C that mirrors `INSTR()` exactly, but in this chapter you'll learn about a couple that come close.

The first function you'll see is the `strcspn()` function. `strcspn()` searches a string for the position of a substring within another string. Here is the format of `strcspn()`:

```
long int strcspn(searchString, subString);
```

Unlike with `INSTR()`, if C cannot find the *`subString`* within the *`searchString`*, `strcspn()` returns the position of the *`searchString`*'s *null zero.* If the string-terminating null zero is located at position 14 in the *`searchString`*, for example, a 14 is returned from `strcspn()`

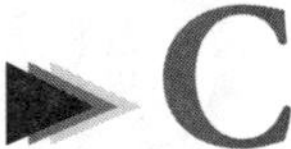

if the *subString* cannot be found. `INSTR()` would return a 0 if the *subString* could not be found. Listing 17.4 contains an example of a QBasic program that searches a string for several substrings.

Listing 17.4. A QBasic program that searches for substrings.

```
' Filename: INSTR1.BAS
' Searches a string for several substrings
searchString$ = "The password, GH76!q, must be kept secret."
subString1$ = "The"
subString2$ = "GH76!q"
subString3$ = "."
subString4$ = "XXXX"
PRINT "Searching: "; searchString$; "..."
PRINT "The location of "; subString1$; " is";
PRINT INSTR(searchString$, subString1$)
PRINT "The location of "; subString2$; " is";
PRINT INSTR(searchString$, subString2$)
PRINT "The location of "; subString3$; " is";
PRINT INSTR(searchString$, subString3$)
PRINT "The location of "; subString4$; " is";
PRINT INSTR(searchString$, subString4$)
END
```

Here is the output of listing 17.4:

```
Searching: The password, GH76!q, must be kept secret....
The location of The is 1
The location of GH76!q is 15
The location of . is 42
The location of XXXX is 0
```

> As you might know, `INSTR()` can accept an optional first integer argument that dictates the starting position of the search. In other words, if each of the `INSTR()` functions in Listing 17.4 started with the argument `10`, the program would begin searching for the substrings at the 10th character in each string. If you omit the first integer argument, QBasic begins searching at the first character in the string. C's string-searching functions always begin searching the first character in the string.

Listing 17.5 contains a C program that searches the same string for the same substrings as done in Listing 17.4. You'll find that Listing 17.5 produces different results because all string positions start at zero in C (string data begins at position 1 in QBasic), and `strcspn()` returns the null zero position rather than `0` if the substring cannot be found.

Listing 17.5. A C program that searches for substrings.

```
/* Filename: STRCSPN.C
   Searches a string for several substrings */
#include <stdio.h>
#include <string.h>
main()
{
  char searchString[] = "The password, GH76!q, must be kept secret.";
  char subString1[] = "The";
  char subString2[] = "GH76!q";
  char subString3[] = ".";
  char subString4[] = "XXXX";
  printf("Searching: %s...\n", searchString);
  printf("The location of %s is ", subString1);
  printf("%d \n", strcspn(searchString, subString1));
  printf("The location of %s is ", subString2);
  printf("%d \n", strcspn(searchString, subString2));
  printf("The location of %s is ", subString3);
  printf("%d \n", strcspn(searchString, subString3));
  printf("The location of %s is ", subString4);
  printf("%d \n", strcspn(searchString, subString4));
  return 0;
}
```

Here is the output of the C program:

```
Searching: The password, GH76!q, must be kept secret....
The location of The is 0
The location of GH76!q is 14
The location of . is 41
The location of XXXX is 42
```

Notice that the first three locations printed are one position less than their QBasic equivalents. The string `"The"` is located at position `0` in the C program but at `1` in the QBasic program. It is because `0` is a possible location that `strcspn()` uses a value other than `0` for substrings that cannot be found. There are 42 characters in the search string, from position 0 through 41. Therefore, the C program prints the value of `42` when the substring cannot be found.

`strspn()` tells where strings differ.

There is an additional C string search function that does not exist in QBasic. Although you might need it only rarely, the `strspn()` function returns the position at which two strings become *different*. For example, consider these two strings:

```
"Roger Ailes"
```

and

```
"Roger Kirkland"
```

The strings are the same for six characters, the `R` through the space between the names. However, at position six (with the first position being zero), the strings differ. The `strspn()` function would return the value of six if you used these two strings as its arguments. Here is the format of `strspn()`:

```
strspn(string1, string2);
```

The return value is the position where *`string1`* starts to differ from *`string2`*. If the strings are completely different from their first character, `strspn()` returns zero. The C program in Listing 17.6 shows a program that applies `strspn()` to the two names shown earlier.

Listing 17.6. A C program that searches for substrings.

```
/* Filename: STRSPN.C
   Searches a string for several substrings */
#include <stdio.h>
#include <string.h>
main()
{
  char string1[] = "Roger Ailes";
  char string2[] = "Roger Kirkland";
  printf("The return value of strspn() when applied to ");
  printf("these strings: \n");
  printf("%s and %s is %d.\n", string1, string2,
          strspn(string1, string2));
  return 0;
}
```

Here is the output of Listing 17.6:

```
The return value of strspn() when applied to these strings:
Roger Ailes and Roger Kirkland is 6.
```

I Want My *LEFT$()* and *RIGHT$()*!

C does not contain functions that mirror the QBasic's old standbys `LEFT$()` and `RIGHT$()`. These functions return the lefthand and righthand portions of strings. If you want the functionality that these routines provide, you have to code them yourself or use routines written by others.

You'll find the C code that performs the same actions as `LEFT$()` and `RIGHT$()` in Chapter 28, "Returning Data." The reason that you have to wait so long is that you must understand both character pointers (an entirely new concept in C that you've never seen in QBasic) and user-defined C functions.

Summary

This chapter taught you how to use several of the ANSI C string functions. C's string functions cannot compare to QBasic's because C does not support string variables. However, C does attempt to give you some low-level functions from which you can build other functions that you need. Most of the functions work on string constants and character arrays that hold strings. When you master character pointers, you'll learn another way to pass strings to the string functions.

Don't ever pass a character array to a string function unless you know that the array contains a string-terminating null zero. If the array does not contain a null zero, there will eventually be a null zero *somewhere* in memory, and the string function will consider the entire section of memory, from the start of the array to the null zero, the string!

C's `strlen()` function works a lot like QBasic's `LEN()` function. Very few of the other C functions have exact QBasic equivalent functions. However, C usually provides enough functions to handle your string-manipulation needs.

The next chapter moves to the other side of the fence by teaching you many of C's numeric functions and compares them to the collection supplied by QBasic.

18

Numeric Functions

C includes several numeric functions, including almost all the scientific and trigonometric functions included in QBasic. Not all readers will use the scientific and trigonometric functions, but many will need the integer functions. You'll see that C even provides a random-number function just like QBasic's that is used in many games.

> It's a good thing the designers of both QBasic and C decided to include so many prewritten mathematical functions. Even if you use a cosine function only once in your life, you'll be glad that you didn't have to write it from scratch.

The numeric functions are easier to use in some ways than the character and string functions. Most of C's mathematical functions have QBasic equivalents; this chapter compares the mathematical functions of each language.

In this chapter, you will learn about the following topics:

- The integer functions
- The double-precision functions
- The scientific and trigonometric functions
- The random-access function

Most of the mathematical functions described in this chapter take numeric constants, numeric expressions, or numeric variables as arguments and require that you include the MATH.H header file.

The Integer Functions

If you look in a C reference manual, you probably won't see the term *integer function.* However, there are a few functions that return whole-number arguments, and they have corresponding functions in QBasic. Although these functions return whole numbers (hence, their nickname, *integer functions*), they return their whole-number values in single-precision data types.

The `ceil()` and `floor()` functions round their arguments up or down to the nearest integer respectively. They are well-named: `ceil()`, for *ceiling,* raises its argument to an integer, and `floor()`, for *floor,* drops its argument to an integer.

QBasic's `INT()` function mirrors the `floor()` function by returning the integer less than or equal to its argument. There is no QBasic equivalent to the `ceil()` function, but by adding `.5` to the `CINT()` (for *convert integer*) function's argument, you can return the next highest integer in QBasic and simulate `ceil()`.

`ceil()` and `floor()` work for negatives too.

The `floor()` and `ceil()` functions work for negative arguments, but remember that the direction of negatives is the opposite from that of positive numbers. In other words, `floor (-9.2)` is `-10`, not `-9`, because `-10` is the next-lowest whole number from `-9`. `floor(9.2)`, however, is `9` because positive `9` is less than positive `9.2`. Listing 18.1 shows a C program that prints the floor and ceiling values of several numbers. Listing 18.2 shows the equivalent QBasic code. As mentioned earlier, you must add `.5` to the argument before QBasic's `CINT()` function can mirror C's `ceil()` function.

Listing 18.1. Working with some C integer functions.

```
/* Filename: INT.C
   Returns integer values for several different arguments */
#include <stdio.h>
#include <math.h>
main()
{
  printf("ceil(9.2) produces %.1f.\n", ceil(9.2));
  printf("ceil(9.8) produces %.1f.\n", ceil(9.8));
  printf("ceil(-9.2) produces %.1f.\n", ceil(-9.2));
  printf("ceil(-9.8) produces %.1f.\n", ceil(-9.8));
  printf("floor(9.2) produces %.1f.\n", floor(9.2));
  printf("floor(9.8) produces %.1f.\n", floor(9.8));
  printf("floor(-9.2) produces %.1f.\n", floor(-9.2));
  printf("floor(-9.8) produces %.1f.\n", floor(-9.8));
  return 0;
}
```

Here is the output from Listing 18.1:

```
ceil(9.2) produces 10.0
ceil(9.8) produces 10.0
ceil(-9.2) produces -9.0
ceil(-9.8) produces -9.0
floor(9.2) produces 9.0
floor(9.8) produces 9.0
floor(-9.2) produces -10.0
floor(-9.8) produces -10.0
```

Notice that the return values for the `ceil()` and `floor()` function calls were printed using the `%f` format code because their integer values are returned as single-precision data types.

If you ever need long double-precision data types returned, use `ceill()` and `floorl()`. They both work like the `ceil()` and `floor()` functions, except that the integer values are returned as long double-precision data types.

Listing 18.2. Working with some QBasic equivalent integer functions.

```
' Filename: INT.BAS
' Returns C-like ceil() and floor() values
CLS
PRINT "ceil()-> CINT(9.2+.5) produces"; CINT(9.2 + .5)
PRINT "ceil()-> CINT(9.8+.5) produces"; CINT(9.8 + .5)
PRINT "ceil()-> CINT(-9.2+.5) produces "; CINT(-9.2 + .5)
PRINT "ceil()-> CINT(-9.8+.5) produces "; CINT(-9.8 + .5)

PRINT "floor()-> INT(9.2) produces"; INT(9.2)
PRINT "floor()-> INT(9.8) produces"; INT(9.8)
PRINT "floor()-> INT(-9.2) produces "; INT(-9.2)
PRINT "floor()-> INT(-9.8) produces "; INT(-9.8)
END
```

Here is the output from listing 18.2. Notice how it mirrors Listing 18.1 as long as you adjust the argument for the `ceil()` values.

```
ceil()-> INT(9.2+.5) produces 10
ceil()-> INT(9.8+.5) produces 10
ceil()-> INT(-9.2+.5) produces -9
ceil()-> INT(-9.8+.5) produces -9
floor()-> INT(9.2) produces 9
floor()-> INT(9.8) produces 9
floor()-> INT(-9.2) produces -10
floor()-> INT(-9.8) produces -10
```

If you want true rounding to occur, in which values with fractions less than .5 round down and others with .5 or higher round up, add `.5` to the argument and use the `floor()` function. For example, to ensure that age is rounded mathematically, not always up or always down, you would do this:

```
roundAge = floor(age + .5);
```

A Few Common Math Functions

There are six C functions that perform useful mathematical routines. These functions are used a lot for business and financial calculations as well as mathematical operations. Table 18.1 lists these functions and gives a description of each.

Table 18.1. Common C math functions.

Function Name	*Description*
`abs()`	Returns the integer argument's absolute value. The positive value of the argument is returned.
`fabs()`	Returns the floating-point argument's absolute value.
`fmod()`	The `fmod()` is the floating-point version of the `%` operator. The function returns the floating-point remainder from the second argument's division into the first argument.
`labs()`	Returns the long integer argument's absolute value.
`pow()`	Raises its first argument to the power of the second argument.
`sqrt()`	Returns the square root of the argument.

Notice that two of the functions, `fmod()` and `pow()`, require two arguments whereas most of the mathematical functions require only single arguments.

QBasic offers `ABS()` *and* `SQR()`.

QBasic supplies equivalent functions for four of Table 18.1's six functions. QBasic's `ABS()` returns the absolute value of its argument. Unlike C's three versions of absolute value functions, `ABS()` works with arguments of any data type. `SQR()` returns the square root of the argument. (The ^ operator does the same thing as C's `pow()`, as you'll see in a moment.) Listing 18.3 contains a QBasic program that prints the absolute value and square root of several numbers.

Listing 18.3. Using *ABS()* and *SQR()*.

```
' Filename: ABSSQR.BAS
' Demonstrates QBasic's ABS() and SQR() functions
PRINT "The absolute value of 25 is"; ABS(25)
PRINT "The absolute value of -25 is"; ABS(-25)
PRINT "The square root of 81 is"; SQR(81)
END
```

Here is the output of Listing 18.3:

```
The absolute value of 25 is 25
The absolute value of -25 is 25
The square root of 81 is 9
```

Listing 18.4 shows a C program that produces the same output as Listing 18.3. QBasic's `ABS()` and `SQR()` functions both return single-precision values, but QBasic hides the fact better than C when the functions produce whole numbers (QBasic does not display a decimal point when the function returns a whole number). Therefore, the C program uses `abs()` rather than `fabs()` or `labs()` because its argument is an integer.

Listing 18.4. Using *abs()* and *sqrt()*.

```
/* Filename: ABSSQR.C
   Demonstrates C's abs() and sqrt() functions */
#include <stdio.h>
#include <math.h>
main()
{
  printf("The absolute value of 25 is %d\n", abs(25));
  printf("The absolute value of -25 is %d\n", abs(-25));
  printf("The square root of 81 is %.0f\n", sqrt(81));
  return 0;
}
```

Don't ever attempt to take the square root of a negative value in either QBasic or C. Square roots are defined only for positive numbers, and you'll get an error message if you pass a negative to `SQR()` or `sqrt()`.

Use the absolute value function when you have to work with positive-only values, such as ages, weights, and distances. Also, store these values in unsigned variables, by preceding the variable definition with the `unsigned` keyword, such as `unsigned int distance;` rather than `int distance;`. All numeric variables are signed by default, and you'll get more storage room for larger positive values if you define the variables with the `unsigned` keyword.

As mentioned earlier, the QBasic ^ operator raises a number to a power, but C uses the `pow()` function to accomplish the same task. Suppose that you wanted to write a program that prints the first eight powers of 2. Listing 18.5 prints the powers in QBasic, and Listing 18.6 does the same in C.

Listing 18.5. Printing the first eight powers of 2.

```
' Filename: POWER2.BAS
' Prints the first eight powers of 2
FOR i = 1 TO 8
  PRINT "2 raised to the power of"; i; "is"; 2 ^ i
NEXT i
END
```

Listing 18.6. Printing the first eight powers of 2.

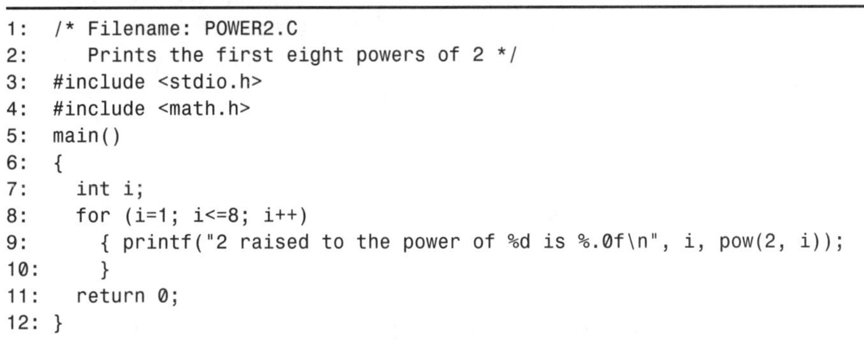

```
/* Filename: POWER2.C
   Prints the first eight powers of 2 */
#include <stdio.h>
#include <math.h>
main()
{
  int i;
  for (i=1; i<=8; i++)
    { printf("2 raised to the power of %d is %.0f\n", i, pow(2, i));
    }
  return 0;
}
```

Here is the output from Listings 18.5 and 18.6:

```
2 raised to the power of 1 is 2
2 raised to the power of 2 is 4
2 raised to the power of 3 is 8
2 raised to the power of 4 is 16
2 raised to the power of 5 is 32
2 raised to the power of 6 is 64
2 raised to the power of 7 is 128
2 raised to the power of 8 is 256
```

You Can Find the nth Root

There is no C or QBasic function that computes the *nth root* of a number. Nevertheless, there are many times in finance and math when you need to take a higher root than a square root. Mathematically, the nth root, such as the 6th root or the 21st root of a number, is that number raised to the 1/n power. In other words, if you wanted to take the cube root of 1,000, you could raise 1,000 to the (1/3) power. By the way, the cube root of 1,000 is 10 because 10 * 10 * 10 equals 1,000 ($10^3 = 1{,}000$).

This equivalent formula for roots enables you to use `pow()` to compute any root of any number. If you wanted to use `pow()` to compute the cube root of 1,000, you would do so like this:

```
cubeRoot = pow(1000, (1/3));
```

If you ever need the remainder of a floating-point division (as opposed to the modulus, or integer remainder, you get using C's `%` operator), use the `fmod()` function. There is no equivalent QBasic function or operator to return the floating-point remainder. If you wanted the remainder of `x` divided by `y`, and both `x` and `y` were floating-point values, you could use `fmod()` like this:

```
fremaind = fmod(x, y);  /* Stores the remainder */
```

If you wanted this value in QBasic, you would have to write a program to produce it.

The Logarithmic Functions

C provides three logarithmic functions, listed in Table 18.2.

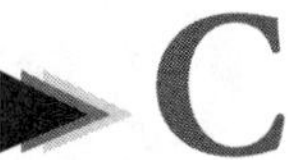

Table 18.2. The logarithmic functions.

Function Name	*Description*
`exp()`	Produces the base of *e*, the natural log, raised to the power of the argument.
`log()`	Produces the natural log of the argument. The argument must be positive. If you are unsure about the argument's sign, take the absolute value of the argument before passing it to the `log()` function.
`log10()`	Produces the base-10 log of the argument. Again, the argument must be positive for the function to work correctly.

> *e* is a mathematical abbreviation for the approximate value of 2.71828. *e* is used a lot in scientific, engineering, and surveying programs.

The QBasic equivalent functions for `exp()` and `log()` are `EXP()` and `LOG()`. There is no QBasic equivalent for C's `log10()` function. Listings 18.7 and 18.8 show equivalent QBasic and C programs that produce the same results using the languages' two common logarithmic functions.

Listing 18.7. Calling *EXP()* and *LOG()*.

```
' Filename: EXPLOG.BAS
' Produces results using EXP() and LOG()
PRINT "EXP(1.5) is"; EXP(1.5)
PRINT "LOG(1.5) is"; LOG(1.5)
END
```

Listing 18.8. Calling *exp()* and *log()*.

```
/* Filename: EXPLOG.C
   Produces results using exp() and log() */
```

continues

Listing 18.8. continued

```
#include <stdio.h>
#include <math.h>
main()
{
  printf("exp(1.5) is %.6f\n", exp(1.5));
  printf("log(1.5) is %.6f\n", log(1.5));
  return 0;
}
```

Here is the output from the QBasic program:

```
EXP(1.5) is 4.481689
LOG(1.5) is .4054651
```

> The QBasic version in Listing 18.7 produces a seventh digit of precision for the `LOG()` function, but the two versions' results are exactly the same other than that extra digit of precision.

The Trigonometric Functions

C supports all the standard trigonometric functions calls, as do most programming languages. Table 18.3 lists C's three most common trigonometric functions and gives a description of each.

Table 18.3. The trigonometric functions.

Function Name	*Description*
`cos()`	Produces the cosine, in radians, of its angle argument from `-1` to `1`.
`sin()`	Produces the sine, in radians, of its angle argument from `-1` to `1`.
`tan()`	Produces the tangent, in radians, of its angle argument.

QBasic supplies equivalents to each of these functions, except that the QBasic function names contain uppercase letters. Listing 18.9 contains a short QBasic program that calls each of the three trigonometric functions, and Listing 18.10 contains the C version of the same program.

QBasic provides identical functions.

Listing 18.9. Calling QBasic's trig functions.

```
1:  ' Filename: TRIG.BAS
2:  ' Calls the 3 primary QBasic trigonometric functions
3:  PI = 3.14159
4:  PRINT SIN(PI / 4)
5:  PRINT COS(PI / 4)
6:  PRINT TAN(PI / 4)
7:  END
```

Here is the output of Listing 18.9:

```
.7071064
.7071072
.9999987
```

Notice that the third value from line 6, the tangent of `PI / 4`, is really `1`, but some rounding caused the output to be slightly less. Listing 18.10 produces the same output (except for minor rounding differences).

Listing 18.10. Calling C's trig functions.

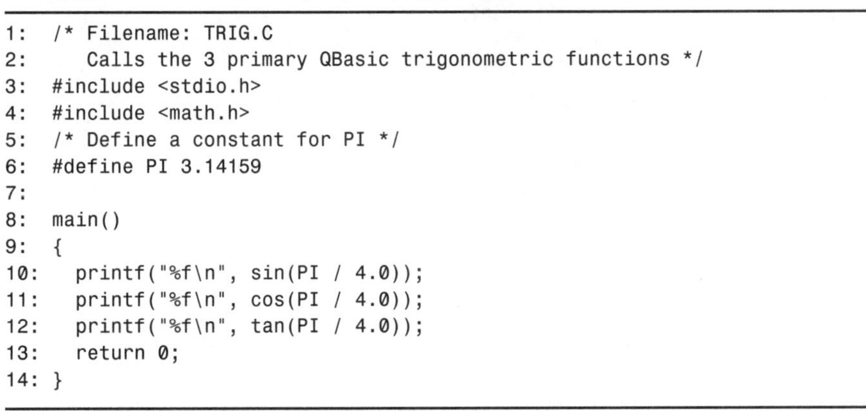

```
/* Filename: TRIG.C
   Calls the 3 primary QBasic trigonometric functions */
#include <stdio.h>
#include <math.h>
/* Define a constant for PI */
#define PI 3.14159

main()
{
  printf("%f\n", sin(PI / 4.0));
  printf("%f\n", cos(PI / 4.0));
  printf("%f\n", tan(PI / 4.0));
  return 0;
}
```

You'll see a defined constant being defined on line 6. Everywhere in the program that `PI` appears, the preprocessor directive replaces the defined constant `PI` with `3.14159`. You first read about defined constants in Chapter 3, "Program Format Differences." When your program contains a value that will not change for the life of the program, using `#define` helps document the program better than using a constant value throughout the code.

Random-Number Generation

Both QBasic and C provide functions that return random numbers. You have to be able to generate random numbers when writing games and simulating certain events. Although both QBasic and C contain similar random-number-generating functions, each language goes about producing random numbers differently.

A little review of QBasic's random-number-generating function, `RND()`, gives you a foundation on which to compare C's random-number-generating function. The random-number-generating functions must be able to produce the *same* random values from program run to program run. That is, even though the function returns different values each time you call it within a program, if you run that same program repetitively, the language must produce the same set of random numbers each run. Certain statistical measurements can be made only from the same set of data. Of course, to make games more interesting, you must also be able to produce a *different* set of random numbers each time a program is run.

QBasic's `RND()` function returns a random number between `0` and `1`. Therefore, if these three QBasic statements appear back-to-back in a program, they print a different number on each line:

```
PRINT RND      ' Prints a number between 0 and 1
PRINT RND      ' Prints a number between 0 and 1
PRINT RND      ' Prints a number between 0 and 1
```

Without changing anything, if you were to run the same program that contained those same three lines over and over, you would get the same set of random numbers each time. `RND()` is one of the few QBasic functions that don't use parentheses if there is no argument.

The `RND()` function can contain arguments, and the arguments control how QBasic generates the random value. If you put a negative number inside the parentheses, `RND()` always returns the *same* number that the previous `RND()` function with the same negative argument generated. For example, the following three `RND()` calls all produce the same number:

```
PRINT RND(-1)
PRINT RND(-1)     ' Repeats the last-generated random number
PRINT RND(-1)     ' Repeats the last-generated random number
```

The following three `RND()` calls all produce a different number from the one generated with `RND(-1)` three times:

```
PRINT RND(-2)
PRINT RND(-2)     ' Repeats the last-generated random number
PRINT RND(-2)     ' Repeats the last-generated random number
```

If you pass a `0` to `RND()`, the last number generated is generated again. For example, the following `PRINT` statements print the same number twice:

```
PRINT RND
PRINT RND(0)
```

And so do these:

```
PRINT RND(-9)
PRINT RND(0)     ' Same as before no matter how it was generated
```

If you pass to `RND()` a number greater than `0`, or omit the argument altogether, you'll get a different random number from the last one generated. Therefore, the following four `PRINT` statements produce four different random numbers between `0` and `1`:

```
PRINT RND(3)     ' Prints a number between 0 and 1
PRINT RND        ' Prints a different number between 0 and 1
PRINT RND(5)     ' Prints a different number between 0 and 1
PRINT RND(3)     ' Prints a different number between 0 and 1
```

How many times do you want a random number between 0 and 1? You rarely do, but with a little ingenuity, you can get a random number to fall within any range you need. The following statement produces a random integer value from `1` to `6`:

Often, you must modify `RND()`'s value.

```
diceRoll = INT(RND * 6) + 1
```

The `INT()` function call and the calculations convert a number from `0` to `1` to the range `1` to `6`, inclusively. The following statement produces a random integer value from `-10` to `+10`:

```
randomNum = INT(RND * 21) - 10
```

> Remember that if the two preceding assignment statements used `RND(10)`, the results would be the same because `RND()` without an argument is the same as `RND()` with a positive argument.

We've yet to discuss how to randomize values from run to run of the same program. For example, if you were to run the program in Listing 18.11 several times, you would get the same set of random values.

Listing 18.11. Always prints the same set of random numbers.

```
' Filename: SAMESET.BAS
' Produces 25 different random numbers
FOR i = 1 TO 15
  PRINT INT(RND * 25) + 1
NEXT i
END
```

Each random-number generation is based, mathematically, on a different *seed value.* The seed value, or *seed* as it's often called, is used by QBasic to start the first number's random generation within a program. If you want the set of random numbers to be different between program runs, you must seed the random-number generator a different number using the `RANDOMIZE` statement. Therefore, the program in Listing 18.12 produces a different result from the program in Listing 18.13 because the seed used in the `RANDOMIZE` statement is different in each program.

Listing 18.12. Prints one set of random numbers.

```
' Filename: SET1.BAS
' Produces a set of random numbers
RANDOMIZE 1
PRINT RND
PRINT RND
PRINT RND
PRINT RND
PRINT RND
PRINT RND
END
```

Listing 18.13. Prints a different set of random numbers.

```
' Filename: SET2.BAS
' Produces a different set of random numbers
```

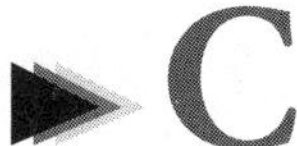

```
RANDOMIZE 35    ' Use a different seed
PRINT RND
PRINT RND
PRINT RND
PRINT RND
PRINT RND
PRINT RND
END
```

You can't go around changing the `RANDOMIZE` statement every time you want a different set of values generated. Therefore, most QBasic programmers know of the trick of putting the `TIMER` keyword after `RANDOMIZE`. `TIMER` returns the number of seconds that have elapsed since midnight. You'll rarely happen to run the same program within the same second of the time of day. Therefore, by putting the statement

```
RANDOMIZE TIMER
```

at the top of all your programs that generate random numbers, you ensure that the program produces a different set of random numbers every time you run the program. The program in Listing 18.14 includes the `TIMER`-based `RANDOMIZE` statement to produce a different set of random numbers each time you run the program as opposed to the two similar programs shown earlier.

Listing 18.14. Ensuring that different numbers always print.

```
' Filename: SETRAN.BAS
' Produces a different set of random numbers each time run
RANDOMIZE TIMER
PRINT RND
PRINT RND
PRINT RND
PRINT RND
PRINT RND
END
```

If you've worked before with QBasic's random-number generator, you've no doubt found this review unneeded. However, it was necessary to refresh your understanding that there is more to random-number generation than just producing a random number. There are several ways to request a random number and several ways to seed the initial value's generation. Luckily, C supports the same random-number generation as QBasic does, but C goes about random numbers slightly differently.

C's `rand()` function produces random numbers, but unlike QBasic's limited range of numbers from `0` to `1`, `rand()` produces a random number from `0` to `32767`. Therefore, adjusting `rand()`'s value to the range you desire is easier (and more efficient due to the lack of a needed `INT()` function call) than using QBasic's `RND()` function. If you want to produce a random-number range, use the `%` operator. For example, the following line stores a random number from `1` to `6` in the variable named `randNum`:

```
randNum = (rand() % 6) + 1;
```

The following line stores a random number from `-10` to `10` in the variable named `randNum`:

```
randNum = (rand() % 21) - 10;
```

You must include the STDLIB.H header file at the top of all programs that use `rand()`.

Never pass a value to C's `rand()` function. Unlike QBasic's `RND()` function, `rand()` never takes an argument. Also, unlike QBasic's `RND()` function, you cannot omit the `rand()` parentheses.

As with QBasic's `RND` and `RND()` with a positive value, C's `rand()` produces a different value each time you call it within the same program. However, from run to run, the set of random numbers differs. The `srand()` function enables you to seed C's random-number generator with a new value to produce a different set of numbers from program run to program run.

If you seed `srand()` with a value of `1` like

```
srand(1);
```

within a program, the random-number generation begins at the same seed as when the program first began. Consider the set of `printf()` statements in Listing 18.15.

Listing 18.15. Resetting the random-number generator.

```
/* Filename: SAMESET.C
   Produces the same three random numbers twice */
#include <stdio.h>
```

```
#include <stdlib.h>
main()
{
  printf(" %d \n", rand());
  printf(" %d \n", rand());
  printf(" %d \n", rand());
  srand(1);                      /* Resets the generator */
  printf(" %d \n", rand());  /* Repeat the set */
  printf(" %d \n", rand());
  printf(" %d \n", rand());
  return 0;
}
```

The first three `printf()` calls all produce different random numbers. The `srand(1)` tells C to reset the random-number generator to the same seed it was set to at the beginning of the program. Therefore, the second set of `printf()`s produces the same three values as the first set. If you run this program several times, you'll get the same output each time: two sets of the same three values.

If you pass a value other than `1` to `srand()`, the program starts producing random numbers based on that new seed value. Obviously, you would like to be able to use a different seed value each time the program executes for programs such as games.

The bottom line is this: If you want the same repeating pattern of random numbers, you must repeat the same call to `srand()` using the same argument to `srand()` before using `rand()` in the program.

C programmers often use the internal clock, as done with QBasic's `TIMER`, to seed the random-number generator to a different value each time the program executes. The `time()` function returns the number of seconds since midnight just as QBasic's `TIMER` does. You must pass `time()` a strange-looking variable defined as `time_t`. `time_t` is not really a data type, but through some advanced commands in the TIME.H header file, `time_t` means the same as `long int`. The `time()` function requires an ampersand before its argument (similar to `scanf()`'s crazy requirement, which you'll understand more after Chapter 21). You must also typecast `time()`'s argument so that it is `unsigned`.

The actual seeding of C's random-number generator is easier to understand when seen than when described. Listing 18.16 shows the code needed to seed the random-number generator with a different value based on the PC's internal clock. The important thing to learn at this point is that you can produce random values between runs as long as you set up the seed value as shown in Listing 18.16.

Listing 18.16. Setting the seed to a new value based on the clock.

```
1:  /* Filename: DIFFRAND.C
2:     Produces a different set of random numbers between runs */
3:  #include <stdlib.h>
4:  #include <stdio.h>
5:  #include <time.h>
6:  /* You must include the header file */
7:  #include <time.h>
8:  main()
9:  {
10:    long t;
11:    srand((unsigned)time(&t));  /* Seed the generator */
12:    printf(" %d \n", rand());
13:    printf(" %d \n", rand());
14:    printf(" %d \n", rand());
15:    printf(" %d \n", rand());
16:    printf(" %d \n", rand());
17:    printf(" %d \n", rand());
18:    return 0;
19: }
```

> Notice that line 5 included the TIME.H header file, needed whenever you seed the random-number generator with the time of day.

Just for fun, Listing 18.17 contains a number-guessing game that uses C's `rand()` function to test your guessing skills.

Listing 18.17. Guess the number.

```
/* Filename: GUESS.C
    Number-guessing game */
#include <stdio.h>
#include <stdlib.h>
#include <time.h>
main()
{
  int ans;     /* Holds the number to guess */
  int guess;   /* Holds the user's guess    */
```

```
   int count=1; /* Keeps track of the number of guesses */
   /* Seed the random-number generator */
   long t;
   srand((unsigned)time(&t));  /* Pass srand() the time of day */
   /* Pick a random number */
   ans = rand() % 100 + 1;     /* From 1 to 100 */
   do
   { printf("Guess the number from 1 to 100!\n");
     printf("What is your guess? ");
     scanf(" %d", &guess);
     if (guess < ans)
       { printf("Sorry, too low. Try again.\n");
         count++; }
     else
       { if (guess > ans)
         { printf("Sorry, too high. Try again.\n");
           count++;}
       }
    } while (ans != guess);  /* Keep looping if needed */
   printf("\aYou guessed it in only %d tries!\n", count);
   return 0;
}
```

Here is a sample run from the program:

```
Guess the number from 1 to 100!
What is your guess? 50
Sorry, too low. Try again.
Guess the number from 1 to 100!
What is your guess? 75
Sorry, too low. Try again.
Guess the number from 1 to 100!
What is your guess? 88
You guessed it in only 3 tries!
```

Summary

In this chapter, you learned about many of C's numeric functions. Because most of the functions overlap those with similar capabilities in QBasic, the transition in this chapter from QBasic to C shouldn't have been too difficult for you.

The integer functions, `ceil()` and `floor`, round their arguments up or down to the nearest integer. When you want numbers rounded to whole amounts, you'll have to pick the method you want to use.

C provides lots of common math functions that return an absolute value, a raised power, and the fractional remainder of floating-point numbers. Two of these functions, `pow()` and `fmod()`, require two arguments, whereas most numeric functions require only one argument.

C also includes support for trigonometric functions that compute the sine, cosine, and tangent in radians. Check your specific compiler's manual to see whether these functions are available for double-precision if you need the higher accuracy.

C, as does QBasic, provides an assortment of random-number options with the `rand()` and `srand()` functions. `rand()` performs a function similar to QBasic's `RND()`, and `srand()` seeds the random-number generator as does QBasic's `RANDOMIZE` statement. Unlike with QBasic's `RND()`, however, you control the reoccurrence of the same random pattern by calling `srand()` with the same argument.

This chapter concludes the internal functions that come with ANSI C compilers. The next chapter begins an exploration into C's data structures by looking at how C supports arrays of types other than character.

Part VI

Advancing Data Power

19

ARRAY MANAGEMENT

This chapter is more of a review than possibly any other in the book. Not only are C arrays similar to QBasic's arrays, but you've already worked with character arrays that held null-terminated string data.

From the viewpoint of the array, a string's null zero is just another character in the array. The null zero just lets C know where to terminate the string when calling string functions and when printing strings with the `%s` format code. Arrays of integers or floating-point values don't have to end with a null zero. (Of course, a zero might happen to be the last array element because integers and floating-point values can be zero.)

You can define an array from any of C's data types. In other words, you can define an array of `int`s, `float`s, `double`s, `long int`s, `unsigned char`s, and any of the other primary data types you learned about in Chapter 4, "Data Differences." You cannot define an array of strings because there is no such thing as a string data type. Before you begin to wonder how you'll do without all those string arrays you've worked with in QBasic, don't worry. With just a little effort that you'll read about in Chapter 21, "Pointers Are New to You," you'll be able to *act* as if C supports string arrays.

In this chapter, you will learn about the following topics:

- The differences between C arrays and QBasic arrays
- How to define arrays
- How arrays are stored in memory
- How C uses row order to allocate arrays

This chapter covers only single-dimension arrays. Multidimensional arrays (often called *tables* or *matrices*) are discussed in Chapter 20, "Table Handling."

An Introduction to C Arrays

All C arrays begin at subscript `0`*.*

All arrays in C begin with a zero subscript. Therefore, whether you define a character array or a double floating-point array (using the `double` data type), the arrays will always begin at a zero subscript, and you will not be able to change that starting subscript.

All array elements must be the same data type. You cannot define an array that contains both `int`s and `long int`s. (You'll learn how to get around this rule, a bit, when you master structures in Chapter 22, "Structure Records.") All array elements, from the first to the last, are laid out sequentially in memory. That is, the first array element (subscript `0`) will *always* appear right before the second array element, and so on. Knowing about this consistent array ordering is important when you begin to work with pointer variables starting in Chapter 21.

The size of each array element differs between array data types. For example, a character array might consist of a single byte of memory for each element (each character) in the array. However, an array of `float` values might consume two or four bytes per element. The size of each element is not fixed by the ANSI C standard. Therefore, you can apply the `sizeof()` operator to an array element if you want to calculate how much memory an array consumes.

Even though arrays of different data types consume different amounts of memory for each element, all arrays are stored contiguously and sequentially, from low to high subscript. Figure 19.1 shows three different types of arrays, a `char`, an `int`, and a `float` array. Although each element in the arrays consumes a different amount of memory, you'll see that each follows these rules for C arrays:

- The arrays begin at subscript `0`.
- The arrays are stored contiguously.
- There is only one data type per array.

Array of chars
[0] A
[1] B
[2] C

Array of ints
[0] 10
[1] 13
[2] 43
[3] 78
[4] 0
[5] 29

Array of floats
[0] 13.4
[1] 73.166
[2] 90.002
[3] 56.453

Figure 19.1. This is how a `char`*, an* `int`*, and a* `float` *array might appear in memory.*

> **Can You Overcome the Zero Subscript?**
>
> There is no rule in C that says you must use the zero subscript for your data. Suppose that you keep track of your employee salaries, and each has an employee number somewhere between 100 and 200. It might make sense in that case to define a 201-element array (for 201 elements beginning with subscript `0` and ending with subscript `200`) and use just the last 100 elements because each subscript would match the employee's number.
>
> Nevertheless, mapping the array in this manner would end up wasting memory without a strong programming need to do so. Also, after you learn how to dynamically allocate memory in Chapter 23, "Dynamic Memory Allocation," you'll see a better way to store data. Therefore, keep in mind that you can ignore the zero-based first array element, but you cannot eliminate it from being there as you can in QBasic with the `OPTION BASE` and advanced `DIM` statement options.

Defining Arrays

As with character arrays, you define arrays of any data type by putting brackets after the array name when you define the array. The brackets and subscript tell C that a variable definition is an array definition rather than a non-array variable. The following statement tells C to reserve a single integer:

```
int i;
```

However, this statement tells C to reserve an array of 14 integers in an array named `i`:

```
int i[14];
```

An array cannot have the same name as another variable in the same block of code. The preceding two statements could never appear within the same function such as `main()`.

After `i`'s definition, C will reserve enough memory for 14 integers in an array called `i`. The elements will range from `i[0]` to `i[13]`. It's important to note that in QBasic, the following array definition reserves *15* elements, from subscript `0` to `14`:

```
DIM I(14)
```

However, a C array definition does not tell C the highest subscript number in the array as done in QBasic's `DIM` statement. Rather, C's array definition tells C the total number of elements that you want reserved for the array.

If the statement `OPTION BASE 1` appears before a QBasic array definition, the first subscript will be `1`. However, QBasic defaults to a zero-based subscript unless you override the starting subscript. It's even possible in QBasic to define *negative* subscripts like this:

```
DIM arrayNeg(-50 TO 65)
```

But such fancy (and often confusing) *designer* subscript ranges aren't currently supported in C and probably never will be.

The following lines define four QBasic arrays of four different data types:

```
DIM i(10) AS INTEGER
DIM l(44) AS LONG
DIM s(100) AS SINGLE
DIM d(200) AS DOUBLE
```

If you want, you can define arrays using the data-type suffix characters like this:

```
DIM i%(10)
DIM l&(44)
DIM s!(100)
DIM d#(200)
```

> Most advanced QBasic programmers use the data-type names rather than the suffix characters. The suffix characters remain in QBasic primarily to maintain compatibility with older versions of BASIC. The data-type names provide better documentation and more closely match the methods used by other programming languages such as C.

The following four lines define four arrays in C (remember that C's `float` and `double` correspond to QBasic's `SINGLE` and `DOUBLE` data types respectively):

```
int i[10];
long l[44];
float s[100];
double d[200];
```

It's worth pointing out again that the C code *almost* but not quite matches that of the preceding QBasic examples because the number in C's array brackets indicates the total number of elements, not the highest subscript. The `long` array named `l` contains exactly 44 elements, subscripted from `0` to `43`. The QBasic's `l` array had 45 elements, subscripted from `0` to `44`. The following rule holds:

> *In QBasic, the subscript number used for defining arrays indicates the highest possible array subscript number. In C, the subscript number used for defining arrays indicates the total number of elements in the array, and the subscript always begins at* `0`.

> You must control your own array subscripts and ensure that you never reference an out-of-bounds array element. If you define an array of 200 floating-point values and then attempt to assign data to the 500th element like
>
> ```
> flArray[499] = 394.54;    /* Oops! */
> ```
>
> C sticks `394.54` in memory exactly 499 floating-point locations from the start of `flArray[0]`. In doing so, C might overwrite a part of your program, other variables,
>
> *continues*

continued

or even part of your operating system's area. QBasic always issues an error if you reference an out-of-bounds element because QBasic always watches your code references during program execution. As long as you maintain array integrity and make sure that you don't reference an out-of-bounds element, you'll reap C's efficiency and won't have the compiler slowing you down by watching your every move.

Using the `#define` preprocessor directive for array sizes helps ensure that you stay within array boundaries. For example, after you define an array size like

```
#define NUMEMPS 200
```

you can then define an array that holds employee salaries like this:

```
float empSalaries[NUMEMPS];  /* Define 200 float values */
```

If you want to loop through the array, use the defined constant `NUMEMPS` rather than `200` like this:

```
for (ct=0; ct<NUMEMPS; ct++)    /* Rest of loop follows */
```

Using `NUMEMPS` makes it less likely that you'll go out of bounds when referencing the array. You'll also have the advantage that you can change the size of the array by changing only the `#define`. If you placed `200` everyplace you defined or referenced the entire array, you would have to change each occurrence of the `200` everyplace it appeared in the program.

Initial Array Values

There are basically three ways to initialize arrays with data:

- Initialize the arrays when you define them.
- Initialize character arrays with strings using the string functions you learned about in Chapter 17, "String Functions."
- Initialize any type of array one element at a time during program execution.

When you first define arrays, you can assign them values. You have done this with character arrays. The following statement both defines a character array named companyName and initializes the array with a string value:

```
char companyName[12] = "EIB Network";
```

If you omitted the 12 from within the brackets, C would count the number of letters in the string, including the null zero, and reserve 12 characters for you.

Never define an array with blank subscripts unless you also, at the same time, initialize the array. For example, the following statement will cause all sorts of problems later in your program:

```
char companyName[];    /* Don't do this! */
```

C assumes that there are *no* values to be held in companyName, and therefore C reserves *no* storage for the array. If you later assign any value to the array, even to the first subscript in the array, you'll overwrite something else in memory. Therefore, if you aren't initializing an array at the same time you define it, always specify the number of elements you want C to reserve, like this:

```
char companyName[12];  /* Later, you can fill this array */
```

Strings are the only kind of constants you can assign, as a group, to arrays using the quotation marks. All other data types require enclosing braces around the data. For example, you could assign the same string to the companyName array one character at a time using braces like this:

```
char companyName[10] = {'E', 'I', 'B', '.', ',', 'I',
                        'n', 'c', '.', '\0'};
```

Single quotation marks appear around the individual letters because each letter is a character and not a string.

Many times, you'll initialize one element at a time.

Obviously, using the consolidated double quotation marks is easier to code and less error prone than putting the individual characters in braces. However, arrays holding individual characters (as opposed to strings), ints, longs, and all the other data types require braces. For example, if you want to initialize an integer array at the same time you define it, you can do so like this:

```
int counts[8] = {9, 4, 6, 1, 3, 7, 9, 7};
```

As with character arrays, if you omit the number inside the brackets, C counts the items inside the braces. There are eight integer values being assigned to the `counts` array, so C would assume `8` as the subscript if you omitted the `8`.

> If you will ever need to initialize the array with additional values later in the program, you'll have to specify a high subscript. For example, the following statement reserves 100 elements for a floating-point array, even though only the first 4 elements are initialized:
>
> ```
> float amounts[100] = {4356.86, 3212.21, 1220.68, 5333.07};
> ```
>
> If you omitted the `100`, C would have reserved only four elements for `amounts`. If you then assigned values to subscripts higher than the fourth one, you would overwrite other areas of memory.

It's true that you will not always know the contents of arrays at the time you define them. Actually, there will be very few times in real-world programming when you know the contents of an array in advance. Usually, your user will enter values into the program's arrays or you'll compute array values or you'll read array values from disk. Nevertheless, there are certainly times when you'll need to initialize arrays when you define them. An array might hold previous sales data, the days in each month, or historical temperature readings. Depending on the application, you might want to assign these values directly to their arrays inside the program.

You can't initialize arrays during their definition in QBasic.

Initializing arrays at their definition time in C is a new feature for you. QBasic requires that you first define arrays, with `DIM`, and then in the program assign values to the arrays. For example, if you want to put the number of days in each month into a month array in C, you can do so when you define the array like this:

```
int monthDays[12] = {31, 28, 31, 30, 31, 30,
                     31, 31, 30, 31, 30, 31};
```

(To make this easy, ignore leap years.) In QBasic, you would have to assign each value like this:

```
DIM monthDays(12) AS INTEGER
monthDays(1) = 31
monthDays(2) = 28
```

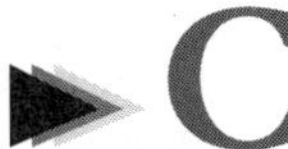

```
monthDays(3) = 31
monthDays(4) = 30
monthDays(5) = 31
monthDays(6) = 30
monthDays(7) = 31
monthDays(8) = 31
monthDays(9) = 30
monthDays(10) = 31
monthDays(11) = 30
monthDays(12) = 31
```

Of course, you could also use READ-DATA statements like this:

```
DIM monthDays(12) AS INTEGER
FOR i = 1 TO 12
  READ monthDays(i)
NEXT i
DATA 31, 28, 31, 30, 31, 30, 31, 31, 30, 31, 30, 31
```

The bottom line is that initializing arrays inside the program is often easier in C because you can directly assign the arrays values when you define the arrays.

> You can directly assign arrays *only* at the time that you define them. The assignment statement can never appear to the right of an array name except during array definition. For example, C would never allow the following code:
>
> ```
> int monthDays[12];
> monthDays = {31, 28, 31, 30, 31, 30, 31, 31, 30, 31, 30, 31};
> ```
>
> After you've defined an array, you are required to initialize the array one element at a time, just as you must do in QBasic. The next section discusses initializing arrays during the program's execution.

Initializing Arrays During Execution

As mentioned in the preceding section, you'll initialize most arrays within your program. You'll make calculations, read user data, and read disk data to come up with the data your arrays need. There is really nothing new here because in QBasic, you must initialize data inside the program instead of assigning arrays values directly during array definition.

The program in Listing 19.1 shows a QBasic program that initializes an integer array with the even numbers from `2` to `30` and then prints the array. This simple program uses the `STEP` value to reach the next even number. Listing 19.2 shows a C version of the program so that you can see the similarities.

Listing 19.1. A QBasic program that stores and prints even numbers.

```
1:  ' Filename: EVEN.BAS
2:  ' Stores and prints even numbers
3:  DIM evens(15) AS INTEGER
4:  subsc = 1   ' Initial subscript
5:  FOR en = 2 TO 30 STEP 2
6:    evens(subsc) = en
7:    subsc = subsc + 1
8:  NEXT en
9:  PRINT "The even numbers:"
10: FOR subsc = 1 TO 15
11:   PRINT evens(subsc)
12: NEXT subsc
13: END
```

The subscript had to move from `1` to `15`, so the `FOR` loop couldn't control the subscript in line 5. The `FOR` loop's job was to step through the even numbers being assigned to the array.

> An array isn't really needed to hold the even numbers before printing them, but this is a simple program with which to start.

Listing 19.2. A C program that stores and prints even numbers.

```
/* Filename: EVEN.C
   Stores and prints even numbers */
#include <stdio.h>
main()
{
```

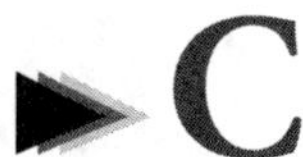

```
6:    int subsc = 0, en;
7:    int evens[15];
8:    for (en=2; en<=30; en+=2)
9:      { evens[subsc++] = en; }
10:   printf("The even numbers:\n");
11:   for (subsc=0; subsc<15; subsc++)
12:     { printf("%d\n", evens[subsc]); }
13:   return 0;
14: }
```

Although Listing 19.2 is one line longer than Listing 19.1, Listing 19.2 is much more efficient because of the way the program increments the `en` variable in line 8 and especially in the way line 9 both assigns `en` to the next array element *and* increments the subscript variable, `subsc`, with a postfix increment.

Here is the output from Listings 19.1 and 19.2:

```
The even numbers:
 2
 4
 6
 8
 10
 12
 14
 16
 18
 20
 22
 24
 26
 28
 30
```

Listings 19.3 and 19.4 further show array manipulation in QBasic and C by initializing integer arrays with random values from 1 to 100, sorting the array, and printing the results. The programs use the *Shell sort,* developed by Donald L. Shell in 1959, which uses three nested loops to sort the array of values. Although the specifics of the sorting algorithm aren't described here, the Shell sort uses a fairly quick and efficient sort algorithm. Despite the efficiency of the sort routine, you'll notice a pause while the QBasic program sorts the 50 numbers, whereas there will be no noticeable pause during the C program.

Listing 19.3. A QBasic program that randomly initializes and sorts an array.

```
' Filename: SORT.BAS
' Sorts an array of 50 random numbers
CONST TOTAL = 50
DIM nums(TOTAL) AS INTEGER
' Seed the random-number generator
RANDOMIZE TIMER
' Fill array with random numbers from 1 to 100
FOR i = 1 TO TOTAL
  nums(i) = INT(RND * 100) + 1
NEXT i
' Print the unsorted array
PRINT "The unsorted numbers:"
FOR i = 1 TO TOTAL
  PRINT nums(i),
NEXT i
PRINT
' Sort the array using the Shell sort
i = TOTAL
DO WHILE (i > 1)
  i = i \ 2
  DO
     ' Scan array until there are no more swaps
     isSwapped = 1  ' Set to true
     FOR j = 1 TO (TOTAL - i)
       n = j + i
       IF nums(j) > nums(n) THEN
         SWAP nums(j), nums(n)
         isSwapped = 0  ' Set to false
       END IF
     NEXT j
  LOOP UNTIL isSwapped
LOOP
' Print the sorted numbers
PRINT "The sorted numbers:"
FOR i = 1 TO TOTAL
  PRINT nums(i),
NEXT i
END
```

Listing 19.4. A C program that randomly initializes and sorts an array.

```
/* Filename: SORT.C
   Sorts an array of 50 random numbers */
#include <stdio.h>
#include <stdlib.h>
#include <time.h>
#define TOTAL 50
main()
{
  int nums[TOTAL];
  int i, j, n, temp, isSwapped;
  time_t t;
  srand((unsigned)time(&t));  /* Seed the random-number generator */
  /* Fill array with random numbers from 1 to 100 */
  for (i=0; i<TOTAL; i++)
  { nums[i] = rand() % 100 + 1; }
  /* Print the unsorted array */
  printf("The unsorted numbers:\n");
  for (i=0; i<TOTAL; i++)
  { printf("%3d\t\t", nums[i]); }
  /* Sort the array using the Shell-sort */
  i = TOTAL+1;
  while (i > 1)
  { i = i % 2;
    do
    { /* Scan array until there are no more swaps */
      isSwapped = 1;  /* Set to true */
      for (j=0; j<(TOTAL-i); j++)
        { n = j + i;
          if (nums[j] > nums[n])
            { temp = nums[j];   /* Swap the values */
              nums[j] = nums[n];
              nums[n] = temp;
              isSwapped = 0;     /* Set to false */
            }
        }
    } while (!isSwapped);
  }
  /* Print the sorted numbers */
  printf("\nThe sorted numbers:\n");
  for (i=0; i<TOTAL; i++)
  { printf("%3d\t\t", nums[i]); }
  return 0;
}
```

Although Listing 19.4 is written in C, you can see that there is very little difference between the programs. There is no `SWAP` command in C, so you'll have to use an intermediate variable to swap two values as done in lines 30–32. Also, having the zero-based C arrays means that you have to print using zero as the first subscript as done on line 40.

Here is the output from Listings 19.3 and 19.4 (your output will differ due to the randomness of the programs):

```
The unsorted numbers:
 21          27          74          79          92
 65          25          55          5           25
 77          22          57          40          40
 36          30          1           46          81
 29          21          60          43          57
 25          14          9           6           64
 62          95          82          53          65
 100         48          35          99          79
 94          73          85          47          33
 58          52          3           19          55

The sorted numbers:
 1           3           5           6           9
 14          19          21          21          22
 25          25          25          27          29
 30          33          35          36          40
 40          43          46          47          48
 52          53          55          55          57
 57          58          60          62          64
 65          65          73          74          77
 79          79          81          82          85
 92          94          95          99          100
```

Part VII of this book, "Using Disk Files," explains how to read from and write arrays to the disk.

Summary

This chapter gave you some insight into how C treats arrays differently from QBasic. Much of what you already know about arrays from QBasic applies to C. However, you must always keep the following differences in mind:

- All C arrays begin with a zero-based subscript.
- You cannot define string arrays. (You'll learn a way to get around this rule in Chapter 21, "Pointers Are New to You.")
- You can initialize C arrays at the same time that you define them, whereas you cannot do so in QBasic.

If you need to initialize arrays within a program, you must do so during program execution. That is, you can never assign an array values using the assignment operator except when you define the array initially. Of course, you can assign values to individual elements within the array.

The next chapter extends the coverage of arrays by teaching you how C handles multidimensional arrays. To round out your knowledge of arrays, you'll then master pointers in Chapter 21. Although there are no pointers in QBasic, you'll see that pointers and arrays (both single- and multidimensional arrays) share commonalities that you cannot ignore when writing C programs.

20

Table Handling

The preceding chapter compared single-dimensional arrays in QBasic and C. This chapter explains multidimensional arrays. Multidimensional arrays have more than one subscript and are sometimes called *tables* or *matrices.*

Multidimensional arrays are often called *tables* because of the two- and three-dimensional feel that these arrays take on. In multidimensional arrays, the values take on less of a linear format but instead "square up" in the way they are laid out in the array.

All table arrays require more than one subscript. The multiple subscripts are supported by both QBasic and C. The multiple subscripts are required both when you define an array and when you access an element from the array. As with single-dimensional arrays, you can create tables of `char`s, `int`s, `float`s, and all the other built-in C data types. (You'll learn how to create arrays of your own user-defined data types in Chapter 22, "Structure Records.")

In this chapter, you will learn about the following topics:

- Defining multidimensional arrays
- The "row order" nature of multidimensional arrays
- Initializing multidimensional arrays at definition time
- Initializing multidimensional arrays during program execution

Both QBasic and C support multidimensional arrays of more than two dimensions. However, the complexity of the data gets severe when you work with arrays greater than two or three dimensions. It gets very difficult visualizing arrays of more than three dimensions. Therefore, this chapter sticks to arrays with a maximum of three dimensions. You'll rarely need more dimensions unless you do a lot of scientific or mathematical data analysis.

Defining Multidimensional Arrays

Multidimensional arrays require more than one subscript.

You'll always define multidimensional arrays using at least two sets of subscripts. C's method of specifying multidimensional arrays differs slightly from that of QBasic. In QBasic, if you want to dimension a table, you can do so like this:

```
DIM table(5, 3)
```

Because of the starting zero-based subscript, `table` contains six rows and four columns. If you want the table to be a data type other than the default of single-precision, you can add the data type like this:

```
DIM table(5, 3) AS INTEGER
```

As with single-dimension arrays, both of the dimensions begin with a zero-based subscript unless you override the starting subscript's default with an `OPTION BASE` command. Also, as with single-dimension arrays, the two subscripts indicate the *highest* subscripts for each dimension, not the total number of elements. Figure 20.1 shows the table that is reserved by the preceding `DIM` statement.

Figure 20.1 shows how each element's subscript set is numbered, from `(0,0)` to `(5,3)`. Even though each dimension's beginning subscript is zero, most QBasic programmers begin storing and accessing tables with the subscript `1`.

C requires that you enclose each subscript in brackets, both when you define a multidimensional array and when you access an element from within a multidimensional array. Here is how you would define the `table` multidimensional array in C:

```
int table[6][4];
```

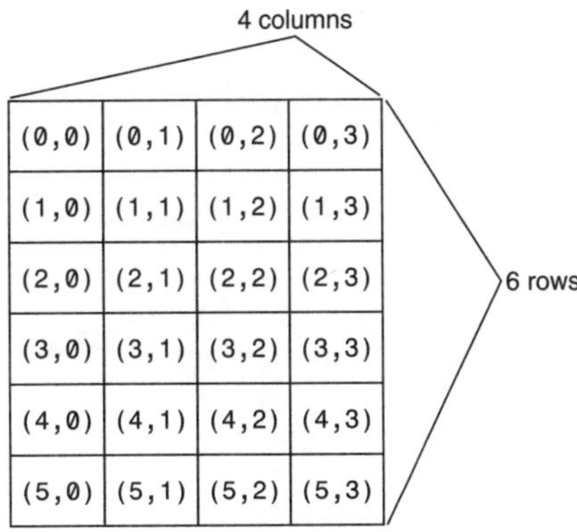

Figure 20.1. After dimensioning `table`.

Enclose each subscript in brackets.

The first difference you'll notice between the two languages is that in C, each subscript is enclosed in brackets, but with the QBasic definition, both subscripts are enclosed in a single set of parentheses. QBasic programmers often have to break the habit of defining a multidimensional array like this:

```
int table[6, 4];    /* Invalid! */
```

The second difference you'll find is that, like single-dimensional arrays, C multidimensional array definitions describe the number of elements in each dimension, not the highest subscript in each dimension. Therefore, to reserve 6 rows and 4 columns, QBasic uses the subscripts `(5, 3)`, but C uses `[6][4]`.

You can define multidimensional arrays of any data type. Here are some tables defined in QBasic:

```
DIM a(10, 10)     ' Defaults to single-precision
DIM b(10, 10) AS SINGLE
DIM c(4, 3, 8) AS DOUBLE
DIM d(2, 2) AS INTEGER
```

Here are the equivalent C table definitions:

```
single a[11][11];
single b[11][11];
double c[5][4][9];
int d[3][3];
```

Notice that each of the three dimensions in the array named is enclosed in brackets.

Arrays of Arrays

In reality, there is no such thing as a multidimensional array in C! Actually, a two-dimensional C table is just an array of arrays, whereas a two-dimensional QBasic table is treated by QBasic as if it were actually a table in memory. Rarely will you care about the C difference, but you should be aware of it.

You'll initialize and access values in a C table, using both subscripts, just as you do in QBasic. When you learn about pointers in the next chapter (haven't you noticed that this book has dropped a lot of hints about pointers lately? It's difficult to separate arrays from pointers in C, as you'll soon learn), you'll gain a little more insight into how C's table storage is accomplished. Meanwhile, keep in the back of your mind that C treats the storage of the table definition

```
char letters[5][8];
```

as an array within an array, as shown in Figure 20.2. You'll learn more about how C accomplishes this array-within-array storage in the next chapter.

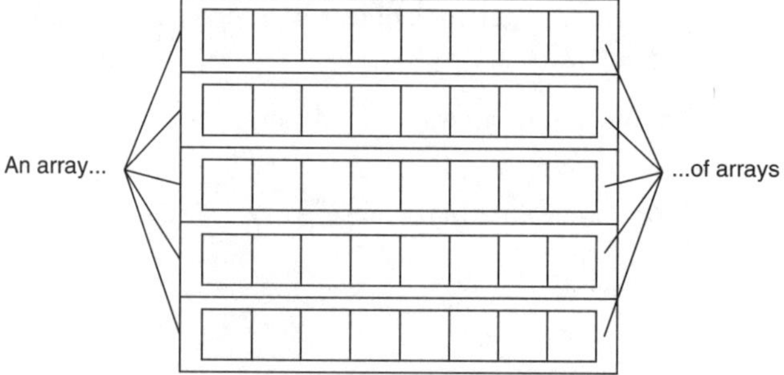

Figure 20.2. Tables are really just arrays in arrays.

Storage by Rows

C stores multidimensional arrays in *row order.* The term *row order* means that one complete row of an array is stored in memory before the next row is stored. The row order storage of arrays becomes critical when you're initializing multidimensional arrays with data.

Multidimensional arrays are stored by rows, called row order.

As with single-dimensional arrays, you can initialize multidimensional arrays in two places:

- When you define the multidimensional array
- During the program's execution an element at a time

To initialize a table at the time you define the table, use an assignment statement and enclose the data within braces. Each set of braces contains a different row of data. For example, the statement

```
int values[4][3] = {{10, 20, 30}, {40, 50, 60},
                    {15, 25, 35}, {45, 55, 65}};
```

stores four rows with three elements each. The first set of braces fills the first row (the row with the `0` subscript) with the values `10`, `20`, and `30`. The second row gets `40`, `50`, and `60`, and so on until the last row gets `45`, `55`, and `65`.

The definition `int values[4][3]` will always define 12 elements, and the *row order* description of C's multidimensional arrays lets you know that the first subscript means rows. The entire first row will fill before the second row gets any data. C doesn't even require that you use the nested braces. In other words, the following definition of `values` is equivalent in every way to the preceding definition:

```
int values[4][3] = {10, 20, 30, 40, 50, 60, 15, 25, 35, 45, 55, 65};
```

Even though the data is listed sequentially, C knows to fit the data into row order, so the table fills as shown in Figure 20.3.

Now you know how C stores tables in memory. Your computer's memory is little more than a huge single-dimensional array. Somehow, C must map a rectangular table to sequential memory. C stores tables by rows. That is, the entire first row appears in memory before the next row.

values

10	20	30
40	50	60
15	25	35
45	55	65

Figure 20.3. Tables are filled by rows.

When you increase the number of dimensions to three, the rightmost dimension always refers to the columns, and the next dimension (from the left) refers to the rows. The leftmost dimension refers to the *slice* or *depth* of the three-dimensional set of data being defined. For example, the statement

```
char initials[2][3][4] = {'A', 'B', 'C', 'D', 'E', 'F',
                          'G', 'H', 'I', 'J', 'K', 'L',
                          'M', 'N', 'O', 'P', 'Q', 'R',
                          'S', 'T', 'U', 'V', 'W', 'X'};
```

creates the cubelike table shown in Figure 20.4. Notice that the first row (subscripted by `0`) in the first depth slice (subscripted by `0`) fills with the letters before the subsequent rows fill with letters.

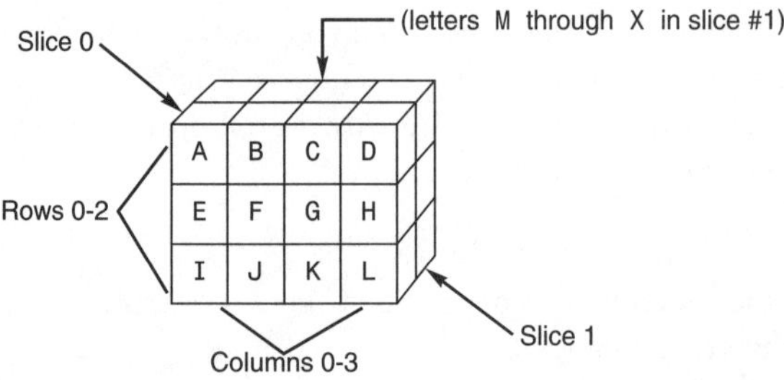

Figure 20.4. A three-dimensional table.

> As with QBasic and virtually every other programming language, many C programmers use nested `for` loops to initialize or work with multidimensional arrays. A few examples that follow show how nested `for` loops improve multidimensional array processing.

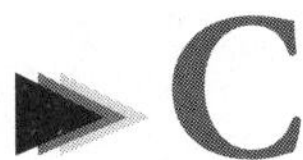

A two-dimensional character array is not the best way to simulate an array of strings in C. A two-dimensional character array is just that: a row-and-column organization of individual characters. It takes way too much time to add and check for a string-terminating character if you treat such tables as arrays of strings. Chapter 21, "Pointers Are New to You," shows you a much better way to represent arrays of strings through the use of pointers. For now, stick to multidimensional arrays made from the primary data types such as `char`, `int`, and `float`, and hold off working with strings in arrays until the next chapter.

Working with Multidimensional Arrays

This section is easy. Now that you've seen how to define and initialize multidimensional arrays, there is really nothing else about C's multidimensional array manipulation that differs from QBasic's. As mentioned in the preceding section, nested `for` loops often streamline array manipulation. This section will present a few programs, in QBasic and then in C, so that you can get used to working with the C-like syntax of enclosing all array subscripts in their own brackets.

Listing 20.1 shows a QBasic program that simply initializes a multidimensional array of weather temperatures and prints them on-screen. The temperatures are stored in a two-dimensional table. The four rows represent four weeks in the month of February, and the seven columns represent the days in each week. Listing 20.2 shows the C equivalent program.

Listing 20.1. A QBasic program that stores and prints February's temperatures.

```
' Filename: TEMP.BAS
' Store and print temperature readings
DIM temps(3, 6)
' This program will use the two zero subscripts
' to more closely resemble the C code.
FOR weeks = 0 TO 3
```

continues

Listing 20.1. continued

```
  FOR days = 0 TO 6
    READ temps(weeks, days)
  NEXT days
NEXT weeks
DATA 76, 78, 75, 68, 67, 69, 71
DATA 73, 69, 70, 70, 73, 74, 76
DATA 75, 76, 73, 76, 77, 78, 79
DATA 80, 81, 80, 79, 81, 82, 81
' Print the temperatures
PRINT "Here are the temperatures:"
FOR weeks = 0 TO 3
  FOR days = 0 TO 6
    PRINT temps(weeks, days); "    ";
  NEXT days
  PRINT    ' Move cursor to beginning of line
NEXT weeks
END
```

Here is the output from Listing 20.1. (Listing 20.2's output is the same.)

```
Here are the temperatures:
 76      78      75      68      67      69      71
 73      69      70      70      73      74      76
 75      76      73      76      77      78      79
 80      81      80      79      81      82      81
```

Listing 20.2. A C program that stores and prints February's temperatures.

```
/* Filename: TEMP.C
   Store and print temperature readings */
#include <stdio.h>
main()
{
  int weeks, days;    /* For the subscripts */
  int temps[4][7] = {{76, 78, 75, 68, 67, 69, 71},
                     {73, 69, 70, 70, 73, 74, 76},
                     {75, 76, 73, 76, 77, 78, 79},
                     {80, 81, 80, 79, 81, 82, 81}};
  /* Print the temperatures */
  printf("Here are the temperatures:\n");
  for (weeks=0; weeks<4; weeks++)
```

```
14:     { for(days=0; days<7; days++)
15:         { printf("%3d    ", temps[weeks][days]); }
16:       printf("\n");    /* Move cursor to beginning of line */
17:     }
18:   return 0;
19: }
```

The C program is shorter than the QBasic version because you can define and initialize the `temps` array in one step (lines 7–10), whereas you must initialize the array separately in QBasic (Listing 20.1's lines 6–10).

Print your tables with ample titles.

Printing a lot of data without titles is like driving without road signs. Your user is left not really knowing where the numbers came from. When printing tables of data, be sure to label the output well so that your user doesn't have to guess at the meaning of the output. Even if the user is expecting to see four weeks of temperature readings, adding a few titles will make the table much easier to understand. Listings 20.3 and 20.4 perform the same jobs as the preceding two listings, but the data contains titles to help explain the numbers.

Listing 20.3. QBasic printing February's temperatures with titles.

```
' Filename: TEMPTITL.BAS
' Store and print temperature readings with titles
DIM temps(3, 6)
' This program will use the two zero subscripts
' to more closely resemble the C code.
FOR weeks = 0 TO 3
  FOR days = 0 TO 6
    READ temps(weeks, days)
  NEXT days
NEXT weeks
DATA 76, 78, 75, 68, 67, 69, 71
DATA 73, 69, 70, 70, 73, 74, 76
DATA 75, 76, 73, 76, 77, 78, 79
DATA 80, 81, 80, 79, 81, 82, 81
' Print the temperatures
PRINT "Here are the temperatures:"
' Print the column titles
PRINT TAB(7); "Day 1  Day 2  Day 3  Day 4  Day 5  Day 6  Day 7"
FOR weeks = 0 TO 3
```

continues

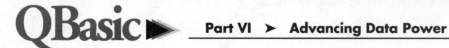

Listing 20.3. continued

```
  PRINT USING "&#"; "Week #"; (weeks + 1);   ' Row title
  FOR days = 0 TO 6
    PRINT temps(weeks, days); "   ";
  NEXT days
  PRINT   ' Move cursor to beginning of line
NEXT weeks
END
```

Listing 20.4. C printing February's temperatures with titles.

```
/* Filename: TEMPTITL.C
   Store and print temperature readings with titles */
#include <stdio.h>
main()
{
  int weeks, days;   /* For the subscripts */
  int temps[4][7] = {{76, 78, 75, 68, 67, 69, 71},
                     {73, 69, 70, 70, 73, 74, 76},
                     {75, 76, 73, 76, 77, 78, 79},
                     {80, 81, 80, 79, 81, 82, 81}};
  /* Print the temperatures */
  printf("Here are the temperatures:\n");
  /* Print the column titles */
  printf("      Day 1  Day 2  Day 3  Day 4  Day 5  Day 6  Day 7\n");
  for (weeks=0; weeks<4; weeks++)
    { printf("Week #%d", (weeks+1));
      for(days=0; days<7; days++)
        { printf("%3d    ", temps[weeks][days]); }
      printf("\n");    /* Move cursor to beginning of line */
    }
  return 0;
}
```

Here is the output from Listings 20.3 and 20.4:

```
Here are the temperatures:
      Day 1  Day 2  Day 3  Day 4  Day 5  Day 6  Day 7
Week #1 76     78     75     68     67     69     71
Week #2 73     69     70     70     73     74     76
Week #3 75     76     73     76     77     78     79
Week #4 80     81     80     79     81     82     81
```

As you can see, the data is much easier to understand in this form. If you want the temperature for the third week's second day, you can easily find it with the row and column titles.

Suppose that three cities' temperatures have to be printed. All you need to do is add depth to the temperature table by adding a third dimension. The programs in Listings 20.5 and 20.6 are identical to the preceding two programs except that two more cities are stored. After you learn how to perform I/O with disk files, you won't need to store so much data in a program (you should know this from your QBasic programming). Right now, you're just trying to get accustomed to multidimensional arrays.

Listing 20.5. QBasic printing three city temperature sets.

```
' Filename: TEMPMORE.BAS
' Store and print temperature readings for three cities
DIM temps(2, 3, 6)
' This program will use the three zero subscripts
' to more closely resemble the C code.
FOR cities = 0 TO 2
  FOR weeks = 0 TO 3
    FOR days = 0 TO 6
      READ temps(cities, weeks, days)
    NEXT days
  NEXT weeks
NEXT cities
DATA 76, 78, 75, 68, 67, 69, 71
DATA 73, 69, 70, 70, 73, 74, 76
DATA 75, 76, 73, 76, 77, 78, 79
DATA 80, 81, 80, 79, 81, 82, 81
' Second city
DATA 56, 55, 57, 55, 55, 58, 59
DATA 59, 58, 60, 61, 61, 60, 58
DATA 57, 57, 56, 58, 58, 60, 61
DATA 62, 63, 64, 63, 64, 65, 66
' Third city
DATA 44, 45, 42, 41, 39, 38, 39
DATA 39, 40, 41, 40, 40, 38, 40
DATA 41, 42, 41, 42, 41, 42, 43
DATA 44, 43, 45, 43, 44, 45, 42
' Print the temperatures
PRINT "Here are the temperatures:"
FOR cities = 0 TO 2
  PRINT USING "&#:"; "City #"; (cities + 1)
  PRINT TAB(7); "Day 1  Day 2  Day 3  Day 4  Day 5  Day 6  Day 7"
```

continues

Listing 20.5. continued

```
  FOR weeks = 0 TO 3
    PRINT USING "&#"; "Week #"; (weeks + 1);     ' Row title
    FOR days = 0 TO 6
      PRINT temps(cities, weeks, days); "    ";
    NEXT days
  PRINT   ' Move cursor to beginning of line
  NEXT weeks
PRINT   ' Move cursor to beginning of line
NEXT cities
END
```

Listing 20.6. C printing three city temperature sets.

```
/* Filename: TEMPMORE.C
   Store and print temperature readings for three cities */
#include <stdio.h>
main()
{
  int cities, weeks, days;   /* For the subscripts */
  int temps[3][4][7] = {{{76, 78, 75, 68, 67, 69, 71}, /* 1st city */
                         {73, 69, 70, 70, 73, 74, 76},
                         {75, 76, 73, 76, 77, 78, 79},
                         {80, 81, 80, 79, 81, 82, 81}},
                         {{56, 55, 57, 55, 55, 58, 59}, /* 2nd */
                          {59, 58, 60, 61, 61, 60, 58},
                          {57, 57, 56, 58, 58, 60, 61},
                          {62, 63, 64, 63, 64, 65, 66}},
                          {{44, 45, 42, 41, 39, 38, 39}, /* 3rd */
                           {39, 40, 41, 40, 40, 38, 40},
                           {41, 42, 41, 42, 41, 42, 43},
                           {44, 43, 45, 43, 44, 45, 42}}};
  /* Print the temperatures */
  printf("Here are the temperatures:\n");
  for (cities=0; cities<3; cities++)
    { printf("City #%d:\n", (cities+1));  /* Adjust zero subscript */
      /* Print the column titles */
      printf("      Day 1  Day 2  Day 3  Day 4  Day 5  Day 6  Day /
      7\n");
      for (weeks=0; weeks<4; weeks++)
        { printf("Week #%d", (weeks+1));
          for(days=0; days<7; days++)
            { printf("%3d    ", temps[cities][weeks][days]); }
```

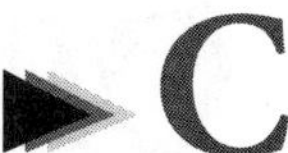

```
             printf("\n");     /* Move cursor to beginning of line */
           }
           printf("\n");     /* Move cursor to beginning of line */
         }
     return 0;
 }
```

Here is the output from both of the preceding listings:

```
Here are the temperatures:
City #1:
      Day 1  Day 2  Day 3  Day 4  Day 5  Day 6  Day 7
Week #1 76     78     75     68     67     69     71
Week #2 73     69     70     70     73     74     76
Week #3 75     76     73     76     77     78     79
Week #4 80     81     80     79     81     82     81

City #2:
      Day 1  Day 2  Day 3  Day 4  Day 5  Day 6  Day 7
Week #1 56     55     57     55     55     58     59
Week #2 59     58     60     61     61     60     58
Week #3 57     57     56     58     58     60     61
Week #4 62     63     64     63     64     65     66

City #3:
      Day 1  Day 2  Day 3  Day 4  Day 5  Day 6  Day 7
Week #1 44     45     42     41     39     38     39
Week #2 39     40     41     40     40     38     40
Week #3 41     42     41     42     41     42     43
Week #4 44     43     45     43     44     45     42
```

Summary

This chapter taught you that other than some definition and initialization differences, both C and QBasic provide virtually identical support for multidimensional arrays. The primary thing that you must remember is to enclose all subscripts in their own brackets when referencing elements from multidimensional arrays.

The full example programs at the end of the chapter showed you how to manipulate multidimensional arrays using nested loops. Be sure to label all your output when you print table data so that your program's user better understands the output.

It's time now for you to learn the most important language distinction between QBasic and C. The next chapter teaches you about C's pointer variables. There are no pointer variables in QBasic, so almost all of the next chapter will be new material that you should master before tackling the rest of the C language. All veteran C programmers realize that after pointers are mastered, the sky's the limit to your programming abilities. When you move into object-oriented programming with C++ and programming for environments such as Microsoft Windows, you have to understand pointers to write such high-level code.

21

Pointers Are New to You

This chapter takes the first major turn away from QBasic. There are no QBasic equivalent data types to pointers. A *pointer* is just a variable in memory that holds the address of data located elsewhere in memory. After you master pointers, you can write some truly powerful code that would otherwise be very difficult to write.

In Chapter 23, "Dynamic Memory Allocation," you'll learn the single most important use of pointers in C: *dynamically allocating* data. A fancy term such as *dynamic allocation* seems very advanced, but you'll have little trouble with it as long as you master pointers here.

Until you get to Chapter 23, one of the biggest advantages that pointers provide you is better manipulation of string data. For once, you'll actually be able to simulate string variables in C! Well, you'll *almost* be able to simulate string variables. Alas, the fact that C does not support string variable data types means that you won't have the full string variable power that QBasic provides, but you'll get close.

In this chapter, you will learn about the following topics:

- Memory addresses
- How to define pointer variables
- The address of, `&`, and dereferencing, `*`, operators
- How to use pointers to refer to data values
- How to mix array and pointer notation
- How to use pointers to define arrays of strings

A Review of Memory

Each memory location has a unique address.

As you might know, each memory location inside your computer has a unique *address.* As with postal boxes, the address differentiates one memory location from another. If your computer contains 4 megabytes of memory, your computer contains approximately 4 million addresses. Memory addresses always begin at zero. The address `0` is the first memory location's address, `1` is the next address, and so on until all memory locations are addressed. Figure 21.1 illustrates the addressing of memory locations.

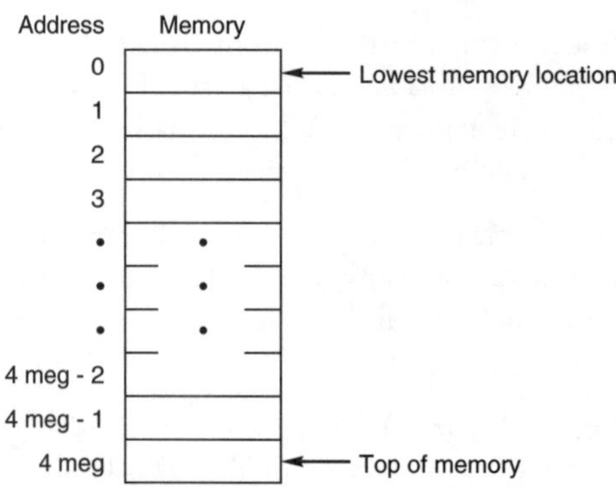

Figure 21.1. Looking at memory addresses.

When you name variables, C (and QBasic) finds an unused memory location and names that memory location. If the variable is an `int` or a `float` or one of the data types that consume more than one byte of memory, C marks as much contiguous memory as needed to hold that data type and treats the chunk of memory as a single variable named with the variable name you give. For multibyte variables, the variable is assumed to begin at the first address in the chunk of addresses reserved for that variable.

> Unused memory is any memory not being used by your operating system, your program's code, and the data you've reserved. When you define an array of 100 elements, C considers all 100 elements of that array as used and will not use any of that memory for new variables defined later in the program. If you decide to play the dangerous game of accessing array elements higher than the number you defined, you'll possibly, and probably, overwrite memory reserved for other variables. C will protect (by flagging the memory as reserved) only as many array elements as you define.

It's important to realize that variable names are nothing more than aliases for memory addresses. Programming language designers don't really have to let you use variable names. If you want to go back to the early machine-language programming days in the 1950s, you could keep track of all addresses where your data begins and refer to addresses such as `837845` and `605096` rather than names such as `myName` and `salary`. You'll have to admit, though, that variable names are much easier to remember than specific addresses (if you follow good naming habits). And using variable names as aliases means that you can finish your programs faster than you otherwise could and can spend more free time playing the latest computer games.

In a way, using pointers means going back to using memory addresses. However, instead of referring to specific addresses, C takes care of remembering the addresses for you. When you want to work with an address, you'll work with that address by name. Therefore, when you're using pointers, your variables can have names and so can your variable addresses. The next section will help clarify pointer names and addresses.

> Remember that pointers are nothing more than variables that hold addresses of other variables. Pointers are often called *pointer variables* because you can change the contents of a pointer variable (which changes the address stored in the pointer variable) as easily as you change the contents of any other kind of variable. You define pointer variables, name them, and give them data types, as you'll learn next.

Defining Pointers

As with any variable, you must define pointer variables before using them. Define pointer variables at the top of functions along with the other variables you define (as you've seen done throughout this book in `main()`). All the variables you've defined until now have been nonpointing variables. For instance, the following statement defines a character variable:

```
char letter;    /* No initial value assigned */
```

The following statement defines an integer variable:

```
int total = 10;
```

Somewhere in memory—you don't know exactly where—C found empty memory locations in which to store `letter` and `total`. There is no way to guess exactly what addresses `letter` and `total` appear at. As the programmer, you really don't care at what addresses C chose to store these two variables; the important thing is that C creates the variables, assigns names to them, and stores a `10` in `total` for you.

How about just guessing at the two addresses C chose to store `letter` and `total` in? Figure 21.2 shows that C stored the two variables at addresses `524500` and `524502`. Although there is no way to predict exactly where C stores the variables, assume that C chose these specific addresses for the time being to streamline the discussion of pointers that's coming up. Compilers often store variables beginning on even addresses. The PC architecture often makes it more efficient to start variables on an even address boundary rather than an odd address boundary.

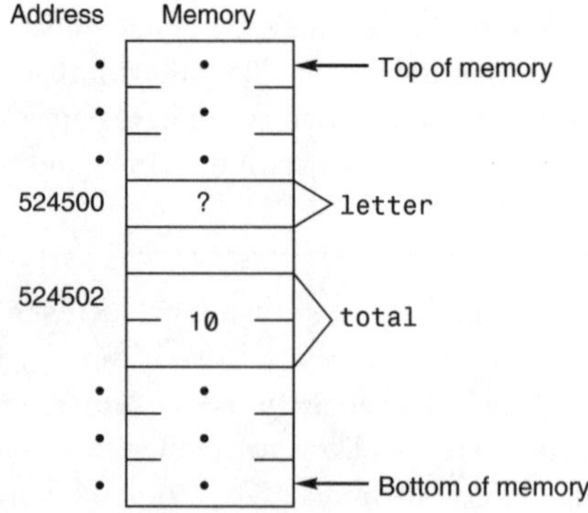

Figure 21.2. Assuming that we know where C stored `letter` *and* `total`*.*

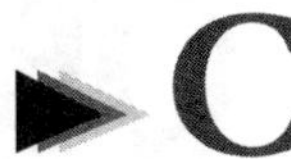

Notice that `total` takes two memory locations and `letter` takes only one. `int`s generally consume two bytes, but only `sizeof()` can tell you for certain how much memory a variable consumes on your particular computer using your particular compiler.

Put your knowledge of regular variable definitions on hold for just a moment. You'll come back to `letter` and `total` shortly.

You'll define pointer variables almost the same way as regular nonpointer variables. You'll have to define the pointers and make up names for the pointer variables. A pointer variable name cannot be the same name as any other variable, pointer or otherwise, or function, or command. (When you learn how C supports *global* and *local* variables in Chapter 26, you'll see that more than one variable in the same program can have the same name, although giving the same names to two variables is not recommended for obvious reasons.)

The dereference operator is `*`.

The `*` operator performs double duty in C. As you know, `*` means multiplication. `*` also means *pointer dereferencing*. C knows which action to perform, multiplication or dereferencing, from the context in which you use the asterisk. The dereferencing operator is used with pointers to do two things:

- Define pointer variables
- Get to data pointed to by the pointer variable

You'll use the `*` to define all pointer variables. As a matter of fact, the `*` is the only way C knows that a variable is to be a pointer and not a regular variable. The following statements define two pointer variables:

```
char * letterPtr;     /* Defines a pointer to a char */
int * totalPtr;       /* Defines a pointer to an int */
```

Without the `*`'s, `letterPtr` and `totalPtr` would be a regular character variable and integer variable. With the `*`'s, C defines the variables as pointer variables. Therefore, whenever you want to define a pointer variable, place the `*` after the data type and before the pointer variable name.

The spacing of the `*` is not critical. All three of the following definitions mean exactly the same thing:

continues

continued

```
int* totalPtr;
int * totalPtr;
int *totalPtr;
```

Use whatever spacing you prefer. The important thing to remember is that the asterisk is not part of the data type or the pointer variable's name. The asterisk simply informs the compiler that the variable is a pointer variable and not a regular, nonpointing variable.

Pointer variable names don't have to contain the letters `Ptr` even though they all will in this book. Appending `Ptr` to the name helps you spot pointer variables in your programs, so naming pointers with `...Ptr` is a good habit to form. However, you can name pointer variables anything you prefer as long as you follow C's variable-naming rules found in Chapter 6, "Numeric Variables."

Pointers have data types just as other variables do.

Notice that you define pointer variables using data types just as you use data types to define nonpointer variables. It's critical that you be as careful with pointer data types as you are with other variable data types. If a pointer is to point to a character variable, the pointer *must* be a character pointer (often called a *pointer to a* `char`). If a pointer is to point to an integer, the pointer must be an integer pointer.

A pointer variable can point *only* to data types that match the pointer's data type. A `float` pointer cannot point to an `int` or a `char`. Therefore, when defining pointer variables, you must define them knowing in advance the type of data they will eventually point to. If you need to point to a `char` later in the program, you'll have to define a pointer to a `char`.

As a review, the following C code defines five different types of pointers:

```
char * namePtr;           /* Define five pointers   */
int * agePtr;             /* that point to five     */
long int * numBooksPtr;   /* different data types. */
float * salaryPtr;
double * spaceDistancePtr;
```

The five pointers are not yet initialized. Until you assign pointer variables values (as shown next), you don't know what the pointer variables contain. As with any other kind of variable, pointers are uninitialized until you initialize them.

Initializing Pointer Variables

The preceding section showed you how to define pointer variables, but it did not show you how to initialize pointer variables. Pointer variables always hold addresses of other variables. Addresses are *all* that pointer variables hold, so after you learn how to store addresses in variables, you'll know all there is to know about initializing pointer variables.

Use the & operator to store addresses in pointers.

In the preceding section, you learned how the dereferencing operator, `*`, enables you to define pointer variables. With another operator, the *address of* operator, `&`, you can store the address of variables into pointer variables.

The *address of* operator is the perfect name for `&`. Any time you see the `&` operator used with pointers, you can think the words "address of" to figure out what's being done with the `&`. Therefore, `&numPages` means "Address of `numPages`." Throughout the rest of this chapter, you'll see how this tip greatly helps clarify the meaning of `&`.

As with the `*`, the `&` performs double duty. If you ever work with the bitwise operators (see Chapter 10), you'll use the `&` to perform bitwise AND. As with `*`, C looks at the context of how you use `&` to determine whether you want a bitwise AND performed or whether you want to take the address of data.

Earlier, you saw the variables `letter` and `total` defined like this:

```
char letter;
int total = 10;
```

To define pointer variables that will eventually point to `letter` and `total`, you can use the `*` operator like this:

```
char * letterPtr;
int * totalPtr;
```

When you assign the address of `letter` to `letterPtr` and `total` to `totalPtr`, you *link up* the data. That is, the two pointer variables will point to the regular nonpointer variables. `letter` does not have to be initialized with any specific data before you point to `letter`. The following two statements create a link between the two pointer variables and their equivalent variables:

```
letterPtr = &letter;    /* letterPtr points to letter */
totalPtr = &total;      /* totalPtr points to total */
```

After these two statements execute, you'll have the situation shown in Figure 21.3. `letterPtr` holds the address of `letter`, and `totalPtr` holds the address of `total`. The figure uses the imaginary addresses shown in an earlier figure for the two variables. It doesn't matter what the addresses of the two variables are; whatever the addresses, `letterPtr` and `totalPtr` hold those addresses when the two pointer variables are initialized.

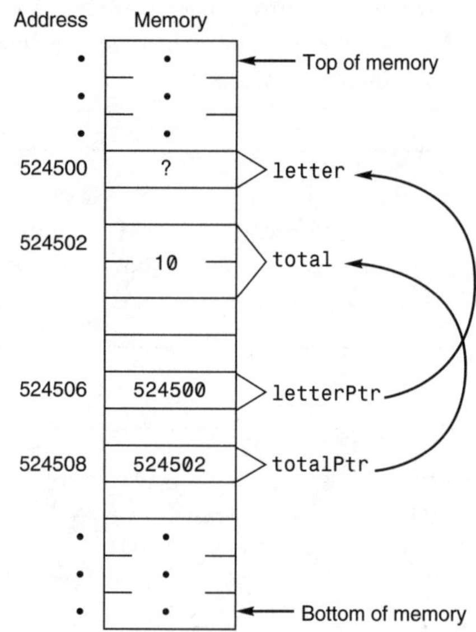

Figure 21.3. Two pointer variables hold the addresses of two variables.

Notice that to a pointer variable, an address is just data. Also, Figure 21.3 only guesses at the addresses and order of the pointer variables in memory. C can place any variable anywhere C finds free memory.

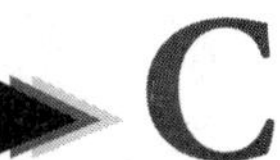

Although Figure 21.3 doesn't show it, C's pointer variables usually take four or more bytes of memory. However, the size of a pointer variable is rarely if ever critical. As with any other variable, however, you can use `sizeof()` to find the size of pointer variable storage on your specific computer and compiler if you want to know.

If you like, you can combine the definition and initialization of pointer variables into the same statements. The following code produces the same memory layout as shown in Figure 21.3:

```
char letter;
int total = 10;
char * letterPtr = &letter;
int * totalPtr = &total;
```

Using the Dereferencing Operator

The dereferencing operator, `*`, is the way in which you access data being pointed to. Therefore, given the variables defined at the end of the preceding section, if you want to store a value in `letter`, you can do so like this:

```
letter = 'P';
```

If you want to print the value of `total`, you can do so like this:

```
printf("%d", total);
```

If you want to, you can also perform these same operations using the pointer variables. The following statement assigns the character `P` to `letter`, but instead of using the variable named `letter`, this statement uses the pointer named `letterPtr`:

```
*letterPtr = 'P';
```

Remember that `letterPtr` did not change with this statement. The `*` tells C to assign the `P` to the variable being *pointed to* by `letterPtr`, rather than to `letterPtr` itself. Therefore, `letter` is assigned the `P` in the preceding statement. If you omitted the `*`, you would mess up the pointer, so this is not correct:

```
letterPtr = 'P';   /* Oops! You just overwrote the address! */
```

Therefore, when a pointer variable points to another variable, you have two references to the regular variable. You can use the pointer (via the dereferencing operator, `*`) or the variable's name to access the contents of the variable.

Here's how you can print the contents of `total` using the pointer to `total`:

```
printf("%d", *totalPtr);  /* Prints total's value */
```

Why Is This Good?

At this point, you might not think that pointers are making life any easier. After all, why define *two* accesses to the same value (through the variable name and the pointer to the variable)?

For now, try to learn how to manipulate pointers without worrying about *why* you're learning them. Right now, using pointers is *not* necessarily any easier than using the variable names themselves.

Later in this chapter, you'll see how to manipulate strings with character variables, and you'll begin to see some advantages to using pointers. More important, in Chapter 23, "Dynamic Memory Allocation," you'll learn how to define memory that cannot have variable names (this memory is called the *heap*). Using pointers is the only method available that enables you to access this memory for your data.

You can now better understand why `scanf()` places such strict syntax requirements on you. When you call `scanf()`, you must pass non-arrays by address to the `scanf()` function. The addresses let `scanf()` know where the data is that you want to fill with user input.

Don't attempt to use `&` to find the address of constants such as `72`. Use `&` just to find the address of variables.

Listing 21.1 defines and works with several pointer variables. Study the program to make sure that you know the difference between the `*` and `&` as applied to pointers. Again, because there is no QBasic equivalent to pointer variables, no comparison can be made to anything in QBasic at this time.

Listing 21.1. Using pointer variables to work with data.

```
/* Filename: POINTER.C
   Works with several kinds of pointers */
#include <stdio.h>
main()
{
  /* First define some nonpointer variables */
  char letter = 'A';
  int number;
  float amount = 12.345;
  double dAmount = 5422345.6544333;
  /* Define some pointer variables */
  char * letterPtr = &letter;
  int * numberPtr = &number;
  float * amountPtr;
  double * dAmountPtr = &dAmount;

  amountPtr = &amount;    /* Could have been done earlier */
  *numberPtr = 23;        /* Assigns 23 to variable named number */
  /* Print the data pointed to */
  printf("The value in letter is %c\n", *letterPtr);
  printf("The value in number is %d\n", *numberPtr);
  printf("The value in amount is %.3f\n", *amountPtr);
  printf("The value in dAmount is %.7lf\n", *dAmountPtr);
  /* Change the contents of the data being pointed
     to without using regular variable names */
  *letterPtr = 'X';
  *numberPtr = 57;
  *amountPtr = 10.991;
  *dAmountPtr = -0.99992;
  /* Print the new values via the pointers */
  printf("After changing the values:\n");
  printf("The value in letter is %c\n", *letterPtr);
  printf("The value in number is %d\n", *numberPtr);
  printf("The value in amount is %.3f\n", *amountPtr);
  printf("The value in dAmount is %.5lf\n", *dAmountPtr);
  return 0;
}
```

Here is the output from Listing 21.1:

```
The value in letter is A
The value in number is 23
The value in amount is 12.345
The value in dAmount is 5422345.6544333
```

```
After changing the values:
The value in letter is X
The value in number is 57
The value in amount is 10.991
The value in dAmount is -0.99992
```

Creating Arrays of Pointers

Individual pointers aren't much help when you want to point to a large amount of data. Therefore, you often need to create a bunch of pointers. The following 10 pointer definitions will be difficult to work with later in the program because of their different names:

```
int * ptr1, ptr2, ptr3, ptr4, ptr5, ptr6, ptr7, ptr8, ptr9, ptr10;
```

Although there is nothing wrong with having 10 integer pointers with 10 different names, an array of pointers is easier to manipulate because you can loop through all the array elements when you want to work with all the pointers. In C, you can define an array of pointers by using the `*` operator. The following statement defines an array of 10 integer pointer variables named `arrayPtr`:

```
int * arrayPtr[10];
```

C's variable definitions can look confusing, but if you read them from right to left, you'll have no trouble understanding them. The preceding statement creates an array of 10 elements, named `arrayPtr`, that contains pointers to integers.

After you define the array of pointers, you can refer to any of the individual pointer elements within the array. Suppose that you wanted to print the contents of each of the 10 locations (assuming that you initialized the locations so that the variables pointed to valid variables somewhere). You could print the 10 dereferenced values like this:

```
for (i=0; i<10; i++)
  { printf("%d\n", *arrayPtr[i]); }
```

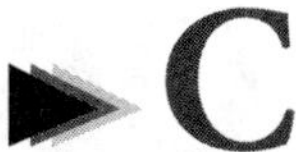

> Without the dereferencing operator, `*`, 10 addresses would print. The `*` is vital so that the data pointed to, not the pointer contents (addresses), prints. Actually, you can't accurately print an address using the `%d` format code, so if you removed the `*`, you would get values that make no sense at all. If you ever do want to print addresses, use `%p` (for *pointer*) format code. However, you must understand the way your PC addresses memory before you'll completely understand printed addresses.

In a way, the `arrayPtr` array creates a table in memory that conceptually looks like the table of memory in Figure 21.4. Each box (each pointer in the array) contains an address that points somewhere in memory.

```
arrayPtr[0]  | + |--->
arrayPtr[1]  | + |--->
arrayPtr[2]  | + |--->
arrayPtr[3]  | + |--->
arrayPtr[4]  | + |--->
arrayPtr[5]  | + |--->
arrayPtr[6]  | + |--->
arrayPtr[7]  | + |--->
arrayPtr[8]  | + |--->
arrayPtr[9]  | + |--->
```

Figure 21.4. An array of 10 pointers.

Array and Pointer Similarities

You might be surprised to learn that there is *very* little difference between arrays and pointers in C. In fact, an array name is nothing more than a special type of pointer. Consider the following character array definition (no string is stored in this character array because there is no null zero that terminates the array):

```
char letters[] = {'a', 'b', 'c', 'd', 'e'};
```

You know that `letters` is an array with five elements. The array is subscripted from `0` to `4`. If you want to print the array, you can do so like this:

```
for (i=0; i<5; i++)
{ printf("%c\n", letters[i]); }
```

All array names are pointer constants.

It turns out that the name `letters` is *just a pointer to the array's first element.* However, unlike pointer variables, the array name `letters` is a *pointer constant.* Suppose that C starts storing the first element, `letters[0]`, at the address numbered 600000. Figure 21.5 shows what the `letter` array would look like in memory given this imaginary starting address.

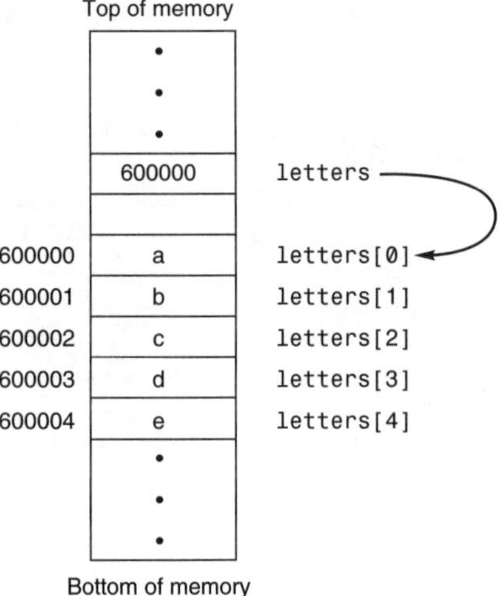

Figure 21.5. `letters` *is a pointer constant as well as an array name.*

> The array elements will not all begin on an even address boundary because all array elements are contiguous in memory with no blank space between the elements. However, the array itself will probably start on an even boundary as shown in the figure.

As you can see, an array name is just a pointer. The array name only points to the first element. However, as mentioned earlier, the array name is a pointer constant. Therefore, you can never change where an array name points. In other words, the array name `letters` will always point to the first element, `letters[0]`. The array name will never point to any other element or to any other address in memory.

Here's the bottom-line difference between an array name and a pointer variable: Array names can never appear on the left side of an equal sign. Well, that's nothing new to you! Throughout this book, you've learned that you cannot change the contents of `letters` with a direct assignment statement like this:

```
letters = {'v', 'w', 'x', 'y', 'z'}; /* Invalid! */
```

The only time you can assign an array values directly with the equal sign is when you first define the array. This special case is possible only because C fills the array before it stores the pointer to the array (the array name).

There is no assignment limitation with pointer variables, however. Pointer variables are *variables,* and the way you change variables is with the assignment operator. Therefore, if you define a character pointer like

```
char * letterPtr;
```

you then can make `letters` point to a new value like this:

```
letterPtr = &initial1;    /* Assume initial1 is a char variable */
```

Later in the program, you can assign `letterPtr` the address of a new variable like this:

```
letterPtr = &initial2;    /* Assume initial2 is a char variable */
```

You could never, however, make the array name point to another address because all array names are fixed constants. Therefore, this would not be allowed given the preceding `letters` array definition:

```
letters = &initial1;  /* Invalid! You can't change array pointers */
```

Array and Pointer Notation

Although you cannot change an array after you define it (except an element at a time), you can refer to an array using pointer notation. Therefore, given the array definition

```
char letters[] = {'a', 'b', 'c', 'd', 'e'};
```

you can print the array an element at a time using a subscript, as you're now used to, like this:

```
for (i=0; i<5; i++)
{ printf("%c", letters[i]); }
```

You can also print the array using *pointer notation* because the array name is nothing more than a pointer to characters. Therefore, the following code also prints the contents of `letters`:

```
for (i=0; i<5; i++)
{ printf("%c", *(letters + i)); }
```

Look at the `printf` a little more closely. When the loop first iterates, `i` is `0`. Therefore, the dereference prints the value at the location of `letters`, which is the first array element containing the letter `a`. The second loop iteration prints the `b` because `letters + 1` is the address of the *second* array element. Dereferencing the second array element produces the `b`. The loop continues until `i` becomes `4` in the last iteration. Assuming that `letters` begins at location `600000`, the character at `600004` prints, so the `e` appears on-screen.

The following statements hold true for the `letters` array:

> `letters` equates to `*letters`.
> `letters` equates to `letters[0]`.
> `letters+1` equates `letters[1]`.
> `letters+1` equates to `*(letters + 1)`.
> `letters+2` equates to `letters[2]`.
> `letters+2` equates to `*(letters + 2)`.

This pattern continues for all five elements of `letters`. Therefore, you can access the individual elements in the array named `letters` using regular array notation or pointer notation. If you want to store a value in `letters[2]`, you can do so like this:

```
letters[2] = 'Q';
```

You can also store the `Q` like this:

```
*(letters + 2) = 'Q';
```

If you work with pointers of data types other than `chars`, when you add one to the pointer, C actually adds *one data type location*. In other words, assume that you defined an integer array like this:

```
int nums[] = {10, 20, 30, 40, 50};
```

If you use pointer notation to access the array, the following statements hold true:

> `nums` equates to `nums[0]`.
> `nums+1` equates to `nums[1]`.
> `nums+1` equates to `*(nums + 1)`.
> `nums+2` equates to `nums[2]`.

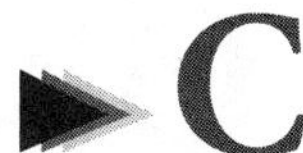

In other words, if you add `1` to the pointer value as in `*(nums + 1)`, C actually adds one integer location. If integers take two bytes on your computer, two actual bytes are added so that `*(nums + 1)` means the same thing as `nums[1]`.

C must be able to perform the proper pointer arithmetic when you manipulate pointer variables and when you reference arrays using pointer notation. C knows how many actual bytes to add by looking at the *type of pointer* being referenced. If the pointer is a `char` pointer, C adds the number of bytes (usually 1) needed to get to the next character location in memory. If the array is a `double`, C adds the number of bytes (usually 4 or 8) needed to get to the next double floating-point location. It is because you sometimes access arrays using pointer arithmetic that C always stores array elements contiguously in memory. All array elements are stored back-to-back. If they were not, if there were blank areas between array elements, you would not be able to use pointer notation to access the elements throughout the array.

The reverse is true as well. To C, a pointer is nothing more than an array name variable that can point to any address. Therefore, you can create a character pointer named `cPtr` and assign it a string of characters like this:

```
char * cPtr = "I am a string";
```

If you like, you can print an individual letter from the string, pointed to by `cPtr`, like this:

```
printf("%c", *(cPtr+2));   /* Prints the a */
```

You can also print using array subscript notation like this:

```
printf("%c", cPtr[2]);   /* Prints the a */
```

Therefore, `cPtr` is not technically an array but is a character pointer. However, you can reference arrays and pointer variables using the same interchangeable notation.

You can print the data pointed to by `cPtr` just as you print character arrays. The following `printf()` prints the contents of the string stored at `cPtr`:

```
printf("%s", cPtr);   /* Prints I am a string */
```

Although you must be careful, you can assign string constants directly to a character pointer anywhere in a program. Therefore, later in the same program that assigned `cPtr` to the string `I am a string`, you could easily make `cPtr` point to a new string using a simple assignment statement like this:

continues

continued

```
cPtr = "A new string!";
```

There is no way you could assign a character array name to a new string. You would have to use `strcpy()` or assign the new string one character at a time.

The preceding tip leads to the primary reason for learning about array and pointer similarities: pointers enable you to work with string data a little more easily than arrays. As a matter of fact, using pointers, you can easily create an array of string data whereas you really couldn't do so in C before learning about pointers. The next section explores arrays of strings.

How Multidimensional Arrays Look in Memory

The preceding chapter explained that C does not actually support multidimensional arrays and that a C multidimensional array is nothing more than an array of arrays. This all sounds a little confusing for one simple reason: It is.

However, as promised, you know enough now to see how multidimensional arrays are stored in sequential memory by C. One note of caution, however, before you see the method that C uses for multidimensional array storage: Mastering multidimensional array storage will not necessarily make you a better C programmer. All the storage of multidimensional arrays is performed by C, and you don't have to worry about the details. Therefore, this sidebar and related figure are offered just for background and completeness.

Suppose that you defined the following multidimensional array:

```
int table[3][4] = {{1, 2, 3, 4}, {5, 6, 7, 8}, {9, 10, 11, 12}};
```

C actually sets up an array that is three elements long. Each element in the array is itself an array of four elements. Figure 21.6 shows you how C actually stores this array. You'll see that the array name, `table`, is just a pointer to `table[0]`. `table[0]` is itself an array, so it in turn points to the first element in the row array. Each row in `table` is just an array pointer to the data within that row. (To save space, only a single memory location was used for each integer. As you now know, however, probably 2 or 4 bytes are used for each C integer stored in memory.)

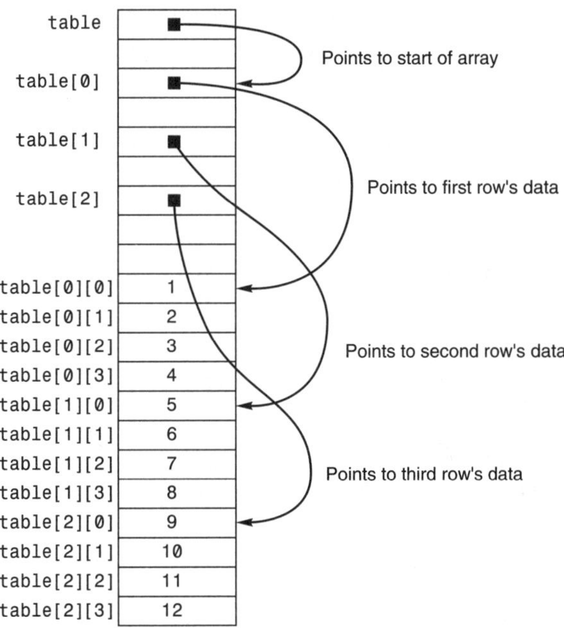

Figure 21.6. Mapping a multidimensional array to sequential memory.

Creating an Array of Strings

Now, you can finally get to something that QBasic finds easy: storing an array of strings. In this final section of the chapter, you'll see some comparisons in the way to define QBasic arrays of strings and C arrays of strings. Here's all you need to know:

> *To create an array of strings in C, create an array of character pointers and make sure that each pointer points to the first element of a null-terminated string.*

A full understanding of how C's arrays of strings work takes a while. The good news is that you'll better understand how arrays of character pointers simulate arrays of strings the more you work with C. For now, when you need an array of string data, adapt one of the following examples to your own program.

Suppose that you wanted to store the names of the months in an array. Here is how you would define an array of 12 character pointers named `months` in C:

```
char * months[12];
```

Listing 21.2 shows how you might store an array of month names in a QBasic string array. Listing 21.3 stores the month names in a C array of pointers.

Listing 21.2. Using QBasic to store and print an array of month names.

```
' Filename: MONTHS.BAS
' Store and print an array of month name strings.
DIM months(12) AS STRING
' Initialize the array
FOR i = 1 TO 12
 READ months(i)
NEXT i
DATA "January", "February", "March", "April", "May", "June", "July"
DATA "August", "September", "October", "November", "December"
' Print the array
PRINT "The months:"
FOR i = 1 TO 12
  PRINT months(i)
NEXT i
END
```

Listing 21.3. Using C to store and print an array of month names.

```
/* Filename: MONTHS.C
   Store and print an array of month names as character pointers */
#include <stdio.h>
main()
{
  int i;  /* Loop counter */
  char * months[12] = {{"January"},
                       {"February"},
                       {"March"},
                       {"April"},
                       {"May"},
                       {"June"},
                       {"July"},
```

```
14:                             {"August"},
15:                             {"September"},
16:                             {"October"},
17:                             {"November"},
18:                             {"December"}};
19:     /* Print the array */
20:     printf("The months:\n");
21:     for (i=0; i<12; i++)
22:     { printf("%s\n", months[i]); }
23:     return 0;
24: }
```

Here is the output from both listings:

```
The months:
January
February
March
April
May
June
July
August
September
October
November
December
```

Of course, you don't have to initialize the `months` array with one month name per line as done on lines 7 through 18. However, spreading the names out helps you distinguish them from one another.

Figure 21.7 shows how the `months` array would be stored. As you can see, each character pointer in the array points to the first character in each month name. C can print each string because the `%s` format code tells C to print until it finds a null zero.

> Using pointer notation, you could also rewrite line 22 like this:
>
> ```
> { printf("%s\n", *(months+i)); }
> ```

There is one problem with arrays of character pointers pointing to strings that QBasic doesn't have to deal with. You don't always know the data you'll eventually point to. For example, what if you wrote a program that asked the user for 25 names of people. How would you assign each person's name to the array?

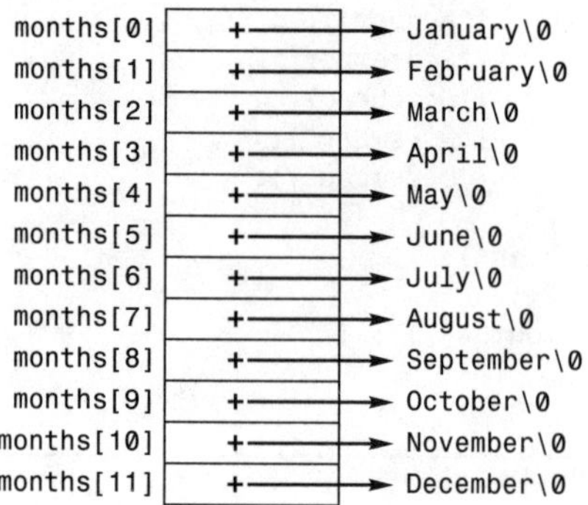

Figure 21.7. The storage of the `months` *pointers.*

You could define the character pointer array that holds the names like this:

```
char * names[25];
```

At first, it might seem as if you could use the following code to get the names from the user:

```
for (i=0; i<25; i++)
{ puts("What is the next name? ");
  gets(names[i]); }     /* Watch out! */
```

The `gets()` causes problems. Each of the `names` elements is a character pointer, but the array is not initialized. Therefore, the 25 elements might be pointing anywhere in memory. The strings entered at the `gets()` would overwrite whatever data each element of `names` points to.

There is never a problem if you want to assign a character pointer to a string constant. For example, the following code causes no problems:

```
names[0] = "Tony Lo Bianco";
names[1] = "Bo Snerdley";
names[2] = "Roger Ailes";
/* Other assignments could follow */
```

C converts all string constants to the addresses where the constants are located. Therefore, the first assignment simply places the address where `Tony Lo Bianco` is stored in `names[0]`.

If, instead of assigning string constants to character pointers, you want to store user input or disk input in the character pointer, you must be sure to first define the pointer so that it points to an area of memory large enough to hold the longest string that will ever be stored there. A multidimensional character array is about the best way to handle this situation.

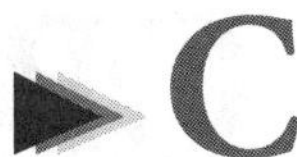

If you want to read names from the disk or use `gets()` (or another user-input function) to fill the array with string data, first define the array as a large multidimensional array like this:

```
char * names[25][80];
```

This statement defines an array of 25 elements, and each element points to 80 initialized characters in memory. The following `for` loop will now cause no trouble as long as the user does not enter a string longer than 80 characters:

```
for (i=0; i<25; i++)
{ puts("What is the next name? ");
  gets(names[i]); }    /* Names must be less than 80 characters */
```

The drawback to defining a multidimensional character array to hold input is that you waste memory unless each string pointed to contains exactly 80 characters including null zeros. After you finish this part of the book, you'll learn about an additional way to grab memory for strings only when you need the memory.

Summary

Congratulations! You just finished one of the most interesting but difficult chapters in the book. Pointers are not necessarily hard, but they have no equivalency in QBasic, so most of this chapter was brand new to you. All chapters until now were able to teach you from a QBasic foundation.

A pointer is just a variable that you define and give a name to. However, unlike nonpointer variables, pointer variables contain addresses of other data. You can then refer to the data being pointed to by the data's original variable name or through pointer notation.

This chapter introduced two new operators, the address of operator, `&`, and the dereferencing operator, `*`. Both `&` and `*` enable you to access and manipulate data pointed to by your pointer variables.

Pointers share a lot with arrays. In fact, an array name is nothing more than a pointer that is constant. You can access arrays as if they are pointers and access pointers as if they are arrays. Given that pointers are variables but arrays are not, you can assign string constants directly to character pointers, whereas you cannot assign string constants directly to arrays.

The last part of this chapter concentrated on arrays of string data. Using an array of character pointers, you can keep track of arrays of string data. QBasic easily handles arrays of strings because the string is one of the fundamental QBasic data types. For C, you must understand pointers before you can understand how to store arrays of string data.

The next chapter moves back into familiar territory. All intermediate and QBasic programmers (those ready for C) have used the `TYPE` statement to define their own data types. In C, `struct` basically does the same thing as `TYPE`. Using `struct`, you'll be able to create records of data that you can then read from and write to disk files.

22

Structure Records

QBasic has the TYPE statement and C has struct. Both create *records* of data. A record is sometimes called an *aggregate data type* because a record is a collection of other data types. By creating records, you can in effect create variables from your own data types instead of being limited to the data types supplied by the language.

In C-speak, a record is called a *structure*. This chapter introduces C structures and shows you how to define your own structure variables using the struct keyword. Because there is almost a one-to-one correspondence between QBasic's TYPE statement and C's struct statement, you'll easily be able to master struct, whereas newcomers to C from some other programming languages might have a problem with struct.

In this chapter, you will learn about the following topics:

- Defining new data types with struct
- How struct relates to TYPE
- The dot operator, .
- Nested structures

- How to work with structure data
- Using pointers with structures

C's dot operator works just like the dot operator in QBasic's TYPE statement. Here you'll learn how to use the dot operator to access individual data items within structure records.

Reviewing *TYPE*

Perhaps the easiest way to learn `struct` is to review QBasic's TYPE statement. The TYPE statement defines the format of QBasic records. A record is just an aggregate collection of data types taken as a whole. If you were to access QBasic's online help and look at the example provided for the TYPE statement, you would see the code shown in Listing 22.1.

Study this review of QBasic's TYPE, even if you've used this advanced command a lot before. The `struct` discussion that comes next refers to several points made in this section.

Listing 22.1. Looking at QBasic's *TYPE* command.

```
TYPE Card
     Suit AS STRING * 9
     Value AS INTEGER
END TYPE
DIM Deck(1 TO 52) AS Card
Deck(1).Suit = "Club"
Deck(1).Value = 2
PRINT Deck(1).Suit, Deck(1).Value
```

The TYPE statement is a multiline statement that begins with TYPE and ends with END TYPE. In Listing 22.1, the TYPE defines a record that has the format shown in Figure 22.1. The two lines between TYPE and END TYPE define the individual *fields* within the record.

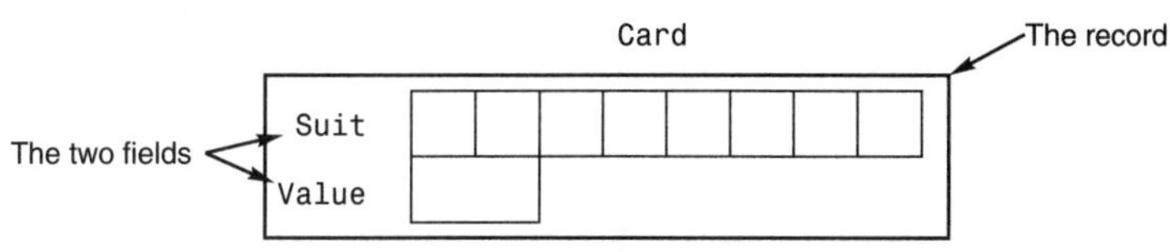

Figure 22.1. After defining the record named `Card`.

Two fields are defined by the `TYPE`. The fields are `Suit` and `Value`. Both fields are considered to be part of the overall record named `Card`.

Most of the time, QBasic programmers use `TYPE` to define data that will later be stored on disk. Disk records are usually fixed in size, so the `STRING * n` format is usually used for individual fields within the `TYPE`'s record rather than just `STRING`, which produces variable-length strings.

> QBasic's `TYPE` statement does not define variables! You must tell QBasic the format of the record with `TYPE` and then use `DIM` to define variables that consist of the `TYPE`'s format. `TYPE` does little more than assign your own data-type name to an aggregate collection of data types.

It is important to understand that instead of defining variables, `TYPE` only defines what variables will eventually look like. There is no QBasic data type that looks like a nine-character string followed by an integer. Therefore, if that kind of combined data type is needed, the programmer must create a record using `TYPE` as shown in Listing 22.1.

A variable is not defined in Listing 22.1 until the `DIM` statement on line 5. Rather than one variable being defined, line 5 defines an array of 52 record values. The array is named `Deck`.

> If only a single variable is needed, you could define one from the record like this:
>
> ```
> DIM aCard AS Card
> ```

After a record variable is defined, you need to be able to assign data to the record's individual fields. If you defined a single non-array variable named `aCard` as just shown, you could assign data to `aCard`'s fields like this:

```
aCard.Suit = "Heart"
aCard.Value = 8
```

Listing 22.1 defined an array of record variables. Any time you work with an array in QBasic, you must specify a subscript. Therefore, lines 6 and 7 store the same pair of values in the first of the 52 array elements. (There is no zero-based subscript in this example because the `TO` keyword was used to define array elements with subscripts that range from `1` to `52`.)

Just to get a better idea of what you can do, the QBasic code shown in Listing 22.2 assigns the data from an entire deck of cards to the array of records.

Listing 22.2. Assign data to the *Deck* array.

```
count = 1     ' Go from 1 to 13
FOR i = 1 TO 13
  Deck(i).Suit = "Club"
  Deck(i).Value = count
  count = count + 1
NEXT i
count = 1     ' Go from 1 to 13
FOR i = 14 TO 26
  Deck(i).Suit = "Heart"
  Deck(i).Value = count
  count = count + 1
NEXT i
count = 1     ' Go from 1 to 13
FOR i = 27 TO 39
  Deck(i).Suit = "Spade"
  Deck(i).Value = count
  count = count + 1
NEXT i
count = 1     ' Go from 1 to 13
FOR i = 40 TO 52
  Deck(i).Suit = "Diamond"
  Deck(i).Value = count
  count = count + 1
NEXT i
```

> The numbers `11`, `12`, and `13` are used to represent the face cards, `Jack`, `Queen`, and `King`.

Using the C *struct*

struct directly corresponds to TYPE.

Again, a C record is called a structure. The `struct` command defines a structure in the same way that QBasic's `TYPE` command defines a record. Here is the format of the `struct` command:

```
struct [structure tag]
  {
    member definition;
    member definition;
      :
    member definition;
} [one or more structure variables];
```

An individual field within a C structure is called a member, and you can define one or more members in a structure. As the brackets in the format indicate, the *`structure tag`* and the *`variables`* are optional. The *`structure tag`* is just the name of the structure in the same way that `Card` was the name of the record in Listing 22.1. C's structures don't have to be named, but if you don't include a *`structure tag`*, you must include one or more variables at the end of the structure definition. The use of the variables at the end of the `struct` is discussed in the next section.

> Don't forget the semicolon at the end of the `struct` statement. All `struct` commands require the ending semicolon.

Here is a `struct` definition that defines the same card record shown earlier:

```
struct Card {
  char Suit[9];
  int Value;
};
```

The structure name (the tag) is `Card`. The `Card` structure contains two members, a character array and an integer. Figure 22.2 shows the similarities between C's `Card` structure definition and QBasic's `Card` record definition.

As you can see, you can easily make the transition from QBasic's `TYPE` to C's `struct`.

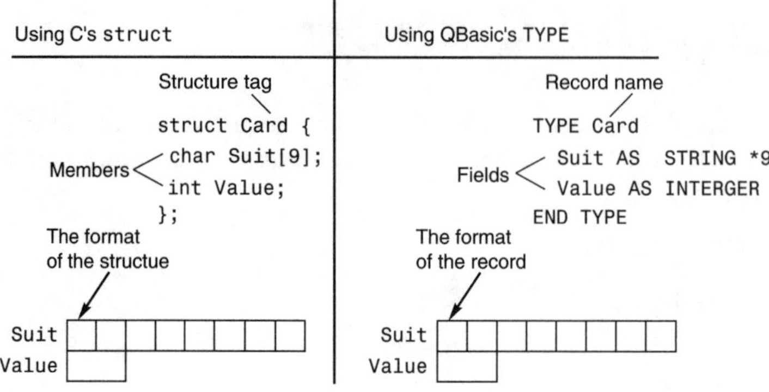

Figure 22.2. The similarities between `struct` *and* `TYPE`.

In a way, you are adding your own data types to both QBasic and C. Whereas there was no `Card` data type in C before the `struct`, there is a `Card` data type after the `struct` statement. The new structure data type is often called a *user-defined* data type because you (you're the "user" of C) defined the new data type. You can define variables using the new data type. The next section shows you how.

Defining *struct* Variables

In QBasic, when you want to define variables from the user-defined data type, you use `DIM` as shown earlier. You can dimension single variables or entire arrays; each variable you define has the format defined by the `TYPE`.

In C, when you want to define variables from the user-defined data type, you do so by prefacing each variable definition with `struct tag`. The *tag* is the name of the structure. Therefore, the following C statement defines a single variable using the `Card` data type:

```
struct Card aCard;    /* Define a structure variable */
```

If you want to define an array of 52 cards, you can do so like this:

```
struct Card aCard[52];  /* 52 cards subscripted from 0 to 51 */
```

> You have to define variables using `struct tag` in the same place that you define other variables (along with the `int` and `float` variable definitions). The following three lines define three variables of three data types. The second variable is a structure variable defined from the `Card` structure.
>
> ```
> char initial;
> struct Card aCard;
> float x;
> ```
>
> You can see that the `Card` data type is not quite known to C as a built-in data type, but it almost is. In other words, you have to repeat the `struct` keyword when defining structure variables. Therefore, `struct` performs a double duty of sorts; `struct` defines structures and also defines structure variables.

Listing 22.3 summarizes the C code needed to define a `Card` structure and an array of 52 `Card` variables.

Listing 22.3. Define the *Card* structure and an array.

```
struct Card {
  char Suit[9];
  int Value;
};
struct Card Deck[52];   /* 52 cards subscripted from 0 to 51 */
```

C provides a faster way to define both a structure and structure variables at the same time. Look back again at the format of the `struct` statement, and you'll see the optional *`[one or more structure variables]`* portion at the bottom of the `struct`. You can define structure variables at the end of all structure definitions if you want to. Therefore, Listing 22.3 can be rewritten as shown in Listing 22.4.

Listing 22.4. Defining the *Card* structure and an array at the same time.

```
struct Card {
  char Suit[9];
  int Value;
} Deck[52];   /* 52 cards subscripted from 0 to 51 */
```

Listing 22.4's line 4 defines an array of 52 cards based on the structure just defined. You're not always ready to define structure variables at the location of the structure definition (see the tip box that follows), but you can do both at the same time if you want.

The structure tag, `Card`, is unnecessary on line 1 if no other `struct Card` variables need to be defined. Therefore, Listing 22.5 accomplishes exactly the same purposes of Listing 22.4 even though the `Card` tag is omitted.

Listing 22.5. Defining an unnamed structure and an array at the same time.

```
1:  struct {
2:    char Suit[9];
3:    int Value;
4:  } Deck[52];   /* 52 cards subscripted from 0 to 51 */
```

There is no need to name the structure on line 1 because the structure variable definition is attached at the end of the `struct`. However, if later in the program you wanted to define additional card variables, you would *have* to use the `Card` tag so that you can later refer to the structure with statements like this:

```
struct Card anotherDeck[52];
```

> Often, a structure is defined before `main()`, and individual structure variables are defined inside `main()` and in the other functions that might follow `main()`. Therefore, the structure definition is global, and the structure variables are local. Every time you define a structure in an early part of your program and the structure variables later, you have to use a structure tag so that you can refer to the structure. If you are unfamiliar with the terms *global* and *local,* you'll learn about them in Chapter 26, "Functions Improve Program Structure."

Just to promote further the fact that a structure definition virtually adds a new data type to C, after you define a structure, you can then define a new structure and use the old structure as a member of the new structure. To clarify this concept, consider the following name-and-address structure definition:

```
struct nameAddr {
  char name[20];
  char address[25];
```

```
  char city[15];
  char state[3];
  long int zip;
};
```

> Actually, ZIP codes are commonly defined as character arrays and not long integers, but the `long int` was used to add some variety to the structure.

Now that the `nameAddr` is defined, you can use the structure within other structure definitions such as these:

```
struct Employee {
  struct nameAddr employeeNA;
  float salary;
  int yrsWorked;
};
struct Customer {
  char custNum[5];
  struct nameAddr custNA;
  double balance;
};
```

How many members do you think `Employee` has? `Employee` has exactly three members. The data types of the members are `struct nameAddr` (because it's now a new data type defined by the user earlier), a `float`, and an `int`. The first member, the structure member, is itself a structure with five members. Figure 22.3 shows what the `Employee` and `Customer` structures look like.

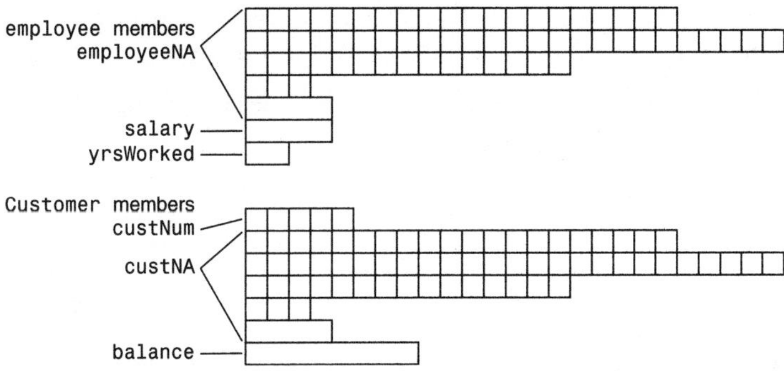

Figure 22.3. The format of the `Employee` and `Customer` structures.

Embedding one structure within another saves you time and effort as a programmer. The Employee and Customer structures could have been defined without the embedded structures like this:

```
struct Employee {
  char name[20];          /* Repeated members... */
  char address[25];
  char city[15];
  char state[3];
  long int zip;           /* ...to here */
  float salary;
  int yrsWorked;
};
struct Customer {
  char custNum[5];
  char name[20];          /* Repeated members... */
  char address[25];
  char city[15];
  char state[3];
  long int zip;           /* ...to here */
  double balance;
};
```

Assigning Data to Structure Variables

To access the individual fields within QBasic's records, you use the dot operator, and you do the same thing with C structures. The dot operator enables you to "get down into the structure" and assign data to individual members of the structure.

Assuming that you've defined a structure variable named aCard, the following C statements assign values to each member:

```
strcpy(aCard.Suit, "Heart");
aCard.Value = 8;
```

The strcpy() stores a string in aCard's first character array member, and the assignment stores the 8 in the integer member. Figure 22.4 shows the resulting structure variable.

The program in Listing 22.6 shows how you would define and assign values to an entire array of playing cards using the Card structure. You can compare this program to the one shown earlier in Listing 22.2 to see how C differs from QBasic when assigning data to structure variables.

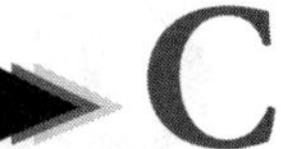

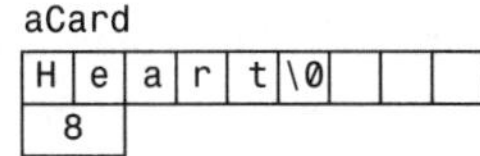

Figure 22.4. After data is stored in the `aCard` *structure variable.*

Listing 22.6. Assigning suit and value data to the cards.

```
/* Filename: DECK.C
   Assign values to the cards */
#include <stdio.h>
#include <string.h>
/* Define the Card structure */
struct Card {
  char Suit[9];
  int  Value;
};
main()
{
  int ctr, count = 1;
  struct Card Deck[52];  /* 52 card structure variables */
  for (ctr=0; ctr<13; ctr++)
  { strcpy(Deck[ctr].Suit, "Club");
    Deck[ctr].Value = count;
    count++;
  }
  count = 1;    /* Go from 1 to 13 */
  for (ctr=13; ctr<26; ctr++)
  { strcpy(Deck[ctr].Suit, "Heart");
    Deck[ctr].Value = count;
    count++;
  }
  count = 1;    /* Go from 1 to 13 */
  for (ctr=26; ctr<39; ctr++)
  { strcpy(Deck[ctr].Suit, "Spade");
    Deck[ctr].Value = count;
    count++;
  }
  count = 1;    /* Go from 1 to 13 */
  for (ctr=39; ctr<52; ctr++)
  { strcpy(Deck[ctr].Suit, "Diamond");
    Deck[ctr].Value = count;
    count++;
  }
  return 0;
}
```

Again, you can see that other than C's limitation imposed by not being able to assign string data directly to character arrays with the equal sign, QBasic and C work almost identically in assigning data to structure variables.

If you want to define a structure variable *and* assign data to the variable at the same time, you can do so in a manner similar to how you dealt with arrays in earlier chapters. The following statement both defines a card variable and assigns data to the card:

```
struct Card aCard = {"Heart", 7};
```

C even enables you to define a structure *and* define a structure variable *and* assign data to that variable all in one statement, like this:

```
struct Card {
  char Suit[9];
  int Value;
} aCard = {"Heart", 7};
```

You can directly assign one structure variable to another as long as you defined the structure variables from the same structure definition. For instance, one card could be assigned to another like this:

```
drawCard = dealCard;  /* Assumes that dealCard already has data */
```

C performs a member-by-member assignment.

Even though both structure variables contain string data, C makes sure that the assignment occurs properly on a member-by-member basis so that the string, character, and numeric data will be copied from one structure variable to the other.

If you want to assign data to a structure that has its own embedded structure as a member, you must use two dot operators. For example, to assign data to the `Employee` structure (shown earlier)

```
struct Employee {
  struct nameAddr employeeNA;
  float salary;
  int yrsWorked;
} person;
```

you must take into account that the first member of `Employee` is itself a structure. It's easy assigning data to the last two members. The following lines put values into `salary` and `yrsWorked`:

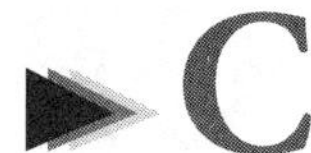

```
person.salary = 45322.00;
person.yrsWorked = 6;
```

To assign data to the embedded structure's members, you must use a dot to get to the embedded structure and another dot to get to the member of the embedded structure. For example, the following statement assigns a value to the `zip` field of an `Employee` variable named `person`:

```
person.employeeNA.zip = zip;
```

If you want to initialize one of the character array members inside the `employeeNA` structure, use `strcpy()` as you would do with any character array:

```
strcpy(person.employeeNA.name, "George Sands");
```

Using Pointers with Structures

Do you think that you can define a pointer to a structure variable? The answer should now be obvious. If you can define an array of structures, you can also define a pointer to a structure. After all, an array name is nothing more than a pointer constant.

The following statement defines a single, nonpointer structure variable:

```
struct Card aCard;
```

As with any other kind of pointer variable definition, if you use an `*` before the variable name, you'll define a pointer to the structure. Therefore, the following statement is a structure pointer definition:

```
struct Card * cardPtr;   /* Defines a pointer to a structure */
```

Note that this structure pointer definition defines a *pointer variable* and *not* a structure! If you want the structure pointer variable to point to a structure in memory, you have to assign the structure pointer variable the address of a structure like this:

```
cardPtr = &aCard;   /* Links a pointer to the structure */
```

Now you can access the structure variable by its name (`aCard`) or by the structure pointer variable (`cardPtr`). However, when accessing individual members within a structure, you cannot use the dot operator with a structure pointer variable; you must learn yet another C operator that enables you to get to a structure pointer variable's members.

The structure pointer operator is ->.

One of the only C operators left for you to learn is the *structure pointer* operator. The structure pointer operator is `->` (formed by typing a dash followed by a greater-than sign). When a structure pointer variable is pointing to structure data (as `cardPtr` is now pointing to `aCard`'s data after the previous assignments), you can still use the dot operator to access the members of `aCard` like this:

```
printf("The value is %d.\n", aCard.Value);
```

You must, however, use the `->` to access the members when using the pointer variable like this:

```
printf("The value is %d.\n", cardPtr->Value); /* Same as before */
```

Here are the only rules you must remember when accessing members with the dot operator and structure pointer operator:

- Use the dot operator if you want to access a member through a nonpointer structure variable.
- Use the structure pointer operator if you want to access a member through a pointer structure variable.

You might wonder why you would ever need to use a structure pointer variable. After all, you have to use a different operator to get to the individual members, and using pointers isn't always as straightforward as using nonpointer variable names. In the next chapter, you're going to learn about a way to store data in *unnamed memory* (memory not named by variable names). The only way to store and retrieve unnamed structure data (and for that matter, any kind of data) is through pointer usage.

Summary

This chapter showed you how C's `struct` command differs very little from QBasic's `TYPE` statement. They both define aggregate data types, called records in QBasic and structures in C. Records contain fields, and structures contain members. Other than the terminology, there is little to distinguish the ways each language works with aggregate data.

If you want to, you can define structure variables either when you define the structure or later, as long as you name the structure format with a structure tag.

Both QBasic and C use the dot operator to access the parts of the aggregate data. If you embed a structure within another structure, you'll have to use two dot operators to get to the actual members of the structure.

As with any other kind of data, you can define pointers to structures. However, if you work with a pointer to structure members, you must use the structure pointer operator, `->`, to get to the members.

The next chapter rounds out your learning of pointers by introducing dynamic memory allocation. Dynamic memory allocation sounds imposing, but it's nothing more than reserving data in memory without assigning a name to that data. Instead of accessing that memory with variable names, you access the memory through pointer variables. You'll learn how to store and access dynamically allocated data of all types, including structures, in the next chapter.

23

Dynamic Memory Allocation

If you've ever used QBasic's *metacommands,* `$STATIC` and `$DYNAMIC`, you'll have a leg up on this chapter's material. Although this chapter is shorter than most others in the book, it opens up the most possibilities for your future programming work. As you progress through the beginning to the more advanced stages of C, you'll find new uses for dynamic memory allocation all the time. Almost every intermediate and advanced C programmer wonders how he or she would ever write a program in a language that didn't support dynamic memory allocation.

Dynamic memory allocation is a fancy term used for a simple concept. Instead of reserving variables at the top of a function, which tells the compiler at compile time to reserve the memory, you can reserve any amount of memory any time you want it. Also, you can release the memory when you're done with it. The allocated memory is not a variable, so you must access allocated memory through pointers.

QBasic doesn't actually support dynamic memory allocation, but the `$STATIC` and `$DYNAMIC` *metacommands* are a start. The keywords are called metacommands because they don't actually execute at runtime but instead send instructions to QBasic before your program starts executing. Another reason `$STATIC` and `$DYNAMIC` don't perform C-like dynamic memory allocation is that the QBasic keywords work only on arrays, whereas C's dynamic memory allocation works for any kind of variables including non-array variables.

As is often the case in this book, you'll see a review of QBasic's `$STATIC` and `$DYNAMIC` before jumping into C's way of allocating memory. After you understand the concepts of QBasic's techniques, you'll learn how inflexible QBasic's support of dynamic memory allocation is when you learn about C's techniques of handling memory.

In this chapter, you will learn about the following topics:

- How QBasic's `$STATIC` and `$DYNAMIC` provide some support for runtime dynamic memory allocation
- The reasons for using dynamic memory allocation
- How C supports dynamic memory allocation
- The heap of memory available for allocation
- The `malloc()` and `free()` functions
- How to use the heap to simulate variable-length strings
- How to dynamically allocate structure data

A Review of QBasic's *$STATIC* and *$DYNAMIC*

The metacommands `$STATIC` and `$DYNAMIC` are two of the strangest keywords in almost any programming language. QBasic recognizes these keywords only when you place them *inside a remark*! In other words, `$STATIC` and `$DYNAMIC` never appear unless preceded by a remark such as this:

```
' $STATIC
```

or

```
REM $DYNAMIC
```

If you omit either metacommand, QBasic assumes `$STATIC`. The difference in the two methods of array allocation can be found in the way QBasic allocates (sets aside) memory for arrays when you run a program.

When statically allocating arrays (the default), QBasic searches your QBasic program for all DIM statements that allocate array storage. Before your program even begins, QBasic allocates *all* array storage and then runs the program. Even if you need an array for only 10 percent of your program's code, that array will be taking up memory while not being used in the other 90 percent of the program.

When dynamically allocating arrays, QBasic does not set aside any memory for your array *until* the DIM statement occurs. *Dynamic* means changing, so your memory usage changes during the program run. The ERASE command releases arrays allocated dynamically. Therefore, if you use $DYNAMIC and ERASE, you can reserve memory for arrays only during those parts of the program that need arrays. Your memory usage shrinks and expands during program execution, and you use memory more efficiently.

You can also tell QBasic whether array storage should be statically or dynamically allocated through the DIM command in a strange fashion. If you allocate an array like

```
DIM myArray(100)
```

then QBasic allocates the array statically (for the entire life of the program). However, if you use a variable for the DIM subscript like

```
n = 100
DIM myArray(n)
```

then QBasic allocates the array dynamically (at the point of the array's DIM statement and not before). $STATIC and $DYNAMIC override the DIM statement if you use either of the metacommands.

Today's programs demand dynamic allocation.

Think of the trend in computers today. The trend is toward multiprocessing, multitasking, and multi-user computers. Networks, peripheral sharing (such as two computers using the same hard disk or printer), and Windows-like operating environments place great strains on the limited memory your computer has. When running Windows, if you start one program, there is less memory left to start another.

An aware programmer will not use resources, especially memory resources, unless that programmer needs the memory to do something. Therefore, programmers concerned about freeing as much memory as possible will always use the ' $DYNAMIC command (or DIM with a variable subscript) to allocate arrays dynamically. After the program is finished with the array, the programmer can then erase the array with ERASE, thereby giving the array's space back to the operating system to dole out to another program or task running at the same time.

Computers used to be easy! When the early versions of microcomputers arrived in the late 1970s, it seemed as though BASIC with its static allocation was more than anybody would ever need. However, times change and computers change even faster. Today's QBasic programmers will always embed a `' $DYNAMIC` at the top of their programs if they want to use only as much array space as necessary.

The C Way of Allocating

C uses a little more advanced method for allocating memory dynamically. As with QBasic's `' $DYNAMIC`, a C programmer can request memory only when needed. Unlike with QBasic, a C programmer can allocate non-array data when needed and keep track of the location (the allocated memory's address) through pointer variables.

C's method of dynamic memory allocation is much more flexible than QBasic's meta-commands can be. If you want to, a C program can use an array of thousands of values, and the only variable in the program might be a single pointer variable that points to the start of the array's value.

Before you go much further, a little terminology is in order. The pool of memory not being used by any other resource in your computer is called the *heap*. The heap is just that portion of memory (RAM) left that is not currently being used. If your program needs to dynamically allocate 100 `floats` at once, the heap decreases in size by 100 `floats`. Figure 23.1 shows the heap.

The heap has not been used by any programs so far in the book. To access the heap, you specifically have to call the dynamically allocated functions described in this chapter that access the heap area.

When you define a variable, whether that variable is local or global, C already allocated the space for that variable before your program began executing. The heap isn't where your program normally gets its data space. The heap, however, is often used by DOS, Windows, and other programs that might be sharing memory along with your program.

Use only what you need when you need it.

Programming in today's multitasking environments requires that you use only as much memory as you need at the time. Windows might need a big chunk of memory for printer spooling, and if your program has reserved a lot of memory but is not currently using that memory, Windows might not be able to have all the memory it needs. There might not be enough heap space left for Windows to do its job.

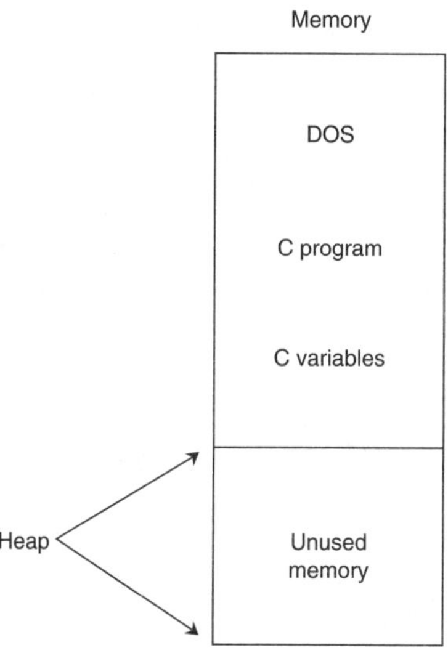

Figure 23.1. The heap is all unused memory.

> Most of the time, you'll want to allocate arrays on the heap, although C, unlike QBasic, enables you to allocate any kind of variable on the heap. A pointer variable must *always* point to each data value on the heap, so allocating a single integer on the heap and then pointing to that single integer with a pointer variable is overkill. After you allocate an array on the heap, you need only a single pointer to access all 100 elements of that heap's array.

There are only two functions you need to know to access the heap:

- `malloc()` allocates heap memory and gives your program the right to use that allocated memory. When you reach the point in your program where you want to allocate new memory from the heap, use `malloc()`.
- `free()` releases the memory that was previously allocated by `malloc()` so that the heap grows by the amount of memory that you release with `free()`.

If your program calls `malloc()` to allocate memory, your program should eventually call `free()` to release that memory. After all, if your program is going to allocate memory and never release it, you might as well forget the heap and use regular variables that are allocated throughout the life of your program. Of course, you should never call `free()` unless you've first called malloc() because without malloc(), there is no heap memory to release with free().

The worst-kept secret in programming is that if you forget to release allocated memory with free(), DOS releases the memory for you when your program ends. Again, why go to the trouble (and slight speed inefficiency) of allocating memory if you're not going to free the memory when you're done with it? When you allocate and free memory, you use only those resources that you need, and other tasks can have the memory you free.

Be sure to include STDLIB.H in all programs that use malloc() and free().

malloc() Allocates

When you allocate a chunk of heap memory with malloc(), malloc() returns a pointer to the newly allocated memory. The heap memory that you allocate does not, and cannot, have variable names as your other variables have. The heap is just a big pool of memory that you can allocate chunks of, and those chunks of memory that you allocate don't have variable names. malloc() returns the exact address to the chunk of memory that you allocate, but you don't want to have to work with addresses. You now know (after Chapter 21, "Pointers Are New to You") that a pointer variable will hold an address and that you can manipulate the value pointed to by the pointer without worrying about the address stored in the pointer variable. Therefore, you will always assign malloc()'s return value to a pointer variable.

The *void* Pointer

malloc() returns a special kind of pointer called the *void pointer.* You know that you can define integer pointers, floating-point pointers, and user-defined pointers. A void pointer is *not* a pointer to a null value as commonly thought by newcomers to C. A void pointer is just a pointer that can point to any kind of data.

int pointers can point only to integers. float pointers can point only to floating-point data. Void pointers, however, can point to any kind of data. Define void pointers using the void data type. Although you rarely have to define void pointers, you can do so like this:

```
void * aPtr;  /* aPtr is a pointer to any data type */
```

There is only one proper way to make a void pointer point to data. You can't arbitrarily assign void pointers to any data type; you must typecast the void pointer before making it point to data.

> If void pointers could be used, without limits, for any data type, there would be no need to allocate pointer variables of specific data types such as `int` pointers.

Therefore, if you want `aPtr` to point to an integer, you must typecast the pointer to point to an integer pointer like this: `(int *)aPtr`. You'll see the primary use of typecasting a void pointer in the next section when you see the specifics of `malloc()`.

Using *malloc()*

At first glance, a `malloc()` function call looks foreboding indeed. Here is the simplest format of `malloc()`:

```
malloc(memoryToAllocate);
```

So far, the function call looks simple because it takes only one argument. The *`memoryToAllocate`* argument is actually an integer that tells C how much memory to allocate. Therefore, `malloc(65)` would tell C to find 65 contiguous bytes on the heap and allocate that memory for your program. When allocating, C in a sense puts a fence around the 65 bytes so that subsequent `malloc()` calls will not infringe on that memory area.

There is more to allocating 65 bytes than `malloc(65)`, but `malloc()` is best learned a piece at a time. Think about this: What if you wanted to allocate 65 *integers*? What value would you pass to `malloc()`? What if you wanted to allocate 65 `double` values on the heap? What value would you pass to `malloc()`? Remember that you cannot predict exactly how much memory an integer or a floating-point value takes because such data sizes vary from computer to computer and among compilers.

You're probably guessing how to solve the size problem. With `sizeof()`, you don't have to worry how much memory each data type consumes. If you want 65 integers, you can call this:

```
malloc(65 * sizeof(int))
```

If you want 65 double floating-point values, you can do this:

```
malloc(65 * sizeof(double))
```

You'll see the `(n * sizeof(dataType))` formula in almost every `malloc()` call. There is still a little left to learn before you see `malloc()` in action.

After C allocates the memory you requested with the `(n * sizeof(dataType))` formula, `malloc()` will find that amount of heap memory, protect it from subsequent allocations, and return a `void` pointer to the first byte in the allocated region. Figure 23.2 shows what happens when C sees `malloc(100 * sizeof(char))`, assuming that a `char` takes exactly one byte of memory.

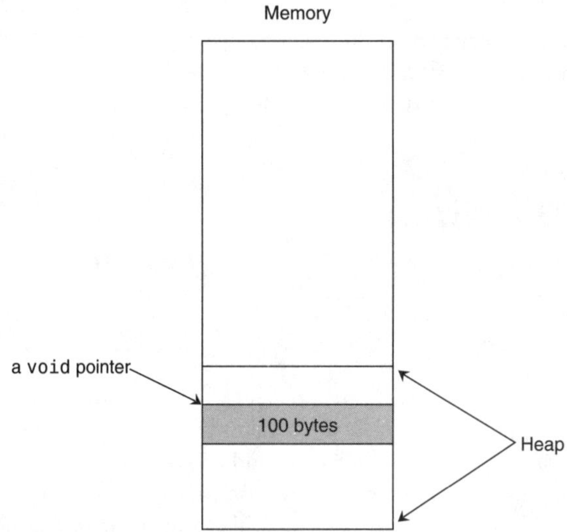

Figure 23.2. After allocating 100 characters.

Your program can't do much with the `void` pointer. After all, there is now an array-like list of 100 characters on the heap, and to access characters, you have to use a character pointer. Therefore, assuming that you've allocated a character pointer named `myLetters`, the following statement is the complete `malloc()` function call needed to allocate 100 characters and link to them `myLetters` so that `myLetters` points to the first character value:

```
myLetters = (char *) malloc(100 * sizeof(char));
```

The `(char *)` typecasts `malloc()`'s returned `void` pointer to a character pointer so that `myLetters` points to the first value.

`myLetters` is now a character pointer pointing to 100 characters on the heap. As you know from Chapter 21, "Pointers Are New to You," you can access a pointer using array

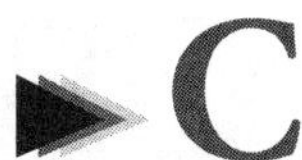

notation and vice versa. Therefore, if you want to store the letter x in each data location allocated, you can do so like this:

```
for (i=0; i<100; i++)
{  myLetters[i] = 'x'; }      /* Store x's on the heap */
```

If you want to use pointer notation, you can use the following loop, which does the same as the preceding one:

```
for (i=0; i<100; i++)
{  *(myLetters+i) = 'x'; }    /* Store x's on the heap */
```

The following code is a section of a C program that defines a `float` pointer and allocates 300 floating-point values on the heap. A loop then zeros the 300 floating-point values on the heap.

```
main()
{
  int i;        /* Loop variable */
  float * fPtr;
  fPtr = (float *)malloc(300 * sizeof(float));
  for (i=0; i<300; i++)
  {  fPtr[i] = 0.0; }    /* Zero the 300 heap values */
```

If There Are Errors

There is a possibility that your computer's heap space will get used up. If you were to allocate hundreds of values on the heap in several arrays, you could use all the heap space. If `malloc()` fails to get any heap memory because there is not enough to fulfill the request, `malloc()` returns a null pointer (a pointer to `0`).

Many times, you'll see error-checking memory allocation code like this:

```
fPtr = (float *)malloc(300 * sizeof(float));
if (!fPtr)
  { fprintf(stderr, "Not enough memory to allocate.\n");
    exit(1);
  }
/* Rest of program could follow */
```

Sometimes, C programmers combine the `malloc()` and `if` into one long section of code like this:

```
if (!fPtr = (float *)malloc(300 * sizeof(float)))
  { fprintf(stderr, "Not enough memory to allocate.\n");
    exit(1);
  }
/* Rest of program could follow */
```

The separate `if` is a little more clear, although not quite as efficient. Use whatever method you feel the most comfortable with and that you can read the easiest.

Freeing the Allocation

After your program is finished with the heap, you can free the memory with the `free()` function call. `free()` is much easier to use than `malloc()`. Here is the format of `free()`:

```
free(pointerToHeap);
```

`free()` knows how much to deallocate.

If `fPtr` points to 300 floating-point values (as set up previously), you can release *all* 300 values with this statement:

```
free(fPtr);
```

Even though `fPtr` points to the first of 300 floating-point values, the `free()` function frees all the memory pointed to by `fPtr`. When you called `malloc()`, C kept track of how much memory `malloc()` allocated, so a subsequent call to `free()` will free an equal amount of memory.

Don't ever change the value of `fPtr`. If you do, you'll never be able to access the heap, and you'll never be able to free the memory pointed to by `fPtr`.

The program in Listing 23.1 contains the same code as the program in Chapter 19, "Array Management," that sorted 50 random numbers. The difference lies in the way the numbers are stored in memory. The values, instead of being stored in an array that's always reserved for the life of the program, are stored on the heap area and pointed to with an integer pointer. After you allocate with `malloc()` and assign the pointer to access the array, the program is identical to the previous version except for a final `free()` at the end that deallocates the memory.

Listing 23.1. Sorting heap memory.

```
/* Filename: SORTHEAP.C
   Sorts an array of 50 random numbers on the heap */
#include <stdio.h>
#include <stdlib.h>
#include <time.h>
```

```
#define TOTAL 50
main()
{
  int * nums;   /* To point to the heap */
  int i, j, n, temp, isSwapped;
  time_t t;
  srand((unsigned)time(&t)); /* Seed the random-number generator */

  /* Allocate */
  nums = (int *)malloc(TOTAL * sizeof(int));

  /* Fill heap with random numbers from 1 to 100 */
  for (i=0; i<TOTAL; i++)
  { nums[i] = rand() % 100 + 1; }

  /* Print the unsorted heap array */
  printf("The unsorted numbers:\n");
  for (i=0; i<TOTAL; i++)
  { printf("%3d\t\t", nums[i]); }

  /* Sort the heap array using the Shell sort */
  i = TOTAL+1;
  while (i > 1)
  { i = i % 2;
    do
    { /* Scan heap array until there are no more swaps */
      isSwapped = 1;  /* Set to true */
      for (j=0; j<(TOTAL-i); j++)
        { n = j + i;
          if (nums[j] > nums[n])
            { temp = nums[j];   /* Swap the values */
              nums[j] = nums[n];
              nums[n] = temp;
              isSwapped = 0;     /* Set to false */
            }
        }
    } while (!isSwapped);
  }

  /* Print the sorted numbers */
  printf("\nThe sorted numbers:\n");
  for (i=0; i<TOTAL; i++)
  { printf("%3d\t\t", nums[i]); }
  /* Deallocate the array */
  free(nums);
  return 0;
}
```

It might seem as if dynamic memory allocation is overkill in Listing 23.1. After all, the heap is allocated toward the beginning of the program and freed at the end. It's true that using a regular variable array would not add much overhead of memory usage and that this program is just an example of how you allocate and free memory. Keep in mind, however, that you'll rarely write one-page programs in the "real world." Often, a program spans several pages, and you might need array memory in only a single section of that program. In such a program, the heap makes a lot of sense.

Allocating String Space

Earlier you learned that if you define a character variable like

```
char *input;
```

you cannot use `gets()` to get a user's value into `input` like this:

```
gets(input);  /* Don't try this */
```

The `input` variable is not pointing to any specific memory location, and hence the `gets()` would place the user's entered string at some unknown, and probably damaging, location in memory. If you want to point to a user's input string, or hold an array of character pointers that will hold user input, allocate each string on the heap. You'll better understand how to use the heap for arrays of strings when you study Listing 23.2. This listing's program asks the user for his or her favorite book titles. An initial 80-character buffer (appropriately named `buffer`) is first allocated on the heap to hold the user's input. As the user inputs each book title, the program uses `malloc()` to store the books in heap memory with each book title pointed to by a different element in the character array.

Listing 23.2. Storing an array of strings on the heap.

```
/* Filename: BOOKHEAP.C
   Store book titles on the heap */
#include <stdio.h>
#include <string.h>
#include <stdlib.h>
main()
{
  int ctr;          /* Look variable */
```

```
9:    char * buffer;     /* Will point to the input string */
10:   char * books[5];  /* 5 books will be stored on the heap */
11:   /* Allocate the input buffer on the heap */
12:   buffer = (char *)malloc(80 * sizeof(char));  /* 80 char input */
13:   /* Get each book title in a loop */
14:   for (ctr=0; ctr<5; ctr++)
15:   {
16:     puts("What is one of your favorite books? ");
17:     gets(buffer);
18:     /* Allocate enough space on the heap */
19:     books[ctr] = (char *)malloc(strlen(buffer) + 1);
20:     strcpy(books[ctr], buffer);  /* Copy the actual title */
21:   }
22:   /* Print the data */
23:   puts("\nHere are the books:");
24:   for (ctr=0; ctr<5; ctr++)
25:   {  puts(books[ctr]);
26:      free(books[ctr]);  /* We're done with that book's heap space */
27:   }
28:   return 0;
29: }
```

Here is sample output from Listing 23.2:

```
What is one of your favorite books?
Moving from C to C++
What is one of your favorite books?
Absolute Beginner's Guide to Programming
What is one of your favorite books?
Teach Yourself OOP with Turbo C++
What is one of your favorite books?
QBasic Programming 101
What is one of your favorite books?
Absolute Beginner's Guide to Access

Here are the books:
Moving from C to C++
Absolute Beginner's Guide to Programming
Teach Yourself OOP with Turbo C++
QBasic Programming 101
Absolute Beginner's Guide to Access
```

Line 10 defines an array of five character pointers. As the user enters each book title at line 17, exactly enough heap space is reserved in line 19 to hold that title (including the null zero). The newly allocated heap space is then sent, via `strcpy()`, the contents of the user's title in line 20.

After each title is printed, line 26's `free()` deallocates the heap space. At line 28's `return` statement, the program occupies no heap space.

Allocating Structures

Nothing new is really needed for the allocation of structures on the heap. `sizeof()` can return the size of a structure variable. After a structure named `Employees` is defined like

```
struct Employees {
  int numYrs;
  char name[20];
  float salary;
};
```

and a structure pointer named `empPtr` is defined like

```
struct * empPtr;
```

the following statement allocates a single structure on the heap and assigns the address of the structure's starting point to `empPtr`:

```
empPtr = (struct Employees *)malloc(sizeof(struct Employees));
```

The two `struct` keywords might seem foreboding to a C newcomer, but you now should have little problem with them. The `(struct Employees *)` typecasts `malloc()`'s returned `void` pointer so that the structure pointer `empPtr` could accurately point to the heap.

You could then assign values directly to the structure members on the heap using the structure pointer operator, `->`:

```
empPtr->numYrs = 8;
strcpy(empPtr->name, "Judith Regan");
empPtr->salary = 53654.90;
```

You'll end up with allocated heap space that conceptually looks similar to that shown in Figure 23.3.

Deallocating the entire structure variable is easy. All you need to do is pass the structure pointer to `free()` like this:

```
free(empPtr);  /* Deallocate the space used by empPtr */
```

There is no need to erase any of the heap values. After the memory is freed, it's up to subsequent programs that happen to allocate that space to initialize the heap memory with new values.

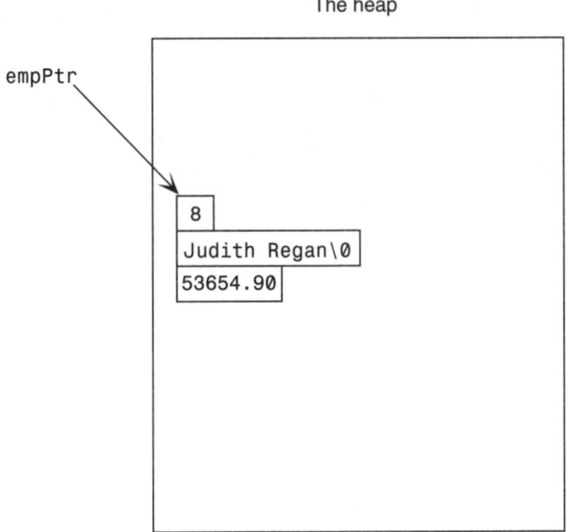

Figure 23.3. After allocating and storing structure data on the heap.

Summary

Dynamic memory allocation is quite a departure from QBasic's `$STATIC` and `$DYNAMIC` metacommands. `$STATIC` and `$DYNAMIC` dictate when QBasic array space is allocated; array space is allocated for the life of a QBasic program with `$STATIC` (the default if you do nothing), and arrays are allocated only when you dimension them if you use `$DYNAMIC`. C provides more flexibility and enables you to directly access the PC's leftover memory, called the *heap*.

The `malloc()` function dynamically allocates heap memory. When you need data space, you can request the space with `malloc()`. `malloc()` returns a `void` pointer that you then can typecast to the appropriate pointer data type you need.

After you are through with memory allocation, you can release the memory back to the heap with the `free()` function. By releasing the memory, you give more resources to other tasks that might need the memory.

An entire book could be written on `malloc()` and `free()`. As your C skills progress, you'll find yourself using these functions more and more. Also, if you study other people's C code in magazines and books (and you should), you'll see how others use `malloc()` and `free()` for specific purposes, such as for character string storage as shown toward the end of this chapter.

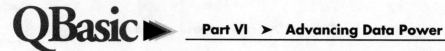

The next chapter takes you into the world of C's file input and output features. You'll find that the designers of C seemed to take QBasic's file I/O commands and turn them into C statements. C's I/O, especially C's sequential I/O, is almost indistinguishable (except for syntax) from QBasic's file I/O methods.

Part VII

Using Disk Files

QBasic → C

24

Sequential Files

C performs sequential file access almost exactly like QBasic performs sequential file access. As you should already know from your QBasic programming experience, disk files are critical for any serious data processing. The disk data is nonvolatile (meaning that its contents aren't erased as memory when you turn off your computer). Not only are disk files more permanent, but disk drives contain much more storage than your computer's internal memory. Your data files will need to be tucked away on the disk, where there is plenty of room and where they'll be safe for future access.

QBasic supports two file I/O methods, *sequential* and *random access.* C also supports these two methods. A file is actually nothing more than a stream of characters, and the way you access the file has nothing to do with the file's contents but with the way your program accesses the file.

This chapter focuses on C's sequential file access, and the next chapter explores how C performs random file access. Of the two methods, C's sequential access more closely mirrors that of QBasic than C's random-access methods.

In this chapter, you will learn about the following topics:

- How you can use sequential access
- How to open files for sequential access
- How to create sequential files

- How to read sequential files
- How to append to sequential files

As with keyboard and screen I/O, C contains several file I/O functions that enable you to direct your I/O to and from disk files as well as to the screen and keyboard.

A Review of Sequential Files

Sequential files are limited.

Not all file data should be accessed sequentially. The needs of your program determine whether you can use sequential file access. These are the only actions you can perform with a sequential file:

- Create sequential files
- Append to sequential files
- Read sequential files

These three sequential methods correspond to QBasic's file *modes.* A mode tells QBasic exactly what kind of access you want. The three methods listed here correspond to QBasic's `OUTPUT`, `APPEND`, and `INPUT` modes. As with tapes, you must read data from sequential files in the same order in which the data was written. When you're reading sequential files, the following rules hold true:

- If the file that you want to read exists, your program reads the data in the order in which the data was originally written.
- If the file that you want to read does not exist, C returns an error condition that you can check for.
- If you reach the end of the sequential file you are reading, C returns an end-of-file condition that you can check for.

When writing to sequential files, you have to keep the following points in mind:

- If the file exists before you open it for writing, all the file's contents will be destroyed when you open the file for writing.
- If the file does not exist before you open it for writing, C creates the file.

When appending (adding) to sequential files, remember this:

- If the file you open for appending does not exist, C creates the file just as if you had opened the file for writing.
- If the file you open for appending does exist, all output you write to the file will add to the end of the file.

All the previous discussion about sequential files holds true for both QBasic and C. The most important thing to remember about sequential files is that you cannot add data to the middle of a sequential file or read the data in an order different from the order in which the data was written originally. If you need to jump around in a file, reading and writing data in various order (as you might access an array), you'll have to open your files randomly as shown in the next chapter.

Sequential files are difficult to change.

Although you can't read and write sequential file data in random order, many times sequential files make lots of sense. Sequential files are perfect for storing history data that you add to over time. If you store text data in a file, you should use a sequential file because random-access file data lengths should be uniform, and text files generally have different line lengths. If you store data that you rarely change, such as backup copies of other files, you'll find that sequential files make the most sense. There's an additional advantage of sequential file processing as well: sequential file I/O code is usually easier to write and maintain than random file access code.

Because all file I/O functions discussed here are described to C in STDIO.H, you don't have to include any additional header files when working with file I/O.

File Openings and Closings

In QBasic, you must open a file before using it, and C is no exception. In QBasic, the `OPEN` statement not only tells QBasic which mode you want to open the file in but also assigns a *file number,* also called a *file handle,* to the file. After the `OPEN` statement, the rest of the program refers to the file by the file number. For example, the following QBasic `OPEN` statement opens a file for output and attaches the file to file number `3`:

```
OPEN "C:\DATAFILE.DAT" FOR OUTPUT AS #3
```

After the `OPEN` finishes, QBasic creates the file named DATAFILE.DAT, located in the root directory of drive C:, and assigns file number `3` to the file. Instead of having to use the filename DATAFILE.DAT throughout the program, all file I/O statements need only refer to file number `3`.

When you're done with the file, you can close it with this `CLOSE` command:

```
CLOSE #3
```

C's open, output, and closing methods are almost identical to the ones described here for QBasic. To open a file in C, use the `fopen()` function. Here is the format of C's `fopen()` function:

```
filePtr = fopen(fileName, accessMode);
```

Rather than a file number, you must assign the return value of the `fopen()` statement to a file pointer, indicated by ***`filePtr`*** in the format. As with the QBasic file number, the rest of the C program accesses the file by the ***`filePtr`*** as described in the next section.

The ***`fileName`*** must be a string constant, a string stored in a character array, or a string pointed to by a character pointer. The filename can contain a disk drive and a complete pathname. It doesn't matter whether you specify the filename in uppercase or lowercase letters. The ***`accessMode`*** must also be a string and can be any of the values listed in Table 24.1.

Table 24.1. The *fopen()* function's *accessMode* values.

`accessMode`	*Description*
`"a"`	Append to the end of the file, equivalent to QBasic's `APPEND` mode.
`"r"`	Read from the file, equivalent to QBasic's `INPUT` mode.
`"w"`	Write to the file, equivalent to QBasic's `OUTPUT` mode.

To open the FILEDATA.DAT for output in C, you would do this:

```
fileOut = fopen("C:\FILEDATA.DAT", "w");
```

The file pointer that you assign `fopen()`'s return value to is a special kind of pointer variable that can point only to files. Before assigning the return value of `fopen()` to `fileOut`, you must properly define `fileOut` like this:

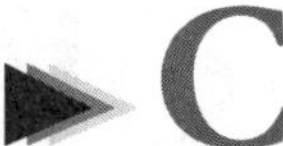

```
FILE * fileOut;    /* Define the file pointer variable */
```

As with any variable, you can use any name you want for the file pointer variable. `FILE` is not a data type. In STDIO.H, the constant `FILE` is actually defined to be a file structure, and the `FILE` structure holds the location of the file on the disk. You never have to worry about the contents of the file pointer variable. The file pointer works like the file number in QBasic. You insert the file pointer in subsequent file I/O function calls so that C knows which file to perform the I/O on.

If you want to open more than one file at a time, be sure to define more than one file pointer and assign them to `fopen()` calls that open different files. The following code shows the first few lines of a `main()` function that defines three file pointers and opens three different files in three different access modes:

```
main()
{
  FILE * fileIn, fileApp, fileOut;
  fileIn = fopen("INPUTDAT.DAT", "r");
  fileApp = fopen("APPENDAT.DAT", "a");
  fileOut = fopen("OUTDAT.DAT", "w");
  /* Rest of program would follow */
```

In QBasic, you could accomplish the same kind of multifile opening like this:

```
OPEN "INPUTDAT.DAT" FOR INPUT AS #1
OPEN "APPENDAT.DAT" FOR APPEND AS #2
OPEN "OUTDAT.DAT" FOR OUTPUT AS #3
```

When you learn to write multifunction programs, as you'll learn to do in Part VIII, define your file pointers before `main()` so that subsequent functions have access to the file.

After writing to the file, you can close the file by calling the `fclose()` function. Here is the format of `fclose()`:

```
fclose(filePtr);
```

To close the three files opened previously, you can do this:

```
fclose (fileIn);
fclose (fileApp);
fclose (fileOut);
```

In QBasic, you could accomplish the same closing of the three files opened previously like this:

```
CLOSE #1
CLOSE #2
CLOSE #3
```

> Resist the temptation to open all your files at the top of a program and close them at the bottom unless you'll use the files throughout the entire program. Try to open a file right before the code that accesses the file and close the file as soon as you're done with it in the program. It's true that if you forget to close a file, DOS closes the file for you when your program ends. However, as mentioned in Chapter 23, "Dynamic Memory Allocation," you shouldn't hold computer resources longer than you need to because other tasks might need the memory and internal file handles consumed by the open files.

As mentioned earlier, if you attempt to open a file for input and the file does not exist, you get an error. C indicates the file-not-found error through the value of the file pointer. If the `fopen()` fails, C returns a null value for the file pointer. A null pointer contains the address of `0`, which means false. Consider the following `fopen()` call:

```
fileOut = fopen("C:\FILEDATA.DAT", "w");
if (fileOut == 0)
  { fprintf(stderr, "The file could not be opened.\n"); }
/* The rest of the program goes here */
```

The `fprintf()` is used for the error message so that the error can be routed to the standard error device named `stderr`. (Chapter 16, "Some I/O Functions," explained `stderr`.) The `fopen()` function assigns a `0` to the file pointer, which is the same as saying that the file pointer is *null*. That is, there is no file to point to.

Many C programmers know that there is a constant defined in STDIO.H named `NULL` that you can use in place of `0` for pointer comparisons if you want to. The following code is identical to that just shown:

```
fileOut = fopen("C:\FILEDATA.DAT", "w");
if (fileOut == NULL)       /* Use the defined constant */
  { fprintf(stderr, "The file could not be opened.\n"); }
/* The rest of the program goes here */
```

TIP

Even though it can be argued that the `NULL` is more readable than a `0` constant when you're testing for a bad file opening, *both* `if` tests just shown are less efficient than this identical code:

```
fileOut = fopen("C:\FILEDATA.DAT", "w");
if (!fileOut)
  { fprintf(stderr, "The file could not be opened.\n"); }
/* The rest of the program goes here */
```

The `!fileOut` means *not false.* Although the NOT operator, `!`, is usually frowned upon as being cryptic, it has good use here. If the `fileOut` file pointer is false, its value will be `0`. The expression `!fileOut` will be true if and only if the open file contained an error. Using `!fileOut` is much more efficient than using `==` to perform an equality test of the `fileOut` value.

Creating Files

After you open a file in QBasic, a simple `PRINT #`, with the same format as a `PRINT` except for the file number, sends data to the file. There is also a `WRITE #` command that writes comma-separated data to a file. Both `PRINT #` and `WRITE #` are easy because they are similar to the `PRINT` you are used to. If you want to format the data as is common before outputting the data, you can use QBasic's `PRINT USING #` command as well.

Use `fprintf()` and `fputs()` to write to C files.

C includes functions similar to `printf()` and `puts()` that write data to disk files you have opened. You've already seen the `fprintf()` command, which works just like `printf()` except that you have to insert a device such as `stderr` or `stdprn` for the first argument. You now can understand that if you use a file pointer for `fprintf()`'s first argument, the output of `fprintf()` goes to the open disk file pointed to by that disk pointer. `fputs()` works the same way; `fputs()` works just like `puts()` except that you pass a file pointer to `fputs()` that dictates exactly where the output is to go.

Consider the QBasic program in Listing 24.1 and the equivalent C program in Listing 24.2. Notice the similarities in the way QBasic and C programs create sequential data files. Most of the differences are solely syntactical, whereas the similarities lie in the method used to open, write, and close the file.

Listing 24.1. Creating a data file in QBasic.

```
' Filename: SEQOUT1.BAS
' Creates a sequential output file
OPEN "BASDATA1.DAT" FOR OUTPUT AS #1
' Write some data to the file
' Write a formatted line
PRINT #1, USING "&, ###, ###.##"; "George"; 15; 34.56
PRINT #1, "Sandy McCloud"
CLOSE #1
END
```

Listing 24.2. Creating a data file in C.

```
/* Filename: SEQOUT1.C
   Creates a sequential output file */
#include <stdio.h>
main()
{
  FILE * outFile;
  outFile = fopen("CDATA1.DAT", "w");
  /* Write some data to the file
     Write a formatted line */
  fprintf(outFile, "%s, %4d %6.2f\n", "George", 15, 34.56);
  fputs("Sandy McCloud", outFile);
  return 0;
}
```

Here is the output file created from each of the two programs:

```
George,   15  34.56
Sandy McCloud
```

Think about subsequent input when performing disk output.

The data written to the data file in these two listings have no consistent format, and you would have trouble reading such data back into a program later. When you write data to a disk file, you have to think ahead about how you'll eventually read that data. In QBasic, the `INPUT #` statement can properly read only comma-separated data. The `WRITE #` command is therefore used much more than `PRINT #` because `WRITE #` automatically inserts the commas and also puts quotation marks around all strings. C's file I/O is a little easier than QBasic's.

If you want to use `fprintf()` for all your file output, a corresponding mirror-image `fscanf()` will read that data back into variables. You'll learn how to read sequential data

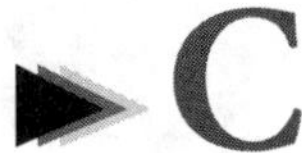

files with `fscanf()` later in this chapter. The only drawback to `fscanf()` is that, like with `scanf()`, you cannot read strings into a character array if the string contains embedded blanks; `fscanf()` skips all whitespace. You couldn't read `Sandy McCloud` with `fscanf()` and a format code of `%s`, although `fgets()` would work. As you are probably guessing, all C I/O function names that begin with `f` can be directed to a disk file pointer that you've opened, so the I/O occurs to the disk rather than the screen or keyboard.

QBasic's `WRITE #` and `PRINT #`, as well as C's `fprintf()` and `fputs()`, are not the best commands to use for writing nontextual sequential data files to the disk. As you might or might not know from your previous programming experiences, random file access is best used for formatted data such as employee records, inventory records, and the like because such data typically is fixed-length in its record format. It's best to use the QBasic `TYPE` statement to format your file data into a record format and then use random file I/O to write that data using `PUT #`. C's `struct` formats data in the same way as `TYPE`. You'll see how to work with such data in the next chapter.

Nevertheless, at times you will simply want to write some data to disk in the easiest way possible. You won't need to randomly access that data because the data might be a small history file that you'll rarely use again. The program in Listing 24.3 asks the user for five inventory items and then writes those items to disk. A program in one of the next sections, Listing 24.6, reads that data back into variables and prints the contents of those variables. Listing 24.4 shows that same data being written using C's `fprintf()`.

Listing 24.3. Writing data to a QBasic sequential file.

```
' Filename: DATAOUT.BAS
' Writes sequential data to a file
OPEN "DATAFILE.DAT" FOR OUTPUT AS #1
' Print a title
PRINT "**Inventory Storage**"
' Loop five times asking for items
FOR i = 1 TO 5
  INPUT "What is the part code (such as X144E)"; part$
  INPUT "How many are in stock"; quant
  INPUT "How much is each item"; cost
  WRITE #1, part$, quant, cost
NEXT i
CLOSE #1
END
```

Here is what a typical data file created in Listing 24.3 might look like:

```
"A121c",41,2.32
"T767p",17,6.43
"E445E",4,9.78
"U845a",67,2.01
"W344M",6,4.65
```

The `WRITE #` command ensures that commas separate each data value and that the strings are written with quotation marks. `WRITE #` helps format the data so that you can read it later with a mirror-image `INPUT #`.

Listing 24.4. Writing data to a C sequential file.

```
/* Filename: DATAOUT.C
   Writes sequential data to a file */
#include <stdio.h>
main()
{
  int i;
  char part[10];  /* Inventory data */
  int quant;
  float cost;
  FILE * outFile;
  outFile = fopen("DATAFILE.DAT", "w");
  /* Print a title */
  printf("**Inventory Storage**\n");
  /* Loop five times asking for items */
  for (i=0; i<5; i++)
  { printf("What is the part code (such as X144E)? ");
    scanf(" %s",part);
    printf("How many are in stock? ");
    scanf(" %d", &quant);
    printf("How much is each item? ");
    scanf(" %f", &cost);
    fprintf(outFile, "%9s%5d%7.2f\n", part, quant, cost);
  }
  fclose(outFile);
  return 0;
}
```

Here is what the data file from Listing 24.4 looks like:

```
A121c    41   2.32
T767P    17   6.43
E445E     4   9.78
```

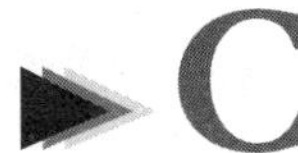

```
U845a    67    2.01
W344M     6    4.65
```

The program wrote the data in columns because each of the `fprintf()` format codes had width specifiers (the character array was written in nine characters, right justified; the integer in five spaces; and so on). No commas or quotation marks are needed because a mirror-image `fprintf()` (shown in a later section) can read these values with no problem.

> Extra spacing was given to the values. The part numbers needed only five characters, and the integers were no larger than two characters each. Listing 24.4's data file consumes much more disk space than the QBasic version, but it didn't have to. The extra spacing was included just so that you can more easily see where the values begin and end. However much or little spacing you put around your data-file values, just be sure that you read the data with the same spacing so that C inputs the values correctly.

No null zero appears in files.

There is no null zero stored in data files. When you read a string of characters using the `%s` format code, C automatically adds the null zero at the end of the input string when it gets into memory.

Use *fopen()* for the Printer

In MS-DOS, the printer devices `LPT1:` and `LPT2:` are nothing more than special files. You can open `LPT1` and `LPT2` as output files and write to the printer as if they were files. Although you earlier learned how to route output to the printer using `stdprn` (Chapter 16), you can now send output to *any* printer or device on your PC by opening the device as a file. The program in Listing 24.5 prints book titles on the second parallel printer port.

> If you don't have a printer attached to `LPT2`, change the `LPT2` to `LPT1` in the following program before compiling and running the program.

Listing 24.5. Writing to the printer on *LPT2:*.

```
1:  /* Filename: PROUT.C
2:     Write book titles on the printer */
3:  #include <stdio.h>
4:  main()
5:  {
6:    FILE * prnOut2;
7:    prnOut2 = fopen("LPT2", "w");
8:    /* Write some data to the printer */
9:    fputs("Moving from C to C++\n", prnOut2);
10:   fputs("QBasic Programming 101\n", prnOut2);
11:   fputs("Teach Yourself OOP with Turbo C++\n", prnOut2);
12:   fputs("Moving from QBasic to C\n", prnOut2);
13:   fputs("Absolute Beginner's Guide to Access\n", prnOut2);
14:   fclose (prnOut2);
15:   return 0;
16:}
```

The `fputs()` in lines 9–13 have to add newline characters to the end of the strings, whereas `puts()` automatically adds the newline character at the end of strings. Here is what you'll see on the printer if you run Listing 24.5:

```
Moving from C to C++
QBasic Programming 101
Teach Yourself OOP with Turbo C++
Moving from QBasic to C
Absolute Beginner's Guide to Access
```

Chapter 16, "Some I/O Functions," told you that the following statement would not work for all C compilers:

```
fprintf(stdprn, "This goes to the printer.\n");
```

Not all C compilers will recognize the `stdprn` as the printer device. However, opening your printer as a file will *always* work. This method has the added advantage of being able to send data to a serial or parallel printer connected to any device, whereas `stdprn` refers only to the first parallel port.

Reading from Files

Before reading the data created earlier, you should know that you can read a file one character at a time using the C function `getc()`. As Chapter 16 explained, `getc()` is identical to `getchar()`, except that `getchar()` always goes to the keyboard (`stdin`), and you can direct `getc()` to any input device including a disk file.

`getc()` reads a character at a time from a file, but the file must be a text file. All files created in this chapter are text files. The files you will create in Chapter 25, "Random-Access Files," are not all text files.

When performing input, you must check for the following two conditions:

- Make sure that the input file exists when you open it. If the file does not exist, you cannot input data from it.
- Check for the end-of-file condition when reading from the file.

Earlier in this chapter, you saw how to check to see whether a file exists when you open the file for input. To check for the end of file, you must use a defined constant defined in the STDIO.H file named `EOF`. The return value upon the end of file is usually `-1` (`EOF` is almost always defined as `-1` in STDIO.H). Therefore, you read character data from a file, but you must somehow check for a negative value as well.

QBasic uses the `EOF()` function to test for end-of-file conditions.

When reading characters from a file, be sure to use an integer variable to hold the character. Remember that `int`s and `char`s work closely together in C. If you define an `int` variable and then read a character into that variable, you can print the character using a `%c` format code. Alternatively, you can use a `signed char` data type. `char` data types are unsigned by default, meaning that you cannot check for negative values in them but only the numbers `0` to `255` (or the corresponding ASCII characters). The `int` data type is much less confusing than the `signed char` data type, and it's almost always used for character input.

The program in Listing 24.6 reads your computer's AUTOEXEC.BAT from the root directory on drive C: one character at a time. If for some reason that file does not exist on your computer, the program prints an appropriate message.

Listing 24.6. Reading AUTOEXEC.BAT a character at a time.

```
1:  /* Filename: AUTOREAD.C
2:     Reads the AUTOEXEC.BAT file a character at a time */
3:  #include <stdio.h>
4:  /* Need the header file for the exit() function */
5:  #include <stdlib.h>
6:  main()
7:  {
8:    int inChar;  /* Input character */
9:    FILE * inFile;
10:   inFile = fopen("C:\AUTOEXEC.BAT", "r");
11:   if (!inFile)
12:     { fprintf(stderr, "You don't have an AUTOEXEC.BAT on C:.\n");
13:       exit(1);   /* Terminate the program */
14:     }
15:   inChar = getc(inFile);       /* Read first character */
16:   while (inChar != EOF)        /* Read while not at end of file */
17:   { putchar(inChar);           /* Print the character on-screen */
18:     inChar = getc(inFile);     /* Get next character in the file */
19:   }
20:   fclose(inFile);
21:   return 0;
22: }
```

The program gets the first character in AUTOEXEC.BAT in line 15 just to get the loop started. As long as the character just read is not the end-of-file character (line 16 checks for `EOF`), the `while` loop continues printing the input character and getting the next one. After all characters in the file have been read and printed, the program closes the input file and terminates.

> If you want to, you can use `putc()` to create a sequential file one character at a time.

Many sequential files are character-oriented, but if you want to read a data file such as the inventory data file created earlier, you can do so using `fscanf()`. `fscanf()` works just like `scanf()` except that you must specify a file pointer for the first argument. Unlike `scanf()`, `fscanf()` isn't considered such a bad function. You must still specify non-array variables with an ampersand (the address of operator) in front of their names, but you're no longer getting input from a user who might not type the data exactly like you expect.

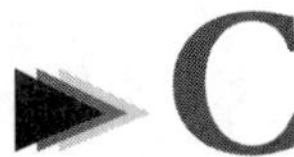

The data file you read is one that you created with your own program, and assuming that you formatted the file correctly when you created it (and after a thorough testing proves that you did), you can be confident that `fscanf()` will read the file with no problem.

`fscanf()` is the cousin to QBasic's `INPUT #`. `INPUT #` offers little in the way of formatting possibilities, however. For `INPUT #` to work, you must ensure that the data values are separated by commas. `fscanf()` can read values from certain columns in your data files. To get an idea of the differences between `INPUT #` and C's `fscanf()`, study the programs in Listing 24.7 and Listing 24.8. The QBasic version in Listing 24.7 reads the QBasic data file created earlier in Listing 24.3. The C version in Listing 24.8 reads and prints the data file created earlier in Listing 24.4.

Listing 24.7. Reading the inventory file in QBasic.

```
' Filename: DATAIN.BAS
' Reads sequential data from a file
OPEN "DATAFILE.DAT" FOR INPUT AS #1
' Print a title
PRINT "**Inventory Listing**"
DO
  INPUT #1, part$, quant, cost
  PRINT "Part Number: "; part$
  PRINT "Quantity:"; quant
  PRINT "Cost:"; cost
LOOP UNTIL (EOF(1))     ' Will quit at end of file
CLOSE #1
END
```

Here's the output from Listing 24.7. Listing 24.8 also produces this output.

```
**Inventory Listing**
Part Number: A121c
Quantity: 41
Cost: 2.32
Part Number: T767p
Quantity: 17
Cost: 6.43
Part Number: E445E
Quantity: 4
Cost: 9.78
Part Number: U845a
Quantity: 67
Cost: 2.01
```

```
Part Number: W344M
Quantity: 6
Cost: 4.65
```

Listing 24.8. Reading the inventory file in C.

```
/* Filename: DATAIN.C
   Reads sequential data from a file */
#include <stdio.h>
#include <stdlib.h>
main()
{
  char part[9];
  int quant;
  float cost;
  FILE * inFile;
  inFile = fopen("DATAFILE.DAT", "r");
  if (!inFile)
    { fprintf(stderr, "The data file does not exist.\n");
      exit(1);
    }
  /* Print a title */
  printf("**Inventory Listing**\n");
  do
    { fscanf(inFile, "%9s%5d%7f", part, &quant, &cost);
      printf("Part Number: %s\n", part);
      printf("Quantity: %d\n", quant);
      printf("Cost: %.2f\n", cost);
    } while (!feof(inFile));
  fclose(inFile);
  return 0;
}
```

Throughout this chapter, you've been told that a mirror-image `fscanf()` will read an `fprintf()`. This is *almost* true. As you might recall from Chapter 8, "Getting Input," you should never specify decimal positions (`.2f` or `7.2f`) when using `scanf()` to read floating-point values. `fscanf()` also cannot deal with decimal precision before a `%f`. Therefore, read all `fscanf()` floating-point values with a width specifier but no decimal specifier. The mirror-image `fscanf()` of the `fprintf()`

```
fprintf(outFile, "%9s%5d%7.2f\n", part, quant, cost);
```

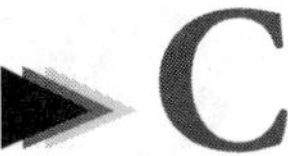

> is this:
>
> ```
> fscanf(inFile, "%9s%5d%7f", part, &quant, &cost);
> ```
>
> Also, as mentioned in Chapter 8, don't ever embed a newline, `\n`, in a `scanf()`, and the same holds true for `fscanf()`, as you can see here.

Listing 24.8 introduces yet another way to check for the end-of-file condition in C. There is an `feof()` function that works almost exactly like the `EOF()` function in QBasic. When reading individual characters in Listing 24.6, the input character would be equal to the defined `EOF` when the last character is read. When reading formatted data with `fscanf()`, you aren't able to test individual characters because you aren't reading individual characters. Therefore, the loop that reads the file's data calls `feof()` on line 23 to see whether further reading is necessary.

Appending to Files

It's easy to add to a sequential file with C. Open the file using the `"a"` mode, and write to it in the same way you would write to the file if you were creating it. Listing 24.9 creates a simple data file with five names; Listing 24.10 then adds five more names to the file. As you can see, the only difference in the two C programs is the mode used in the `fopen()`s.

Listing 24.9. Creating a file with five names.

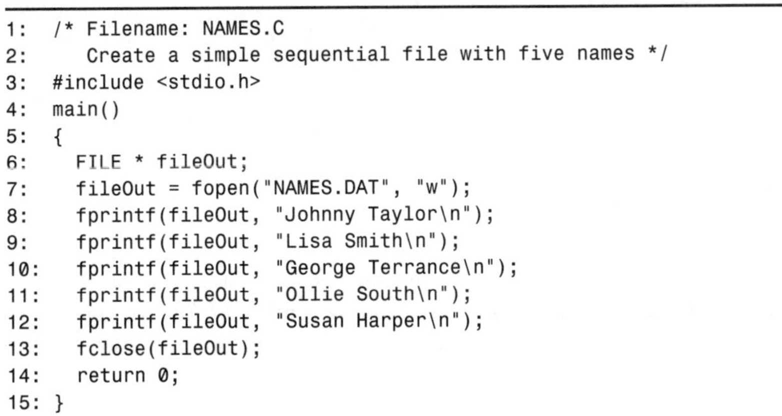

```
/* Filename: NAMES.C
   Create a simple sequential file with five names */
#include <stdio.h>
main()
{
  FILE * fileOut;
  fileOut = fopen("NAMES.DAT", "w");
  fprintf(fileOut, "Johnny Taylor\n");
  fprintf(fileOut, "Lisa Smith\n");
  fprintf(fileOut, "George Terrance\n");
  fprintf(fileOut, "Ollie South\n");
  fprintf(fileOut, "Susan Harper\n");
  fclose(fileOut);
  return 0;
}
```

Listing 24.10. Adding to the name file.

```
/* Filename: NAMESADD.C
   Adds to a simple sequential file */
#include <stdio.h>
main()
{
  FILE * fileOut;
  fileOut = fopen("NAMES.DAT", "a");  /* Append mode */
  fprintf(fileOut, "Michael Rogers\n");
  fprintf(fileOut, "Tina Jane Reynolds\n");
  fprintf(fileOut, "Paul Peters\n");
  fprintf(fileOut, "Mary Lin\n");
  fprintf(fileOut, "Betty Quincy\n");
  fclose(fileOut);
  return 0;
}
```

After both programs have run, the NAMES.DAT data file looks like this:

```
Johnny Taylor
Lisa Smith
George Terrance
Ollie South
Susan Harper
Michael Rogers
Tina Jane Reynolds
Paul Peters
Mary Lin
Betty Quincy
Michael Rogers
Tina Jane Reynolds
Paul Peters
Mary Lin
Betty Quincy
```

Summary

C performs sequential file I/O in almost the same manner as QBasic. You can write to a sequential file, read from a sequential file, or add to a sequential file. After you open a file and assign the file location to a file pointer, you use the file pointer in all subsequent I/O routines.

Although C uses functions for file I/O and QBasic uses commands, most of the programs that read and write sequential data are similar in format between the two languages. Actually, using `fprintf()` (for output) and `fscanf()` (for input) is many times easier than using `PRINT #` and `WRITE #` (both for output) and `INPUT #` because the formatting that the format codes provide give you the ability to specify exactly how you want data stored in a data file.

The `getc()` reads one character at a time from a sequential file if you ever need to do that. When using `getc()`, you must be sure to check for the end-of-file condition by comparing the character you last read to the defined `EOF` constant (defined in STDIO.H).

When using functions other than `getc()` for input, you must call the `feof()` function, passing to `feof()` the file pointer, so that you can determine exactly when you reach the end of the file. You never have to worry about end-of-file conditions when outputting data to a disk file.

The next chapter explores C's random file access methods. C and QBasic differ in their approaches to random file access, but the spirit is the same in both languages. Both languages enable you to read from and write to the same file randomly, without reopening the file, just as you can access array elements in any order. A sequential file enables you to only read or write (not both at once), and you must perform I/O in the order of the data in the file.

25

Random-Access Files

Unlike with sequential files, you can access (read, write, or add to) random-access file records in any order. Not only can you randomly access a random-access file but you can both read from *and* write to the file with a single `fopen()` function call.

Not every application can use random-access files, however. Each record in a random-access file must be the same length. Without fixed-length records, you have to use sequential files. Not all data fits within fixed-length record formats (such as text data), but a lot of data does. As a matter of fact, most data that computers store is made up of fixed-length records such as employee data, inventory data, and customer data.

The underlying concepts in the way that QBasic programs access random-access files and the way that C programs access random files are similar. However, QBasic and C use two different methods when accessing random-access files. Whereas there was a strong correlation between the two languages regarding sequential files, there is only a conceptual similarity with random-access files.

If you use QBasic's `FIELD` statement rather than `TYPE` to generate record data for files, you might be a little lost here. The `FIELD` statement has been considered to be archaic since the `TYPE` statement was added to the first version of QBasic. The good news is that Chapter 22, "Structure Records," reviewed `TYPE` quite a bit for those readers who have not worked with `TYPE` much. Not only is `TYPE` a more flexible statement than `FIELD`, but the C `struct` more closely matches `TYPE`. You'll use C's `struct` a lot with random-access file data, as this chapter shows.

In this chapter, you will learn about the following topics:

- Why you use random-access files
- File record layout
- Special file open modes
- Moving around the file with `fseek()`
- Reading and writing with `fread()` and `fwrite()`

Often, new programmers want to know why sequential file access is even needed. After all, if random access enables you to access a file in any order, why can't you use random access to access a file sequentially, from the first record to the last? As explained at the top of this chapter, some data will not fit into the random-access file methodology because random files have to be fixed-length records, and not all data fit into fixed-length records. Also, you'll find that random-access files take a little more work (although not much more) than sequential files. Therefore, if you don't need the advantages that random-access files provide, use sequential files to save programming effort.

A Review of Random-Access Files

Random-access files are sometimes called random files or direct access files.

You'll almost always use C's `struct` statement to prepare random-access file data just as you use `TYPE` to prepare random-access file data in QBasic. Although C programmers call

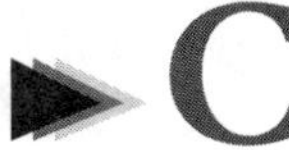

`struct` data *structures,* after that data goes to the file, they use the general term *records* (QBasic makes it easier by calling both in-memory formatted data and file data *records*). Figure 25.1 shows what a typical random-access file might look like for a customer file.

Smith, Larry	350.61	4	41A
Adams, Pauline	4693.89	1	56D
Washington, Jim	27.80	2	31A
Wheeler, Tom	954.98	2	67I
Elk, Mary Anne	2305.64	5	85T
Johnson, Jill	689.31	2	77E
Donner, Adam	1992.35	3	64D

Figure 25.1. A customer file's layout.

> The figure's file contains four columns and seven rows.

On the disk, the file is actually a stream of individual bytes following one another, but random-access files are conceptually seen as being formatted in a rectangular format as the figure shows. Each field in a random-access file is fixed-length, and because each record should contain the same kind and number of fields, the records themselves are fixed-length too. Here is the QBasic `TYPE` statement that might prepare such a file for I/O:

```
TYPE Customer
  custName AS STRING * 15
  balance AS SINGLE
  yrsAsCust AS INTEGER
  custCode AS STRING * 3
END TYPE
```

Notice that file strings defined with a `TYPE` statement always contain length specifiers, so fixed-length strings save to disk maintaining the fixed-length integrity that random-access files require. All the numeric data types such as `SINGLE` and `INTEGER` (as well as C's numeric data types) take the same amount of disk space no matter what the value of the number is. Here is the equivalent C `struct` statement that might produce such a file:

```
struct Customer
{  char custName[15];
   float balance;
   int yrsAsCust;
  char custCode[3];
};
```

Think Ahead

You must plan ahead when writing programs that create and manipulate random-access file data. If you set up a field to be 10 characters wide, store hundreds of records, and then find a record that requires *11* characters in the field, you'll have to truncate (ignore) part of the data, abbreviate the data value, or create the file all over again with a larger record size.

If you have to re-create the file, you'll have to write a program that copies all the data from the first file to the second file that contains the larger record size.

Plan ahead to eliminate as many file-structure changes as possible. Try to predict the extreme values that your file will consume. Of course, finding the correct record size is always more of an art than a science. You don't want to pad with more space than you'll ever need because that would slow down your file access and waste disk space too.

Think of random-access files like arrays on disk.

As with arrays, you can access the records in a random-access file in any order. Although moving around in a random-access file might not be as straightforward syntactically as using an array element's subscript, random-access files aren't at all difficult to use.

The Position Pointer

You learned about the file pointer in the preceding chapter. When you open a file for any kind of access, the file pointer enables you to refer to the open file throughout the program. You can open several files at once, in several different modes, and the file pointer lets your code refer to whichever open file you need to access at the time.

There is another kind of file pointer, called the *position pointer*. As you read or write data in a file, the position pointer moves to the next subsequent byte in the file to access. In a way, the file's position pointer works a lot like the cursor that shows exactly where the next character will appear on your screen.

The position pointer exists for all kinds of files, even sequential files. Figure 25.2 shows the relative placements of the position pointer when you open a file in one of the three sequential access modes.

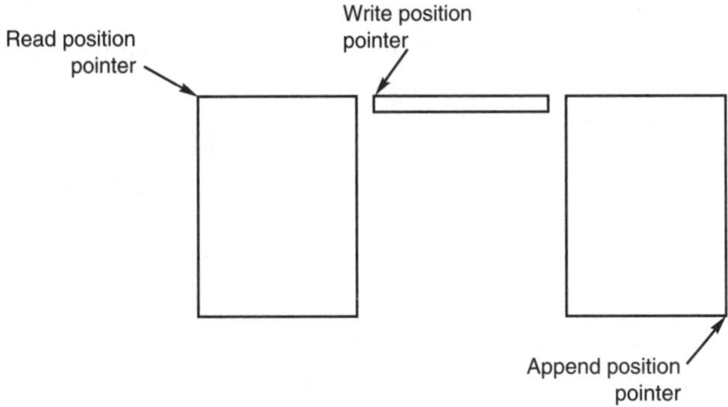

Figure 25.2. The position pointer upon opening sequential files.

The position pointer moves forward sequentially as you read a file, write to a file, or append to a file. You cannot back up the position pointer if you open the file sequentially. To reposition the position pointer to the random location of your choice, you must open the file in one of the *update* modes that make random file access possible.

Opening for Random Access

To open a random-access file, use the `fopen()` just as you did with sequential files. The only difference is the mode you use. Table 25.1 lists the modes available for random file access.

Table 25.1. Random file access modes.

Access Mode	*Description*
`"r+"`	Open for reading and writing. The file must exist first.

continues

Table 25.1. continued

Access Mode	*Description*
"w+"	Open for writing (and reading). The file should not first exist. If the file does exist, the file will be overwritten, and the original data will be lost.
"a+"	Open a file for appending, reading, and writing. If the file does not exist, C creates it. If the file exists, the position pointer will point to the end of the file as is usual when appending files.

In QBasic, when you wanted to open a file for random access, you had to use the RANDOM access mode. For example, the following OPEN statement opens a file for random access:

```
OPEN "CUST.DAT" FOR RANDOM AS #1
```

QBasic defaults to the RANDOM access mode, so the following statement is identical to the preceding one:

```
OPEN "CUST.DAT" AS #1
```

Using the FOR RANDOM keywords helps document your QBasic code and clarifies your desire for random file access.

In C, you must decide how you want the position pointer to appear when you first open the file. Although all the random-access modes enable you to read, write, and add to the file, the difference between the modes, as shown in Table 25.1, is the *initial* location of the position pointer. Subsequent file access will have to use the starting location as a guide when moving the position pointer, as the next few sections demonstrate.

If you want to open a file that already exists and you want to read from and write to the file randomly, you can do this:

```
FILE * randFile;
randFile = fopen("CUST.DAT", "r+");
```

Or you can do this:

```
randFile = fopen("CUST.DAT", "a+");
```

The choice depends on what you want to do after opening the file. If your program will add data to the file before backing up the position pointer and reading or changing other records, use the "a+" mode because the position pointer will be located at the end of the file initially. If you want to read the file from the beginning (as is often the case) and change data that fits a specific criteria along the way, use the "r+" access mode.

> Be sure to check the file pointer's initial value when using the "r+" access mode specifier. If the file does not exist (as it should if you use "r+"), the file pointer comes back equal to NULL.

In C, if you want to create a file, but possibly read from the file after you've written data to it, use the "w+" access mode like this:

```
randFile = fopen("CUST.DAT", "w+");
```

Close As Usual

To close a random-access file, use the fclose() function just as you do when working with sequential files. After you've opened the CUST.DAT file in any of the three access modes shown in the preceding section, the following C line will close the file:

```
fclose(randFile);     /* Close the file */
```

Seeking Randomly

QBasic's method of random file access is a little more straightforward than C's method. QBasic uses the record number to move around in a file, and in QBasic you can read or write a record at a time. The GET # and PUT # commands tell the QBasic program exactly which record to read or write.

For example, suppose that a data file existed on the disk that contains the Cust format shown earlier. If you want to read and print the contents of every other record starting with the first one, you would read the record numbers 1, 3, 5, and 7. The following section of a QBasic program would do just that:

```
' Assume that the file already exists as shown in Figure 25.1
TYPE Customer
  custName AS STRING * 15
  balance AS SINGLE
  yrsAsCust AS INTEGER
  custCode AS STRING * 3
END TYPE
DIM fullRec AS Customer    ' Must create a record variable
OPEN "CUST.DAT" FOR RANDOM AS #1
' Read every other record
GET #1, 1, fullRec    ' First record
PRINT "Customer: "; fullRec.custName
PRINT "Balance:"; fullRec.balance
PRINT "Years here:"; fullRec.yrsAsCust
PRINT "Customer code: "; fullRec.custCode
GET #1, 3, fullRec    ' Third record
PRINT "Customer: "; fullRec.custName
PRINT "Balance:"; fullRec.balance
PRINT "Years here:"; fullRec.yrsAsCust
PRINT "Customer code: "; fullRec.custCode
GET #1, 5, fullRec    ' Fifth record
PRINT "Customer: "; fullRec.custName
PRINT "Balance:"; fullRec.balance
PRINT "Years here:"; fullRec.yrsAsCust
PRINT "Customer code: "; fullRec.custCode
GET #1, 7, fullRec    ' Seventh and final record
PRINT "Customer: "; fullRec.custName
PRINT "Balance:"; fullRec.balance
PRINT "Years here:"; fullRec.yrsAsCust
PRINT "Customer code: "; fullRec.custCode
CLOSE #1
END
```

Of course, using a FOR loop with a STEP value of 2 makes more sense. The following code is identical to the preceding code:

```
' Assume that the file already exists as shown in Figure 25.1
TYPE Customer
  custName AS STRING * 15
  balance AS SINGLE
  yrsAsCust AS INTEGER
  custCode AS STRING * 3
END TYPE
DIM fullRec AS Customer    ' Must create a record variable
OPEN "CUST.DAT" FOR RANDOM AS #1
' Read every other record
FOR rec = 1 TO 7 STEP 2
  GET #1, rec, fullRec    ' Next record
```

```
  PRINT "Customer: "; fullRec.custName
  PRINT "Balance:"; fullRec.balance
  PRINT "Years here:"; fullRec.yrsAsCust
  PRINT "Customer code: "; fullRec.custCode
NEXT rec
CLOSE #1
END
```

If, in the middle of a larger program that accessed the CUST.DAT file randomly, you wanted to change some data, you could do so by writing this:

```
' Zero the data
fullRec.custName = ""    ' Writes a null string
fullRec.balance = 0.0
fullRec.yrsAsCust = 0
fullRec.custCode = ""    ' Another null string
PUT #1, fullRec, 5       ' Changes the fifth record
```

The last line writes the zeroed record to the fifth record in the file. Although the fifth record now contains null strings and zeros, it still consumes exactly as much disk space as it occupied before the fields were set to zero and strings.

C randomly seeks characters, not records.

In C, when you want to move the position pointer around in a file, you must call the `fseek()` function. *Seek* is the term applied to the act of randomly moving the position pointer from one location to another. (You cannot access one part of a random-access file until you move the position pointer to that desired location.)

In other words, with QBasic, you only had to specify the record number you wanted to access. In C, you must get to the proper record by moving the position pointer to the exact *byte,* or character, that you want to access. After the position pointer points to the first character of the record you want, via `fseek()`, you can use subsequent I/O functions to read or write that record's data.

Here is the format of `fseek()`:

```
fseek(filePtr, longNum, origin);
```

The *`filePtr`* is the file pointer variable you opened with `fopen()`. Of course, you had to use one of the random-access modes listed in Table 25.1. *`longNum`* is a `long int` value—a constant, a `long int` variable, or an `int` variable that C typecasts to `long int`. The *`longNum`* tells C exactly how many characters to move the position pointer forward or backward. In other words, if you wanted to move the position pointer forward 3 bytes, you would pass `3` for the *`longNum`* value. If you wanted to move the position pointer backward 10 bytes, you would pass `-10` for the *`longNum`* value.

You can move forward or backward a record at a time through a little ingenuity. If you want to move the position pointer ahead five records, you can pass this expression to `fseek()`:

```
(5 * sizeof(struct CustRec))
```

The *`origin`* is one of the three defined constants listed in Table 25.2. The values are defined in STDIO.H.

Table 25.2. Origin values.

Origin Value	*Description*
`SEEK_SET`	Beginning of file
`SEEK_CUR`	Current position in the file
`SEEK_END`	End of file

C's `fseek()` function combines the *`longNum`* and *`origin`* values to determine exactly where you want to move the position pointer. For instance, if you want to locate the position pointer to the 20th byte in the file, you would specify this `fseek()`:

```
fseek(filePtr, 20, SEEK_SET);
```

If, however, you wanted to position the file pointer 20 bytes from the *end* of the file, you would do this:

```
fseek(filePtr, -20, SEEK_END);
```

To be extremely clear and accurate, place an `L` at the end of the *`longNum`* value. If you place an `L` at the end of an integer constant, C immediately converts that integer constant to a long integer value before passing the value to `fseek()`. Although both do the same thing (through C's automatic typecasting in this case), the following `fseek()` function call is identical to the preceding one, but it passes a `long int` for the second argument:

```
fseek(filePtr, -20L, SEEK_END); /* Use a long int value */
```

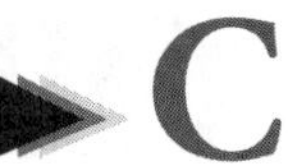

If you've been accessing a random file and want to position the file pointer forward one record from the current position in the file, you would do this:

```
fseek(filePtr, (1*sizeof(struct Cust)), SEEK_CUR);
```

Reading and Writing Records

Before looking at some complete C random-access programs, you should learn one more pair of functions that often work together. `fread()` and `fwrite()` are perhaps C's two most important functions for I/O. `fread()` reads data from a file, and `fwrite()` writes data. However, unlike `fprintf()` and `fscanf()`, `fread()` and `fwrite()` don't write formatted text data; instead, these functions compress the data before writing or after reading the data. Therefore, files created with `fwrite()` often consume much less disk space than files created with `fprintf()`.

> If you will ever need to look at the C data file from another program such as a word processor or database program, you'll have to use `fprintf()` or `fputc()` to write the data so that the data appears as text that the other programs can read.

With `fread()` and `fwrite()`, you can read and write *entire* arrays of structures with one simple function call. Here are the formats of the two functions:

```
fread(addressOfData, sizeOfData, count, filePtr);

fwrite(addressOfData, sizeOfData, count, filePtr);
```

The *`addressOfData`* is an array name, a pointer to a value or list of values (the values can be on the heap), or a variable with the address of operator placed in front of it. The *`sizeOfData`* is generally just an embedded `sizeof()` for the data you want to write. The *`count`* is the number of items you are writing. *`count`* is usually specified as `1`. The *`filePtr`* is the file pointer you've assigned in a previous `fopen()` function call. If you are writing the data, use `fwrite()`, and if you are reading the data, use `fread()`. Always maintain consistency; a mirror-image `fread()` will always read file data written with `fwrite()`.

QBasic's `GET #` and `PUT #` commands don't compare at all to C's `fread()` and `fwrite()`. For instance, `PUT #` cannot read an entire file in one line of code, but `fwrite()` can if the file's entire contents are stored in an array of structures. If you want to read or write a

single record at a time, both `fread()` and `fwrite()` can read and write individual records just like `GET #` and `PUT #` can. If you read or write one record at a time, `fread()` and `fwrite()` automatically update the file's position pointer for you.

It is because QBasic offers no equivalents to `GET #` and `PUT #` that it is difficult to show you direct language comparisons between the two languages. If you first saw a QBasic program that wrote random data to a file and then saw a C program that did the same, there would be so many differences in the two methods that the QBasic version would hamper your learning of C's way of performing random file access. Therefore, the rest of this chapter presents several C programs to teach you the "C way" of performing random file I/O.

Random-Access C Programs

Listing 25.1 shows you a program that writes an array of 10 integers to a random-access disk file and then reads the file in reverse order. The array elements are written one at a time. `fwrite()` and `fread()` can read and write entire arrays in one step (as done in the subsequent program). Using these functions for single integers values is OK, but probably not the most efficient method. This example program, however, is a good place to start seeing how to work with random-access files.

Listing 25.1. Writing 10 integers and reading them backward.

```
/* Filename: INTBACK.C
   Writes 10 integers and reads them backward */
#include <stdio.h>
/* Need header file for rand() function */
#include <stdlib.h>
#define TOTAL 10
main()
{
  FILE * rFile;
  int ctr;
  int val;          /* Holds random values */
  int newPosition;  /* To locate position pointer */
```

```
13:
14:   /* Print title */
15:   printf("Here are the %d values I'll write to disk:\n", TOTAL);
16:
17:   /* Write the data to a file one value at a time */
18:   rFile = fopen("NUMS.DAT", "w+"); /* Create and update randomly */
19:   for (ctr=0; ctr<TOTAL; ctr++)
20:   { val = rand();
21:     printf(" %d\n", val);
22:     fwrite(&val, sizeof(val), 1, rFile);
23:   }
24:
25:   /* Read the file backward without having to close it */
26:   /* Locate the file's position pointer to the end of the file */
27:   printf("Here are the %d values read backward:\n", TOTAL);
28:   newPosition = -1 * sizeof(val);
29:   fseek(rFile, newPosition, SEEK_END);  /* Point to last integer */
30:   for (ctr=1; ctr<=TOTAL; ctr++)
31:   {
32:     fread(&val, sizeof(val), 1, rFile);
33:     printf(" %d\n", val);
34:     newPosition = -2 * sizeof(val);    /* Read one, skip back two */
35:     fseek(rFile, newPosition, SEEK_CUR);
36:   }
37:
38:   /* Always close before exiting */
39:   fclose(rFile);
40:   return 0;
41: }
```

You'll notice that the program makes good use of the `fopen()` and `fclose()` function calls because the output file is not opened until just before the values are written to it on line 18.

Listing 25.1 generates and writes 10 random integers to the file in lines 19–23. As mentioned earlier, using `fwrite()` to write 10 individual integers is a little like overkill because with `fwrite()`, you can read and write an entire array at once (as subsequent programs will demonstrate). Nevertheless, `fwrite()` does write data as efficiently as possible. If you used `fprintf()` to print the integer `12345`, the integer would take five bytes in the file (one for each character). Using `fwrite()`, the integer would probably take only two bytes because `fwrite()` writes the data as stored internally, and integers generally take two bytes.

Line 28 locates the position pointer to the last integer in the file (literally, the function reads, "Position the pointer one integer from the end of the file"). Lines 30–36 then start the loop to read 10 values. Each time an integer is read, the position pointer automatically moves forward an integer size, so line 34 must back up the position pointer *two* integer places so that the next `fread()` will read the file properly.

The program in Listing 25.2 takes the reading and writing of large amounts of data to the next level. A list of 200 random floating-point values is saved in heap memory (no array has to be defined for the entire program, only a pointer to the first heap value) and then is written to a file using one `fwrite()` function call. Listing 25.2 then opens the file and reads all the values back into heap memory using a corresponding `fread()` function call.

Listing 25.2. Writing an array with *fwrite()*.

```
/* Filename: ARRAYWR.C
   Writes an array from the heap to disk */
#include <stdio.h>
/* Need header file for rand() function */
#include <stdlib.h>
#define TOTAL 200
main()
{
  FILE * rFile;
  int ctr;
  float * floatPtr;     /* Points to values on heap */
  /* Reserve the heap space */
  floatPtr = (float *)malloc(TOTAL * sizeof(float)); /* 200 floats */

  /* Store 200 random values on the heap */
  for (ctr=0; ctr<TOTAL; ctr++)
  { *(floatPtr+ctr) = (float)rand(); }

  /* Open the file */
  rFile = fopen("ARRAY.DAT", "w+");

  /***************************************************************/
  /* Save all 200 values */
  fwrite(floatPtr, sizeof(float), 200, rFile);
  /***************************************************************/

   /* Always close before exiting */
  fclose(rFile);
  return 0;
}
```

Listing 25.3. Reading the array with *fread()*.

```
/* Filename: ARRAYRD.C
   Reads an array from the disk into the heap */
#include <stdio.h>
#include <stdlib.h>
#define TOTAL 200
main()
{
  FILE * rFile;
  int ctr;
  float * floatPtr;    /* Points to values on heap */
  /* Open the file */
  rFile = fopen("ARRAY.DAT", "r+");
  /* Reserve the heap space to hold the disk's data */
  floatPtr = (float *)malloc(TOTAL * sizeof(float)); /* 200 floats */

  /*****************************************************************/
  /* Read all values */
  fread(floatPtr, sizeof(float), TOTAL, rFile);
  /* The floatPtr points to the heap, so the previous fread()
     automatically reads all values from the file to heap memory */
  /*****************************************************************/

  /* Close file because we're done with it */
  fclose(rFile);

  /* Print the values on the heap */
  printf("Here are the numbers: \n");
  for (ctr=0; ctr<TOTAL; ctr++)
  { printf("%10.1f\t", *(floatPtr+ctr)); }

  return 0;
}
```

> Listings 25.2's and 25.3's files are opened in `"w+"` and `"r+"` modes, but there happens to be no random access performed on the file in these programs. The purpose here is just to show you how simple `fread()` and `fwrite()` are.

First concentrate on the sections in each program with commented asterisks surrounding the code. In reality, the little code in each of these sections does the most work in both programs. The surrounding code simply defines variables, allocates heap memory, and prints the random numbers (in Listing 25.3). It's really amazing that one line, line 24 in Listing 25.2, writes the entire contents of the 200 heap floating-point values to the heap, and line 18 in Listing 25.3 reads those 200 values. No loop is necessary to read all the values.

Write structures just as easily.

Listing 25.4 contains a program that asks the user for inventory values. `fwrite()` writes the inventory structures to the disk. The program in Listing 25.5 then uses the inventory file created here by reading the data from the file and changing certain parts of it.

Listing 25.4. Storing inventory data.

```
/* Filename: INSTORE.C
   Stores inventory items in a disk file */
#include <stdio.h>
#include <stdlib.h>
#include <ctype.h>
#include <conio.h>
/* Define the structure format */
struct invRec {
  char partNo[6];     /* 5 characters and space */
  int quant;
  float price;
};
main()
{
  struct invRec * inv;  /* Define a pointer, not structure data */
  FILE * invFile;
  char ans;
  /* Reserve the heap space to hold the disk record */
  inv = (struct invRec *)malloc(sizeof(struct invRec));

  /* Open the data file */
  invFile = fopen("INV.DAT", "w+");

  /* Loop and prompt the user for the data */
  do
  { printf("\nWhat is the 5-character part number? ");
    scanf(" %s", inv->partNo);
    printf("What is the quantity? ");
    scanf(" %d", &inv->quant);
    printf("What is the price? ");
    scanf(" %f", &inv->price);
    fwrite(inv, sizeof(struct invRec), 1, invFile);
    printf("Do you want to enter another item (Y/N)? ");
    ans = getch();   /* Need CONIO.H */
```

```
35:     putch(ans);      /* Echo the input character */
36:   } while (toupper(ans) == 'Y');
37:
38:   /* Close file */
39:   fclose(invFile);
40:   return 0;
41: }
```

In lines 27–31, the structure pointer is used to access each of the members because the `inv` variable is a pointer to the structure and the dot operator would not work. There was no need to reserve an entire array of inventory items because each item was written to the disk as soon as the user filled the structure variable.

If you couldn't write the entire inventory item with `fwrite()`, you would have to use `fprintf()` to write a structure one member at a time. It's much easier to write each structure data using a single `fwrite()` as done in Listing 25.4.

When a Bug Is Not a Bug

Programs such as the one in Listing 25.4 sometimes produce the following strange error:

```
scanf : floating point formats not linked
Abnormal program termination
```

This often happens with Borland products when you reference floating-point structures with the `->` operator. In Borland's words, "This is not a bug."

Borland offers this solution: Place the following code at the end of any program that produces the message, and the error will go away:

```
#pragma warn -aus
void LinkFloat (void)
{
    float f=0, *ff=&f;   /* forces linking */
}
#pragma warn .aus
```

continues

continues

You be the judge. Can you understand this solution? Do you think there's something wrong that should be fixed? Well, for the time being, as superb as Borland's C products are, the `Abnormal program termination` problem seems to cause a lot of frustration for those who don't know the solution.

Here is the output from Listing 25.4:

```
What is the 5-character part number? XYZ12
What is the quantity? 12
What is the price? 5.87
Do you want to enter another item (Y/N)? y
What is the 5-character part number? ABC62
What is the quantity? 53
What is the price? 1.01
Do you want to enter another item (Y/N)? y
What is the 5-character part number? IJK90
What is the quantity? 4
What is the price? 5.43
Do you want to enter another item (Y/N)? y
What is the 5-character part number? QRS04
What is the quantity? 87
What is the price? 5.29
Do you want to enter another item (Y/N)? n
```

The program in Listing 25.5 is one of the most powerful programs you've seen so far in the book. The program asks the user for an inventory part number and searches the file (created in Listing 25.4) for the record. If the record is found, the program prints the data. If it's not found, the program informs the user that the search failed. It's true that only 4 items were written to the file (given the previous output), but if 3,000 items were written, the program would still work as is. `fread()` is used to read the records in the file.

Just to show the power of random file access, the program changes the price value of whatever item is found by increasing the price by 20 percent. Therefore, after the user's inventory item is found and the data is printed on-screen, that price is then updated in the file by 20 percent. If you run the program more than once and search for the same item, you'll see that the item's price increases on each run.

Listing 25.5. Searching for a part and updating the part if found.

```
/* Filename: INREAD.C
   Reads inventory items from a disk file */
#include <stdio.h>
```

```
#include <stdlib.h>
#include <string.h>
#include <ctype.h>
#include <conio.h>
/* Define the structure format */
struct invRec {
  char partNo[6];    /* 5 characters and space */
  int quant;
  float price;
};
main()
{
  struct invRec * inv;  /* Define a pointer, not structure data */
  FILE * invFile;
  char searchPart[6];    /* User's search part number */
  int found = 0;         /* 1 (True) if search is successful */
  int reposition;
  /* Reserve the heap space to hold the structure */
  inv = (struct invRec *)malloc(sizeof(struct invRec));

  /* Ask the user for a part number */
  printf("What part number do you want to see ");
  printf("before its price increase? ");
  scanf(" %s", searchPart);

   /* Open the data file */
  invFile = fopen("INV.DAT", "r+");

  /* Loop, reading until finding the structure */
  /* Perform first read for search */
  fread(inv, sizeof(struct invRec), 1, invFile);
  do {
    if (!strcmp(inv->partNo, searchPart))
      { /* Found the item */
        printf("Here is the inventory item:\n");
        printf("Part number: %s\n", inv->partNo);
        printf("Quantity: %d\n", inv->quant);
        printf("Price: $%.2f\n\n", inv->price);
        found = 1;   /* Set found flag */
        break;
      }
    fread(inv, sizeof(struct invRec), 1, invFile);
   } while (!feof(invFile));
  if (found)
    { inv->price *= 1.2;   /* Increase the price 20% */
      reposition = -1 * sizeof(struct invRec); /* Back up */
```

continues

Listing 25.5. continued

```
50:       fseek(invFile, reposition, SEEK_CUR);
51:       fwrite(inv, sizeof(struct invRec), 1, invFile); /* Write rec */
52:     }
53:   else
54:     { printf("Your requested part number could not be found.\n"); }
55:   /* Close file */
56:   fclose(invFile);
57:
58:   return 0;
59: }
```

Although the program is fairly long, the `fread()`s in lines 34 and 45 (line 34 gets the first record to get things started) read individual records from the file, and the `strcmp()` on line 36 attempts to match the record's part number with the part number entered by the user.

Later chapters will build on this program a bit. When you get to the next part of the book, you'll learn how to organize this program so that it is more manageable.

When you write programs such as the preceding two, you have the choice of saving all the user's data in an array of structures before writing the entire array with `fwrite()` and then reading an entire array of structures, with a single `fread()`, before processing the data. Programs with fewer I/O calls are more efficient than those that call lots of small I/O functions. The trade-off, however, is memory. A rather large inventory array (5,000 items) could be too big to fit in memory at one time.

The programs in this chapter are longer than many you've seen so far. As a matter of fact, most C programmers would consider them too long for `main()`. In the next chapter, you'll learn how to break your programs into separate and more manageable functions.

Summary

You now have the groundwork for developing programs with file I/O. You saw in this chapter that although QBasic performs random file access a little differently from C, they both offer methods that enable you to read and write forward, backward, and randomly from your data files.

Random-access methods require that the data in the random-access files be uniform in record lengths. As long as you use a `struct` for your record definitions, you'll have no problem using the random I/O routines found in this chapter.

The `fseek()` enables you to locate the position pointer anyplace in a random-access file that you want it to appear. After you move the position pointer, you can read or write (or both) the record in question with `fread()` and `fwrite()`.

The next chapter shows you how to structure your programs so that they become more manageable. QBasic supports local variables, global variables, and separation of routines (using subprocedures and function procedures). However, QBasic's separation of routines is fairly difficult. It almost seems as though Microsoft made QBasic into a language that is just too difficult to properly structure into separate routines. How often have you wondered whether you needed a `COMMON` or `DIM` when passing values from one procedure to another? Should your variables be defined with the `STATIC` keyword? How do you delete a procedure?

The next chapter explores C's methodology of separating programs into smaller, more manageable functions. Very little comparison will be made to the QBasic way of doing things because C's function separation is much easier than the requirements QBasic places on you to do the same thing.

Basic C

Part VIII

Organizing Your Code

QBasic → C

26

Functions Improve Program Structure

So far, all the programs you've worked with in this book have contained one and only one function (other than the built-in functions such as `printf()`). That function is `main()`. Actually, `main()` was not designed to hold a lot of code. As you saw toward the end of the preceding chapter, `main()` can get large if it's the only function in your program.

It's time to structure your programs better by breaking them into separate functions. There are several equivalent names for *functions* in QBasic: *subroutines, functions, subroutine procedures, and function procedures.* C doesn't confuse the issue with several names for the same language feature. A C function is a section of code, separated from the rest of the program, that works like a building block. Sometimes, a program contains several functions. The first function is always `main()`, but starting in this chapter, you'll learn the advantages of writing additional functions as well.

If you've worked much with QBasic's `COMMON`, `CALL`, `SUB PROC`, and `FUNCTION PROC`, you'll have no problem here. These QBasic keywords are fairly advanced, and not all QBasic programmers have used them. As mentioned at the end of the preceding chapter, this chapter doesn't dwell much on QBasic's equivalent routines for functions because QBasic's methods are fairly difficult, whereas C's are easy. If you've never worked with anything other than a `GOSUB` in QBasic, that's fine too, because this chapter teaches you the importance of separating your code into smaller and more manageable functions.

> This last part of the book focuses on truly making your programs more structured so that you'll finish programming faster and with fewer bugs. Structured programs are also easier to maintain than unstructured programs.

In this chapter, you will learn about the following topics:

- Writing separate functions
- Making `main()` more high level
- Prototyping your functions
- What header files really do
- How to define local and global variables

main() Is Not Enough

The preceding chapter began to show longer programs than those you saw in the earlier chapters of the book. When your program gets longer than a single screen, you probably need to break that program into more than one function. `main()` is OK for short programs that demonstrate a C language element as done throughout this book so far. However, when programs (such as the real-world programs that you'll write) get longer than one screen length or so, `main()` is doing too much.

One function, one screen, makes programming easier.

There are always exceptions to every rule. Not every program that's longer than one screen requires separate functions. The screen length, however, is a good suggestion to follow because if you can't see an entire function on one screen, you can't see the overall goal of the function. You'll have to press Page Up and Page Down to see sections of the function, and it's easy to get confused.

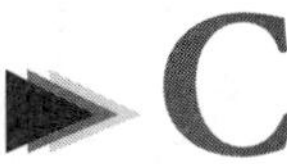

The first C program function will always be `main()`, which is required in all C programs. When you execute a program, `main()` is always the first function executed. Until now, all programs have consisted of a single (sometimes long) `main()` function. If you want to put 400,000 lines of code in `main()`, you can. However, the original purpose of `main()` was not to hold the entire program. `main()` should just be a high-level function caller that calls functions you list after `main()`.

> If you have worked with separate procedures in QBasic, you'll understand that C's `main()` function corresponds to QBasic's *main module.* Generally, the main module controls (via `CALL` statements) other QBasic modules such as function and subroutine procedures. As mentioned earlier, C's support of separate modules is easier than QBasic's, so very little of this part of the book discusses QBasic's awkward methods for separating programs into modules.

In a way, `main()` is a lot like the table of contents in a book. `main()` should be a high-level listing of function calls, and very little code should go inside the `main()` function. It's important to get the "big picture." You should be able to glance at `main()` and see names of functions called by `main()`. Unless those functions are built-in C functions, you should supply the code for the functions that `main()` calls after `main()` or include the code for the functions with an `#include` preprocessor directive.

> By breaking a long program into smaller sections (functions), you'll write the program more quickly because you can test each function as you write it. Also, you can more easily isolate errors during debugging.

It's natural for people to classify large collections into groups. If you collect books, you probably group them in some way, such as biographies, humor, computers, fiction, and so on. By breaking large collections into small and related groups, you can focus more on the "forest" without getting lost in all the "trees." Put another way, you can manage your collection more easily by grouping related subjects together. Grouping related subjects enables you to work from a high-level perspective in the collection.

When you first begin to write a program, try to separate the parts of the program into logical units. There might be a data-entry section, a reporting section, and a disk I/O section. Each section will eventually be a C function. Remember that there is no distinction between a function and a subroutine in C; both are known as *functions.* Functions might return a value (as a QBasic function procedure does), or they might just perform a programming task that produces no return value, such as printing a report (as a QBasic subroutine procedure does).

The C functions you write will look like `main()` in their format, except that you'll call them something other than `main()`. The function name should indicate the function's purpose; for example, `printfTotals()` would be a perfect name for a function that produces summary totals on-screen. You can distinguish a function name from a variable because of the parentheses that always follow a function name.

A Function in Action

Perhaps the easiest way to learn functions is to see an example program that contains separate functions. The program in Listing 26.1 contains the following three functions:

```
main()
printOddNums()
printEvenNums()
```

The functions are almost overkill in this case because they do nothing more than print odd or even numbers from 1 to 25. Nevertheless, starting with a simple example helps speed your understanding of how to write your own functions.

Listing 26.1. Printing odd and even numbers in functions.

```
/* Filename: SIMPLFUN.C
   Simple program with three functions */
#include <stdio.h>
printOddNums(void);    /* Prototypes */
printEvenNums(void);

main()
{
  printf("Get ready for the numbers...\n");
  printOddNums();        /* Calls a function */
  printEvenNums();       /* Calls a function */
  printf("\nJust returned from the functions.\n");
  return 0;              /* Go back to DOS */
}
/*************************************************************/
printOddNums()
{
```

```
18:    /* This function prints odd numbers from 1 to 25 */
19:    int num;
20:    printf("The odd numbers:\n");
21:    for (num=1; num<=25; num+=2)
22:      { printf("%5d", num); }
23:    return 0;      /* Back to main() */
24: }
25: /**************************************************************/
26: printEvenNums()
27: {
28:    /* This function prints even numbers from 1 to 25 */
29:    int num;
30:    printf("\nThe even numbers:\n");
31:    for (num=2; num<=25; num+=2)
32:      { printf("%5d", num); }
33:    return 0;      /* Back to main() */
34: }
```

Here is the output from Listing 26.1:

```
Get ready for the numbers...
The odd numbers:
    1    3    5    7    9   11   13   15   17   19   21   23   25
The even numbers:
    2    4    6    8   10   12   14   16   18   20   22   24
Just returned from the functions.
```

Although Listing 26.1 is a simple program, it offers much for discussion. First, the program defines the three functions listed in the paragraph before the program listing. However, the program also calls a built-in function, `printf()`, on lines 9, 12, 20, 22, 30, and 32. Therefore, the program uses four functions, three of which are defined in the program and one of which is supplied by the compiler.

You already know that you call C functions by just using the function name, such as `printf()`. Unlike in QBasic, no `GOSUB` or `CALL` is allowed. It is hoped that you will write meaningful function names so that `main()` basically reads like English rather than C code. Although it's a stretch to say that a non-C programmer would understand Listing 26.1, it's true that looking at `main()` tells a person that a title will print, then even numbers will print, then odd numbers will print, and then a closing message will print. Although Listing 26.1 did not call any of the program's defined functions more than once, your program can call a function over and over (such as in a loop) as many times as necessary.

Figure 26.1 shows the order of execution in this program. First, as is always the case, `main()` begins executing. `main()`, at line 10, is put on hold while `printOddNums()` executes. On line 10, `main()` turns over the program's execution to the `printOddNums()` function.

The `printOddNums()` function retains control until its `return` statement on line 23. The program's control is then passed back to `main()`, and immediately line 11 calls another function, turning control over to `printEvenNums()`. When `printEvenNums()` finishes, control returns to `main()`, and upon `main()`'s `return` statement at line 13, control is again passed to the operating system or to your C editing environment.

```
main()
{
 printOddNums();
 printEvenNums();
 return 0;              /* Go back to DOS */
}
/**********************************************/
printOddNums()
{
      :
 return 0;     /* Back to main() */
}
/**********************************************/
printEvenNums()
      :
 return 0;     /* Back to main() */
}
```

Figure 26.1. The order of the program.

C's `return` fills the same purpose as QBasic's `RETURN`. As the figure shows, program control always returns to the *calling* function when the *called* function's `return` statement executes. In a way, MS-DOS or your program's editing environment (however you compiled and ran the program) called `main()`, so `main()`'s final `return 0;` statement returns control to MS-DOS or your compiler's editing environment.

> Don't yet worry about the zero that follows each `return` statement. In Chapter 28, "Returning Data," you'll finally see why functions always end with `return 0;`, rather than simply `return;`. It turns out that the three functions in Listing 26.1 really don't require a `return` statement, but using `return` makes your code clearer and helps eliminate problems later in functions that will require `return`.

> **Make Things Readable**
>
> The asterisks on lines 15 and 25 in Listing 26.1 help separate the three functions from each other. Even if you put ample whitespace throughout a program, it's still difficult to find where some functions end and the next begin.
>
> Most C programmers use some kind of separating comment such as the asterisks. When searching through a long program listing, you can more easily find the start of each function because each function begins immediately following the line of asterisks.
>
> Often, C programmers put a comment or two after the separating asterisks or after the function's name that describe the overall purpose of the function.
>
> As you write your programs, think ahead and include as much whitespace, separating comments, and documenting comments as you can so that later when you debug or change the program, you'll be able to finish more quickly.

When you call a function, you must put a semicolon after its name. All `printf()` function calls and `scanf()` function calls that you've seen in this book have semicolons after their names, and the functions you write also must be called by names followed by semicolons.

When you place the actual function code, called *defining the function,* you never put a semicolon after the function name. Semicolons appear only after complete *executable* program lines, and the function names on lines 16 and 26 of Listing 26.1 don't really execute; they define the function by naming the code that follows. Lines 10 and 11, however, do have semicolons after their names, so they are function calls.

I know that your eyes keep going back to lines 4 and 5 and that you're asking, "What's up with *those* two lines?" I'll not leave you wondering too much longer. The next section of the book explains the two lines preceding `main()`. Understanding the function-calling mechanism is much more important at this point than understanding lines 4 and 5.

> Lines 19 and 29 define *local* variables, and Listing 26.1 will not work without those variable definitions. A little later in this chapter, you'll see why these variables are needed. Although they have the same name, they are two different variables in the program. If you've worked with local and global variables before, you'll understand how two variables with the same name can be entirely different variables. If you haven't worked with local or global variables, the explanation that follows later in the chapter will clarify everything.

Prototypes

Always prototype your functions.

A *prototype* is a model of something. Every time you use a function in your program—with the single exception of `main()`, which is self-prototyping because it appears first in your program—you must *also* prototype the function. Although most C compilers only generate warning messages when you forget to prototype functions, the experts agree that you should prototype even if prototypes are not strictly required by your compiler.

> A compiler warning is less severe than an error message. Warnings occur when you compile a program that defines a variable but never uses the variable for anything. As just mentioned, warnings also occur when you fail to prototype functions. Your program will often run correctly when you get warning messages, but you usually should correct the problem causing the warning. More likely than not, the warning is a good suggestion that there's something you should look at and correct. Defining a variable but not using it is a waste of memory. Not prototyping a function can cause lots of problems if you add extras to the function later (such as passed values and return values that you'll read about in the next two chapters).

You'll learn more about prototypes in the last two chapters of this book. In the meantime, you should know that a prototype is just a model of your function. In Listing 26.1, lines 4 and 5 are prototypes. The prototypes model the actual first lines of the `printOddNums()` and `printEvenNums()` functions. Notice, however, that the prototypes always end with a semicolon, whereas a function definition (the first line in a function that names the function) does not have a semicolon. The prototype is a special kind of executable statement that tells C, "This function is coming up, so be ready for it."

The purpose of prototypes will become more obvious throughout the next two chapters. For now, think of a prototype as a hint to the compiler that you'll use those functions later. The idea is not to surprise the compiler when it finds lines 10 and 11 in `main()`. The compiler has not yet seen the definition for `printOddNums()` and `printEvenNums()` when `main()` calls them in lines 10 and 11. If you don't prototype, the compiler has to trust you that the two functions appear later. Sometimes, the function call is too complex for the compiler to trust your function call, as you'll see in the next two chapters.

Simple functions that operate like pure subroutines, as both `printOddNums()` and `printEvenNums()` do, need only simple prototypes. Any function definition that has empty

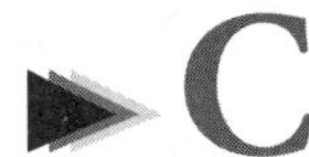

parentheses after its name and nothing before the name (as on lines 16 and 26) is a simple function that is the easiest to prototype. Here are the guidelines to follow for such functions:

1. Copy the function's definition line, where the function name appears, to an area of the program before `main()`.
2. Add a semicolon to the end of the prototype line.
3. If the function's parentheses are empty, place the keyword `void` in the prototype's parentheses.

It's actually more accurate and consistent to put `void` inside a function's empty parentheses when you define the function, although you don't have to. In other words, lines 16 and 26 could have looked like

```
16: printOddNums(void)
```

and

```
26: printEvenNums(void)
```

and C would not have complained. Many programmers choose not to put `void` in the parentheses because `void` is not required, but because you're going to copy that line to the top of the program and turn it into a prototype, you might as well use `void` when you first define the function.

> As you are probably guessing, programmers usually prototype after they've written their program and before they compile the program for the first time. It's difficult to prototype before you define a function because it's hard to tell in advance exactly what format the function will take on. If you insert `void` when you define the function, you won't have to mess with it later when you copy the function's first line to your prototype area.

The `void` is a keyword that tells C you are not passing data to the function from the calling function. In other words, `main()` passes no values to `printOddNums()` and `printEvenNums()`. If you've ever passed values to QBasic function procedures or subroutine procedures, you know that the passed values appear in parentheses after the procedure name and passed values also appear in C's function parentheses. Chapter 27, "Passing Data," explains everything you need to know about passing values between functions.

Prototype All Functions!

You should prototype *all* functions in your program except `main()`. There are no exceptions to this rule. You prototype not only your own functions but also the built-in functions. In other words, if your program uses `printf()`, `puts()`, or `fseek()`, you should prototype those functions too!

How do you prototype `printf()`? It's both difficult and easy to do! Here's the scoop: If you were to write out the prototype to `printf()`, you would have to learn a lot more about C than you and most advanced C programmers know. There's a way around writing out the prototype. Your C compiler writer wrote the prototype for `printf()` for you and stored that prototype in a file named STDIO.H.

Every program in this book has included the STDIO.H header file because every program uses some function from this file. Sometimes, a built-in string function was used, so the header file STRING.H had to be included. Every time one of these header files was included, all the function prototypes defined within those header files were placed at the top of your program.

You've been blindly including those header files, and now you can see why. By doing so, you prototype the built-in functions that you're using, and you make it easier for the compiler to compile your program when you use a `printf()` or `strcpy()`.

If you don't prototype, your programs will often run anyway. Therefore, if you forgot to include STDIO.H, your `printf()` function calls should still work, although you'll get compiler warnings.

Global and Local Variables

When your programs consist of one big `main()` function, you don't have to worry about variables as much as you do when you begin writing separate functions. The problem arises with separate functions because the variables you've seen so far in the book were defined after `main()`'s opening brace.

Local variables have little visibility.

All variables defined right after an opening brace are *local* variables. Local variables are *visible,* meaning that they can be seen and used, only within the block of code you define them in. Variables aren't always local for the entire function. Consider this incorrect `main()` function:

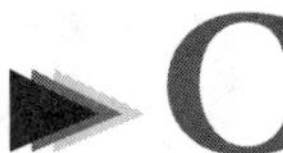

```
main()
{
  int i = 5;    /* Visible throughout entire block & function */
  printf("i is %d\n", i);
  {
    int k=4;    /* Visible throughout this block only */
    printf("i is %d and k is %d\n", i, k);
  }             /* k is NO longer available
  printf("i is %d and k is %d\n", i, k);  /* Error! */
  return 0;
}
```

Two blocks are shown in this code. The entire function consumes one of the blocks. (Remember that a block of code is any code enclosed within braces.) `i` is defined at the top of `main()`'s block, so `i` is known until the closing brace of `main()`.

There is also a second block inside `main()`. (There is no good reason to begin a new block in the middle of `main()`, but this block exists solely to demonstrate local variables. Many times, a new block appears because of `while` and `for` loops.) `main()`'s inner block defines the variable `k`, and `k` is visible only until the closing brace three lines later. `k` cannot be printed in the last `printf()` because `k` is no longer visible. The C compiler will issue an error because of the final `printf()`. As far as the compiler is concerned, there is no `k` variable at the last `printf()`. There is a `k` only inside the middle block of code. However, `i` is visible for the entire program.

Global variables are visible for the rest of the program.

You can also define variables before a function. If you define variables before function definitions, rather than after a block's opening brace, those variables are *global* variables. Unlike local variables, global variables are known from their point of definition *down* in the source file. Therefore, in Listing 26.2, no variable is defined inside `main()`, yet `main()` prints the contents of a variable and the program compiles without any errors.

Listing 26.2. Using a global variable.

```
/* Filename: GLOBAL.C
   Define a global variable and print it in main() */
#include <stdio.h>
/* The global variable is next */
int gl = 9;
/* gl is visible to all code that follows */
main()
{
  printf("gl is %d\n", gl);
  gl++;
```

continues

Listing 26.2. continued

```
11:    printf("gl is now %d\n", gl);
12:    gl++;
13:    printf("gl is now %d\n", gl);
14:    return 0;
15: }
```

Here is the output of the program:

```
gl is 9
gl is now 10
gl is now 11
```

The `main()` function is accessing the global variable named `gl` that is defined in line 5. `gl` exists for the entire program, and its value is known to any and all functions following its definition.

Global variables aren't as safe to work with as local variables. Although local variables take slightly more effort to use, the effort is made up for by the safety of local variables. When you define one or more variables globally, any function throughout the rest of the program can access and change the variable. If you write a long program and use global variables, you might call one of the variables `amount` and forget what you're using the variable for. You might have two different amounts to track in two separate parts of the program. When you change one, you're also changing the other.

Local variables keep variables inside the functions that need them. You can have more than one variable with the same name as long as you define both of them locally in separate functions. Back in Listing 26.1, there were two local variables, one in each of the two bottom functions, named `num`. Although you shouldn't name important variables such as totals and averages the same name because of the programmer confusion that could result, loop-counter variables are fine.

> Two or more variables can have the same name only if you define them locally and in separate functions.

The program in Listing 26.3 shows an example of a structured program that prints a menu in `main()` and then calls a function based on the user's response to the menu item. The user's input value is stored in a global variable. The user's value is used in every function, so the variable might as well be global. Each of the functions that follow `main()` uses a local variable to hold the result of a specific calculation.

Listing 26.3. Printing odd and even numbers in functions.

```
/* Filename:
   Program that uses a global and several local variables */
#include <stdio.h>
#include <math.h>
#include <stdlib.h>
doubleIt(void);  /* Prototypes */
tripleIt(void);
trigIt(void);
/* The user's input goes into the following global variables */
float userVal;

main()
{
  int menuAns;
  printf("What number do you want to work with? ");
  scanf(" %f", &userVal);
  do
  {
    printf("Do you want to:\n");
    printf("1. Double your number\n");
    printf("2. Triple your number\n");
    printf("3. Perform trigonometric calculations on your number\n");
    printf("4. Quit the program\n");
    printf("What is your choice? ");
    scanf(" %d", &menuAns);
    switch (menuAns)
    { case 1 : doubleIt();
               break;
      case 2 : tripleIt();
               break;
      case 3 : trigIt();
               break;
      case 4 : exit(1);
               break;
      default : printf("You didn't answer properly.\n\n");
                break;
    }
   } while ((menuAns < 1) || (menuAns > 4)); /* Keep looping until
                                              you get a good number */
   return 0;
}
/*****************************************************************/
doubleIt(void)
{
  float db;
```

continues

Listing 26.3. continued

```
  db = userVal * 2.0;
  printf("The doubled value is %.1f\n", db);
  return 0;
}
/*****************************************************************/
tripleIt(void)
{
  float tp;
  tp = userVal * 3.0;
  printf("The tripled value is %.1f\n", tp);
  return 0;
}
/*****************************************************************/
trigIt(void)
{
  float trig;
  trig = cos(userVal);
  printf("The cosine is %.1f\n", trig);
  trig = sin(userVal);
  printf("The sine is %.1f\n", trig);
  trig = tan(userVal);
  printf("The tangent is %.1f\n", trig);
  return 0;
}
```

Here are two sample runs from the program:

```
What number do you want to work with? .7
Do you want to:
1. Double your number
2. Triple your number
3. Perform trigonometric calculations on your number
4. Quit the program
What is your choice? 1
The doubled value is 1.4

What number do you want to work with? .8
Do you want to:
1. Double your number
2. Triple your number
3. Perform trigonometric calculations on your number
4. Quit the program
What is your choice? 3
The cosine is 0.7
The sine is 0.7
The tangent is 1.0
```

No Function Is an Island

As recommended earlier, most of your variables should be local. About the only variables that make more sense as globals than locals are those variables that are used in every function throughout the program. If all functions have a need for the variable, it must be visible to all those functions, so you might as well make it a global variable. File pointers are also good candidates for global variables because the file is outside the scope of the entire program, and all functions should have access to a file without being passed a pointer.

There's a problem, however, when your program contains lots of functions and each function has access only to the variables defined within the function. Sometimes, a function must use the value from another function. If, however, the variable is local from the first function, how can you use the variable in the second function?

Perhaps you've passed data between QBasic procedures. If you have, you'll have no trouble understanding how to do so in C. Even if you've never passed a value from one routine to another in QBasic, you'll still learn all there is to know about passing data in the next chapter.

Summary

You can now write your own functions. Doing so enables you to break your programs into more manageable sections. A well-structured program contains separate functions that perform separate tasks. When you localize your code, you improve the program's readability.

`main()` should primarily consist of a series of function calls. By making `main()` more high level and placing the working code in separate functions, you provide an overview of the program in `main()`, and you classify your functions in the same way that you classify other kinds of collections of data in the real world.

You must prototype all separate functions in your program. The prototype tells the C compiler what to expect when your function gets called. When you include header files, you are prototyping the compiler's built-in functions.

After your program contains separate functions, you also have to worry about the concept of local and global variables. A local variable is visible only within the function you define it in. A global variable is visible throughout the rest of the program. It's too easy to damage the contents of a global variable, so use global variables sparingly. By making as many variables as possible local, you'll have fewer conflicts when you work with long programs that use lots of variables.

When two or more functions have to share local variables, you must pass data between the functions. Passing data means that one function gets passed the value of another's local variable. The next chapter explores the ways that C passes variables from function to function.

27

PASSING DATA

The preceding chapter began showing you how to structure your programs better by breaking them into separate functions. Also, you learned that using local variables as much as possible is safer than using global variables, but if you use only local variables, you'll have a problem communicating between functions. A local variable is visible only within the block and function in which it's defined.

This chapter shows you how to pass data between functions. Be warned in advance that this chapter teaches only a one-way passing direction. In other words, you'll learn how to pass a variable (or more than one variable) to a function, but you won't learn how to pass any data back from the called function. (Chapter 28, "Returning Data," completes this loop by showing you how to return values to a called function.)

This entire chapter is devoted to passing data to functions because there are actually different ways to pass data. The method you use depends on what you need to do in the calling function. If your QBasic programming required the use of procedures and you passed data to those procedures, you know that QBasic passes data *by address* or *by value*. C supports both methods. Sadly, C's support of passing data by address is not quite as simple as QBasic's, but the result is the same. Passing by address and passing by value both send data from a called function to a calling function, but you can do certain things with variables passed by address that you cannot do with variables passed by value.

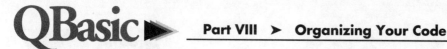

In this chapter, you will learn about the following topics:

- Some data-passing terminology
- Prototyping issues
- Passing non-array data by value
- Passing non-array data by address
- Passing array data by address

Some Terminology

Arguments and parameters are very similar.

In C, as in QBasic, you can pass one or more variables from one function to another. You pass local variables so that more than one function can share the same variable. The variable is still visible only in the calling function, and depending on how you pass the variable, the called function can get a copy of the local variable.

The terms *calling function* and *called function* are important to distinguish. As they sound, the calling function is the function that calls or triggers the called function. In Listing 27.1, `main()` is the calling function, and `calledFn()` is the called function. A called function should always return control to the calling function.

Listing 27.1. Helping to distinguish the calling function from the called function.

```
/* Filename: CALL.C
   main() is calling and calledFn() is called function */
#include <stdio.h>
calledFn(void);   /* Prototype */

main()
{
  printf("In main()\n");
  calledFn();
  printf("After return to main()\n");
  return 0;      /* Returns control to you */
}
/*****************************************************************/
calledFn(void)
{
```

```
16:   printf("In calledFn()\n");
17:   return 0;
18: }
```

The terms *calling* and *called* apply to C's built-in functions as well. When you call `printf()`, your program's function is the calling function, and `printf()` is the called function.

When you call `printf()`, the function parentheses are not empty as they have been in all user-defined functions you've seen so far in this book. For example, in line 9 of Listing 27.1, nothing appears in the parentheses, and in line 14, the `void` indicates that nothing is going to appear in the function's parentheses. `void` actually tells the C compiler that if you do attempt to pass that function a value, the compiler will give you an error message. This hints at the need for prototypes. A prototype informs C of what to expect in your program. If you call a function before the function's definition, the prototype tells C whether you're calling the function correctly. If you don't prototype, C doesn't always find your function-calling mistakes.

The variables that you pass between functions always go in the function parentheses. There must be a one-to-one correspondence between the passed data and the receiving data. In other words, if you pass a function named `myFunc()` three values, the definition of `myFunc()` must be set up to receive three values, and those three values must appear in the called function definition's parentheses.

Technically, you pass *arguments*, and functions receive *parameters*. Consider the program in Listing 27.2. `main()` passes the function named `newFun()` two values, an `int` and a `float`. Those two variables are called arguments. Even though the two variables are also local to `main()`, they are known as arguments in the function call. The function definition for `newFun()` is set up to receive two variables. Those received variables are called parameters, even though they act like local variables inside `newFun()`. Although you'll look at such details shortly, you can see here that a called function's parameter list must specify data types as well as parameter names. Also, the prototype looks just like the function's definition as should be the case.

Listing 27.2. Passing two arguments and receiving the two parameters.

```
/* Filename: ARGPARAM.C
   Passing arguments and receiving parameters */
#include <stdio.h>
```

continues

Listing 27.2. continued

```
newFun(int i, float x);   /* Prototype */

main()
{
  int i = 10;
  float x = 18.9;
  printf("In main(), i is %d and x is %.1f\n", i, x);
  newFun(i, x);         /* Don't specify data types here */
                        /* i and x are arguments being passed */
  return 0;             /* Returns control to you */
}
/*****************************************************************/
newFun(int i, float x)    /* Receive the parameters */
{
  float total;            /* Just a variable local to newFun() */
  total = x + (float)i;
  printf("In newFun(), i and x are still %d and %.1f\n", i, x);
  printf("The local variable called total is %.1f\n", total);
  return 0;
}
```

Here is the output from the program:

```
In main(), i is 10 and x is 18.9
In newFun(), i and x are still 10 and 18.9
The local variable called total is 28.9
```

On a need-to-know basis.

Although `newFun()` had no access to `main()`'s local variables (the variables `i` and `x` are not visible to `newFun()`), `main()` passed those variables to `newFun()` as arguments. `main()`, in other words, is giving `newFun()` permission to use its local variables. If four more functions were defined in the program, `main()` might or might not pass its local variables to those functions. The idea is to let `main()` pass its local data only to the functions that should have access to that data.

Figure 27.1 helps show the data passing of `i` and `x`. (The figure shows only a skeleton of Listing 27.2 with the pertinent code shown.) Notice that the data is a one-way pass. You'll see how to return values to the calling function in the next chapter.

By the way, some books and magazines are a little lenient about the terms *argument* and *parameters.* Some say that you pass and receive parameters. Some say that you pass and receive arguments. Don't worry about what terms they actually use.

> Often, it's clear just to say that you are "passing variables from one function to another." The important thing is not the terminology but your understanding of the need for local variable data sharing between some functions.

```
/* Filename: ARGPARAM.C
   Passing arguments and receiving parameters */
#include <stdio.h>
newFun(int i, float x); /* Prototype */
   :
main()
{
 newFun(i, x);
   :
 return 0;
}

newFun(int i, float x) /* Receive the parameters */
{
   :
 return 0;
}
```

Figure 27.1. Passing data.

After a called function receives the parameters, those parameters are just like variables within that function. The names in the parentheses of the called function and calling function don't have to match, although most C programmers make them match. For example, Listing 27.3 works *exactly* like Listing 27.2. Unlike in the preceding listing, however, the receiving parameters are named something other than `main()`'s passed arguments. Notice that the body of `newFun()` must use the same variable names as the parameters it received.

Listing 27.3. Different argument and parameter names.

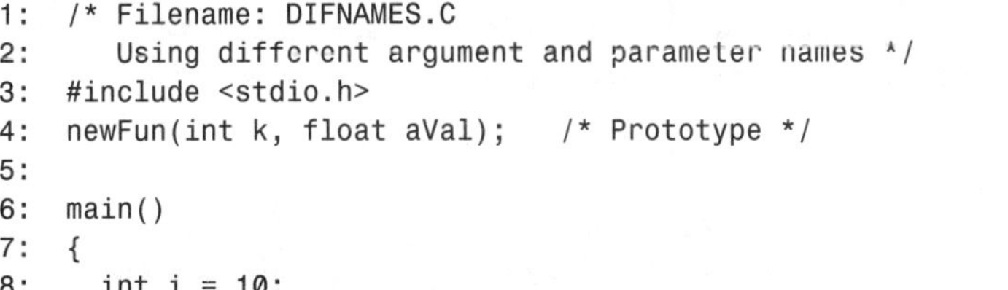

```
/* Filename: DIFNAMES.C
   Using different argument and parameter names */
#include <stdio.h>
newFun(int k, float aVal);   /* Prototype */

main()
{
  int i = 10;
  float x = 18.9;
  printf("In main(), i is %d and x is %.1f\n", i, x);
```

continues

Listing 27.3. continued

```
11:   newFun(i, x);          /* Don't specify data types here */
12:                          /* i and x are arguments being passed */
13:   return 0;              /* Returns control to you */
14: }
15: /*****************************************************************/
16: newFun(int k, float aVal)     /* Receive the parameters */
17: {
18:   float total;             /* Just a variable local to newFun() */
19:   total = aVal + (float)k;
20:   printf("In newFun(), k and aVal are still %d and %.1f\n", k, aVal);
21:   printf("The local variable called total is %.1f\n", total);
22:   return 0;
23: }
```

Often, you will want to send several different variables to the same function at different times. For instance, you might write a payroll-increasing function that prints a person's salary after applying a 5 percent salary increase. You might want to pass hourly salaries, executive salaries, and professional salaries to the same function. The function should increase *whatever* value is passed to it by 5 percent. The variables you pass from different parts of the program won't all be called the same name. Therefore, as long as the called function is consistent and uses the same received names throughout its body, there's nothing wrong with naming a parameter list differently from an argument list. The data types must match, but the names are trivial.

As a matter of fact, your prototypes don't have to list any variable names. The following prototype would work in line 4 of Listing 27.3:

```
4:  newFun(int, float);   /* Prototype */
```

Many times, you'll see variable names listed in a prototype next to the data types, but the names mean nothing to the prototype. Prototypes check for data types, not names. The reason you'll often see the programmer list the parameter names is that the programmer copied the function's definition (which always has to include variable names) to the prototype section of the program before compiling.

> Have you noticed that a C prototype does the same thing as a QBasic procedure's `DECLARE` statement? If you've worked much with QBasic procedures (and not all QBasic programmers have), you know that a `DECLARE` statement prepares the main module for all procedures that the main module calls. That's exactly what C prototypes do.

The Receiving Data Types

Sometimes newcomers to C have a hard time remembering whether to put data types in an argument list or a parameter list. The placement of the data types is easy to remember. When you call `printf()` to print two integers, you never insert the `int` data type in `printf()`'s parentheses. The following statement just isn't right:

```
printf("%d  %d", int i, int j);  /* Incorrect */
```

Think of how you use the built-in functions, and you'll have no trouble remembering that you never insert the data type names when calling a function. You insert the data type names only when receiving parameters. For example, line 16 in Listing 27.2 included both parameters' data types. Without the data types, `newFun()` would have *no* idea what the data types for `i` and `x` are. After all, `i` and `x` are local to `main()`, not to `newFun()`. The prototype also needs to include data types because all function prototypes should look just like the function definition's first line. If the function definition line has data types (and all should have data types, or have `void`), then so should the prototype for that function.

More Insight into Prototypes

A prototype, especially one with parameters and data types, helps the C compiler keep *you* more accurate. For example, consider the following definition line of a function named `addThem()`:

```
addThem(int a, float b, double c)
```

Suppose that you were to call this function, from `main()`, like this:

```
addThem(2.15434543, 4, 6.1);    /* Oops! */
```

What's wrong? As you know, a `2.1543432` will not fit in the receiving integer value. C would have to perform an automatic typecast data conversion and truncate data. It's obvious that the function was called with arguments that were out of sequence from those expected by the called function.

If there were no prototype for `addThem()`, your compiler would *not* issue an error on the previously incorrect function call. Instead, C would typecast the data as needed, and you would lose significance, especially with the first double floating-point constant.

continues

continued

If the program included the following prototype, however, C would know ahead of time how the function call should look:

```
addThem(int a, float b, double c);    /* Prototype */
```

If you, after properly prototyping a function, switch arguments as done here, the compiler catches the error and refuses to compile the program until you correct the error. Therefore, prototypes help ensure that you don't accidentally switch data types between a function's calling and a function's receiving.

The called function can, in turn, call other functions, but eventually control must be returned to the original calling function.

Don't ever pass global variables. First of all, there is no need to pass a global variable because all global variables are known throughout the entire program. Also, if you pass a global variable, a new local variable will be created in the called function, and the new temporary local variable will "hide" the global variable's value. Anything done to the new local variable will not be done to the global variable.

Just to put you back into more familiar territory, Listing 27.4 shows a QBasic program that includes a subroutine function which is passed an integer and a single-precision value similar to the simple C programs you've seen so far in this chapter. If you've worked with QBasic procedures, you know that QBasic separates procedures from the main module, and you must switch back and forth between them by pressing F2 and selecting from a procedure listing menu. Actually, such physical separation is quite nice because it promotes the separate data and procedure concept that is so important when you're writing structured programs. When you type `SUB`, type a procedure name, and press Enter, QBasic puts you in a new editing window for that procedure. In C, all functions follow one another, hence the common practice of separating functions with a line of asterisks.

Listing 27.4. Passing data between QBasic procedures.

```
1:  DECLARE SUB newFun (i AS INTEGER, x AS SINGLE)
2:  ' Filename: ARGPARAM.BAS
3:  ' Passing arguments and receiving parameters
4:
5:  DIM i AS INTEGER
6:  DIM x AS SINGLE
7:  i = 10
8:  x = 18.9
9:
10: PRINT "In the main module, i is"; i; "and x is"; x
11:
12: CALL newFun(i, x)   ' Don't specify data types here
13:                     ' i and x are arguments being passed
14: END   ' Control returns to you
15:
16:
17: SUB newFun (i AS INTEGER, x AS SINGLE)
18:   DIM total AS SINGLE         ' Just a variable local to newFun()
19:   total = x + i               ' QBasic doesn't need a typecast
20:   PRINT "In newFun(), i and x are still"; i; "and"; x
21:   PRINT "The local variable called total is"; total
22: END SUB
```

If you were to type Listing 27.4 into your QBasic editor, you would see that QBasic separates the subroutine procedure, `newFun()`, from the rest of the program. Again, press F2 if you want to switch between the main module and the procedure. Line 1 is the QBasic-like prototype for the called function. The two `int` and `float` arguments are passed in line 12 when the procedure is called, and they are received in line 17 as parameters to be used in the procedure.

> Here's an advantage of QBasic over C: If you forget to write a function's `DECLARE` prototype, QBasic inserts one at the top of the main module for you! It would be nice if C were that kind.

The parameters in the procedure don't have to be named `i` and `x`. As with C, QBasic's received parameter names don't have to match the passed names.

Passing Differences

C passes arguments differently from QBasic.

No comparison between C and QBasic would be complete without a discussion of the differences between the two languages in the way they handle the passing of data. In QBasic, all data is passed by address unless you override QBasic's default method of passing. In C, all data is passed by value unless you override C's default method of passing. Here is the difference between the terms *by value* and *by address:*

- If you want the called function to change a variable, and you want that change to remain in effect when the calling function regains control, you must pass the variable by address.
- If you want the called function to change a variable, and you *don't* want that change to remain in effect when the calling function regains control, you must pass the variable by value.

Consider the simple QBasic program in Listing 27.5. The main module assigns `5` to the variable named `var`. The subroutine procedure named `changeVar()` then receives `var` as a parameter. The procedure assigns `10` to `var`. After the main module regains control, `var` is still `10`. In other words, the procedure changed the variable, and that change was still in effect in the main module. Therefore, `var` was passed by address.

Listing 27.5. Passing QBasic data by address.

```
DECLARE SUB changeVar (var AS INTEGER)
' Filename: ADDRESS.BAS
' Pass a variable by address. Its change will remain in effect.

DIM var AS INTEGER
var = 5
PRINT "In the main module, var is"; var; "before calling changeVar()"

CALL changeVar(var)

PRINT "In the main module, var is"; var; "after changeVar() returns"

END

SUB changeVar (var AS INTEGER)
  var = 10
END SUB
```

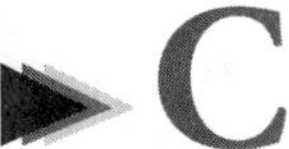

Here is the output from Listing 27.5:

```
In the main module, var is 5 before calling changeVar()
In the main module, var is 10 after changeVar() returns
```

As you can see, when a QBasic procedure receives a variable, that procedure receives the variable by address. In other words, the address of the variable is sent so that the same memory location is used by both the calling function's argument and the called function's parameter.

Passing by address has its advantages and disadvantages. Often, you'll need to send several variables to a function, and you will want the function to change one or more variables and for that change to remain in effect in the calling function. However, passing by address also has its disadvantages. Sometimes, you want to pass a data value to a function and you want that function to work with the data, changing it possibly, but you want the value to retain its original value in the calling function. When you pass by value, the called function cannot change the calling function's value. The called function works on a copy of the value, not the same memory location as is the case when passing by address.

> Often, the term *by value* is called *by copy.* A copy of the variable's value is passed, not the address.

If you want to pass a variable by value in QBasic, you only have to enclose that variable in a set of parentheses. Listing 27.6 looks just like Listing 27.5 except that the main module's `var` is passed enclosed in its own set of parentheses (making a double set of parentheses including the procedure's). The extra pair of parentheses overrides the default *by address* passing that QBasic would do otherwise.

Listing 27.6. Passing QBasic data by value.

```
DECLARE SUB changeVar (var AS INTEGER)
' Filename: VALUE.BAS
' Pass a variable by value. Its change will not remain in effect.

DIM var AS INTEGER
var = 5
PRINT "In the main module, var is"; var; "before calling changeVar()"

CALL changeVar((var))

```

continues

Listing 27.6. continued

```
PRINT "In the main module, var is"; var; "after changeVar() returns"

END

SUB changeVar (var AS INTEGER)
  var = 10
END SUB
```

With only the extra set of parentheses, look how the output changes:

```
In the main module, var is 5 before calling changeVar()
In the main module, var is 5 after changeVar() returns
```

Notice that even though the `changeVar()` procedure changes the parameter to `10`, that change does not stick after the main module regains control. `main()` passed the value of `var`, not the address of `var`, so `changeVar()` was passed a copy of `var`'s value.

> As mentioned earlier, the primary difference between how C passes data and how QBasic passes data is in their default methods. C passes all data by value unless you override the default to pass by address. C also requires more than just an extra set of parentheses to override the by-value default.

C is safer than QBasic.

The designers of C wanted to make C as safe as possible. Therefore, the designers thought that functions shouldn't be able to change calling function's arguments unless the calling function gave the called function permission by passing the value by address.

> There is one major exception to C's by-value default method of passing data. All arrays are passed by address! Nothing you can do will override this. Therefore, if you pass an array to a function and that function changes the array, the array remains changed when the called function regains control. C passes only non-array variables by value, but you can override that method as shown later in this chapter.

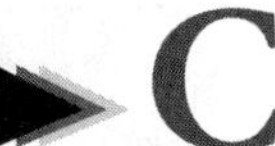

Passing by Value

Starting with C's default (and easiest) passing method, consider Listing 27.7. In `main()`, the user is asked to enter an integer. The first function, `doubleIt()`, prints the user's value multiplied by two. The second function, `tripleIt()`, prints the user's original value multiplied by three. If the value were passed by address, the `tripleIt()` function would be working with twice the value that the user entered. Here is a program that demands that its arguments be passed by value.

Listing 27.7. Passing C data by value.

```
/* Filename: VALUE.C
   Passing an argument by value (C's default) */
#include <stdio.h>

doubleIt(int num);    /* Prototypes */
tripleIt(int n);

main()
{
  int num;
  printf("Please enter an integer: ");
  scanf(" %d", &num);
  doubleIt(num);
  tripleIt(num);
  return 0;             /* Returns control to you */
}
/*********************************************************/
doubleIt(int n)         /* Receive the parameter by value */
{
  n *= 2;
  printf("Your number doubled is %d\n", n);
  return 0;
}
/*********************************************************/
tripleIt(int n)         /* Receive the parameter by value */
{
  n *= 3;
  printf("Your number tripled is %d\n", n);
  return 0;
}
```

Here is the output from Listing 27.7:

```
Please enter an integer: 5
Your number doubled is 10
Your number tripled is 15
```

If the value had been passed by address, this would be the output:

```
Please enter an integer: 5
Your number doubled is 10
Your number tripled is 30
```

The `doubleIt()` function would have changed `main()`'s argument, so when `main()` passed that same argument to `tripleIt()`, the doubled value, not the user's original value, would have been tripled.

Passing by Address

This section of the chapter shows you how to pass a C variable by address. When passing by address, remember, if the called function changes the variable, the variable is also changed in the calling function.

When passing by address in C, you must preface all passed arguments with the address of, `&`, operator. That makes sense, doesn't it? If you want to pass a variable's address, do so by passing the address of that variable. If `i` is an integer variable, the following statement calls the `doIt()` function and passes `i` by value:

```
doIt(&i);    /* Pass i by address */
```

Passing by address isn't difficult. However, when receiving variables by address, you have to do something else that few people like doing. When you receive parameters that were sent by address, you must preface each by-address parameter with a dereference operator, `*`, everywhere in the function you use the variable.

All those asterisks get confusing, but they provide the only means you have in C to pass by address. Listing 27.8 shows a program that first defines a variable in `main()`, passes that variable by address to a function for initialization, and returns to `main()`, where the value is printed. There is no way `main()` could know what the calculated value is unless the variable were passed by address from `main()`.

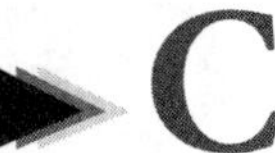

Listing 27.8. Passing C data by address.

```
1:  /* Filename: ADDRESS.C
2:     Passing an argument by address (Not C's default) */
3:  #include <stdio.h>
4:  getNum(int *num);
5:  main()
6:  {
7:    int num;
8:    getNum(&num);        /* Pass num by address */
9:    printf("The calculated value is %d", num);
10:   return 0;            /* Returns control to you */
11: }
12: /*********************************************************/
13: getNum(int *num)       /* Receive the parameter by address */
14: {
15:   /* Perform some calculations */
16:   *num = 10;               /* Everywhere num is used, it MUST */
17:   *num += 15;              /* be preceded by an asterisk */
18:   *num = 20 / *num - 2;    /* because it was passed by address */
19:   *num = 15 + 10 + *num;
20:   return 0;
21: }
```

Here is the output from the program:

```
The calculated value is 23
```

As you can see from line 4, when you receive parameters passed by address with an address of operator, the prototype also includes the address of operator. Always, the prototype should look just like the first line of the function you are prototyping.

You'll Always Pass Arrays by Address

As you might recall, an array name is nothing more than an address to the start of the array. Therefore, when you pass an array, you automatically pass by address. As a matter of fact, there is nothing you can do to pass arrays by value. When you pass an array, the calling function must assume that the array might be different when the called function returns.

If you want to pass an array for use in a function, but you don't want the array changed in the calling function, make a copy of the array before passing it. Use the copy if you want an unchanged array after the calling function regains control.

Listing 27.9 contains a program with a function that asks the user for his or her first and last names. The name arrays are passed to an input function. After the user enters the names inside the function, the arrays are printed in `main()` to show that the function changed `main()`'s arrays.

Listing 27.9. Getting a name by address.

```
/* Filename: ARRAYADR.C
   Initializing an array in a function and
   printing the contents in main() */
#include <stdio.h>
getNames(char first[], char last[]);
main()
{
  char first[15], last[15];
  getNames(first, last);        /* Pass arrays by address */
  printf("List your name like this:\n");
  printf("%s, %s\n", last, first);
  return 0;                     /* Returns control to you */
}
/*********************************************************/
getNames(char first[], char last[]) /* Receive by address */
{
  printf("What is your first name? ");
  gets(first);
  printf("What is your last name? ");
  gets(last);
  return 0;
}
```

Here is the output from the program:

```
What is your first name? Alice
What is your last name? Howard
List your name like this:
Howard, Alice
```

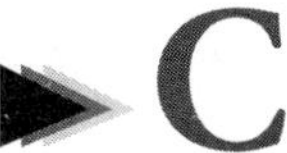

Notice that you don't have to list the array subscripts in the receiving parameter list. The brackets are enough to tell C that the array is being passed by address. If you want to put the subscripts in the brackets, that is fine. The following line is identical to line 15:

```
15: getNames(char first[15], char last[15]) /* Receive by address */
```

The same holds true for the prototype. You don't have to specify array sizes, but you can if you want.

If you pass a multidimensional array, you can omit only the first subscript in the receiving parameter list. For example, if you define a multidimensional array in `main()` like

```
float values[10][14][15][27];   /* 4-dimensions */
```

then you must receive the multidimensional array like this:

```
aFun(values[][14][15][27])
```

You also can specify the first subscript like

```
aFun(values[10][14][15][27])
```

but only the first subscript is optional.

Some *scanf()* Remarks

Hmm...`scanf()` now makes perfect sense!

Throughout this entire book, `scanf()` has been a necessary evil. For a newcomer's first learning experience with C, `scanf()` is a good function to use because it mirrors `printf()`. Also, alternatives to `scanf()` require lots of code or the use of special I/O such as `gets()` that demand an understanding of character arrays and so forth. Nevertheless, `scanf()` is cryptic, and telling a beginner to put an `&` in front of non-array variables and not array variables, without giving an explanation, is difficult.

Now that you understand how C passes arrays and non-arrays, you can understand all there is to know about `scanf()`. For instance, the following two `scanf()` calls get first an integer and then a character array from the user:

```
scanf(" %d", &myNum);       /* Get an integer */
scanf(" %s", myFirstName);  /* Get a character array */
```

If you didn't pass the integer variable by address, your program would have no idea what was stored there by the `scanf()` function! Remember that if you pass non-arrays by value, the default, the calling function's variables remain unchanged. When you call a `scanf()` function, you *want* the variables changed because you want whatever the user types to appear in the variables.

The array doesn't have an ampersand because arrays are automatically passed by address, as you learned in the preceding section.

Here's one last `scanf()` tip: If a `scanf()` appears in a called function, and if you've passed the `scanf()` variable to the function by value, the `scanf()` will look something like this:

```
scanf(" %d", &*myNum);   /* Fill a variable passed
                            by address */
```

Remember that if the integer `myNum` is passed by value, its name *always* has to appear with a dereference operator. However, `scanf()` requires that you pass the address of all non-array variables. In this case, the `&` and `*` cancel each other out. The preceding `scanf()` is identical to this one:

```
scanf(" %d", myNum); /* Fill a variable passed by address */
```

Again, you can omit the `&` from a non-array `scanf()` variable only if the `scanf()` appears inside a function of yours that was passed the variable by address.

Summary

Now your functions can communicate with each other. Through the passing of variables, one function can share its local variables with other functions while still maintaining control over that variable. Only functions that require access to variables get access.

When you pass a variable, the variable is known as an argument. The receiving function's variable is then called a parameter. The important thing to remember is that a function cannot work with another function's local variable unless you pass that variable as an argument.

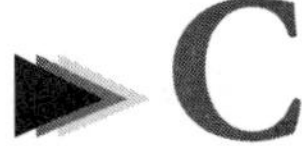

There are three ways to pass data in C. All non-arrays are passed by value unless you override that default. In QBasic, however, all variables are passed by address unless you do something to change that default. C's default (by value) is safer because a function cannot inadvertently change a parameter unless specifically passed that parameter by address.

All C arrays are always passed by address because an array is just the address to the data. When you pass an array to a function, be aware that when your calling function regains control, that function might be different from when it was passed.

The next chapter finally completes this book's part on structuring your programs. You now know how to pass data from one function to another. If all you passed were variables by address, you wouldn't need to know anything about returning values. However, you often pass by value to protect a variable, but at the same time, you want a function to return a value. The next chapter explains how to return values from called functions.

28

Returning Data

This chapter teaches you how to return a value from a C function. The preceding chapter showed you how to send data *to* a function, and this chapter closes the loop by showing you how to write functions that return values.

At the end of every `main()` function you've seen so far in this book, you've seen the statement `return 0;`. `main()` is always returning a value, and that value is zero. The `return` statement returns the value; without a `return`, a function cannot return a value.

This chapter shows you how to return values of different data types and how to capture those return values back in the calling function. At a high level, C's function return values work like QBasic's `DEF FN` and `FUNCTION` statements. The designers of C, however, streamlined functions so that a function that returns a value is coded very much like a function that does not return a value. One of the reasons QBasic includes more than 200 commands is that there are commands to do all sorts of things that actually could be done using one command, as C proves. For instance, why have five kinds of `LOOP` statements? C does the same things with two `while` loops, as you saw in Chapter 13, "The *while* Loops." Also, there are commands for subroutines (`GOSUB`, `RETURN`), functions (`DEF FN`), subroutine procedures (`SUB`, `END SUB`), and function procedures (`FUNCTION`, `END FUNCTION`), and a C function duplicates all those possibilities.

After you begin to return values, you have to understand a little more about prototypes. You'll see here how the prototype acts to set up a function for a return value.

In this chapter, you will learn about the following topics:

- The need for returning values
- Specifying the return values
- Prototyping the return values

The Need for Returning Values

A function often needs to return a value to the calling function. The calling function might need a complicated calculation performed on some data. Instead of putting the calculation directly inside the code that needs it, the programmer chooses to put the calculation in a function to make the program more structured and modular. After the return value is computed, the calling function receives that return value and uses it.

Figure 28.1 illustrates the concept of return values. As you can see from the figure, a function might have one or more arguments sent to it. No matter how many arguments are sent, there is always one and only one return value sent back to the calling function.

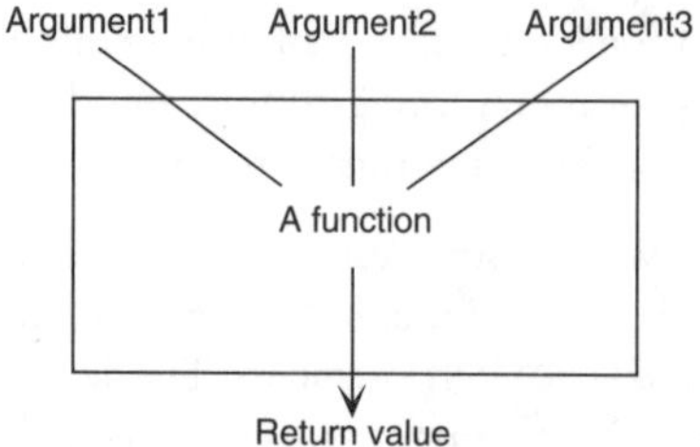

Figure 28.1. A function can receive several arguments but return one value at most.

Some newcomers to programming think that a single return value is too limiting and that a function should be able to return more than one value. They say that they might need more than one return value. First of all, where would all those return values go? How could you collect those return values in the calling function? As you already know from your QBasic programming, a variable usually holds the

return value from a function, and if multiple return values were allowed, perhaps an array could be set up to hold the multiple return values. However, using an array would be difficult to implement. There's another point to be made here: If you need a function that returns more than one value, perhaps that function is doing too much, and you should break the function into two or more smaller functions. The functions would probably be more manageable.

On those rare times when you *really* want a function to calculate more than one value and the calling function needs to use those values, pass some arguments by address. Although doing so won't ensure the safety that passing by value provides, your calling function can use values changed by the called function.

Return Values Have Their Roots in Math

Programming logic is often related to mathematics. Although you don't have to be good at math to be a good programmer (thank goodness), the kinds of logical thinking that both math and programming often require are similar.

In mathematics, as in programming, there are functions. Often, such math functions are written like this:

```
f(x, y) = (x + y) * (x + y)
```

(You might recognize the syntax similarity to QBasic's `DEF FN` or to C's function calling argument lists.)

As with C and QBasic, a math function always returns a single value, but you can pass more than one value to the function.

A function doesn't have to return a value. Such functions work like QBasic subroutines. Consider the function in Listing 28.1. The function's sole purpose is to print a menu of choices on-screen. The function doesn't have to get user input, make a calculation, or do anything else that requires sending a return value back to the calling function. This subroutine-like function doesn't have to have a `return` statement at the end, but in keeping with the tradition set up much earlier in the book, the function should have a `return` statement.

Listing 28.1. A simple subroutine-like C function.

```
prMenu(void)
{
  printf("Please make your choice from the following menu:\n");
  printf("1. Add employee records\n");
  printf("2. Edit employee records\n");
  printf("3. Delete employee records\n");
  printf("4. Print a report of employee records\n");
  printf("5. Quit this program\n");
  return 0;
}
```

In QBasic, simple subroutines that you call with `GOSUB` require a `RETURN` statement. However, the function's ending brace is all that C needs in order to know that your subroutine is at its endpoint and should return to the calling function. A QBasic subroutine procedure that you call with `CALL` returns when the `END SUB` statement is reached in the procedure.

Getting Ready for Return Values

As mentioned earlier, you must place the value that you return from a function at the end of the function's `return` statement. In a QBasic function, you specify the return value by assigning the return value to the name of the function somewhere in the body of the function. The following short function does nothing but return a `7`:

```
days(void)
{
  return 7;    /* Return number of days in a week */
}
```

This function, named `days()`, receives no arguments. Remember that the `void` is usually placed inside empty parameter lists. The prototype for `days()` would look just like the first line in the function's definition, like this:

```
days(void);     /* Prototype */
```

The 7 is returned to the calling function. Think about the return value for a moment. If you wanted to call `days()` from `main()`, would the following statement be appropriate?

```
days();    /* Call the function */
```

You should do something with the return value.

Calling `days()` by placing it on the line by itself, as done here, is fairly useless. After seeing the contents of the `days()` function earlier, you know that `days()` returns a `7`. Something should be done with that `7`, and if you place the function call on a line by itself in `main()`, as just shown, nothing is done with the return value. You might as well place this line in `main()`:

```
7;     /* Kind of strange, isn't it? */
```

There is nothing about return values that *requires* you to do something with a function's return value. In other words, you can call `days()` without doing anything with the return value, and C will not issue an error (most C compilers will warn you that the function call has no effect, and calling `days()` would be useless if you didn't capture the return value somehow).

In C, you literally could run the program shown in Listing 28.2!

Listing 28.2. A useless but interesting C program.

```
/* Filename: DONOTDO.C */
main()
{
   3; /* What? THIS is a C program?? */
   1445;
   0;
   30112;
   7;
   23;
   return 0;
}
```

You wouldn't want to write a program like this, but it's important for you to realize that, other than generating a few possible compiler warnings, the preceding program compiles and runs. Of course, nothing is produced by the program because there is no output, but it does run.

Obviously, a point is being illustrated here. The point is that you don't have to do anything with return values. If you don't, your program will still run, but it's silly to do nothing with the return value.

In QBasic, you *must* do something with any function's return value. Listing 28.3 shows a QBasic program that includes a multiline `DEF FN` definition. The program attempts to call the function without doing anything with the return value (such as assigning the value, using it in a calculation, or printing the value).

Listing 28.3. Defining a function and trying to ignore the return value.

```
1: ' Filename: DONOTDO.BAS
2: ' A program that does nothing with a function's return value
3: ' First, define the function that returns a value
4: DEF FNdoubleIt (x)
5:   FNdoubleIt = x * 2
6: END DEF
7: ' The "real" program appears next
8: INPUT "What value do you want to double"; aNum
9: FNdoubleIt (aNum)     ' You'll have a problem here!
10: PRINT "The doubled value is"; dNum
11: END
```

When you run the program in Listing 28.3, QBasic issues a syntax error on line 9 because QBasic can't figure out what to do with the return value.

So getting back to the simple `days()` function, how can you capture the return value? You can assign the value to a variable, you can use the value in an expression, or you can print the value somehow. The program in Listing 28.4 calls `days()` several times and does something with the return value each time.

Listing 28.4. Using the return value.

```
/* Filename: WORKRETN.C
   A program that uses the return value from days() in 3 ways */
#include <stdio.h>
days(void);   /* Prototype */
main()
{
  int wkHours, monthHours;
  printf("There are %d days in a week.\n", days());
  wkHours = days() * 24;  /* Hours in a week */
```

```
  printf("There are %d hours in a week.\n", wkHours);
  monthHours = days() * 24 * 4;
  printf("There are about %d hours in a month.\n", monthHours);
  return 0;
}
/****************************************************************/
days(void)
{
  return 7;    /* Return the number of days in a week */
}
```

Here is the output from Listing 28.4:

```
There are 7 days in a week.
There are 168 hours in a week.
There are about 672 hours in a month.
```

Don't get confused here about the simpleton code inside `days()`. The function is simple only because you are learning about function return values. You'll move into more detailed example programs in a moment.

Specifying *int* Return Values

Study the program in Listing 28.5. This program is exactly the same program as in Listing 28.4, but Listing 28.5 has two differences. See whether you can find the differences.

Listing 28.5. Using the return value with something extra.

```
/* Filename: NEWRETN.C
   A program that uses the return value from days() in 3 ways */
#include <stdio.h>
int days(void);   /* Prototype */
main()
{
  int wkHours, monthHours;
  printf("There are %d days in a week.\n", days());
  wkHours = days() * 24;  /* Hours in a week */
```

continues

Listing 28.5. continued

```
10:    printf("There are %d hours in a week.\n", wkHours);
11:    monthHours = days() * 24 * 4;
12:    printf("There are about %d hours in a month.\n", monthHours);
13:    return 0;
14: }
15: /**************************************************************/
16: int days(void)
17: {
18:    return 7;     /* Return the number of days in a week */
19: }
```

Do you spot the two differences? Look at lines 4 and 16. You'll see something that you've never seen so far in this book. The keyword `int` appears before the function's definition line in line 16. The prototype on line 4 also includes the `int`, but the prototype line should always look like the function's definition line.

When a data type appears before a function name, that data type *is the return value's data type.* In other words, the compiler knows from the prototype on line 4, and later verifies on line 16, that the `days()` function returns an integer. If the programmer says that he or she will return an integer but returns a `float` or any other non-integer data type, the compiler issues an error.

> Think of a prototype as your promise to the compiler. You promise to pass the function certain (or no) data types, and you promise to return a certain data type. If you break your promise, the compiler issues an error. If you didn't prototype, the compiler does *not* catch your data type errors.

Always specify the return data type. If you don't, the compiler will not be able to compile and check your program as accurately as might otherwise be possible. However, you might say that Listing 28.4 didn't include the return data type before the function (and prototype) name. In reality, it did contain the `int` return data type.

If you don't specify a return data type, C assumes `int`. Therefore, no program in this book, until this chapter, has included a specified return data type. You never saw `main()` with an `int` before, but C always assumes that there is an `int` before `main()`. That's why each `main()` included a `return 0;` rather than just a `return;` for the last statement. (It took only 28 chapters to explain something you've seen since the first section of the book!)

If you don't want to return a data type, you can't just leave the data type off the function's definition, because C assumes `int` if you don't specify anything else. Therefore, if you really don't want to return a value, put `void` before the function name. A `void` tells the compiler that the function works like a subroutine and not to expect a return value.

If you want to eliminate the `0` from `main()`'s `return` statement, preface `main()` with `void` like this:

```
void main()      /* main() will not return a value */
```

There's a potential problem here. Older computers required that all programs return values to the operating system. When the designers of C were writing the language, they decided to require that `main()` return a value, even if that value is `0`. Therefore, `main()` should always return a value if you want to be ANSI C compatible. ANSI C dictates that the definition line for `main()` should always be one of the following lines:

```
main()
```

or

```
int main()      /* Same as the preceding one because
                   int is assumed */
```

If you want to grab the return value in MS-DOS, you'll find that the MS-DOS `ERRORLEVEL` variable captures your C program's return value. If you are unfamiliar with `ERRORLEVEL`, that's OK because many programmers don't mess with it.

The only reason such great lengths are being taken here to teach you about the ANSI C requirement of `main()`'s return data type is that your compiler might issue a warning (few, if any, would issue an error) if you don't return a value from `main()` or if you preface `main()` with `void`.

Remember that `main()` is self-prototyping because `main()` appears first in the program and is not called from any other function. Therefore, you don't need a separate prototype for `main()`. All you need to do is specify the return data type before `main()`'s definition line, or omit the return data type if `main()` returns an `int` (as ANSI C requires).

Specifying Return Values of Any Data Type

If you want to return a `float`, specify `float` as the return data type. If your function returns a `double`, specify `double` as the return data type. Whatever you do, if you return any data type other than `int`, be sure to specify a return data type. C assumes that you are returning an `int` if you don't put the correct data type before the function name. Therefore, if you return a `float` but don't do anything to specify the `float` return data type, C truncates your `float` return data type to an `int`, and more likely than not, you'll get a bad return value. Such errors are difficult to find. (If, however, you prototype properly and specify the correct return data type, C catches your return data type error for you.)

Listing 28.6 contains a C program that includes three functions. The first function, `fun1()`, returns an integer. Notice that no return data type is specified, and that's OK because C assumes `int`. The second function, `fun2()`, returns a `float`, and the third function, `fun3()`, returns a `double` value. Only the middle function, `fun2()`, receives parameters just to show you that return data types and argument lists have nothing in common and that you can have one without the other.

Listing 28.6. Returning three data types.

```
/* Filename: RETURN3.C
   This program returns three different data types */
#include <stdio.h>
/* The prototypes follow */
fun1(void);
float fun2(float x, int k);
double fun3(void);
main()
{
  int i;
  float f;
  double d;
  i = fun1();
  printf("fun1()'s return value is %d\n", i);
  f = fun2(20.0, 5);
  printf("fun2()'s return value is %.1f\n", f);
  d = fun3();
  printf("fun3()'s return value is %.2f\n", d);
  return 0;    /* Must satisfy main()'s return data type */
}
```

```
/*****************************************************************/
fun1(void)
{
  return 9;
}
/*****************************************************************/
float fun2(float x, int k)
{
  /* Define a local float variable */
  float temp;
  temp = x + (float)k;
  return temp;     /* Return the sum of the parameters */
}
/*****************************************************************/
double fun3(void)
{
  return -93440039.43;
}
```

Here is the output from Listing 28.6:

```
fun1()'s return value is 9
fun2()'s return value is 25.0
fun3()'s return value is -93440039.43
```

You can return any data type, including pointers. Consider the following function:

```
char * left(char a[], int len)
{
  /* Define a temporary array */
  char temp[10];
  int ctr;
  if (len > strlen(a))
    { len = strlen(a); }   /* Length can be no longer than string */
  for (ctr=0; ctr<len; ctr++)
    { temp[ctr]=a[ctr]; }
  temp[ctr] = '\0';
  return temp;
}
```

What do you think this code does? It's a reproduction of QBasic's `LEFT$()` function. C doesn't provide a function that returns the left side of a string. The preceding code returns a character pointer to the start of the requested substring.

Summary

You now can return values from the functions that you write. A little extra care is needed when you return non-integer values because you have to properly specify the return value. Until this chapter, the default return value, `int`, was returned from all functions. That's why `main()` returned a `0` in each program.

When a function returns a value, you should do something with that value. You can assign the value to a variable, use the return value in an expression, or print the value. Whatever you do, be sure that you properly prototype all functions that return values so that C will catch any return errors if you make them. The prototype is like a promise or a contract to C that you will pass the argument data types that you list and that you'll return the data type that you specify.

This chapter wraps up the book. You have enough material behind you now to convert your QBasic programs to C. Are you an expert C programmer yet? Perhaps, but there's a lot of C coding that you must do to ensure that you'll remember the language. Although it is cryptic, C becomes second nature when you work with it for a while. You'll soon be programming with the pros.

Part IX

Appendixes

A

ASCII Table

Dec X_{10}	Hex X_{16}	Binary X_2	ASCII Character
000	00	0000 0000	null
001	01	0000 0001	☺
002	02	0000 0010	☻
003	03	0000 0011	♥
004	04	0000 0100	◆
005	05	0000 0101	♣
006	06	0000 0110	♠
007	07	0000 0111	●
008	08	0000 1000	■
009	09	0000 1001	○
010	0A	0000 1010	■
011	0B	0000 1011	♂
012	0C	0000 1100	♀
013	0D	0000 1101	♪
014	0E	0000 1110	♪♪
015	0F	0000 1111	☼
016	10	0001 0000	►

Dec X_{10}	*Hex* X_{16}	*Binary* X_2	*ASCII Character*
017	11	0001 0001	◄
018	12	0001 0010	↕
019	13	0001 0011	!!
020	14	0001 0100	¶
021	15	0001 0101	§
022	16	0001 0110	–
023	17	0001 0111	↨
024	18	0001 1000	↑
025	19	0001 1001	↓
026	1A	0001 1010	→
027	1B	0001 1011	←
028	1C	0001 1100	FS
029	1D	0001 1101	GS
030	1E	0001 1110	RS
031	1F	0001 1111	US
032	20	0010 0000	SP
033	21	0010 0001	!
034	22	0010 0010	"
035	23	0010 0011	#
036	24	0010 0100	$
037	25	0010 0101	%
038	26	0010 0110	&
039	27	0010 0111	'
040	28	0010 1000	(
041	29	0010 1001	)
042	2A	0010 1010	*
043	2B	0010 1011	+
044	2C	0010 1100	,
045	2D	0010 1101	-
046	2E	0010 1110	.
047	2F	0010 1111	/

Dec X_{10}	Hex X_{16}	Binary X_2	ASCII Character
048	30	0011 0000	0
049	31	0011 0001	1
050	32	0011 0010	2
051	33	0011 0011	3
052	34	0011 0100	4
053	35	0011 0101	5
054	36	0011 0110	6
055	37	0011 0111	7
056	38	0011 1000	8
057	39	0011 1001	9
058	3A	0011 1010	:
059	3B	0011 1011	;
060	3C	0011 1100	<
061	3D	0011 1101	=
062	3E	0011 1110	>
063	3F	0011 1111	?
064	40	0100 0000	@
065	41	0100 0001	A
066	42	0100 0010	B
067	43	0100 0011	C
068	44	0100 0100	D
069	45	0100 0101	E
070	46	0100 0110	F
071	47	0100 0111	G
072	48	0100 1000	H
073	49	0100 1001	I
074	4A	0100 1010	J
075	4B	0100 1011	K
076	4C	0100 1100	L
077	4D	0100 1101	M
078	4E	0100 1110	N

Dec X_{10}	Hex X_{16}	Binary X_2	ASCII Character
079	4F	0100 1111	O
080	50	0101 0000	P
081	51	0101 0001	Q
082	52	0101 0010	R
083	53	0101 0011	S
084	54	0101 0100	T
085	55	0101 0101	U
086	56	0101 0110	V
087	57	0101 0111	W
088	58	0101 1000	X
089	59	0101 1001	Y
090	5A	0101 1010	Z
091	5B	0101 1011	[
092	5C	0101 1100	\
093	5D	0101 1101	]
094	5E	0101 1110	^
095	5F	0101 1111	_
096	60	0110 0000	`
097	61	0110 0001	a
098	62	0110 0010	b
099	63	0110 0011	c
100	64	0110 0100	d
101	65	0110 0101	e
102	66	0110 0110	f
103	67	0110 0111	g
104	68	0110 1000	h
105	69	0110 1001	i
106	6A	0110 1010	j
107	6B	0110 1011	k
108	6C	0110 1100	l
109	6D	0110 1101	m

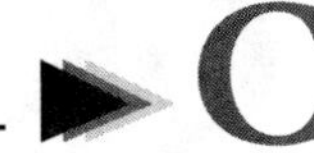

Dec X_{10}	Hex X_{16}	Binary X_2	ASCII Character
110	6E	0110 1110	n
111	6F	0110 1111	o
112	70	0111 0000	p
113	71	0111 0001	q
114	72	0111 0010	r
115	73	0111 0011	s
116	74	0111 0100	t
117	75	0111 0101	u
118	76	0111 0110	v
119	77	0111 0111	w
120	78	0111 1000	x
121	79	0111 1001	y
122	7A	0111 1010	z
123	7B	0111 1011	{
124	7C	0111 1100	¦
125	7D	0111 1101	}
126	7E	0111 1110	~
127	7F	0111 1111	DEL
128	80	1000 0000	Ç
129	81	1000 0001	ü
130	82	1000 0010	é
131	83	1000 0011	â
132	84	1000 0100	ä
133	85	1000 0101	à
134	86	1000 0110	å
135	87	1000 0111	ç
136	88	1000 1000	ê
137	89	1000 1001	ë
138	8A	1000 1010	è
139	8B	1000 1011	ï
140	8C	1000 1100	î

Dec X_{10}	Hex X_{16}	Binary X_2	ASCII Character
141	8D	1000 1101	ì
142	8E	1000 1110	Ä
143	8F	1000 1111	Å
144	90	1001 0000	É
145	91	1001 0001	æ
146	92	1001 0010	Æ
147	93	1001 0011	ô
148	94	1001 0100	ö
149	95	1001 0101	ò
150	96	1001 0110	û
151	97	1001 0111	ù
152	98	1001 1000	ÿ
153	99	1001 1001	Ö
154	9A	1001 1010	Ü
155	9B	1001 1011	¢
156	9C	1001 1100	£
157	9D	1001 1101	¥
158	9E	1001 1110	Pt
159	9F	1001 1111	ƒ
160	A0	1010 0000	á
161	A1	1010 0001	í
162	A2	1010 0010	ó
163	A3	1010 0011	ú
164	A4	1010 0100	ñ
165	A5	1010 0101	Ñ
166	A6	1010 0110	ª
167	A7	1010 0111	º
168	A8	1010 1000	¿
169	A9	1010 1001	⌐
170	AA	1010 1010	¬
171	AB	1010 1011	½

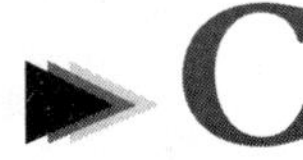

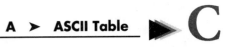

Dec X_{10}	Hex X_{16}	Binary X_2	ASCII Character
172	AC	1010 1100	¼
173	AD	1010 1101	¡
174	AE	1010 1110	«
175	AF	1010 1111	»
176	B0	1011 0000	░
177	B1	1011 0001	▒
178	B2	1011 0010	▓
179	B3	1011 0011	│
180	B4	1011 0100	┤
181	B5	1011 0101	╡
182	B6	1011 0110	╢
183	B7	1011 0111	╖
184	B8	1011 1000	╕
185	B9	1011 1001	╣
186	BA	1011 1010	║
187	BB	1011 1011	╗
188	BC	1011 1100	╝
189	BD	1011 1101	╜
190	BE	1011 1110	╛
191	BF	1011 1111	┐
192	C0	1100 0000	└
193	C1	1100 0001	┴
194	C2	1100 0010	┬
195	C3	1100 0011	├
196	C4	1100 0100	─
197	C5	1100 0101	┼
198	C6	1100 0110	╞
199	C7	1100 0111	╟
200	C8	1100 1000	╚
201	C9	1100 1001	╔
202	CA	1100 1010	╩

Dec X_{10}	Hex X_{16}	Binary X_{2}	ASCII Character
203	CB	1100 1011	╦
204	CC	1100 1100	╠
205	CD	1100 1101	═
206	CE	1100 1110	╬
207	CF	1100 1111	╧
208	D0	1101 0000	╨
209	D1	1101 0001	╤
210	D2	1101 0010	╥
211	D3	1101 0011	╙
212	D4	1101 0100	╘
213	D5	1101 0101	╒
214	D6	1101 0110	╓
215	D7	1101 0111	╫
216	D8	1101 1000	╪
217	D9	1101 1001	┘
218	DA	1101 1010	┌
219	DB	1101 1011	█
220	DC	1101 1100	▄
221	DD	1101 1101	▌
222	DE	1101 1110	▐
223	DF	1101 1111	▀
224	E0	1110 0000	α
225	E1	1110 0001	β
226	E2	1110 0010	Γ
227	E3	1110 0011	π
228	E4	1110 0100	Σ
229	E5	1110 0101	σ
230	E6	1110 0110	μ
231	E7	1110 0111	τ
232	E8	1110 1000	Φ
233	E9	1110 1001	θ

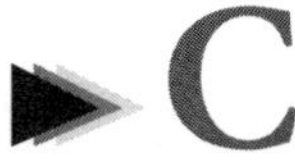

Dec X_{10}	*Hex* X_{16}	*Binary* X_2	*ASCII Character*
234	EA	1110 1010	Ω
235	EB	1110 1011	δ
236	EC	1110 1100	∞
237	ED	1110 1101	ø
238	EE	1110 1110	∈
239	EF	1110 1111	∩
240	F0	1111 0000	≡
241	F1	1111 0001	±
242	F2	1111 0010	≥
243	F3	1111 0011	≤
244	F4	1111 0100	⌠
245	F5	1111 0101	⌡
246	F6	1111 0110	÷
247	F7	1111 0111	≈
248	F8	1111 1000	°
249	F9	1111 1001	•
250	FA	1111 1010	·
251	FB	1111 1011	√
252	FC	1111 1100	η
253	FD	1111 1101	²
254	FE	1111 1110	■
255	FF	1111 1111	

The last 128 ASCII codes listed in this table, numbers 128 through 255, are specific to IBM PCs and IBM compatibles.

B

C Order of Operators

Level	*Operator*	*Description*	*Associativity*
1	++	Prefix increment	Left to right
	--	Prefix decrement	
	()	Function call and subexpression	
	[]	Array subscript	
	->	Structure pointer	
	.	Structure member	
2	!	Logical negation	Right to left
	~	1's complement	
	-	Unary negation	
	+	Unary plus	
	(type)	Typecast	
	*	Pointer dereference	
	&	Address of	
	sizeof	Size of	
3	*	Multiplication	Left to right
	/	Division	
	%	Modulus	
4	+	Addition	Left to right
	-	Subtraction	
5	<<	Bitwise left shift	Left to right
	>>	Bitwise right shift	
6	<	Less than	Left to right
	<=	Less than or equal to	
	>	Greater than	
	>=	Greater than or equal to	

Level	*Operator*	*Description*	*Associativity*
7	`==`	Equality test	Left to right
	`!=`	Not-equal test	
8	`&`	Bitwise AND	Left to right
9	`^`	Bitwise exclusive OR	Left to right
10	`¦`	Bitwise OR	Left to right
11	`&&`	Logical AND	Left to right
12	`¦¦`	Logical OR	Left to right
13	`?:`	Conditional	Right to left
14	`=`	Assignment	Right to left
	`+=`	Compound addition	
	`-=`	Compound subtraction	
	`*=`	Compound multiplication	
	`/=`	Compound division	
	`%=`	Compound modulus	
	`<<=`	Compound bitwise left shift	
	`>>=`	Compound bitwise right shift	
	`&=`	Compound bitwise AND	
	`^=`	Compound bitwise exclusive OR	
	`¦=`	Compound bitwise OR	
15	`,`	Sequence point	Left to right
	`++`	Postfix increment	
	`--`	Postfix decrement	

This order-of-operator table presents the *practical* order that you'll find the most comfortable. Technically, this table contains errors! If you were to look at an official ANSI C order of operators, you would find that the postfix increment and postfix decrement appear *before* the prefix increment and prefix decrement. Yet, as you are well aware, prefix always operates before postfix operators in expressions. The truth is that the technically correct order-of-operator table exists to interpret such awful expressions as this one: `x = i+++j++;`. Given the technically correct interpretation, this expression would be solved like this: `x = i++ + j++;`. If you're writing such expressions, use lots of parentheses instead of relying solely on the order-of-operator table, or you'll drive yourself into programmer madness!

C

Command and Function Cross-Reference

This appendix includes QBasic cross-references for C commands and functions.

> A complete cross-reference is given for all of C's commands, even though a few are too obscure to have been explained in this book (such as `register`). Where there is no QBasic equivalent, you'll see *n/a*. All C functions described in this book are cross-referenced in Table C.2.

Table C.1. C/QBasic command cross-reference.

C Command	*QBasic Equivalent(s)*
auto	n/a
break	n/a
case	CASE
char	n/a
const	CONST
continue	n/a
default	CASE ELSE
do	DO
double	DOUBLE
else	ELSE
enum	n/a
extern	n/a
float	SINGLE
for	FOR
goto	GOTO
if	IF
int	INTEGER
long	LONG
register	n/a
return	RETURN
short	INTEGER
signed	n/a
static	STATIC
struct	TYPE
switch	SELECT CASE

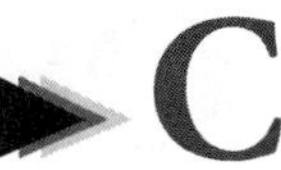

C Command	QBasic Equivalent(s)
`typedef`	n/a
`union`	n/a
`unsigned`	n/a
`void`	n/a
`volatile`	n/a
`while`	`WHILE-WEND, DO WHILE-LOOP, DO UNTIL-LOOP, DO-LOOP WHILE, DO-LOOP UNTIL`

Table C.2. Common C/QBasic function cross-reference.

C Function	QBasic Equivalent Function or Statement
`abs()`	`ABS()` function
`ceil()` and `ceill()`	`CINT()` function after adding `.5` to the argument
`cos()`	`COS()` function
`exp()`	`EXP()` function
`exit()`	`QUIT` or `END` statement
`fabs()`	`ABS()` function
`fclose()`	`CLOSE` statement
`feof()`	`EOF()` function
`fgetc()`	`INPUT #` statement
`fgets()`	`INPUT #` statement
`floor()` and `floorl()`	`INT()` function
`fmod()`	n/a
`fopen()`	`OPEN` statement
`fprintf()`	`PRINT #` and `PRINT # USING` statements
`fputc()`	`PRINT #` statement

continues

Table C.2. continued

C Function	*QBasic Equivalent Function or Statement*
`fputs()`	`PRINT #` statement
`fread()`	`GET #` statement
`fscanf()`	`INPUT` and `INPUT #` statements
`fseek()`	n/a
`fwrite()`	`PUT #` statement
`getc()`	`INPUT` statement
`getchar()`	`INPUT` statement
`gets()`	`INPUT` statement
`isalnum()`	n/a
`isdigit()`	n/a
`islower()`	n/a
`isupper()`	n/a
`labs()`	`ABS()` function
`log()`	`LOG()` function
`log10()`	n/a
`pow()`	^ operator
`printf()`	`PRINT` or `PRINT USING` statements
`putc()`	`PRINT` statement
`putchar()`	`PRINT` statement
`puts()`	`PRINT` statement
`rand()`	`RND()` function
`scanf()`	`INPUT` statement
`sin()`	`SIN()` function
`sqrt()`	`SQR()` function
`srand()`	`RANDOMIZE` statement

C Function	*QBasic Equivalent Function or Statement*
`strcpy()`	Assignment statement
`strcat()`	String concatenator operator, +
`strcmp()`	`IF` statement
`strlen()`	`LEN()` function
`strcspn()`	`INSTR()` function
`strspn()`	`INSTR()` function
`tan()`	`TAN()` function

D

Additional Resources to Help You Make the Move

This appendix lists some books that you might want to read now that you know C. All are from Sams Publishing, and many are listed on the book order form included with this book.

Teach Yourself C in 21 Days

With this best-selling book, users can achieve C success now! Each lesson can be completed in two to three hours or less. Shaded syntax boxes, Q & A sections, and "Do/Don't" sections reinforce the important topics of C. (Beginning to Intermediate)

Advanced C

Here's the next step for programmers who want to improve their C programming skills. This book gives tips and techniques for debugging C programs and for improving the programs' speed, memory usage, and readability. (Intermediate to Advanced)

Moving from C to C++

An invaluable guide for C programmers who want to learn how to move from C to C++. This book shows how one application written in C is converted to C++ with more efficient code. It includes tips and techniques for making the transition from C to C++. It also shows the "why" of object-oriented programming before teaching the specifics. (Beginning to Intermediate)

C++ Programming 101

Readers take an active approach to learning C++ in this step-by-step tutorial/workbook. Special features such as Find the Bug, Try This, Think About..., Finish the Program, and Still Confused? give the reader a thorough understanding of the language. (Beginning)

Advanced C++

This comprehensive guide is the next step for programmers who have achieved proficiency with the basics of C++ and want to learn about advanced topics. (Intermediate to Advanced)

Absolute Beginner's Guide to C

This is your quickest and easiest guide to the basics of C programming! In 30 short chapters, it covers everything you need to know to get started with C, learn programming fundamentals, and have fun at the same time! (Beginning)

The Waite Group's New C Primer Plus

The friendliest yet most comprehensive introduction to every aspect of C programming, from the most elementary to the most advanced! Goes into full detail about control

structures, functions, and even low-level bit-twiddling. An international best-seller, with more than 400,000 copies sold! (Beginning to Intermediate)

C for Fun and Profit

Learn how to have fun and make money—all in the key of C! This book is your guide to special tricks for using C to create music, stunning animation, and eye-catching computer entertainment. Includes tips on getting started in the software business. A must-read! (Intermediate)

Tom Swan's Code Secrets

Learn the most advanced tricks of C++ programming from the acknowledged master of both programming and teaching! Tom Swan shows you the ins and outs of C++ programming that you won't find in ordinary programming books! (Intermediate to Advanced)

Index

Symbols

A

B

D

G

H

J–L

M

N

O

P

Q

R

S

T

U

V

W

X–Z

Add to Your Sams Library Today with the Best Books for Programming, Operating Systems, and New Technologies

The easiest way to order is to pick up the phone and call

1-800-428-5331

between 9:00 a.m. and 5:00 p.m. EST.

For faster service please have your credit card available.

ISBN	Quantity	Description of Item	Unit Cost	Total Cost
0-672-30341-8		Absolute Beginner's Guide to C	$16.95	
0-672-30326-4		Absolute Beginner's Guide to Networking	$19.95	
0-672-30282-9		Absolute Beginner's Guide to Memory Management	$16.95	
0-672-30343-4		Even You Can Soup Up and Fix PCs	$16.95	
0-672-30306-X		Memory Management for All of Us, Deluxe Edition	$39.95	
0-672-30372-8		Teach Yourself Visual C++ in 21 Days	$26.95	
0-672-30365-5		C for Fun and Profit	$29.95	
0-672-30370-1		Visual C++ Developer's Guide	$49.95	
0-672-30286-1		C Programmer's Guide to Serial Communications, 2nd Edition	$39.95	
0-672-30399-X		The Waite Group's C Programming Using Turbo C++, 2nd Edition	$34.95	
❑ 3½" Disk		Shipping and Handling: See information below.		
❑ 5¼" Disk		TOTAL		

Shipping and Handling: $4.00 for the first book, and $1.75 for each additional book. Floppy disk: add $1.75 for shipping and handling. If you need to have it NOW, we can ship product to you in 24 hours for an additional charge of approximately $18.00, and you will receive your item overnight or in two days. Overseas shipping and handling adds $2.00 per book and $8.00 for up to three disks. Prices subject to change. Call for availability and pricing information on latest editions.

201 W. 103rd Street, Indianapolis, Indiana 46290

1-800-428-5331 — Orders 1-800-835-3202 — FAX 1-800-858-7674 — Customer Service

Book ISBN 0-672-30250-0

Order Your Program Disk Today!

You can save yourself hours of tedious, error-prone typing by ordering the companion disk to *Moving from QBasic to C.* This disk contains the source code for all the programs in the book.

Samples include all example code for testing all the QBasic and C routines. You can see how to perform I/O, calculate, access files, manage arrays, and much more, giving you approximately 200 programs to help you master C. With the disk, you'll be able to better concentrate on the book's training. Each disk is only $15.00 (US currency only). Foreign orders must enclose an extra $5.00 to cover additional postage and handling. Disks are available only in 3½-inch format.

Just send the following information with your check or postal money order to:

Greg Perry
Dept. QC
P.O. Box 35752
Tulsa, OK 74153-0752

Please *print* the following information:

Number of disks: ____ @ $15.00 (US Dollars) = ______________________

Name: ____

Address: ____

City: ________________________________ State: __________

ZIP: ________________

On foreign orders, use a separate page if needed to give your exact mailing address in the format required by your postal service.

Make checks and postal money orders payable to **Greg Perry**. Sorry, but we cannot accept credit cards, checks drawn on a non-U.S. bank, phone orders, or purchase orders. Please do not staple your check to the order form.

(This offer is made by the author, not by Sams Publishing.)